HERB OF GRACE

by

Rosa Nouchette Carey

AUTHOR OF "RUE WITH A DIFFERENCE," "THE
MISTRESS OF BRAE FARM," ETC.

" We may call it herb of grace o' Sundays"

OPHELIA

PHILADELPHIA

J. B. LIPPINCOTT COMPANY

1901

ELECTROTYPED AND PRINTED BY J. B. LIPPINCOTT COMPANY, PHILADELPHIA, U. S. A.

CONTENTS

5

CONTENTS

HERB OF GRACE

❧❧

CHAPTER I

INTRODUCES A LOVER OF THE PICTURESQUE

Our adventures hover round us like bees round the hive when preparing to swarm.—MAETERLINCK.

FROM boyhood Malcolm Herrick had been a lover of the picturesque. In secret he prided himself on possessing the artistic faculty, and yet, except in the nursery, he had never drawn a line, or later on spoilt canvas and daubed himself in oils under the idea that he was an embryo Millais or Turner. But nevertheless he had the seeing eye, and could find beauty where more prosaic people could only see barrenness: a stubble field newly turned up by the plough moved him to admiration, while a Surrey lane, with a gate swinging back on its hinges, and a bowed old man carrying faggots, in the smoky light of an October evening, gave him a feeling akin to ecstasy. More than one of his school-fellows remembered how, even in the cricket field, he would stand as though transfixed, looking at the storm clouds, with their steely edges, coming up behind the copse, but the palms of his hands were outstretched and he never failed to catch the ball.

" Nature intended me for an artist or a poet," Malcolm would say, for he was given at times to a hard, merciless introspection, when he took himself and his motives to pieces, " but circumstances have called me to the bar. To be sure I have never held a brief, and my tastes are purely literary, but all the same I am a member of the legal profession."

7

Malcolm Herrick used his Englishman's right of grumbling to a large extent; with a sort of bitter and acrid humility, he would accuse himself of having missed his vocation and his rightful heritage, of being neither " fish, flesh, nor good red herring;" nevertheless his post for the last two years had pleased him well: he was connected with a certain large literary society which gave his legal wits plenty of scope. In his leisure hours he wrote moderately well-expressed papers on all sorts of social subjects with a pithy raciness and command of language that excited a good deal of comment.

Herrick was a clever fellow, people said; " he would make his mark when he was older, and had got rid of his cranks;" but all the same he was not understood by the youth of his generation. " The Fossil," as they called him at Lincoln, was hardly modern enough for their taste; he was a survival of the mediæval age—he took life too gravely, and gave himself the airs of a patriarch.

In person he was a thin spare man, somewhat sallow, and with dark melancholy eyes that were full of intelligence. When he smiled, which he did more rarely than most people, he looked at least ten years younger.

In reality he was nearly thirty, but he never measured his age by years. " I have not had my innings yet," he would say; " I am going to renew my youth presently; I mean to have my harvest of good things like other fellows, and eat, drink, and be merry;" but from all appearance the time had not come yet.

Malcolm Herrick's chambers were in Lincoln's Inn. Thither he was turning his footsteps one sultry July afternoon, when as usual he paused at a certain point, while a smile of pleasure stole to his lips.

Familiarity had not yet dulled the edge of his enjoyment; now, as ever, it soothed and tranquillised him to turn from the noisy crowded streets into this quiet spot with its gray old buildings, its patch of grass, and the broad wide steps up and down which men, hurrying silently, passed and repassed intent on the day's work.

As usual at this hour, the flagged court was crowded by pigeons, strutting fearlessly between the feet of the passers-by, and filling the air with their soft cooing voices.

"Ah, my friend the cobbler," he said to himself, and he moved a little nearer to watch the pretty sight. A child's perambulator—a very shabby, rickety concern—had been pushed against the fence, and its occupant, a girl, evidently a cripple, was throwing corn to the eager winged creatures. Two or three, more fearless than the others, had flown on to the perambulator and were pecking out of the child's hands. Presently she caught one and hugged it to her thin little bosom. "Oh dad, look here—oh daddy, see, its dear little head is all green and purple. I want to kiss it—I do—I love it so."

"Better put it down, Kit—the poor thing is scared," returned the man, and the child reluctantly let it fly. It made straight for the distant roofs behind them, but the rest of the pigeons still strutted and pecked round the perambulator with tiny mincing steps, like court ladies practising the minuet. Malcolm looked on with unabated relish—the homely idyll always charmed him.

He had never spoken to the crippled child or her father, although they had often crossed his path at this hour; nevertheless he regarded them as old friends.

More than once he had made up his mind to accost them, but he was reserved by nature and it cost him an effort to take the initiative. In his case silence was always golden; in his own cynical language, he refused to tout for a cheap popularity by saying pleasant things to strangers.

They were not an attractive pair. The cobbler was a thin meagre little man, with a round back, bow-legs, a sharp pinched face, and pale blue eyes that seemed to look dejectedly at life.

The child was the image of her father, only in her case the defects were more accentuated: her face was still more pinched, and absolutely colourless, and the large blue-gray eyes were out of proportion to the other features. A fringe of red hair, curled very stiffly, and set round the small face like a large frill, gave her a curiously weird look. Some woman's hand must have curled it and tied the wide limp bows of her sunbonnet under the sharp little chin.

Neither of them seemed to notice Malcolm Herrick's scrutiny, they were so absorbed by the pigeons; but the scanty supply of corn had soon been scattered, and the guests were flying off by twos and threes.

"Oh see, dad!" exclaimed the child in her shrill little voice. "Oh, my! ain't it heavenly to cut capers like that in the air; it is like the merry-go-rounds at the fair;" and then Kit clapped her hands as another pretty creature rose softly and fluttered away in the distance.

The air had been growing more sultry and oppressive every moment; a heavy storm was evidently gathering—already a few heat-drops had fallen. Malcolm was a man who noticed details; he perceived at once that the ragged cover of the perambulator offered a flimsy and insufficient protection. Then he glanced at the umbrella in his hand; it was a dandified article, with a handsomely carved handle.

The two voices that usually wrangled within his breast for the mastery made themselves heard.

"It is perfectly impossible for you to offer the umbrella that Anna gave you to that brat," murmured common-sense; "very likely her father would pawn it for gin."

"But the child looks ill," remonstrated impulse. "Anna would be sure to think of the poor mite first." But it was doubtful which voice would have prevailed but for a chance word.

"Oh, dad, there is a big drop—it quite splashed my face. Ma'am said the rain would drown us." Then the man, whose wits had been wool-gathering, looked up in alarm, and began fumbling with Kit's shawl.

"Dear sakes," he muttered, "who would have thought it! But it is just my luck. You will be drenched before I get you in, Kit, and Ma'am will scold us for the rest of the day."

"Will you take this umbrella for the child, my good man?" observed Malcolm pleasantly. "I am close to my chambers. You can let me have it back to-morrow morning." Then, as the man regarded him in dazed astonishment, he gave him his address. "Perhaps you may as well let me know your name," he continued,

"Caleb Martin, sir," replied the cobbler; "and we live in Todmorden's Lane, leading out of Beauchamp Street. It is Mr. Bennet's the bootmaker, and I works for him and lives in the basement, 'long of wife and Kit."

"Beauchamp Street—oh yes, I know. Then you had better get the child home." He nodded and smiled at Kit as he moved away.

Caleb gazed after him with open mouth and pale eyes full of speechless gratitude; but Kit had unfurled the umbrella proudly, and sat like a queen in a silken tent.

"Ain't he a gentleman!" she exclaimed with a joyous chuckle; "seems to me the angels must be his sort. Wasn't he just splendid, dad!" But Caleb, who was trundling the perambulator down a side street, only shook his head in silence.

Malcolm felt a warm glow of exhilaration, which secretly moved him to astonishment, as he ran lightly up the long bare flights of stairs to his chambers. "A mere trifle like that," he said to himself contemptuously, as he entered the outer room, where a small and exceedingly sharp office boy, rejoicing in the euphonious name of Malachi Murphy, beguiled the tedium of the waiting hours by cutting the initials of his family on the legs of the table.

When Malcolm wanted to amuse a friendly visitor, he would question Malachi blandly and innocently on his brothers' and sisters' names.

"You are all minor prophets," he would say carelessly. "I think Mr. So-and-So would be interested to hear how you came by these names." And thus encouraged, Malachi would twist his face knowingly, until it resembled a gargoyle rather than a human face, and start away as though he had been wound up afresh.

"Well, it was like this, sir. Father was just reading Hosea on Sunday evening, when mother took bad, and so they made up their minds that they would call my eldest brother Hosea; the next one was Joel, because father liked the name; and by-and-by mother put in her word for Amos. Obadiah only lived five weeks; and the next was a girl, and they called her Micah. Father wouldn't have none of us christened Jonah, because he said he was real mean; but we had Nahum, and Habakkuk Zephaniah and Haggai Zechariah; and when my time came there was nothing left but Malachi, and father said we had better finish the job; and so Malachi I was. It is a blessing," continued Malachi frankly, "that Habakkuk Zephaniah and Haggai Zechariah died when they were babies; for none of us would have known what to call them; as it is, I am mostly called Mealy Murphy down my way."

"There's a gentleman waiting to see you, sir," observed Malachi, dropping his clasp knife dexterously into the waste-paper basket. "Wouldn't give his name. Seems in a mighty hurry by the way he has been walking all over the shop," he continued, *sotto voce,* as he dipped his pen into the ink again. "I wonder what the governor would say if he had heard him whistling like a penny steamer and playing old Sallie with the pen-wipers and sealing-wax. A lively sort of bloke as ever I see."

Malcolm walked rapidly to the door and opened it; as he did so, a look of surprise and pleasure crossed his face at the sight of a handsome, fair-haired youth, lying back on his easy-chair, with his feet resting on a pile of ledgers.

"Hallo, Cedric!" he exclaimed in a cordial tone. "What on earth has brought you up to town on the hottest day of the year? No, stay where you are," as his visitor attempted to rise, and Malcolm put his hands lightly on the boy's shoulders, pressing him gently back against the cushions. "I never sit there myself unless I am lazy."

"All right, old chap," returned the other easily. "I didn't want to move; only manners maketh man—I always was the pink of courtesy and politeness, don't you know. Ask old Dinah, and she will tell you."

"Oh yes, we all know that," returned Malcolm drily. "Now, will you answer my question—what brings you up to Lincoln's Inn in this unexpected manner?"

"Keep cool, old fellow, and take a seat, and I will tell you," returned the lad in a patronising tone. "You see I am staying at Teddington. Fred Courtenay was spliced yesterday, and I had promised to be at the show."

"Oh, I forgot Courtenay was to be married yesterday," muttered Malcolm.

"It went off all right," continued Cedric. "No one forbade the banns, and the happy couple drove away with half-a-dozen satin slippers reposing on the roof of the carriage. But now the business is over, it is a trifle dull. Fred's sisters are all in the schoolroom, you know, so I told Mrs. Courtenay that I had a pressing engagement in town."

"Oh, I begin to see light."

"I did some shopping in the Strand, and then I thought I would look you up in your grimy old diggings. My word, we are going to have a storm, Herrick," as a flash of lightning lit up the dark room.

" Yes, but it will soon be over, and you are in no hurry to catch your train."

" No, you are right there. The house is all in a muddle from the wedding, and we are to have a sort of nondescript meal at eight. Herrick, old fellow, I want you to put me up for a couple of nights. You are coming down to Staplegrove on Tuesday, so I told Dinah that we might as well travel together."

" Does your sister really expect me?" asked Malcolm dubiously. " My dear boy," as Cedric grew rather red and pulled his budding moustache in an affronted manner, " I know you were good enough to invite me, but I understood from you that your sisters were the owners of the Wood House, and as I have not yet made their acquaintance——"

" Hang it all, Herrick, I suppose a fellow can see his friends sometimes, even if he is dependent on his sisters," and Cedric's tone was decidedly sulky. " Besides, Dinah sent you a message—she and Elizabeth will be delighted to see you, and all that sort of thing, and they hoped you would stay as long as possible."

" I am glad you told me that," returned Malcolm, with a relieved air. In reality he had been secretly much embarrassed by Cedric's invitation. " You know, my dear fellow, how pleased I am to be introduced to your people, and it is most kind of Miss Templeton to send me that message.'"

" Oh, Dinah is a good old sort," returned the lad carelessly. The cloud had vanished from his face. " Well, Herrick, what do you say about putting me up? There are two or three things I want to do in town, and it is a bore staying on at the Briars now old Fred has gone."

" When do you want to come to me?'" asked Malcolm. " I am to sleep at Queen's Gate the next two nights, and I have promised to take Miss Sheldon out to-morrow. She is my mother's adopted daughter, you know—Anna Sheldon. I have often mentioned her to you."

Then Cedric nodded.

"I shall be back at Chelsea on Friday, if you like to come to me then; but the guest-chamber is remarkably small—at present it holds all my lumber and little else." But as Cedric professed himself indifferent on the subject of his own comfort—an assertion that drew a covert smile from his friend's lips—the matter was soon settled.

An animated conversation ensued, consisting mainly of a disjointed monologue on Cedric's part; for Malcolm Herrick only contributed a laconic remark or question at intervals, but there was a kindly gleam in his eyes as he listened, as though the fair, closely-cropped head lying back on the shabby cushion, with the eager bright young face, was a goodly spectacle.

At first sight the friendship between these two men seemed singularly ill-assorted; for what possible affinity could there be between a thoughtful, intellectual man like Malcolm Herrick, with his habitual reserve, his nature refined, critical, and yet imaginative, with its strong bias to pessimism, and its intolerance of all shams, and Cedric, with his facile, pleasure-loving temperament, at once indolent and mercurial—a creature of moods and tenses, as fiery as a Welshman, but full of lovable and generous impulses?

The disparity between their ages also seemed to forbid anything like equality of sympathy. Malcolm was at least eight or nine years older, and at times he seemed middle-aged in Cedric's eyes. "He is such a regular old fossil," he would say—"such a cut and dried specimen of humanity, that it is impossible to keep in touch with him; it stands to reason that we must clash a bit; but there, in spite of his cranks, Herrick is a good fellow." But, notwithstanding this faint praise, the inhabitants of the Wood House knew well that there was no one whom Cedric valued more than his friend Malcolm Herrick.

CHAPTER II

FALLEN AMONG THIEVES

Why insist on rash personal relations with your friend? Why go to his house, or know his mother and brother and sisters? Why be visited by him at your own? Are these things material to our covenant? Leave this touching and clawing. Let him be to me a spirit.—EMERSON.

MALCOLM HERRICK was a devout disciple of Emerson. He always spoke of him as one of the master minds that dominated humanity. "He is the chosen Gamaliel at whose feet I could sit for ever," he would say; "on every subject he speaks well and wisely;" and once, when he was strolling through Kensington Gardens with his sister-friend, Anna Sheldon, he had electrified her by quoting a favourite passage from his essay on friendship.

"Frien'ship requires that rare mean betwixt likeness and unlikeness that piques each with the presence of power and of consent in the other party. Let me be alone to the end of the world, rather than that my friend should overstep, by a word or look, his real sympathy. I am equally baulked by antagonism and by compliance. Let him not cease an instant to be himself. . . . Better be a nettle in the side of your friend than his echo."

Malcolm had uttered the last sentence in rather a tragic tone, but he was somewhat offended when the girl laughed. "What an odd idea!" she observed innocently. "I should strongly object to anything so stinging as a nettle; perhaps it is because I am a woman that I should prefer the echo;" but Malcolm, who had received a douche of cold water from this feminine criticism, declined to be drawn into a discussion on the subject.

"Women are so illogical," he muttered angrily, and

Anna's heaven of content was suddenly clouded. Malcolm's approval was vitally necessary to her happiness—a chilling word from him had power to spoil the fairest landscape and blot out the sunshine; nevertheless she took her rebuff meekly and without retort.

A mere chance, an accident in the destinies of both men, had brought about this acquaintance between Malcolm Herrick and Cedric Templeton. The vice-president of Magdalene was an old friend of the Herrick family, and was indeed distantly related to Mrs. Herrick; and after Malcolm had taken his degree and left Lincoln, he often spent a week or two with Dr. Medcalf. He was an old bachelor, and one of the most sociable of men, and his rooms were the envy of his friends. Malcolm was a great favourite with him, and was always welcome when he could spare time to run down for a brief visit.

About two years before, he was spending a few days with his friend, when one evening as he was strolling down Addison's Walk in the gloaming, his attention was attracted by a young undergraduate. He was seated on a bench with his head in his hands; but at the sound of passing footsteps he moved slightly, and Malcolm caught sight of a white boyish face and haggard eyes that looked at him a little wildly; then he covered his face again.

Malcolm walked on a few steps; his kind heart was shocked at the lad's evident misery, but to his reserved nature it was never easy to make the first advance; indeed, he often remarked that he had rather a fellow-feeling with the Levite who passed by on the other side.

"I daresay he was sorry for the poor traveller in his heart," he observed, "but it takes a deal of moral courage to be a Good Samaritan; it is not easy for a shy man, for example, to render first aid to a poor chap with a fractured limb in the middle of a crowd of sympathising bystanders—one's self-consciousness and British hatred of a scene seem to choke one off."

2

So, true to his diffident nature, Malcolm walked to the other end of Addison's Walk; then something seemed to drag at him, and he retraced his steps slowly and reluctantly; finally, as though constrained by some unseen power that overmastered his reserve, he sat down on the bench and touched the youth lightly on the arm.

"You are in trouble, I fear; is there anything I can do to help you?"

The words were simple almost to bluntness, but they were none the worse for that, for they rang true from a good heart.

Malcolm's voice was pleasant; when he chose, it could be both winning and persuasive; to the lad sitting there in the Egyptian darkness of a terrifying despair, it sounded honey-sweet. He put out a hot hand to his new friend, and then broke into a fit of tears and sobs. "Oh, can you help me?" he gasped out. "I wanted to drown or hang myself, sooner than disgrace them; only I thought of Dinah and I couldn't do it;" and then as he grew calmer a little judicious questioning and a few more kind words brought out the whole story.

He had fallen into bad hands; two or three men older and richer than himself had got hold of him for their own purposes, and had led him into mischief. The culminating misfortune had happened the previous evening, when they had induced him to play at cards; the stakes were high, though the boy was too much fuddled by champagne to guess that.

"They made me drunk, sir," groaned Cedric; "and there was a professional sharper there—Wright has just told me so—and he will not let me off. If they found out things at headquarters I should be rusticated, and I am only in my first term. The Proctor has vowed to make an example of the next fellow caught gambling, and they say he always keeps his word."

"How much do you owe?" asked Malcolm; and when

Cedric in a low voice mentioned the sum, Malcolm gave a whistle of dismay. No wonder he was in despair.

"If I had not drunk too much, I should have stopped playing when I saw I was losing," went on Cedric in a contrite tone; "but they plied me with liquor, and I got reckless, and then I knew no more till I found myself in bed with my clothes on."

Cedric was not shirking the truth certainly. The young prodigal already realised the nature of the husks given to him; he was so low and abject in his abasement that a word of rebuke would have seemed cruel. One thing was certain, that matters were serious—gambling and drunkenness were no light offences.

Malcolm had already been put into possession of the youth's domestic history. His name was Cedric Templeton; his parents were dead, and he was dependent on his half-sisters; his father had had heavy losses, and Cedric's inheritance had been small. The first Mrs. Templeton had brought her husband great wealth, but the money had been settled on the daughters. Mr. Templeton's second wife was a penniless girl. She had died two or three years after Cedric's birth, and Dinah, the elder sister, had mothered him.

"You must put a good face on it and write to your sister," continued Malcolm. "If you take my advice, Templeton, you will keep nothing back—'the truth, the whole truth, and nothing but the truth'—and hang the consequences." Malcolm finished his sentence with a touch of impatience, for the boy's scared face almost frightened him.

"No, no, no!" returned Cedric vehemently. "I would sooner drown myself a hundred times over. Look here," plucking at Malcolm's coat-sleeve with his feverish, restless hand, "you don't understand—you don't know Dinah; she would break her heart, and Elizabeth too.

They are such good women, they don't allow for a fellow's temptation; and—and I have broken my word."

" How do you mean, my dear lad?"

" I gave them my sacred promise not to play for money. I don't know why Dinah was always so afraid of that. They never thought of the other thing," and Cedric hung his head in shame—" they would not believe it was possible; it was always debt and not paying one's bills that Dinah feared."

" Your sister was right, Templeton," returned Malcolm somewhat sternly. " Wait a moment, I must think over things and see what is to be done;" and then he rose from the bench and paced slowly up and down. " A hundred and twenty pounds lost in a single night to a professional card-sharper," he thought. " The rogues ought to be shown up, only this would involve the end of the lad's university career." Malcolm knew the Proctor well—not even a first offence would receive a merciful verdict.

If only the boy would throw himself upon his sisters' compassion—women were so soft-hearted and forgave so easily. But Cedric had refused this; he had even used strong language when his adviser pressed it.

" Obstinate young beggar," he growled; " it would serve him right to let him get out of the mess by himself;" and then he relented from his severity, and rapidly added up some sums in his head. The result of his calculation was satisfactory. He had just that amount lying idle at his banker's. His mother made him a liberal allowance, and he was beginning to turn an honest penny by literary work. At that time he was still an occupant of his mother's house, so his expenses were not great.

" Yes, I will risk it," he thought, with one of those sudden impulses that took other people as well as himself by surprise, and then he walked quickly up to Cedric.

" Look here, Templeton," he exclaimed, " I have made

up my mind to go bail for the whole amount. It is too late now to do anything, but to-morrow I will see those fellows and give them a bit of my mind. Your friend the card-sharper will have to make tracks. Anyhow, I will pay up."

"Good heavens, Mr. Herrick, you don't mean—you don't mean;" but here Cedric could not utter a word more, for his voice was choked with sobs. Malcolm could just gather a few incoherent expressions—"benefactor" —"God bless him"—"eternal gratitude," or some such phrases.

"Tut, nonsense," returned Malcolm testily; but his eyes were not quite clear, and he laid a kindly hand on the boy's shoulder. "I want no thanks, only you must promise me, on your word as an English gentleman, never to play for money as long as you are here."

"I promise—I will vow if you like—there is nothing —nothing that I would not promise you. Mr. Herrick, you have saved me from disgrace, and Dinah from a broken heart."

"Hush, hush!"

"No, please let me say one thing more. It is a loan —of course I understand that; it may be years before I pay it back, but if I live it shall be paid back, every penny."

"Oh, we can talk about that in the future," returned Malcolm quickly. He had little hope that Cedric would ever be able to repay him.

"It shall be paid," replied the lad firmly. "My sisters are very good to me—and I have more than I need;" and Malcolm's good sense and knowledge of human nature made him hold his tongue.

It would be a pity to damp the lad's good resolution, and probably the small sacrifices and petty self-denials necessary to the settlement of the debt would be valuable training, and help to make a man of him; so he said nothing further on the subject, and a few minutes later they parted.

Malcolm kept his promise, and before the next day was over he had paid Cedric's debt of honour, with a stern word of caution to his tempters that turned them chill with dismay.

From this day Cedric attached himself to his benefactor with a dog-like fidelity and devotion that secretly touched Malcolm. During the latter's brief visits to Oxford they were seldom apart; and in spite of the disparity between their ages, and the marked difference in their tastes, a warm mutual attachment sprang up between the two. Malcolm was soon put in possession of Cedric's history and manner of life from his boyhood; he listened to copious anecdotes of his home and school-days.

He was soon made aware of Cedric's crowning ambition to take part in the Oxford and Cambridge race, and that this honour was the dream and purpose of his life.

His other purpose, to compete for the Civil Service Examination at the close of his university life, seemed relegated to the background and scarcely entered into his thoughts at all; and though Malcolm dropped a warning word from time to time, he dared not put too much pressure on the lad, for he recognised intuitively how body and mind were developing under an athlete's training. Cedric's fame as an oarsman soon reached the ears of authority, and at the time of his visit to Lincoln's Inn it was already a foregone conclusion that his name would be entered for the next race.

They talked of this for some time; and then, as the storm still raged, Malcolm handed his visitor his own copy of the *Times*, and sat down to answer one or two pressing letters. As soon as these were finished and Malachi had received his instructions for the next day, he tilted his chair back from the table and disposed himself comfortably for further talk.

But first there was a little dumb-show on Cedric's part; for he drew from his breast-pocket a Russian leather cigarette-case and held it out with a significant smile. But Malcolm waved it away.

"Avaunt, Satanus," he said with dignity. "Are you aware, my dear fellow, that you are in a place of business—a venerable institution sacred to the Muses—and that I have to live up to my reputation?"

"Oh, I thought you were boss of the whole concern," returned Cedric in a discomfited tone. "You are pretty safe from visitors on such an afternoon."

"Even if there are no clients, we have a minor prophet always on hand," replied Malcolm.

Then Cedric laughed.

"Mealy Murphy! Oh my prophetic soul, I forgot the youthful Malachi. I say, Herrick, I was just thinking, as you were writing just now, how odd it seems that I have known you just two years, and you have never been near the Wood House yet."

"It has not been for want of invitations," returned his friend with a smile. "Don't you remember that when you first kindly asked me I had arranged to take my mother abroad, and the next time I was going to Scotland with a friend?"

"Oh yes, and the third time you were moving into your new diggings in Cheyne Walk." Cedric spoke with a touch of impatience.

"But we have often met at Oxford," observed Malcolm smilingly. And then he coloured slightly and continued in an embarrassed voice, "I am afraid, my dear fellow, that you have rather wondered that you have not been invited to No. 27 Queen's Gate; but, as I once explained to you, the house belongs to my mother."

"Just as the Wood House belongs to Dinah and Elizabeth," returned Cedric.

"Ah, just so; but there is a difference. My mother is

not quite like other ladies. Her life, and I may say the greater·part of her fortune, are devoted to charitable objects. If I had invited you to stay with us you would have been simply bored to death. Amusement, social obligations, the duties we owe to society, do not belong to my mother's creed at all. If I might borrow a word from a renowned novelist, I would call her ' a charitable grinder,' for she grinds from morning till night at a never-ceasing wheel of committees, meetings, and Heaven knows what besides."

"She reminds me of the immortal Mrs. Jellyby," observed Cedric airily; but Malcolm shook his head.

"No, there is no resemblance. My mother is a clear-headed, practical woman. She manages her house herself, and the domestic machinery goes like clockwork. The servants know their duty and do their work well: and I have heard our old nurse say that one could eat off the floor; but in spite of all this the word ' comfort' does not enter my mother's vocabulary."

"Good gracious! Herrick."

"She has splendid health," continued Malcolm gravely, "and work is a perfect passion with her. She is energy incarnate, and among her fellow-workers she is much respected. Unfortunately she expects her belongings to live up to her standard." Here Malcolm paused.

"You mean Miss Sheldon has to work too?" observed Cedric.

"Yes, I mean that," returned Malcolm slowly. "She is very fond of my mother—they are much attached to each other—but there is no doubt that Anna works too hard. You can see now," he went on hurriedly, "why I thought it better to take rooms for myself. I was not in sympathy with my mother's pursuits; and when I left Oxford I soon began to realise that life was impossible under my mother's roof. The separation was painful to us both, and it nearly broke Anna's heart, but at the present moment I do not think that any of us repents of my action."

"You are all right now, Herrick?"

"Yes, I am all right, as you will see for yourself on Friday. My crib just suits me. I have excellent companionship when I want it, or solitude if I prefer it, and though life at Cheyne Walk is a trifle Bohemian after Queen's Gate, I would not exchange it for a palace."

"I am so glad to hear you say that. But, Herrick, I begin to be afraid, don't you know, that you will find the Wood House slow. Of course I think no end of my sisters; but you see they are not young."

"So I imagine," returned Malcolm, who was secretly disposed to agree with Cedric. Two maiden ladies of uncertain age might be endeared to their brother; but Malcolm, who was rather fastidious on the subject of female beauty, was not over-anxious to cultivate their acquaintance.

"Dinah is much older than Elizabeth," continued Cedric confidentially. "There were two or three brothers and sisters between them, only they died. She is over forty, you know, and Elizabeth is nearly thirty. There is a good bit of difference—only she never makes herself out young. You will be sure to like them," went on the lad eagerly; "they are good women, and just your sort."

"Oh, I daresay we shall get on first-rate," returned Malcolm mendaciously, for he was anything but certain of it. "Hallo, old fellow," interrupting himself, "the storm is over and we can make tracks now." And then they went out together.

As they parted at the Temple station, Cedric pushed a little sealed packet into his friend's hand.

"It is the first instalment," he whispered, growing very red; "don't open it till you get back." But Malcolm's curiosity would not allow him to wait; and when Cedric had disappeared into the station he broke the seal. To his surprise there were fifty pounds in notes and gold, the saving and scrapings of two years.

" Good lad," he murmured approvingly, as he stowed it carefully away in a breast-pocket, and a thrill of pride and pleasure shot through him. Yes, he must keep it, he thought; he could not affront his young manliness and independence by returning it. " It is what I should have done in his case," he said to himself. And then he thought that he would lay out part in buying a keepsake for Anna. There was a little brooch she had much admired, a mere toy of a thing, a tiny quiver full of arrows, studded with small diamonds and tipped with a pearl. The shop where they had noticed it was close by, and he would buy it at once. But as Malcolm hurried off on this kindly errand he little realised what the joy of that possession would be to Anna Sheldon.

CHAPTER III

A PAGE OF ANCIENT HISTORY

Before we can bring happiness to others, we must first be happy ourselves; nor will happiness abide within us unless we confer it on others.—MAETERLINCK.

DURING the preceding hour or two Malcolm's face had worn its brightest and most youthful aspect—the society of Cedric had roused him and taken him out of himself; but as he approached the handsome and imposing-looking house where his mother lived, his countenance resumed its normal gravity.

To him it had been a house of bondage, and he had never regarded it as a home; his environment from boyhood had not suited him, and though he loved his mother, and gave her, at least outwardly, the obedience and honour that were due to her, there had not been that sympathy between them that one would have expected from an only son to a widowed mother.

Malcolm's father had died when he was about six years old, but his infant recollections of him were wonderfully vivid. He remembered waking up one night from some childish dream that had frightened him, to see a kind face bending over him, and to feel warm, strong arms lifting him up.

"Never mind, Sonny, father's with you," he heard a cheery voice say.

"Daddy's wid baby," he repeated drowsily, as he nestled down in his father's arms. "Nice, nice daddy," and two hot little hands patted his face.

Then a voice in the distance said, "You are spoiling him, Rupert. Malcolm ought to be a brave boy and not

27

cry on account of a silly dream." Of course it was his mother who spoke; even from his infancy her method of education had been bracing. "Baby isn't a boy, movver," he had once said in extenuation of some childish fault; "movver must not punish Baby."

The memories of early childhood are always vague and hazy; but in the distance, among shifting forms and changing prospects, there was always a big, big figure, with kind eyes and strong arms, looming largely in his recollection.

"If my father had lived, I know we should have been such friends," Malcolm would sigh to himself in his growing youth; and though his mother never suspected it, he often looked at his father's portrait that hung in her dressing-room, until his eyes were full of tears. "If father had lived, I shouldn't have been so lonely and out of it all," he would say as he turned away with a quivering lip.

Mrs. Herrick tried to do her duty by the boy; but she was a busy woman, and had no leisure to devote to his amusement. The long holidays were more pleasant in anticipation to both mother and son than they proved in reality.

In the working hive at 27 Queen's Gate there seemed no place for the restless, growing lad. His mother was always shut up in the library, where she wrote her endless letters and reports and added up her accounts, and Anna was with her governess.

Malcolm would be put in Anderson's charge, the steady, reliable butler and factotum, and introduced to all the sights of London—Westminster Abbey and St. Paul's, the Tower, and the British Museum, the Zoological Gardens, and Madame Tussaud's. Sometimes they went to Kew, or Richmond Park, or took the steamer to Hampton Court. The nearest approach to dissipation was an afternoon spent with the Christy Minstrels. Mrs.

Herrick would not hear of the theatre; but once, sad to relate, when Anderson was indisposed, and the footman, a rather feeble-minded young man, had been sent with Malcolm to see a panorama that was considered interesting and instructing, Malcolm, by sundry bribes and many blandishments, had seduced his guardian into accompanying him to Drury Lane, where they sat in the pit, side by side, and watched with breathless interest the never-to-be-forgotten pantomime of " Jack and the Bean-Stalk."

" They'll run you in for this, Master Malcolm," Charles had observed ruefully, as they hurried through the dark streets. " If I lose my place it will be all along of you, and it is a good place too, though Mr. Anderson is a bit down on one." But, strange to say, they escaped scot-free. Mrs. Herrick had not returned from a monster meeting at St. James's Hall, and Anderson had retired to bed to nurse his cold. Malcolm confided the whole story of his escapade to Anna, and she had wept with grief and dismay. " Oh, Mally, how wicked of Charles to take you!" she sobbed. " I never did think he looked quite good. Mother would be so angry and unhappy if she knew; she says theatres are not good for young people."

" It is just a crank on mother's part," returned Malcolm loudly; his eyes were bright with excitement. " It was the loveliest thing you ever saw, Anna. The Princess was a beauty, and no mistake; even Charles thought so, and he has seen princesses by the score. I am glad I went; the boys won't think me such a duffer when I tell them. Don't shake your head, Anna; you are a girl, and you don't understand how much one has to put up with from the fellows. They call me the Puritan, and ask if I wear pinafores at home. But I stopped that," and here Malcolm doubled up his fists in a singularly suggestive manner.

Malcolm's only sister, a pretty, fair-haired girl, had

died of fever when she was eight years old, and for years Mrs. Herrick had felt her loss too deeply to mention her name. " If Florence had lived," she once said rather bitterly to her son, " she would have been my close companion, and we should have thought alike on all points;" but it may be doubted if this maternal dream would ever have been realised.

A mere accident had led to the adoption of Anna Sheldon shortly after Florence's death. She was the orphan child of a young artist in whom Mrs. Herrick had interested herself, and when the broken-hearted wife had followed her husband, Mrs. Herrick had taken the lonely child home.

The kind action had brought its own reward. Anna's gentleness and sweetness of disposition soon won the affection of her adopted mother. She was submissive by nature, and yielded readily to the opinions and wishes of those she loved. Mrs. Herrick's ideas on the subject of education might be bracing and invigorating, but there was nothing oppressive in her rule. Perhaps she understood girls better than boys, for Anna thrived under her system. The old nurse, Mrs. Dawson, who still officiated as Mrs. Herrick's personal attendant, taught her needlework; an excellent governess, who was both judicious and reasonable, presided over the schoolroom and accompanied her in her walks; nor was she entirely without companions, for she attended dancing and deportment classes with the young daughters of their vicar, a much-esteemed guide, philosopher, and friend to the Herrick family.

Until the governess, Miss Greenwood, left them to be married, and Anna grew up to woman's estate, her life was as happy as most girls'. The chief events in it were Malcolm's holidays. Anna looked forward to them for months beforehand, and she always cried herself to sleep the day he left.

She and her adopted mother were the best of friends. Anna regarded Mrs. Herrick as one of the noblest of women, and her dutiful submission and anxiety to please her benefactress secretly surprised Malcolm.

Mrs. Herrick was not a demonstrative woman, but in her own way she was very good to Anna; she encouraged her to call her mother, bought her pretty dresses and ornaments such as girls loved, but there Anna's list of privileges was at an end. It never struck Mrs. Herrick that she had simply no life of her own—that at seventeen or eighteen a girl craves for congenial companionship, pleasant occupation, and a fair amount of amusement.

When Anna was liberated from the schoolroom, she would have liked to go to picture-galleries, attend concerts, and mix with interesting people; in spite of her shyness and gentleness, she had plenty of mind and character, and Malcolm had already cultivated her artistic tastes. One summer, indeed, they had gone abroad, and Malcolm had been with them, and for two months Anna felt they had been in the anteroom of Paradise.

"The summer we spent in Switzerland and in the Austrian Tyrol," were words perpetually on Anna's lips. Poor child, she little guessed, as she built up wonderful castles in the air, that it would be long before she had such a holiday again.

It was an evil moment for Anna when she volunteered to learn typewriting, that she might help her adopted mother; from that day she became the willing slave bound at the chariot wheels of a good-natured despot. No amount of work tired Mrs. Herrick; she had the strength and vitality of ten women. It never entered her head that a growing girl in her teens was liable to flag and grow weary, and so the pretty pink roses that had bloomed among Alpine snows faded out of Anna's cheeks, and the soft brown eyes grew heavy.

Anna never complained; if her back ached and her head was hot and throbbing, Mrs. Herrick never knew it, and she was quite indignant when Malcolm spoke to her of Anna's changed looks.

"She is not strong, and she is doing far too much. Dawson and I both think so." Perhaps he spoke with some degree of bluntness, for Mrs. Herrick responded with unusual irritability.

"I am very much obliged to you and Dawson," she returned rather sarcastically, "for your solicitude on Anna's account, but I believe I am still quite equal to the charge of looking after her."

"Oh, if you take it in that way," retorted Malcolm in an offended voice; and then Mrs. Herrick resumed her smooth manner. She was a good-tempered woman, and seldom indulged in sarcasm; but things had gone wrong that morning, and her young secretary had made several mistakes. Anna had at last been obliged in her own self-defence to own that she had a severe headache.

Mrs. Herrick had just sent her to her own room to lie down, and had rung for Dawson to attend her. She was sadly inconvenienced by this untoward accident, and it was at this inauspicious moment that Malcolm lodged his complaint.

"If these headaches continue I shall ask Dr. Armstrong to look in," she continued tranquilly. "Anna's services are most valuable to me. I almost feel lost without her. It was a good day for me when she threw herself into the work; it makes me regret my dear child less, to feel that Anna sympathises with me so entirely;" and, in spite of himself, Malcolm felt a little touched by these words.

A few weeks later he spoke to Anna; the girl had not recovered her looks, and Nurse Dawson told him privately that she was losing her appetite and getting thin; but Anna's eyes filled with tears at the first words.

" Oh hush, dear Malcolm, please," she said, encircling
his wrist with her soft hand; it was a favourite caress
with her, and Malcolm used playfully to term it " Anna's
handcuff," or the " Sheldon shackles." In spite of their
close intimacy as brother and sister, he had never kissed
her, but there was entire confidence between them.

" Please, please, Malcolm, do not say any more; it
was very wrong of nurse to put these ideas in your head.
You know mother spoke to Dr. Armstrong, and he is
giving me a tonic; he says I must go out more, so mother
is trying to spare me all she can."

" And the headaches are better?" Malcolm looked at
her quite sternly as he put the question.

" Yes, I think so—I hope so," rather hesitatingly, for
Anna was absolutely truthful. " I still feel rather stupid
of an evening; but mother is so good, she lets me go to
bed early."

She sighed rather heavily. " I wish I were stronger,
Malcolm. Nurse says I have never been robust. I do
so love to help mother. I always feel as though I can
never do enough to show my gratitude to her. What
would have become of me when my parents died if
she had not brought me here. We were so dreadfully
poor, and had so few friends. Oh Malcolm, think of
it," and then she whispered in his ear, " they would
have taken me to the workhouse—there was nothing
else."

" Nonsense—rubbish," began Malcolm wrathfully; but
Anna put her hand upon his lips.

" No, dear, not nonsense. I am telling you the sober
truth—mother would endorse it. Do you think I do not
owe her a life's service and love for all her dear care of
me !

" If I am tired, I glory in my fatigue, for it is for my
adopted mother and her poor that I am working;" and
Anna's eyes were very soft and bright. " Malcolm, you

have no idea how much happier she is now I share her work. I know she never complained of her loneliness —it is not her way to complain—but she has missed Florence so terribly. We talk of her sometimes, mother and I," continued the girl thoughtfully, " and she tells me what a sweet daughter she would have been, and how we should have been sisters. It is so dear of her never to exclude me, even when she is thinking and talking of Florence. ' If my little girl had lived,' she said once, ' I should have had two daughters.' "

Malcolm had to hold his tongue at last, but he grumbled freely to Nurse Dawson. In her he had a staunch ally; the old woman was devoted to Anna, and by no means sided with her mistress.

" You see it is just this way, Mr. Malcolm, my dear," she said to him once; " the mistress, bless her heart, thinks of nothing but them charitable societies, from morning till night; they are more to her than meat or drink or rest. She is as strong as a horse, and so she is never tired like other folks. Why, my dear, I have known her spend a whole day going from one meeting to another, speechifying and reading reports, and yet when I have gone up to dress her in the evening she has been as fresh as paint. She is made of cast-iron, that's my belief," continued Dawson, who secretly adored her mistress; " but cast-iron is one thing and a fragile blossom like Miss Anna is another, as I made bold to tell my mistress the other day; ' for it stands to reason, ma'am,' I said to her, ' that a young creature like Miss Anna is not seasoned and toughened like a lady of your age, and I never did think much of her constitution.' "

" And what did my mother say to that, Dawson?"

" Well, dearie, she had a deal to say, for I am free to confess that my mistress is never at a loss for words. She argued with me for pretty nigh half an hour—until

she made things look so different that I did not know
whether I was on my head or my heels.

"She would have it that every one ought to work, old
or young, rich or poor; that she loved Miss Anna all
the better for so readily offering herself for the work.
'I should have left her free,' she said that, Mr. Malcolm—'no one in my house should be compelled or
urged to put their hand to the plough; but when she
came to me of her own accord I could have wept with
joy.'"

"Did my mother really say that, Dawson?"

"Ay, Mr. Malcolm, she did; and begging your pardon, dearie, you do not half understand my mistress.
She is quiet-spoken, and does not show her feelings;
but she has a warm heart. I know as well as you do
that our poor child is put upon and overworked, but she
is the sunshine of my mistress's life; that's what makes
things so difficult, for Miss Anna is bent on helping her,
and will not listen to a word."

Malcolm soon found he must hold his peace, and very
soon his mind was too much absorbed by his own concerns. After a time he got used to Anna's pale cheeks;
she had refused to listen to his advice, and must dree
her weird.

He had his own battles to fight, and victory was not
easily achieved; nevertheless his masculine will prevailed.

It was no hastily considered resolution that determined
Malcolm to leave his mother's roof and set up in chambers of his own, neither did he effect his purpose without
a good deal of pain; but, as he told Cedric, life at 27
Queen's Gate was becoming impossible to him.

But it was one of the worst moments of his life when
he announced his intention to his mother. She listened
to his embarrassed explanation silently, and without
offering any interruption; but her pleasant, strong-

featured face grew set and stern, and when he had finished she looked at him almost solemnly.

"He was the only son of his mother, and she was a widow," she said slowly and sadly, and no word of reproach could have stung him more deeply. It made him angry.

"Mother, you have no right to say that, and to speak as though I were failing in my duty towards you," he returned indignantly; "it is not fair—all my life I have tried to please you, and to carry out your wishes."

"I am not complaining of you, Malcolm," she replied quietly; "your own conscience is accusing you, not your mother. Would you have me suppress the truth or tell you a lie? Do you think any mother could listen unmoved to what you have told me just now—that you intend to leave my roof, that my only son finds his home so uncongenial, and his life here so irksome, that he is forced to quit it?"

"Mother, you are making things worse and worse," returned Malcolm passionately; "you are putting matters in a wrong light. Will you listen to me a moment?"

"Have I ever refused to listen to you, my son?" and a softer and more motherly expression came into the gray eyes.

"No, you have always been kind," he replied; but there was a slight quiver in his voice. "Mother, it is not my fault—at least I hope not—that we think so differently on most subjects. I am nearly eight-and-twenty, and at that age a man is bound to do the best for himself."

"I hoped you would have married before this, Malcolm."

"There is no question of marrying at present," he returned in a constrained voice. "I have not yet seen the woman whom I wish to make my wife."

Then a singular expression crossed Mrs. Herrick's face.

"I am sorry to hear that, Malcolm; I would have willingly given you up to a wife, but life in chambers seems to me so Bohemian."

"It is only an idea," he returned impatiently. "Mother dear, try to believe that I am doing it for the best—for both our sakes. I am not leaving you alone—you have Anna; and in spite of all your kindness to me, I am well aware that I have never been any real help or comfort; if I thought you needed me—that you relied on me for assistance or protection—I would never have carved out this independent life."

"It is the spirit of the age," she returned a little bitterly; "it is the children who make terms, and the parents who have to yield and submit."

"That is an old argument, mother," replied Malcolm wearily; "how often we have gone over that ground, you and I. When our wills have clashed it seems to me the concessions have all been on my side. How many men of my age do you suppose would have yielded to you in the matter of a latch-key? Poor old Anderson has been the chief sufferer, and the victim of your strictness; do you think it has not troubled me to keep him up night after night?"

"Anderson is my servant, and has to do his duty," replied Mrs. Herrick rather stiffly.

"And he has done it," was Malcolm's answer; "he has been perfectly conscientious; if he grumbled a bit now and then, no one could wonder, at his age. Mother, it is no good talking—it is not only the question of the latch-key, I want to have a place where I can be free to lead my own life and see my own friends; there is no room for them here—your busy life is too much crowded up with work to have leisure for society."

"I have never refused to entertain your friends, Malcolm;" and a dull red flush crossed the mother's face, as though this reproach had gone home.

"Possibly not," rather coldly, "I do not think I have ever asked you; but, mother, let us make an end of this. The first break will be painful to all of us, but we shall soon shake down, and then you and Anna will own that it was for the best. When you want me I shall always be at your service. I shall see you every few days—Cheyne Walk and Queen's Gate are not very far apart. As soon as I am settled, you and Anna must come and have tea with me, and I must introduce you to the Kestons. Now, mother dear, say something comforting to a fellow;" and then Mrs. Herrick smiled faintly. She loved her son far too well to hurt him by her reproaches; in her secret heart she strongly disapproved of the step he was taking, but she was a sensible woman, and knew that it was no good crying over spilt milk.

At eight-and-twenty a man may refuse with some show of reason to be attached to his mother's leading-strings, and may also be permitted to strike out new paths for himself. Nevertheless, for many a long day Mrs. Herrick carried a heavy heart, and only her adopted daughter guessed how sorely Malcolm was missed by his mother.

CHAPTER IV

ANNA

Better to feel a love within
  Than be lovely to the sight!
Better a homely tenderness
  Than beauty's wild delight!
                MacDonald.

Malcolm often spent a night at Queen's Gate; he made a point of never refusing his mother's invitations, and would even put off an engagement if she needed him. On this occasion he had promised to remain two nights.

A meeting on behalf of a college in Japan, for training native candidates for holy orders, was to be held at 27 Queen's Gate that evening, and some excellent speakers—women as well as men—had been announced for that occasion. Mrs. Herrick thought the whole subject would appeal to Malcolm, and in this she was not wrong. Hitherto he had fought shy of zenana meetings, barmaid associations, working girls' clubs, open-air spaces, and people's parks, and even cabmen's shelters and drinking fountains.

"They were all good and worthy objects," he had observed to Anna, and he could have tackled them singly, but not when they were piled on *ad nauseum*. But the Japanese college had been largely discussed in his special circle, and also in the paper of which he was the editor—the *Times* had even devoted one of its columns to the subject; and Mrs. Herrick had been secretly much gratified by Malcolm's readiness to be present.

"The Bishop will be with us," she said, with an inflexion of pride in her tone; "he is over here just now

on account of his wife's health, and has promised to take
the chair." Then Malcolm signified his perfect willing-
ness to make his Lordship's acquaintance, and to listen
to any amount of speeches; and Mrs. Herrick had gone
to her bed that night a happy woman.

Why could not Malcolm be always like that? she
thought, and then she sighed gently as she took her Bible
in her hand.

It opened of its own accord at Samuel's childhood and
Hannah's solemn dedication of her first-born; no passages in the well-read book had been more frequently
perused.

Of all the characters of holy writ, this Jewish mother
appealed most forcibly to her imagination: the little coat
brought year by year to the Temple child, the precious
sacrifice and oblation made in gratitude for an answered
prayer, the pride and joy of the mother's heart, as she
stood in the court of the women and saw her boy minis-
tering in his fair linen ephod, seemed to touch her irre-
sistibly, and in her secret soul she had envied Hannah.

The evening was to be devoted to this important meeting, but the next day Malcolm had promised to take Anna
for an outing—it would be her birthday—and already
they had made and rejected many plans. Kew, Richmond, Hampton Court, and Henley had all been proposed; but Anna had been indifferent to each. She had
been to the Royal Academy more than once, and all the
best concerts were over; the weather was too hot for
sight-seeing, and in her present state of languor she
dreaded fatigue and crowds. "What did the place matter after all," she said to herself, "as long as Malcolm
was with her? Her rest and enjoyment were in his
society—to sit beside him and listen to his dear voice, and
tell him all her little joys and troubles."

The programme was still a blank when Malcolm
knocked at his mother's door. Anderson received him

with a beaming face. The old man had grown a trifle
stiff and rheumatic of late years, but he still kept a sharp
eye on his coadjutor—the weak-minded and erring
Charles.

"They are not expecting you just yet, Mr. Malcolm,"
observed Anderson respectfully; "the mistress has a
committee in the library, and Miss Anna is in the drawing-room along with Charles and the carpenter, arranging
the seats."

"What time do they dine, Anderson?" Malcolm put
the question with some indifference—he knew quite well
what the answer would be.

"Why, you see, Mr. Malcolm, it is past six now," returned Anderson apologetically, "and the meeting's for
eight, and the mistress said there would be no time for
dinner as the committee would not break up until seven,
so she will have a cup of tea and a sandwich."

"Oh, indeed," returned Malcolm drily. "I suppose
Miss Anna and I are to be regaled on the same fare."

"No, sir, I think not. I believe Miss Anna and Dawson have contrived some sort of meal for you in the
schoolroom. They have done their best, Mr. Malcolm;
but what with committees and deputations and Heaven
knows what, my mistress has been driven almost out of
her senses. The maids are in the dining-room now, for
there's to be tea and light refreshment; and they've been
behindhand too with the plants from Covent Garden,
drat them," muttered the old man irritably. He was a
faithful servant, and true to his mistress's interests; but
he was growing old, and there were times when he longed
to sit quietly under his own fig tree, in the Surrey village
where he was born, where meetings and committees were
unknown.

"Never mind, Anderson," returned Malcolm pleasantly, "we cannot entertain a Bishop without some degree
of fuss and discomfort. I will go up and find Miss Anna;

I daresay she has nearly finished." But as he ascended the handsome staircase, he was not so certain in his own mind that this was a foregone conclusion; and again he blessed the day when he had pitched his tent in the quiet pasturage of Chelsea, where bishops and committees and drawing-room meetings never interrupted his lawful meals, or impaired his digestion; for Malcolm, like many other men, abhorred that nondescript meal so dear to the feminine mind, a meat tea. The wide, softly-carpeted staircase led to a spacious landing-place, fitted up with couches and easy-chairs, and ending in a small but pretty conservatory.

The drawing-room was a large, well-proportioned room, with a curtained archway opening into a smaller one, which went by the name of the music room. Here there was a grand piano and a fine harmonium; the latter was Mrs. Herrick's special instrument. The drawing-room wore its usual aspect on these occasions; rows of chairs and cushioned benches occupied the entire floor space, and overflowed into the inner apartment.

A crimson covered dais or platform, decorated with plants in full bloom, and tall spreading palms, with a semicircle of comfortable easy-chairs, was the chief feature in the arrangements; and here, with the evening sunshine streaming on her, stood a tall slim girl in a white dress, with a loose cluster of Shirley poppies in her hand.

It made such a pretty picture that Malcolm stood quite spell-bound: the crimson dais was such a rich background to the soft creamy white of the girl's dress, while the poppies held so carelessly added to the effect; even the sunshine filtering through the partially drawn curtains gilded the fair hair until it shone like gold. Malcolm was almost sorry when Anna caught sight of him, and ran down the steps towards him with a bright smile of welcome, and two hands outstretched.

" Oh, Malcolm, I never thought you would be here yet,"

she said, and her voice was very soft and clear; "but I am so glad to see you, and I have quite finished."

Anna Sheldon was not a pretty girl, but people always said she was so interesting. Her figure was well formed and graceful, and her expression and smile were remarkably sweet; but her features were by no means faultless, and her want of colour was certainly a defect. She had beautiful hair, which was fine and fluffy as a baby's; its tint was rather too colourless, but she wore it in a style that exactly suited her. At this moment, when her eyes were bright with pleasure and there was a flush on her face, Anna certainly looked pretty, but such moments were transient with her.

Malcolm pressed her hands affectionately; then he looked her over with brotherly freedom.

"You look very nice, dear. I see you are dressed for the evening; are those poppies part of the toilette?"

Then Anna laughed and fingered her pearl necklace as though she were embarrassed by his scrutiny. "No, of course not—what an absurd question. Fancy flowers at a drawing-room meeting. I am going to put them in a vase directly. Now, as mother is engaged just now, I am going to take you to the schoolroom, and nurse will give us something to eat."

"Feminine nectar and ambrosia, I imagine," muttered Malcolm to himself, for he had partaken frequently of these schoolroom feasts. But he was determined to make the best of things during his short visit, so he linked his arm in Anna's and said cheerfully, "Lead on, Hebe, and don't scatter poppies as you go," which was exactly what she was doing. The schoolroom was still Anna's special room, although it had changed its character of late years. It was a large, cheerful front room, two floors above the drawing-room, and Anna had made it very pretty and comfortable. Here she kept her books and all her treasures, and here her canaries twittered and sang in the sunshine. Malcolm, who loaded her with presents, had himself selected the handsomely framed prints that adorned the walls; his favourite " Huguenot," and " The Black Brunswicker," and Luke Fildes's " Doctor," and some of Leader's landscapes, had their places there. In this room Anna spent her leisure hours, few and far between as they were; here she read and thought and wrote her letters to Malcolm—sweet, maidenly letters, which he read lightly and tossed aside with a smile, not unkindly, but with the preoccupied carelessness of a busy man.

The sound of their voices brought Dawson to the door. She was a little pincushiony woman, with bunched-up gray curls, which she wore in defiance of all prevailing fashions, and of which she was secretly very proud; her complexion was still as clear and pink as a girl's; and her somewhat wide mouth was garnished by the whitest of teeth. It was Dawson's boast that she had never sat in a dentist's chair in her life.

" I am sixty-five if I am a day," she would say, with a quick little birdlike nod that always emphasised her statements; " but there, mother was eighty-three when the palsy took her, and she hadn't a gap in her mouth, dear soul."

Malcolm always kissed his old nurse, for there was a warm attachment between them; and indeed he never forgot that he had owed all his childish comfort to her.

" Blessed is he who expecteth nothing," observes the wise man, and Malcolm, who had indulged in moderate expectations in which the teapot loomed largely, was somewhat surprised by the agreeable sight of quite a tasteful little dinner-table laid for two, with a half-filled vase in the centre for which the poppies were evidently intended. Anna smiled delightedly when she saw his face, and at once proceeded to arrange her flowers, while Dawson bustled about and rang the bell, and chattered like an amiable magpie. In a very short time the weak-minded Charles, now a reformed and steady character and engaged to the head housemaid, brought in the tray, and a modest and appetising little meal was served. Cutlets with sauce piquant and pigeon pie, salad such as Malcolm loved, and a delicate pudding which seemed nothing but froth and sweets, while an excellent bottle of hock, sent up by Anderson, completed the repast.

"I wish mother could have joined us," observed Anna regretfully; "I did my best to persuade her, but she said there was no time. The people have not gone yet, and she has to dress, you see, so she said she would have some tea in her dressing-room and talk to you later."

"I must just see about getting the mistress's things ready," interrupted Dawson, but she spoke in a grumbling tone. "Don't you fash yourself, Mr. Malcolm,—I told Charles to unpack your Gladstone and put out your clothes ready for the evening. My mistress won't be dressed, you may take my word for it, for a good three-quarters of an hour. There is nothing like a committee for dawdling along, and keeping one standing on one leg as it were, like a pelican in the wilderness, or a stuffed goose, or anything you like to call it. Don't you let Mr. Malcolm hurry his dinner, Miss Anna, for there is nothing so bad for the digestion; a good digestion comes next to a good conscience in my opinion," and Dawson hurried away, all ready primed with a scolding for her mistress—sandwiches being like the proverbial red rag to a bull to this excellent woman.

"Such a pack of nonsense," she ejaculated, as she took down the black satin dress from its place in the wardrobe and shook out its lustrous folds, "a lady of her age, just passed fifty, and acting as though she were in her teens;" for Dawson, who was a privileged person, always spoke her mind to her mistress; indeed, it was rumoured in the household that Mrs. Herrick stood somewhat in awe of her faithful retainer, and it was certainly the fact that if any of the servants had incurred their mistress's displeasure, Dawson was always the mediator, and brought the apology or conciliatory message. Mrs. Herrick had a great respect for the straightforward, honest little woman, who was never afraid to speak the truth on any occasion, and she was sufficiently magnanimous to forgive her sharp speeches.

"Dawson is worth her weight in gold," she would say sometimes. "When the children were young I was never afraid to leave them in her charge, I knew I could trust her;" and once she said with a sigh, "I cannot forget her devotion to my dear Florence. She watched beside her night and day, and yet there were other nurses. I shall never forget her saying to me, 'Dear Miss Flo mustn't wake up and find herself amongst strangers, or she will be scared, poor lamb. She will like to see her old nurse's face, bless her,' and it seemed to us all as though she lived without sleep. She was right too," went on Mrs. Herrick softly, "for when Florence caught sight of her she put out her arms with such a smile. 'It is my own dear nurse,' they heard her say—those were my darling's last words."

When Dawson had left the room Malcolm looked at Anna with a smile.

"Well," he said tentatively, "have you made up your mind about to-morrow; is it to be Kew, or Cookham and Henley?" But to his surprise the question seemed to embarrass the girl.

"We have been so often to Kew," she returned in a hesitating voice; "and though the Quarry woods are delightful, it will be so hot on the river. There is something I should like so much better, but I am afraid you will laugh at me." But as Malcolm continued to look at her with an indulgent smile, she went on with renewed courage—

"I hope you will not think me absurd, but I should so

love to see your chambers in Lincoln's Inn, and Malachi, and the pigeons, and little Kit with the curly red fringe, and the old cobbler; and afterwards," and here Anna caught her breath with excitement, "we could go to Cheyne Walk and have tea and look at the river and talk."

"My dear child," in quite a startled voice, "what a programme for a birthday!"

"It will be just lovely," returned Anna with sparkling eyes. "I do so long to see Goliath and Yea-Verily and Babs. You know, Malcolm, I have only been twice to your rooms in Cheyne Walk—once with mother, and once when we had been to the Albert Hall—and each time the Kestons were away."

"And you want to see little Verity. I am not sure that she is quite up to your mark, Anna; she and Goliath are rather Bohemian."

"Oh, but you like her, and she makes you so happy and comfortable. I want to know your friends, Malcolm; it seems to bring you nearer," and Anna's eyes grew wistful.

"Are you sure my mother will approve of your programme?"

Then Anna smiled and nodded assent.

"She will call me a silly, fanciful child," she replied laughing. "Mother does not understand sentimentality; but I am a privileged person on my birthday. Now, Malcolm, please do not throw cold water on my little scheme."

"Certainly not; we will go to the Seven Dials if you like. Only I wish I had known beforehand. Verity is occasionally like the renowned Mother Hubbard, her cupboard is bare. You will have to put up with plain bread and butter, I expect."

"What does that matter!" returned Anna scornfully. "Thank you, Malcolm dear. Then we will have a real good time."

"I think we shall be able to carry out your modest programme," replied Malcolm. "Wait a moment, I have an idea. Suppose 'we beard the lion in his den;' in other words, look up Caleb Martin and my umbrella in Todmorden's Lane?" And then he gave Anna a graphic account of the little adventure, and, as he expected, received her warm approval.

"Oh yes, you shall take me there too," she observed. "I must see that poor little Kit; it was so like you to think of her comfort;" and here Anna laid a soft little hand on his coat-sleeve. "Malcolm, I am afraid I ought not to let you talk any longer. I heard mother go into her dressing-room ten minutes ago, and she is never long over her toilet."

"That means I must get into my war paint too, or Dawson will be coming in search of me;" and then he went off to his old room, leaving Anna looking thoughtfully out of the window.

"To-morrow I shall be one-and-twenty," she said to herself; "it seems a great age, but Malcolm is nearly nine years older." And then she added to herself in a whisper, "And from morning to night we shall be together, just he and I, our own two selves," and there was a soft look of contentment on Anna's face.

CHAPTER V

MRS. HERRICK OBJECTS TO BOHEMIA

We fear originality as a coat which is too new, and do our utmost to be like the rest of the world.—CARMEN SYLVA.

Life is work. . . . Life without work is unworthy of being lived.—BISHOP EDWARD BICKERSTETH.

TWENTY minutes later Malcolm knocked at the door of his mother's dressing-room. A deep, sonorous voice bade him enter. As he did so Mrs. Herrick laid down the book she was reading on the toilet-table, and turned to greet him. "My dearest boy, how glad I am to see you!" she exclaimed with a warm, motherly kiss. Then she put her hands on his shoulders and regarded him with an affectionate smile that quite lighted up her homely face. Even in her youth Mrs. Herrick had never been handsome. Indeed, her old friends maintained that she was far better-looking in her middle age, in spite of all her hard work and that burning of the candle at both ends which is so abhorrent to the well-regulated mind. Her features were strongly marked, and somewhat weather-beaten, and the lower part of the face was too heavily moulded, but the clear, thoughtful gray eyes had a pleasant light in them. Malcolm was secretly very proud of his mother. He liked to watch her moving among her guests in the dignified, gracious way that was habitual to her.

"She is the very personification of an old-fashioned English gentlewoman," he said once to Cedric; "but she is hardly modern enough in her ideas. She takes things too seriously, and that bores people."

It must be confessed that to her young acquaintances

4   49

Mrs. Herrick was rather awe-inspiring. Mere pleasure-seekers—drones in the human hive and all such ne'er-do-weels—were careful to give her a wide berth. Her quiet little speeches sometimes had a sting in them. "She takes the starch out of a fellow, don't you know," observed one of these fashionable loafers, a young officer in the Hussars—"makes him think he's a worm and no man, and that sort of thing; but she doesn't understand us Johnnies." Perhaps Mrs. Herrick would willingly have recalled her crushing speech when, years after, she read the account of Charlie Gordon's death. "He would have had the Victoria Cross if he had lived," exclaimed his weeping mother to Mrs. Herrick. "They say he was the bravest and the finest officer that they had ever known. You can read the account for yourself. All those lives saved by his gallantry." But here the poor woman could say no more. How could any woman bear to think of her boy standing at bay in that dreadful defile, to gain a few precious moments until help came?

"I wish I had not been so hard on him," thought Mrs. Herrick with a remorseful recollection of the young officer's hurt look. "What right had I to climb up into the judgment seat and rebuke one of these little ones?" and for a long time after that she was more gentle in her speeches.

"You look well, Malcolm," continued his mother with a satisfied air, "in spite of the heat and thunder. Anna has been complaining of a headache all day; but it was impossible for her to rest. However, Dawson tells me she is better."

"Oh yes, I thought she looked much as usual. She is always rather pale, you know. I need not ask how you are, mother—you look as fit as ever."

"Yes, I am very well, thank God! I sometimes think I have more than my fair share of good health. Malcolm, as you are here, I want to show you what I have chosen for Anna to-morrow," and she handed him a small case. It contained one of those minute toy watches, set very prettily with brilliants.

Malcolm lifted his eyelids in some surprise. "It is a perfect beauty," he observed; "but you must have paid a goodish bit for it."

"It was certainly rather extravagant of me," returned Mrs. Herrick apologetically; "but you know how girls love pretty things. Anna did so long for one of these little watches, and you know it is her one-and-twentieth birthday. By the bye, Malcolm, what have you two arranged for to-morrow?" But when her son briefly sketched out Anna's modest programme, Mrs. Herrick's pleasant face clouded a little.

"What a singular choice the child has made!" she observed. "Malcolm, I am not particularly anxious for her to be introduced to your Bohemian friends. Oh, I don't mean to say anything against the Kestons," warned by a certain stiffness of manner on Malcolm's part—" I have never even seen them; but Anna and Mrs. Keston move in such different worlds."

"Yes, of course," he returned rather impatiently; "but a mere introduction need not lead to intimacy. Verity is a good little creature, and her Bohemianism will not hurt Anna for one afternoon."

Mrs. Herrick's firm lips were pressed together rather closely as Malcolm spoke, and her manner became still graver.

"Will you forgive my speaking plainly, Malcolm?" she said quietly, "but I do think it such a grievous mistake for you to call Mrs. Keston by her Christian name. You know I have mentioned this before." Then Malcolm reddened; but though he laughed, he was inwardly annoyed.

"I spoke without thinking," he returned, trying to control his impatience, "but I suppose habit was too strong for me. There is really no harm in it, mother.

You know Keston is my most intimate friend—he is one of the best fellows in the world—and it stands to reason that his wife should be my good friend too."

" Yes, but there are limits, Malcolm."

" Of course there are limits," rather irritably; " but if I were to talk for ever I should never make you understand, mother.   In the first place, you have never seen Verity—I mean Mrs. Keston.   She is the product of a modern age.   From babyhood she has lived among artists. She has imbibed their Bohemianism and learnt to talk their jargon.   A studio has been her nursery, playroom, and schoolroom, and as soon as she grew up she married an artist."

" But all this does not prove that she is not to be treated with the respect due to a married woman, Malcolm."

" My dear mother, there is no question of respect. There is not a man who knows Mrs. Keston who does not esteem, and hold her in honour.   She is an original little person certainly, but a more loyal wife and devoted mother never lived.   He would be a bold man who ventured to take a liberty with her, or to overstep the limits laid down by her.   He would soon feel the measure of Goliath's foot—in plain words, he would find himself kicked downstairs by Amias Keston."

Mrs. Herrick shrugged her shoulders.   The conversation bored her, and as usual she found Malcolm a little impossible; he seemed so determined to maintain his point.

" From the first Mrs. Keston wished me to call her by her Christian name," he went on, " and Amias wished it too.   We were on such brotherly terms," he said, " that Verity—you see habit is too much for me, mother— wished me to regard her as a younger sister."

" I thought you looked upon Anna as your sister, Malcolm;" but Mrs. Herrick's keen gray eyes had a curious look in them—an acute observer might almost have thought that she was hoping that her son would contradict this statement.

"Oh, Anna," and then he laughed. "My dear mother, one cannot draw comparisons between them—they are utterly dissimilar."

"So I imagine," was the dry response; and then Mrs. Herrick made an effort to recover her wonted placidity. "Malcolm," she said, putting her hand through his arm, "we must go downstairs now or the Bishop will be arriving. I expect Anna is wondering what has become of us." Which proved to be the case.

Malcolm soon regained his good-humour. His mother had rubbed him up the wrong way, as usual, but his good sense told him that it was no use resenting her plain-spoken remarks.

She had her own fixed opinions on every subject, and nothing could move her out of her groove. She was a good woman and a kind-hearted one, but the sense of humour was lacking in her. She disliked all that she did not understand, and under the comprehensive term Bohemianism, she embodied all that was irregular and contrary to her creed.

"Herrick mère is a Philistine of the purest type," Amias Keston once said to his wife. "No, I have never seen her, but I can draw my own conclusions. Yea-Verily, my child, far be the day when that British matron crosses our humble threshold."

Malcolm had determined not to disappoint his mother that evening, so he banished all thoughts of his friends from his mind, and a few minutes later he was showing people to their seats and chatting pleasantly with his acquaintances.

Now and then, in the midst of her duties as a hostess, Mrs. Herrick's eyes rested on her son's dark face with motherly pride and tenderness.

He was doing his part so well—in his quiet, unobtrusive manner he was making himself so agreeable. Oh,
if he would only have stayed with her, and been indeed
the son of her right hand, and given himself to the work;
and then for a moment there was a filmy look in the
mother's eyes, and she listened a little absently to her
favourite speaker.

Malcolm did his part like a man. He applauded the
speakers at exactly the right moment, and when the meeting was over he actually made a neat, telling little speech,
conveying the vote of thanks to the chairman; and both
the manner and matter were so good that more than
one of Mrs. Herrick's friends observed to her that her
son would make his mark in the House.

Malcolm felt rewarded for his exertions when his
mother wished him good-night.

"You have been my right hand this evening, Malcolm," she said, looking at him with unusual tenderness.
"Thank you so much, my son;" and these few words
gave Malcolm quite a thrill of pleasure.

The heavy storm had tempered the extreme heat and
the night had been comparatively cool, and the little
group gathered round the breakfast table the next morning looked as bright as the day itself.

Anna had been charmed with her watch; but when
she opened Malcolm's case and saw the tiny diamond-
studded quiver, she was almost speechless with surprise
and delight. "Oh, Malcolm, how could you—how could
you be so kind to me!" was all she could say. But Malcolm only laughed and fastened the brooch in her white
dress. Then he took some half-open pink rosebuds from
a vase on the table and bade her wear them. "You are
too pale, and these will give you colour," he said in a
cool, critical tone.

Anna took them from his hand rather shyly. She
had put on her daintiest white frock in his honour, but

the rosebuds savoured of vanity to her. She never disputed Malcolm's opinion on any subject, but as she adjusted the flowers she gave Mrs. Herrick a deprecating glance, which the latter met with an indulgent smile.

" No, dear, you look very nice," she observed, as though in reply to this mute question; " you are not at all too smart. Now I must go and read my letters. Have a good time, children; and, Malcolm, remember Anna must not be overtired," and then Mrs. Herrick nodded cheerfully and withdrew to the library. Anna ran off to put on her hat, while Malcolm read his paper.

They went first to Lincoln's Inn, and Anna stood on the wide steps looking at the pigeons fluttering over the old buildings, quite unaware, in her innocent excitement —though Malcolm was not—that many an admiring glance rested on her.

In spite of her lack of beauty, Anna's pretty girlish figure and youthful grace often attracted people—her expression was so guileless and sweet, and the fair fluffy hair so softly tinted; and as she stood there in the morning sunshine, in her white gown and shady hat, Malcolm felt secretly proud of his young companion, and his manner became still more affectionate.

They interviewed Malachi, and to Anna's delight Malcolm put him through his paces. Then they went into the inner room, and Anna sat down on the chair Cedric had occupied, and looked round her with undisguised amazement: the shabbiness and ugliness of the surroundings almost shocked her.

" Oh, Malcolm, it is not a bit nice and comfortable," she said with an anxious frown; " fancy your spending your days in this dreary room."

Then Malcolm gave an amused laugh.

" Poor little girl, so you are disappointed in my literary den. I suppose you thought I should have carved oak and Russia leather bindings; but we don't go in for æsthetic furniture in Lincoln's Inn."

"But it is so ugly and so dingy, Malcolm."

"Is it?" he returned, quite surprised at this severe criticism. "I think it quite snug myself. I have done some good work here, Anna, so I suppose the ugliness and dinginess are somewhat inspiring." And Malcolm glanced at his littered writing-table rather proudly.

As Anna felt no temptation to linger, they started off briskly in search of Todmorden's Lane.

They found it with little difficulty. It was a small side street, of somewhat unprepossessing appearance, leading out of Beauchamp Street. Bennet, boot-maker and um-brella-maker, had a dark, dingy little shop just at the corner. It had evidently been an ordinary dwelling-house in old times, but a bow window had been added to transform it into a shop. A flight of broken steps led to the basement, where the cobbler and his household lived; but as they carefully descended, Malcolm suddenly paused.

"What on earth is that noise?" he asked in a puzzled tone. And Anna, drawing her dainty white skirts closely round her, stood still to listen.

It was certainly an extraordinary combination of sounds. It seemed at first as though two people were singing a duet in different tunes and without any re-gard to time; there was persistent melody and yet there was utter discord, and it seemed accompanied by the clanging of fire-irons.

Presently Anna began to laugh. "Do let us go in and see what it means," she whispered. "Somebody—a man, I think—is singing 'Rule Britannia' and 'Hark, hark, my soul' by turns, and there is a woman talking or scold-ing at the same time."

"I believe you are right," was Malcolm's answer. "Take care of that last step, child, it is quite worn away." And then, as they stood side by side in the dismal little area, he looked vainly for a bell. Finally, he rapped so smartly at the door with Anna's sunshade that they distinctly heard an irate voice say, " Drat their imperence," and a tall, bony-looking woman, in a flowered gingham dress and a very red face, bounced out on them.

She was so tall and so excessively bony, and so altogether aggressive-looking, that Anna felt inclined to hide herself behind Malcolm. Indeed, he remarked afterwards himself, that he had never seen a finer specimen of a muscular Christian, barring the Christianity, in his life.

" What's your pleasure?" observed the Amazon, folding her arms in a defiant manner, while through the open door they could now hear distinctly the cobbler's subdued and singularly toneless voice meandering on —" O'er earth's green fields, and ocean's wave-beat shore."

" Deuce take the man!" continued the woman wrathfully. " Will you hold your old doddering tongue, Caleb, and let the gentlefolk speak!" But there was no cessation of the dreary, dirge-like sounds. They found out afterwards that Caleb always worked with cotton-wool in his ears, so his wife's remonstrance failed to reach him.

" You see, it is like this, sir," he observed to Malcolm afterwards, when they became better acquainted with each other: " Ma'am's tongue is like a leaking water-butt. It is bound to drip, drip from week's end to week's end, and there's no stopping it. It is a way she has, and Kit and me are bound to put up with it. She means no harm, doesn't Kezia; she is a hard-working crittur, and does her duty, though she is a bit noisy over it; she is good to us both in her way, and I am not quarrelsome by nature, so, as I like to work in peace, I just stop my ears and hum to myself, and if she scolds I mind it no more than I do the buzzing of the blue-bottles on the glass."

"But the child Kit?" questioned Malcolm a little anxiously. Then a queer little twisted smile came to Caleb's face.

"She is used to it, is Kit, and she don't take it to heart much. I have heard her cheek Ma'am sometimes. Ma'am wouldn't hurt a hair of her head, for all her bouncings and flinging of pots and kettles when she is in a temper. It is the basement tries her, poor soul. She says she has never been used to it. Her first husband was in the tin trade, and they had a tidy little shop in the Borough."

"Oh, Mrs. Martin has been married before," observed Malcolm. He was rather surprised at this piece of intelligence.

"Lord love you, yes, sir; and when she became Josh Leggett's widow she just took up with me because she said she felt lonesome. She did it with her eyes open as I often tell her, but she has never got over the basement. It does not agree with her constitution, and it never will."

"I suppose Kit is Mrs. Martin's child?" asked Malcolm, as he digested this information.

Then Caleb gave a dry little laugh.

"Bless you, no, sir. Kezia never had any family. That was always a sore point with her. She said that was why she was so lonesome, and I believe she married me mostly on Kit's account. Oh, she has a good heart, has Ma'am," continued Caleb in his slow, ruminative way, "though she would talk a dozen men stupid, one after another, and be as fresh as paint herself." And with this graphic description of the second Mrs. Martin, Caleb touched his old hat and slouched away.

CHAPTER VI

YEA-VERILY AND BABS

We will have a swashing and a martial outside.—*As You Like It.*

The direct influence of good women is the greatest of all forces under Divine Grace for making good men.—KNOX LITTLE.

NEVER had that much-loved hymn "The Pilgrims of the Night" sounded so flatly and discordantly in Anna's ears as when she listened to Caleb's monotonous croak; but her sense of irritation changed to alarm when Mrs. Martin suddenly shook her fist at the open door and vanished. Malcolm, who promptly followed her, was just in time to see her shaking the cobbler by his coat-collar, much after the fashion of a terrier shaking a rat.

"Are you a born natural?" she screamed. "Pilgrims of the night, indeed! I'll pilgrim you, you chuckle-headed idiot. Here are your betters trying to make themselves heard." Then Caleb slowly unstopped his ears, and rose rather stiffly to his feet.

"You have got no call to be so violent, Kezia," he returned meekly. "Oh, it is the gentleman who lent us the umbrella. Kit and I were going to bring it back this afternoon, sir, but I had to finish a job I had in hand."

"There is no hurry," returned Malcolm. "We were in this direction, so I thought I would save you the trouble." Malcolm looked curiously round the room as he spoke.

He was not surprised when he learnt afterwards that the second Mrs. Martin objected to the basement. It was certainly a gloomy little place, though scrupulously clean and neat. The sunshine of a July day filtered reluctantly

59

through the small, opaque-looking window. Caleb's bench and tools were placed just underneath it, and above his head a linnet hopped and twittered in a green cage. Kit's perambulator occupied one corner, while Kit herself, seated at the table in a high chair, was busily engaged in ironing out some ragged doll-garments with a tiny bent flat-iron. Anna regarded her pitifully—the small shrunken figure and sunken chest, and the thin white face with its halo of red curls. But Kit was almost too absorbed with her endeavour to get the creases out of a doll's petticoat to heed her scrutiny. She only paused to nod at Malcolm in a friendly way.

" I wasn't wet one little bit, though Ma'am scolded dad so," she exclaimed in her high shrill voice. " I was like a queen in a big tent, wasn't I, dad? I was awful comfortable."

" She might have been drowned dead for all the care he took," returned Mrs. Martin with a contemptuous sniff, as she planted her arms akimbo in her favourite attitude. Her elbows were so sharp and bony that Anna thought of the Red Queen in *Alice in Wonderland*. " If it weren't for me that blessed lamb would be a corpse every day of her life—though I beg and pray him on my bended knees not to run her into danger."

She was only a coarse-tongued virago, but even Anna, who had shrunk from her, felt a little mollified and touched as she saw how tenderly the rough hand rested on the child's curls. But Kit pushed it pettishly away. " Don't, Ma'am, you've been and gone and spoiled Jemima's ball dress, and she is going to wear it to-night," and Kit held up a modicum of blue gauze which certainly did not bear the slightest resemblance to a garment, and regarded it anxiously. Jemima herself, a mere battered hulk of a doll, lay in a grimy chemise staring with lacklustre eyes at the ceiling.

" I suppose Kit is not able to walk?" asked Anna, looking rather timidly at the formidable Mrs. Martin; but to her surprise the rugged, forbidding features softened and grew womanly in a moment.

"Law bless you, miss, the poor lamb has never stood on her feet in her life, and never will as long as she lives. The doctors at the hospital yonder say that when she gets older and stronger she will be able to use crutches; but she is as weakly as a baby now, for all she has turned eight."

"Kit's a slight stronger than she was last year," interposed Caleb, laying down the boots he was cobbling; but Ma'am was down on him in a moment.

"You may as well shut your mouth, Caleb, if you have got nothing better to say than that, and if you have not eyes to see the dear lamb is dwindling more and more every day in this cellar of a place. 'Plenty of fresh air and light,' says the doctor, 'and as much nourishment as you can get her to swallow,' and all the winter we have to burn gas or sit in darkness through the livelong day, and the fog choking the breath out of one."

"It is our misfortune, sir, as Kezia knows," began Caleb feebly; but his pale blue eyes grew watery as he spoke; "it is not much of an 'ome when one has seen better days, but to my thinking Solomon was in the right when he talked of that dinner of herbs. If Kezia had a contented mind we should maybe all of us get on better."

"A contented fiddlestick!" exclaimed Mrs. Martin, so angrily that Malcolm thought it wise to make a diversion, especially as a warm fishy odour in the adjoining kitchen heralded the near arrival of the noontide repast. When he saw more of the Martins he invariably noticed the smell of fish; it seemed to be their principal diet—fish broiled or fried or boiled, or even at tea-time shrimps or periwinkles. He saw that Anna found the atmosphere oppressive, and determined to beat a hasty retreat.

"Well, we must be going," he observed. "Good-day,

Kit. Now I wonder, if I were to give you a doll, what sort you would like?" Then Kit, who had been frowning fiercely over the ball dress, looked up at him with astonished blue eyes.

"A real new dollie for me," she said breathlessly. "Oh my, Ma'am, do you hear that? Oh please may I have a baby that shuts its eyes, and that I can love?"

"Oh yes, I think we can manage that very well, Kit. You may look for your new baby in a few days." And then Anna kissed the sharp little face, and Mrs. Martin smiled at her quite affably.

"She'll talk of nothing else from morning to night. Thank you kindly, sir—and you too, young lady."

"Who is she?" whispered Kit, so loudly that both Malcolm and Anna overheard her. "Who is that nice lady, dad, in the white dress? Is she the gentleman's wife?"

Malcolm laughed in amused fashion as he assisted Anna up the crazy steps, but for once the girl did not respond. "It was so hot in that room," she said rather impatiently, putting up her hands to her burning cheeks. "Oh, Malcolm, what a dreadful woman and what a miserable place!"

"Oh I don't know," he returned. "Mrs. Martin's bark's worse than her bite, and one can see she is fond of the child. We may as well buy that doll, Anna, and then we will have some luncheon. There is a place I know where they do cutlets remarkably well, and their ices are capital," and then they set out in search of a toy-shop.

The shop where Malcolm proposed they should eat their luncheon had an upper window overhanging Piccadilly. Here they secured a small table to themselves.

At first Anna seemed a little thoughtful and abstracted. Kit's innocent suggestion had startled her out of her maidenly unconsciousness. It was such a strange thing to say. It was so terrible that people could think such things, and that Malcolm should only laugh as though he were amused. Somehow that laugh seemed to hurt her more than anything.

Malcolm was quite aware of the girl's discomposure; his gentlemanly instincts were never at fault. He knew that many of his mother's friends often hinted that his position with regard to her adopted daughter must be somewhat difficult. At such times he was given to affirm that no tie of blood could be stronger. " She is my sister in everything but name," he would say.

His influence over her was so great that he charmed her out of her quiet mood, and they were soon laughing and chatting in their old way.

They got into a hansome presently and drove to Cheyne Walk. As they passed Cheyne Row, and looked up at the grim old figure of the Sage of Chelsea, looking so gray and weather-beaten, Malcolm proposed that they should make a pilgrimage to No. 5, but Anna refused.

"We have been there three times," she objected, " and I do so dislike that dismal, dreary old house. I don't wonder that bright, clever Mrs. Carlyle was moped to death there."

"Hush, you little heretic," returned Malcolm good-humouredly. " To me No. 5 Cheyne Row is a shrine of suffering, struggling genius. When I stand in that bare, sound-proof room and think of the work done there by that tormented, dyspeptic man with such infinite labour, with sweat of brow and anguish of heart, I feel as though I must bare my head even to his majestic memory."

Malcolm had mounted his favourite hobby-horse, but Anna listened to him rebelliously. They had been over this ground before, and she had always taken Mrs. Carlyle's part. " Think of a handsome, brilliant little creature like Jane Welsh," she would say indignantly, " thrown away on a learned, heavy peasant, as rugged and ungainly as that ' Hill of the Hawk,' that Craigenputtoch, where he buried her alive. Oh, no wonder she became a neurotic invalid, shut up from week's end to week's end with a dyspeptic, irritable scholar in an old dressing-gown." Indeed, it must be owned, in spite of all Malcolm's eloquence, Anna was singularly perverse on this subject, and absolutely refused to burn incense to his hero.

As Anna must have her way on her birthday, Malcolm said no more, and the next moment they arrived at their destination—a gray, dingy-looking old house, somewhat high and narrow, overlooking the river.

The first floor windows opened on a balcony, which had an awning over it. Two or three deck-chairs had been placed there, and on summer evenings Malcolm loved to sit there, either alone or with a congenial spirit, enjoying the refreshing breezes from the river.

The house belonged to his friend Amias Keston, and some years before he had built himself a studio in the back garden. As his income was remarkably small, and his work at that time far from remunerative, he was obliged to let the upper floor. The situation charmed Malcolm, and the society of his old friend was a strong inducement, so they soon came to terms. Malcolm was an ideal lodger; he gave little trouble, beyond having his bath filled and his boots well polished. He breakfasted in his own apartment, but he always dined with the Kestons. A solitary chop eaten in solitude was not to his taste, and he much preferred sharing his friends' homely meals. " Plain living and high thinking suit me down to the ground," he would say—" a laugh helps digestion;" but in spite of his philosophic theories, many secret dainties found their way into the Keston larder, and were regarded doubtfully and with awe by an anxious young housekeeper.

Anna felt a little quickening of excitement as they walked up the flagged path—she could not look indif-

ferently at the house where Malcolm lived. It seemed
an age to both of them before the door was opened. Malcolm had knocked twice, and was meditating a third
assault, when they heard footsteps, and the next moment
a little brown girl appeared on the threshold with a child
in her arms.

"I am so sorry, Mr. Herrick, but Hepsy has just gone
for the milk," she whispered to Malcolm, who did not
seem a bit surprised by the intelligence.

He had grown used to these domestic episodes. The
milkman was generally late, and Hepsy, otherwise Heph-
zibah, was for ever on his track with a yellow jug in her
hand; they called it the "Hunting of the Snark," for
they were wont to treat the minor accidents of life in a
playful fashion.

"Anna, this is Mrs. Keston," observed Malcolm—"my
friend Verity, and Babs." Then Anna, in some confusion
and much astonishment, shook hands with this very
singular young person.

Verity! could this be the Verity that Malcolm had
eulogised with such enthusiasm—this little brown girl
who was regarding her so gravely and fixedly?

Anna was obliged to own afterwards that her appearance had given her a shock. She was so small and sallow
and insignificant, and her short curly hair was parted on
one side like a boy, and cropped quite closely behind. The
baby was small and brown too, a tiny edition of herself,
and they both had dark eyes that looked preternaturally
solemn; Babs, indeed, wore an injured expression, and a
puckered look of anguish spoke of the pangs of hunger
and the delinquencies of milkmen.

"Babs wants her tea," observed Verity cheerfully; "I
am going to give her a crust to amuse her. Will you
bring Miss Sheldon into the studio, Mr. Herrick? Amias
will be so pleased to see her, though he is very busy. I
know your name," she continued smilingly to Anna—she

5

had a fresh clear voice that sounded pleasantly on Anna's ear; " I have heard so much about you, that of course I recognised you directly, though Mr. Herrick did not introduce you properly."

Verity spoke with so much ease and frankness that Anna began to feel interested in her; she seemed so utterly oblivious of her shabby cotton dress and ridiculous bib-apron. Babs presented a far more imposing appearance in a white frock and pink ribbons, underneath which the bare little brown feet were peeping. Anna would willingly have made friends with her, but Verity advised her to wait. "Babs will not be sociable until she has had her tea," she remarked; " we had better take no notice of her for the present," and indeed that much-enduring and long-suffering infant was at that moment so reduced by famine as to attempt swallowing her own dimpled fist.

"What a capital boy she would make!" thought Anna as she followed Mrs. Keston into the dining-room; for the dark, closely-cropped head and a certain boyish freedom of step and bearing gave her this idea.

The dining-room was rather a gloomy apartment; the front windows were high and narrow, and the overhanging balcony rather obscured the light; the folding-doors had been taken away, but though this added to the size of the room, there was no additional cheerfulness gained, as the glass door in the inner room, which once had opened into a pleasant garden, now merely led into a covered way to the studio.

This sombre apartment was furnished in a curious manner, which made people open their eyes with astonishment until they found out that Amias Keston had acquired his household goods at second-hand sales.

The table of good Spanish mahogany had been a bargain, but it hardly harmonised with a Sheraton cabinet and a light oak sideboard, though both were good of their kind. Then the chairs had been picked up singly, and were of all sizes and patterns. Amias always sat in a grandfather chair of carved dark oak at the bottom of the table, and Verity in a high-backed chair in light oak and red morocco, while others were rosewood, mahogany, or Sheraton. Nothing matched, nothing harmonized; it was merely a curiosity shop in which they stored their purchases. So there were plush curtains and Japanese screens, a bronze Mazeppa, and an alabaster boy and butterfly, while blue dragon china and some lovely bits of Chelsea were in a corner cupboard. Anna, who knew there was no other living room, looked vainly round for some feminine occupation, and Verily, who was as sharp as a needle, seemed to guess her thought.

"Oh, I never sit here," she said confidentially, "it is too dark; Babs and I prefer the studio," and Anna did not wonder at the preference. The studio was a delightful room, high and well-proportioned, and with plenty of light. The part used by Amias Keston as his workshop was quite bare with the exception of the sitter's throne and an easel or two; this could at any time be curtained off to secure privacy.

The rest of the studio was fitted up as a sitting-room, with rugs, easy-chairs, and a couch, and a table with work and writing-materials. Here, in a retired nook behind an old screen, stood "Babs's" bassinette, where she took her mid-day naps.

"This is Verity's and Bab's playroom," explained Malcolm with a patronising air; "here the Martha of the establishment takes her well-earned rest." Then Verity flashed a sudden look at him which expressed unmitigated indignation.

"Hit one of your own size, Malcolm, my boy," observed a voice genially from the distance; and then, as Verity drew back a curtain, Anna saw a big, burly-looking man, with shaggy hair and a fair moustache, painting at an easel.

He was so big, so colossal in fact, that he seemed to shake the floor as he walked; everything was big about him, his hands and feet, his voice and his laugh, and when he whispered his words were audible at the other end of the room. This giant among men wore an old brown velvet coat, very frayed about the elbows, and though he was by no means handsome, there was such a pleasant, kindly expression on his face that Anna felt drawn to him at once.

"How do you do, Miss Sheldon?" he said, as Malcolm introduced them; "my wife and I have long wished to make your acquaintance," and here his big hand seemed to swallow Anna's up.

"Go on with your painting, Goliath," interrupted Malcolm. "He is working against time, Anna, and every daylight hour is of consequence to him; it was Verity who drew that curtain that he might not be disturbed;" and then Amias Keston stretched his huge arms and gave himself a shake.

"The Philistines are upon thee, Samson! Yea-Verily, my child, if the Snark is back, you had better tell her to bring us some tea." But here Malcolm again interposed. Goliath was far too busy, they would have tea upstairs, and then sit on the balcony afterwards; and Verity understood him at once. "Hepsy is back," she said composedly; "please take Miss Sheldon upstairs, and then Amias will go on with his work, and I will send up tea as soon as possible;" but before they were out of the studio Goliath was back at his easel and painting away for dear life.

CHAPTER VII

MORE ANCIENT HISTORY WITH VERITY

Heart, are you great enough
  For a love that never tires?
Oh heart, are you great enough for love?
  I have heard of thorns and briers?
                                    TENNYSON.

As the studio door closed behind them, Anna said regretfully, "I wish we could have stayed longer, Malcolm, I wanted to see more of that nice Mr. Keston; and I did so long to peep at his picture."

"Did you?" observed Malcolm in a surprised tone, but he was evidently gratified at this expression of interest. "Well, we will go back there presently, when he has finished that bit of drapery that is bothering him. Goliath is as nervous as a cat when he is working against time. He and Verity have arranged a regular code of signals," he went on: "when the curtain is drawn right across the arch, it means no admittance except on business, and all loafers and trespassers will be prosecuted. On these occasions Verity is a perfect dragon, and he would be an audacious man who would try to force his way in."

Anna nodded as though this explanation satisfied her, and then she followed Malcolm up the steep, narrow staircase into a pleasant, well-furnished room, with two windows opening on to the balcony.

Everything was in good taste and thoroughly well chosen. The dark oak bureau and writing-table, the book-shelves filled with well-bound volumes, the proof engravings on the walls, and a handsome bronze group on the mantelpiece; while the deep easy-chairs and couch gave it an air of comfort.

Anna had been there before, but she always reiterated her first remark on seeing it, " that it was the most comfortable room she had ever entered. You have such good taste, Malcolm," she would say; " even your paper-weight and the coal-scuttle are artistic."

" I am a lover of the picturesque," he would return solemnly, " and anything ugly or unsuitable would jar on me. I like subdued tints and mellow rich tones; that is why I bind my books in buff-coloured Russian calf. They harmonise so splendidly with the dark oak and the faded russet and brown and blue of the rug. Take my advice, Anna, cultivate your eye, and you will add much to the pleasures of life."

When Anna had inspected the latest engraving and tested the Chesterfield couch—a recent purchase—they went out on the balcony until tea was ready. A red-haired, buxom-looking maid brought it in.

It was evident that the mistress of the establishment was not without resources, for quite a pretty, tempting little meal was spread on the oval table. There was sponge-cake and shortbread, a dish of fruit, and delicious bread-and-butter. The beautiful teacups were Malcolm's own property, and had been picked up by him at a fabulous price in Wardour Street, and the little melon-shaped teapot had been a present from his mother. Verity always washed up these teacups herself. She said it was just for the pleasure of handling such lovely things, but in reality she knew Hepsy's clumsy fingers were not to be trusted.

Anna had only taken her place at the tea-tray, and was manipulating the curiously-shaped sugar-tongs rather carefully, when Malcolm looked at her a little searchingly. "Hurry up," he said severely; "how long do you suppose I am going to wait for your opinion of the Keston family?"

Then Anna, who had been vaguely alarmed by his judicial tone, filled up the teacups with a reassured air and in a leisurely manner. "You can hardly expect me to judge of any human being in five minutes," she answered with some show of reason.

"That sounds very plausible, my dear, but I can read you like print," and here Malcolm looked at her squarely. "You may as well confess, Anna, you are far more struck with Goliath than with poor little Verity."

Anna looked rather guilty; as usual, Malcolm's penetration had not deceived him. She had been most favourably impressed with the good-humoured giant, with his honest face and kindly blue eyes; but Verity, a brown slip of a girl with big solemn eyes, how was she to perjure herself by pretending that she was attracted by such a unique little piece of eccentricity.

"I wish she did not look so like a boy," she observed in a deprecating voice. But Malcolm took this remark in good part.

"Oh, you mean her hair," he replied coolly. "Oh, poor girl, that is the result of brain fever. She had the most wonderful hair you ever saw. When she let it down it quite swept the floor, and though it was so dark it had such splendid shades in it. Have you ever seen Keston's 'Leah and Rachel at the Well'?" Then, as Anna shook her head, "Well, Verity was his model for Leah. Leah is filling her pitcher and looking down into the well, so the eyes are hidden, but it is Verity's small brown face to the life. I always say that was his best picture. His Rachel was marvellous, but I liked Leah best; she was more human somehow, and those dark plaits of hair escaping from her turban were so beautiful. Poor little Leah! a month later they robbed her of her chief beauty by cutting off her hair. Old Goliath nearly sobbed as he told me."

Anna's face was full of sympathy. " Mr. Keston must be very fond of her," she returned in such a surprised and dubious tone that Malcolm laughed outright.

" You are not very flattering to poor little Verity," he observed, " but I can assure you that Goliath worships the ground she walks on. They are the happiest couple in the world. Amias is a good fellow and a fine artist, who will make his mark some day when he has got rid of his cranks, but he has not an ounce of his wife's brains; she is the cleverest and brightest little woman I ever met, and she has a heart big enough to hold the whole world."

Anna pondered over this splendid eulogium with some surprise; then she said quickly—

" You must allow me a little time before I can fairly judge of your friends, Malcolm. I know so little about Mrs. Keston. I remember you once promised to tell me about her early life, but somehow there has been no opportunity."

" Let us go out on the balcony and have our talk there, while I enjoy a cigarette," was Malcolm's answer to this. " We must not go back to the studio for another hour;" and then Anna took possession of one deck-chair while Malcolm occupied the other.

There was a short silence while Malcolm lighted his cigarette. Anna looked down on the broad gray river and a passing steamer with eyes shining with happiness. To her the hour was simply perfect. Malcolm was beside her, and in his kindest and most brotherly mood. What did it matter on what subject they talked? Verity or Cedric or Lincoln's Inn—anything that interested him would interest her. When Malcolm held forth on his favourite theories, Anna would listen with unflagging attention, and never once hint at her lack of comprehension, although the effort to understand him had made her head ache. The very sound of his voice was music in her ears, and this unconscious flattery was very soothing to his masculine intellect.

Malcolm, who had masterful ways of his own, was bent on convincing Anna that she was wrong in her estimate of Verity Keston, and he was very willing at this moment to tell her all he knew of her.

" I have heard all about things from Goliath," he began, " and Verity often talks about her old life to me. Neither of them make any secret about it. She was only seven or eight when he first saw her; she had just lost her mother. Her father's name was Westbrook; he was a scene-painter, a thriftless ne'er-do-weel, whose intemperate habits had brought them to poverty and broken his wife's heart; but in his sober moments he was good to the child, and she certainly seemed devoted to him."

" Oh dear, how sad it sounds, Malcolm!"

" My dear, it was far sadder in reality. Think of that lonely little creature, with no one to guide and befriend her except the woman of the house.

" In her rough way Mrs. Parker kept watch over the child, but she had children of her own and a sick husband, and had to drudge and slave for her family and lodgers from morning until night. Oh, I must tell you her answer to a well-meaning district visitor one day, Anna. The lady had just said very sweetly, ' It is so good for us to count our blessings, Mrs. Parker; we are so apt to forget our thanksgivings.'

" ' Humph,' returned Mrs. Parker, ' I don't reckon that I shall take long in counting mine—unless backaches and singing in your ears are amongst them. But then we have got something to look forward to in t'other world —there'll be no wash-tubs and no district visitors there, with their texts and high-falutin' nonsense.' "

Anna laughed merrily. In her quiet way she had a strong sense of humour.

"I think I like Mrs. Parker, Malcolm."

"Verity liked her too; she always says that she owes a great deal to her motherly care. 'I got a few cuffs sometimes,' she once said to me, 'but I daresay I deserved them, and, poor woman, she had troubles of her own to bear. But on cold nights I can't forget how she would come upstairs to tuck me up, and see if I were warm enough; and once, when I could not sleep for shivering, she brought me up some hot drink, and covered me up in an old shawl of her own;' and as long as Mrs. Parker lived Verity never forgot her.'

"I am beginning to feel interested in her, Malcolm."

"My dear child, if you could only hear Goliath talk on this subject your heart would ache for many a day. Think of that poor child growing up to womanhood in such surroundings; spending her days in a dirty, bare studio, with only rough, dissipated men for her companions—though to do them justice they treated her with respect and kindness. Somehow she picked up a desultory education among them. One broken-down old scene-painter taught her to read and write, and another, a French artist, taught her the rudiments of French, and also to play on the violin. 'They all treated me as a plaything,' she once said to me, 'and poor as they were, they would bring me toys and sweets. I think, nay, I am sure, that they were careful of their talk before me, but it was a strange life for a child. Very often I could not see their faces for the cloud of tobacco smoke, and sometimes the atmosphere was so stifling that I preferred to sit outside on the cold dark landing.'"

"Poor mite, what a life!"

"Amias told me once that he should never forget the first time he saw her. He was a mere lad himself of sixteen or seventeen, and a student in a life academy.

" Some errand had brought him to Westbrook's lodgings. It was a dull, cold January afternoon, and though it was only three o'clock, he said the light was so dim that he nearly stumbled over the child. She was sitting huddled up in the doorway of the studio, with an old red shawl over her head to protect her against the draughts, and a tiny black kitten was mewing piteously in her arms.

" ' Kitty's crying for her mother pussy,' she said, looking at him without the least shyness, ' but I want her to keep me company out here. It is not kind of her to cry.'

" ' But it is too cold for you and Kitty too,' observed Amias; ' you had better come in with me.' But the child shook her head.

" ' No, I durst not,' she whispered; ' daddy's drunk, and he is flinging things about so hard that Kitty and me might get hurt; so I am making believe we are the Prince and Princess in the enchanted forest. Will you stop and play with me?' and actually Amias—he was always a good fellow—squatted on the ground beside her and entered into the game. From that day they were the best of friends, and he was Verity's favourite playmate. On Sunday afternoons he took her out to feed the ducks in St. James's Park, or to watch the boys sail their boats on the pond in Kensington Gardens. He was only a poor art student, but he would forego a meal cheerfully to provide some little treat for his protégée. As the days grew darker with trouble, and Westbrook grew more hopeless and degraded in his habits, the neglected child turned to Amias for help and sympathy. There were terrible scenes towards the last, but I will spare you the fearful details; it was a miracle how any girl of fifteen could endure what Verity had to bear. For some months Westbrook's friends were fully aware that he was hardly accountable for his actions, and there was an attempt made to shut him up in an asylum. It was certain that the man was insane, and that his daughter was not safe from his violence. Amias concurred in this opinion, and the necessary steps were taken. Unfortunately, either the thing was bungled or Westbrook was too cunning for them, but before they could secure him he had hidden himself in Verity's room, and when the poor child entered he thought she was his keeper and felled her brutally to the ground. They were only just in time to save her. Don't look so pale, Anna, I am not going to harrow up your feelings. It is not a nice story. Westbrook was raving in a strait waistcoat before night, but he did not live many months afterwards;" and then Malcolm related the rest of the story.

It was after that terrible experience that Verity had brain fever and lost her beautiful hair. She had only just left the hospital when the news of her father's death reached her. It was Amias who told her.

The good fellow had visited her constantly, and as soon as she was strong enough to be moved, he took lodgings for her in a farmhouse in Kent where he had often stayed. The woman of the house was a simple, kindly creature who had grown-up daughters of her own, and Amias knew he could safely trust Verity to her care.

No environment could have been better for the girl: the beautiful air, the fresh country sights and sounds, soothed and strengthened her worn nerves. When Verity woke in the morning, instead of the rumbling of carts and waggons, she heard the fluting of blackbirds and thrushes in the orchard below, and the lowing of cows for their pastures. Everything was new and fresh to her; every flower in the hedgerow, every bird singing in the copse, was a miracle and revelation; the old miserable life had slipped away from her like a disused and faded garment, and her soul seemed new-born and steeped in beauty. "Oh, the peace and the loveliness of it all!"

she would say to Amias when he came down for his Sunday visit. "Am I really Verity—Verity Westbrook, who used to live in that dreadful Montagu Street?" And then she would look wistfully at him—for she had grown strangely timid and self-distrustful. But he would only laugh at her in his kindly way. "Yea-Verily, my child, it is certainly you yourself," he would answer; "when Nature made you she broke her mould, there could not be two editions of Verity." Sometimes, when she was low and weak, and memories of the past horrors were too vivid, and even his big laugh and little jokes failed to drive them away, she would cling to his arm and entreat him not to send her back. "If I see that place again I shall die," she once said, and the look in her eyes, and the way her small hand went to her throat, as though the very thought impeded her breathing, told him that she spoke the truth.

What was he to do with her? That was the question that occupied him for many a day. The summer had passed, and autumn was well advanced before he found the right answer.

One October afternoon he had taken her out for a walk as usual, and they had sat down to rest on a bench under a wide-spreading chestnut tree overlooking a village green. An aged donkey and some geese were feeding near them, but there was no one in sight. The old gammers and gaffers of the village were sitting by their firesides, for, in spite of the sunshine, the air was cold, and more than once Verity shivered as she sat.

"This wind is too cold for you, my child," he said presently; "let us walk on." But she shook her head.

"No, please let us stay a little longer. I do so love this village. If I were an artist I would paint it. Amias," interrupting herself, "there is something I want to say to you. I have been at dear Colbrook seven months— seven happy, beautiful months—but I am well now, and quite strong, and it is time for me to work and get my own living."

Verity spoke with great determination, but he noticed that her lips were white and drawn, and that there was a strained look in her eyes, and a sort of pitiful feeling came over him, such as a mother would feel for a suffering child. In spite of her brave words, he knew how she dreaded to face the world, though her womanly pride and spirit would prevent her from telling him so. More than once she had hinted to him that she felt herself a burden on his generosity; but at the first word he had checked her.

" How old are you, dear?" he asked by way of answer to her remark. The question seemed to surprise her.

" Oh, Amias, don't you remember I was seventeen on the first of May, and Mrs. Craven gave us a syllabub in honour of the occasion?" and Verity's dark eyes were a little reproachful. It seemed so strange to her that he could have forgotten that day. But Amias only tugged at his moustache and pondered deeply.

" I have it," he said briskly. " Verity, you shall be married on your eighteenth birthday, and you shall marry me." Then, as the girl shrank from him, and her thin face was covered with a burning blush at these unexpected words, his manner changed and grew very gentle. " Darling, you need not be afraid of me. Every hair of your head is sacred to me, for I love you dearly. I will take such care of you, my little Verity. You will be my child as well as my wife. You can trust your old friend Amias, can you not?" and though such an idea had never entered her head, Verity's confidence in him was so great that she actually put her hand in his and promised to marry him.

Never for one moment did she repent her resolution, and before the wedding day arrived she had learned to love him dearly. Amias had not long lost his mother, and the old house at Chelsea was empty when he took Verity there after their brief honeymoon. She was almost frightened at its magnificence until her husband explained to her that they would be too poor to keep it all for themselves, and that a friend of his had taken the drawing-room floor and would live with them.

Such were the outlines of the story related by Malcolm, but in reality much of it was only learnt later on from Verity's lips; but even the slight sketch as Malcolm told it affected Anna almost to tears.

"Oh, how she must have loved him!" were her first words when he had finished. "Malcolm, I know you will laugh at my enthusiasm, but I think Mr. Keston is one of the grandest and noblest of men. What a friend he has been to her all her life—she owes her life and peace and happiness to him! What would have become of her when she left the hospital if he had not cared for her and placed her with those kind people at the farm?"

"One can easily answer that question," returned Malcolm; "she would not have been alive now. Her nerves were fearfully shattered, Anna, and she was as weak as a baby when she arrived at the Hill Farm. Amias told me himself that he carried her into house like an infant. There, dry your eyes, lady fair, all's well that ends well. Now, as our hour is up, I think we may safely venture into the studio again."

CHAPTER VIII

THE RECORD OF AN IMPOTENT GENIUS

And whether you climb up the mountain or go down the hill to the valley, whether you journey to the end of the world or merely walk round your house, none but yourself shall you meet on the highway of fate.—MAETERLINCK.

THE door of the studio was slightly ajar, and the sound of a singularly sweet voice crooning out a lullaby was plainly audible. Malcolm, who was about to knock, changed his mind and peeped in through the aperture; then he beckoned to Anna to do likewise.

It was certainly a pretty picture before them. Verity was sitting in her low nursery chair, in the shadow of the heavy, ruby-coloured curtains, hushing her child to sleep, while her husband, at a little distance, stood before his easel; but she was so utterly transformed that Anna would not have known her.

She wore the dress of a Roman peasant; heavy gilt beads were clasped round her throat and fell over her white pleated chemisette, a gay-coloured scarf was arranged picturesquely on her head and gave warmth and colour to the small brown face. On her lap lay Babs. open-eyed and rebellious, kicking up her bare little feet and humming baby fashion in pleased accompaniment.

"Oh, Amias," exclaimed Verity at last in a laughing voice, "what am I to do with this naughty girlie, who refuses to go to sleep and only laughs in her mother's face? Oh, you darling, you darling!" and here Verity smothered the little one with kisses.

"Behold the stern parent!" observed Malcolm mockingly at this point. "Verity, that rogue of a Babs is a

match for you already. Why don't you put her in her cot
and order her to go to sleep, instead of crooning absurd
ditties over her? Oh, I thought so," severely, as Babs
grasped her toes with her dimpled hands in the practised
style of an acrobat, and gurgled defiantly in his face;
" she is just exulting over her own victory as an emanci-
pated daughter."

"Babs takes after her great-grandmother," observed
Amias cheerfully from the background; " it is the law of
heredity, you see. Her name was also Barbara—Barbara
Allen, and she was remarkable for her brown skin, her
gipsy beauty, and her incorrigible self-will. She had
lovers by the score, and flouted them all except my great-
grandfather, whom I have reason to believe wished himself dead before he had been married a week. She was
the mother of fifteen, and lived to a good old age, and was
a pride and terror to the neighbourhood, and the mantle
of her self-will has fallen upon Barbara Maud Keston.
Yea-Verily, my child, the oracle has spoken," and Amias
went on with his work, while Babs gurgled at him in delighted appreciation of these paternal sentiments.

"Would Miss Sheldon care to see my picture, Malcolm?" he asked the next minute in his usual voice; " it
is nearly finished, and I shall be glad of an opinion;"
and then he drew back from the canvas, and Malcolm and
Anna took his place.

It was one of those little studies from life that appeal
so strongly to the popular taste, and in spite of its simplicity and absence of breadth, it was exquisitely painted.
It was only a couple of organ-grinders resting during
the noontide heat. The man was sitting on the curb with
a short pipe in his mouth—a handsome rascal of a fellow,
evidently an Italian, with gold rings in his ears. The
woman, in peasant costume, looked heated and weary, and
had a baby in her arms. Both mother and child were
painted from life.

6

" How beautiful!" whispered Anna, looking reverently at the giant beside her.

" It is one of your best pictures, Goliath," observed Malcolm, " but I suppose you do not intend to exhibit it next year?"

" Oh no," he returned, " it is already bespoken by a rich Australian.   Rainsford brought him here to see if he would give me an order, and he fell in love with my organ-grinders at once.   I had a sort of idea that I would keep it myself, for the sake of Verity and the kid; but with a family"—here Amias smoothed his yellow moustache proudly—" one is bound to keep the pot boiling."

" I did not want it to go," sighed Verity, who had just then sidled up to her husband—she looked a mere child beside him—" it is such a perfect likeness of Babs." And then she withdrew with the rebel, while the others made a turn round the studio; and Amias showed them sketches, and also a more important picture that was to be exhibited at the Royal Academy the following year. Verity was the model again—this time as a sick gipsy girl lying on a heap of straw in a barn, while the caravan and encampment were painted most realistically, even to the old horse and shaggy donkey hobbled to the trunk of a tree, with a thin yellow cur near them.   When completed it would be a striking picture: the smoky sunset tints of a November afternoon were faithfully depicted; and a woodman's hut, just falling into decay, with golden lichen on the rotting roof, was marvellously painted. Malcolm stood before it in a rapt mood of ecstasy, then he struck himself dramatically on the breast.

" Goliath," he said sorrowfully, " I am the most miserable of men, a ' mute inglorious Milton' is nothing to me. Nature has created me a lover of the picturesque.   In heart and soul I am an artist, I dabble in colours, I dream of lights and shades and glorious effects; but the power of working out my ideas is denied me.   If I try to paint a tree my friends gibe at me. I am a poor literary hack; but I give you my word, my dear old Philistine, that I would willingly change places with you." Anna smiled, she was accustomed to this sort of talk; but to her surprise Verity, who had just rejoined them, looked grave.

"I am always so sorry for Mr. Herrick when he says this sort of thing," she observed in a low voice aside to Anna. "He means us to laugh, but he is quite serious. Amias and I just know how he feels. It must be so sad to love the beautiful with all one's heart and not have the power to create—to be just a thought and word painter and nothing else."

"Perhaps if Malcolm took lessons he might be able to paint in time," suggested Anna. She felt rather culpable, as though all these years she had not sympathised enough with him; but then it was so difficult for any one to know when he was serious.

It was evident that Verity understood him.

"Oh no, it is too late now," she remarked; "besides, the gift has been denied him. But he helps Amias so much by his clever suggestions. He would not tell you, of course, but this caravan scene is all his idea. He came upon a gipsy encampment in a Kentish lane one afternoon, and he made Amias go down the next day and see it. There was the woodman's hut, and the barn, and the hobbled horse and donkey. Amias was down there at the inn three days, making sketches for the picture, and getting some of the gipsies to sit to him. There was one woman ill in the tent, but Amias declared she looked more like a sick ape, she was so ugly—so I had to be the model."

"Isn't it rather tiring work, Mrs. Keston?"

"Oh dear, no," returned Verity smiling; "it never tires me to do things for Amias; and then he lets me talk to him all the time. I like to feel I am useful to him, and can help him a little with his work."

"Oh yes, I can understand that," returned Anna softly. She thought Verity looked quite beautiful as she spoke; perhaps the costume of a Roman peasant suited her, but Anna, who was standing quite close to her, noticed the wonderful softness of the brown eyes and the length of the curling lashes. Babs had grown drowsy at last, and Verity had placed her in the cot. Then they all sat down for a brief chat before it was time for Malcolm to take Anna home.

They had been talking about Amias Keston's unfinished picture, and, as usual, Malcolm had been holding forth in his rôle of art critic, when one of those sudden pauses which seem to drop softly between intimate friends followed his concluding speech. Verity held up her finger with the hackneyed allusion to a passing angel, at which Malcolm laughed scornfully.

"You are too poetical, my dear Verity," he observed; "it was no white-robed celestial vision brushing past us in the twilight and fanning us with plumed and balmy wings; the gliding shadow that moved between us was merely the guardian genius who presides over my destiny. But as he passed I touched his mantle"—and here Malcolm regarded his audience with infinite meaning.

No one hazarded an observation. Amias, who had been filling his pipe with tobacco, looked at it longingly and returned it to his pocket. This process he repeated at intervals from sheer force of habit. With his pipe alight he was an ideal listener; without it his attention wandered and grew drowsy. But Malcolm, wrapt up in his own visionary conceits, did not see the pathos of the action.

He was on his favourite hobby-horse—life, and its limitations, its enforced denials and futile sacrifices, was opening before his eyes.

"I am going to write a book," he announced abruptly. "I mean to take the world by storm—to say my say—for once. It will not be a novel. The public is inundated by the flood of fiction that threatens to engulf it. We have biographies by the ton, in two, three, or four volumes; in every public place in England we set up our golden image, and we bid men, women, and children fall down and do it homage. Hero-worship is our favourite cult; woe to that man who refuses to burn incense before it!"

"I suppose you intend to bring out a volume of essays?" queried Amias lazily.

"No, my dear fellow," returned Malcolm rather mendaciously, for he was planning a series of essays at that very time. "No trifles and syllabubs for me—froth above and sweetness and jam beneath. Every one writes essays nowadays, and tries to stir with his little Gulliver pen the yeasty foam raised by a Carlyle or an Emerson. One might as well watch the effort of a small hairy caterpillar to follow in the wake of a sea-serpent. Oh ye gods and little fishes, could anything be more grotesque!"

"But the book?" growled Amias, with a surreptitious glance at his pipe.

"Oh, the book," returned Malcolm loftily, "it is a sudden inspiration, but I feel the grip of my Frankenstein already; I have not yet let go the mantle of my guardian genius. It will be autobiographical, expansive, and deep as human nature itself, and I shall call it ' The Record of an Impotent Genius.' "

"Good lack!" observed Amias in a disgusted tone, " what a drivelling title! Why impotent, in the name of all that is rational?"

"My dear old Philistine," returned his friend in a measured voice, " I use the word impotent in the meaning attached to it in Holy Writ, and as my beloved and well-thumbed Thesaurus uses it: impotent, powerless, unarmed, weaponless, paralytic, crippled, inoperative, ineffectual, inadequate. Think of the strong man bound for a lifetime, Goliath—of a dumb and palsied genius gazing out of a prison-house. Could even a blinded Samson equal the pathos of such a picture?"

Amias shook his head mutely, and felt a third time for his pipe, and plugged the tobacco tenderly with his finger. In some moods he never argued with Malcolm.

"I shall write the autobiography of this poor tormented soul," went on Malcolm—"this dumb poet, this crippled artist, to whom the birthright of failure has descended, who has to look on for a lifetime at other men's labours, and to whom the power of expression and creation is denied, who has been gifted with the seeing eye in vain."

"Oh that seeing eye!" groaned Amias, who had heard this observation at least a hundred times. Then Verity began to laugh, and, to Anna's surprise, Malcolm followed suit. Then he clapped Amias heavily on the shoulder.

"Where's your pipe, Goliath? Poor old Philistine, he is a gone coon without his baccy. Fetch him a match somebody." And as Amias feebly protested against this, he went on—"Anna is quite a Bohemian, and rather likes the smell of tobacco. I will have a cigarette to keep you company," and in another minute Amias's broad countenance wore its usual expression of placid enjoyment.

The conversation turned on Cedric Templeton, and Malcolm asked Verity if she could transform the lumber-room into a bedroom for two or three nights for the use of his friend. This she at once cheerfully undertook to do, and promised to have it ready by the following evening, and then he informed them of his intended visit to Staplegrove.

Verity's eyes at once challenged her husband. "Staplegrove," she said in a surprised voice, "do you mean Staplegrove in Surrey? Why, that is the very place where the Logans live."

"Are you speaking of Matt Logan?" asked Malcolm.

"Of course he lives down there; but I heard the other day that he had come in for some money, and had gone abroad for his wife's health."

"Oh, that's right enough," returned Amias. "Verity and I saw them off two days ago. They have gone to the Black Forest. I meant to have told you before, but something put it out of my head—that he has lent us his cottage."

"What a piece of good luck! Upon my word, I am inclined to envy you, Goliath."

"There is no need for you to do that," returned Amias cordially. "There will be a 'prophet's chamber' ready for you when you feel inclined to run down. It is a nice little place enough. 'The Crow's Nest' they call it, though I am not sure there are any crows about. Verity and I ran down to have a look at it. The house is a mere cottage, only just room to swing two cats and a kitten— not a corner for any impotent genius to woo the drowsy god in," and here Amias gave a great laugh; "but there is a queer sort of garden room Logan has built which he calls his workshop, and part of it is partitioned off as a bedroom. It is a bit airy in the winter, he says, but simply perfect in the summer. You can sleep with your window wide open, and great tea-roses nodding in at you, and now and then a night-jar or a black-winged bat flitting between you and the moon."

"It is a little bare certainly," observed Verity, "but so pleasant, and I think I could make it comfortable for you, Mr. Herrick. The side window looks out on a flower-border. There are great yellow clumps of evening primroses and milky white nicotiana, and the roses are simply everywhere."

"How long shall you stay?" asked Malcolm in an interested voice.

"Well, the Logans have offered it to us until the end of October," returned Verity; "and as it is so hot in

town, Amias proposed this morning that we should try
and get off in another ten days. I think we shall stay
there until the end of summer."

"And what am I to do without you both—a lonely
bachelor?" exclaimed Malcolm. "For selfishness and
want of feeling commend me to married people. With
regard to their less fortunate fellows they have simply no
conscience."

"My dear fellow, you will be as right as a trivet,"
returned Amias. "You will have the Snark to attend to
your comforts, and the maternal Snark—a sad-faced but
most respectable woman—to attend to her daughter's.
We have the Logan's servant, and a slip of a girl besides,
a sort of Marchioness, who answers to the name of
Miranda. Verity will find her a comfort with Babs."

"And I am to run down to the Crow's Nest when I
like?" Then Amias nodded a cheerful assent.

"We shall expect you from Saturday till Monday, and
as many more days as you like to give us. You are part
of the household, my dear fellow. I wish we could offer
a room to Miss Sheldon; but we shall have to turn the
spare room into a nursery. By the bye, Malcolm, I
strolled down the road with Logan and passed the Wood
House. It looks a charming place, and it is only a stone's
throw from the Crow's Nest."

Malcolm felt vaguely interested. What a small world
it was after all! He was going to make acquaintance
with Cedric's people in this remote corner of Surrey, and
lo and behold, Goliath and his belongings were following
him.

Well, he was sick of the heat and turmoil of town, and
it would not be a bad plan to take possession of the garden room, and make Verity find a quiet nook where he
could write undisturbed. He really had a brilliant scheme
in his head—some essays which should interlace and
overlap each other like a linked chain of curious work-

manship. He had already accumulated his material, and he only wanted leisure to write. He knew his trade well, and his strong, vigorous style, his admirable choice of words, his pure English, and above all, his complete knowledge of his subject, were already bringing him into notice with the critics.

Yes, his summer holiday should be spent at the Crow's Nest, and he would work and play at his own sweet will. It was a pity Anna could not join them for a week or two. She and Verity would have become such friends; and then he remembered his mother's prejudices. Besides, she was thinking of going to Whitby, and if so she would expect Anna to accompany her.

It was time for them to go now; but, as they drove home in a hansom, Malcolm suddenly laid his hand on Anna's. "You are very quiet, dear," he said gently. "Have I tired you, or has your day disappointed you?" But he was amazed when the girl turned her face to him, for he saw her eyes were full of unshed tears.

"Oh no, it has been perfect—you and your friends have been so good to me, Malcolm. It will be like a beautiful picture—the river and the studio and the sunset. But why must pleasant things come to an end?" And then she sighed, and said half to herself, "There will be no Wood House or Crow's Nest for me;" and Anna's voice was so sad as she said this that Malcolm felt quite a pang of pity cross him. Why was Anna's life so dull, and his so full of interest?

CHAPTER IX

THE WOOD HOUSE

Without love there is no interior pleasantness of life.—SWE-
DENBORG.

IT was a lovely July afternoon when Malcolm Herrick
and his friend arrived at Earlsfield. A smart dog-cart,
Cedric's own especial property, was waiting for them at
the station. As they mounted to their places, and Cedric
took the reins from the groom, he pointed out the good
points of the mare with an air of complacency and satisfaction that somewhat amused Malcolm; but the next
moment he said in a boyish manner, " You see, Herrick,
I have not got quite used to my new toy. My sisters
gave me the trap on my last birthday. I have had Brown
Becky for two years. She is good for either driving
or riding; but I dropped a hint once, in Dinah's hearing,
that I longed for a dog-cart, and though she said nothing at the time, she and Elizabeth put their heads together, and they got Mr. Brodrick, a neighbour of ours,
to choose it."

" Your sisters are very good to you," observed Malcolm in rather a patronising manner. He even smiled
to himself furtively at the thought of the two gentle
spinsters. " A good-looking boy like Cedric is always
spoilt by his womankind," he said to himself. " If I
ever get on intimate terms with them, which is very un-
likely, I shall tell them that all this petting and spoiling
is not good for the lad, and will only unfit him for his
work in life. Women have no sense of proportion," he
continued rather irritably; " they either do too much
or too little, and the Misses Templeton seem to be no
exceptions to the rule."

90

They had left Earlsfield behind them, and were now climbing the long, winding ascent that led to Staplegrove. As the road grew steeper, Brown Becky slackened her pace.

The heavy storms had tempered the great heat, and though the sky was cloudless and the sunshine brilliant, the trees meeting overhead gave them a pleasant shade, and a soft, refreshing breeze blew in their faces. Malcolm drew a long breath of delight.

"There is nothing like the country after all," he observed. "When I have made my pile, I shall pitch my tent or build myself a hut far from the madding crowd, and bid good-bye to Lincoln's Inn, and Piccadilly, and club-land, and all the delights of modern civilisation."

"Not you, old fellow," returned Cedric sagaciously. "Why, you would be bored to death in no time." But Malcolm shook his head.

"Am I not a lover of the picturesque, my dear boy? Nature intended me for a country gentleman." Malcolm so dearly loved argument for its own sake that he did not always consider it necessary to weigh the accurate truth of his words. He liked to take different views of the same subject. On more than one occasion in Cedric's hearing he had compared himself with Charles Lamb. "Custom had made the presence of society, streets and crowds, the theatre and the picture-gallery, an absolute necessity." Why, in some moods he would take this as his text, and discourse most eloquently on what he called the spectacle of the streets. "There are few days when there are not groups of Hogarth-like figures," he would say—"sketches from the life, abounding in humour or infinite pathos. There is a blind beggar and his dog over in a corner by the Temple station," he continued, "that I never can pass without putting a penny in the box. The dog's face is perfectly human in its expression. The eyes speak. I gave him a bone once—a meaty bone it was, too"—and here Malcolm looked a little ashamed of himself—"in fact, it was a mutton chop, and I stole it off the luncheon table. I kept the beggar in conversation while he ate it. Sir," for he was addressing Amias Keston at that moment, "that dog positively grovelled at my feet with affection and gratitude."

"How many mutton chops has he had since?" asked his friend.

"He never had another," responded Malcolm sadly. "The carriage of a greasy paper full of meat is too much even for my philanthropy; but I take him dry biscuits—sometimes Spratt's meat biscuits—and tobacco for the beggar. He is an old soldier and wears his medal; and the dog—Boxer is his name—is like Nathan's ewe lamb to him. He has got a crippled son—a natural he calls him—who fetches him home in the evening. I saw him once," went on Malcolm, puffing slowly at his cigarette, "an uncouth sort of chap on crutches; and when Boxer saw him he nearly knocked him down, jumping on him for joy; and they all went home together, quite a cheerful family party."

"You would not be happy away from town, Herrick," persisted Cedric; "that's such a jolly crib of yours at Cheyne Walk;" for he had been greatly struck by the Keston ménage, and had quite fallen in love with his quaint little hostess; while Verity, on her side, had taken very kindly to the handsome lad, and made much of him for Malcolm's sake.

"Oh, I am comfortable enough," returned Malcolm. "Chelsea is sacred ground to me. Did not Carlyle live and die there! Besides, there is the river and the bridges, and Battersea Park in the distance, and the house where Gabriel Dante Rossetti lived, and an old historical church, and the grand old Hospital, and all sorts of gray secluded old nooks and corners over which I can gloat when I take my walks abroad."

"What a queer chap you are, Herrick," Cedric returned in a puzzled tone. He felt rather like the bewildered Satyr when the traveller blew hot and cold. But Malcolm was perfectly sincere. No man loved the country more truly and sincerely. Nevertheless, the town was equally necessary to him; and if he had been compelled to choose between them, his casting vote would have been for town.

"We are at the top of the hill now," observed Cedric presently, with a jerk of the reins to remind Brown Becky that she must not go to sleep, and then they bowled swiftly down a wide open road. They had just passed a cross-road, which, as Cedric informed Malcolm, led to Rotherwood, where the nearest church and shops were, when Malcolm's attention was attracted by a house they were passing. It was a small gray house, standing rather back from the road, with a garden at the side full of gay flower-borders.

"Oh, that's the Crow's Nest," observed Cedric, "where the Logans live; that is where your friends the Kestons are coming. Oh, there is no need of looking at it now," as Malcolm craned his neck in his effort to see more of it; "we can go over it any day we like. Here we are at the Wood House," and Cedric drove in at an open gate.

Malcolm looked round in pleased surprise. At that moment the house was not visible. They seemed driving through a little wood—only the carriage road winding between the fir trees was beautifully kept. Now and then there was an open glade, but the greater part was thickly fringed with heather, bracken, and whortleberry bushes.

The next moment Cedric turned a corner sharply, and a low gray house and a well-kept tennis lawn were before them.

"What a charming place!" exclaimed Malcolm. "It certainly merits its name—it is indeed a Wood House."

"Dinah is going to build a lodge next year," returned Cedric. "Lots of people refuse to believe there is a house in the wood, and lose themselves a dozen times before they find it. Ah, there's Dinah on the look-out for us. Jump down, Herrick; I will follow you directly. I want to speak to Forbes about the mare."

Malcolm did as he was told, and entered the long, softly-lighted hall. Perhaps the sunshine had dazzled his eyes a little, but at that instant he thought it was a young girl who was advancing to meet him. The figure was so rounded and graceful, and there was such alertness and youthfulness in the bearing; but as she came closer to him he saw that her hair was quite gray.

"I am very pleased indeed to see you, Mr. Herrick," she observed in a pleasant voice. "We have heard so much of you from Cedric that you seem quite an old friend. I am afraid you will find us very quiet, homely people; but I daresay Cedric will have prepared you for that. He grumbles dreadfully, poor boy, at our old-fashioned, humdrum ways."

"I can assure you, Miss Templeton, that the quiet will be very restful after the turmoil of town," returned Malcolm seriously; "and, as far as I can judge at present, Staplegrove seems a perfect paradise;" and then Miss Templeton smiled and led the way into a pleasant, cosy-looking drawing-room, with three windows opening on to a terrace, below which lay a charming garden. On this side of the house the wood ended abruptly; but in the distance, beyond a rose arch, Malcolm caught sight of a little rustic bridge which seemed to span a sort of green ravine.

Miss Templeton had taken her place at the tea-table; but Malcolm did not at once follow her. "After all, town has its drawbacks," he said half to himself; but Miss Templeton understood him.

"You mean one has to do without gardens there,"

she returned. " That would never suit either my sister or myself; our garden is very dear to us. You have not seen all its beauties yet, Mr. Herrick," she continued brightly; " it is full of surprises. When I have given you some tea we will go in search of my sister. She is sure to be down at the Pool—we call it Ophelia's Pool, because it reminds us so of a picture we have seen in the Royal Academy. It is our favourite haunt on a hot summer's afternoon."

Malcolm made an appropriate reply, and for the next few minutes they talked pleasantly of Staplegrove, and the short cut that led to Rotherwood church and village; and then Cedric joined them, and began chatting volubly to his sister; and Malcolm drank his tea and watched them both. He owned to Anna afterwards that Dinah Templeton was a revelation to him, and that all his preconceived notions of her fell as flat as a pack of cards.

The demure and somewhat stately spinster he was expecting to see was certainly not *en évidence* in this gray-haired, radiant-looking woman; the soft, girlish bloom and the silvery hair were wonderfully attractive; and yet what struck him most, with a sort of indefinable surprise, was the mingled gentleness and brightness of expression; there was such a wonderful clearness in the eyes—it somehow reminded him of the innocent look of a happy child.

And it was to this sweet woman that Cedric was talking in that cavalier fashion—with much affection certainly, but little reverence, after the manner of the nineteenth-century youth. More than once Malcolm muttered " Jackanapes " under his breath, and once he interposed.

" Our young friend is too modern in his notions, Miss Templeton," he observed. " Young Oxford is so cock-sure of everything under the sun—it is a fault of the age."

"Oh, do you think so?" and Miss Templeton looked relieved; for the moment her serenity had seemed slightly clouded with what her sister always called her "hen and duckling look."

"Oh, you may laugh, Cedric," looking at him fondly, "but I intend to believe Mr. Herrick, he is older and more experienced. Oh, we have such arguments sometimes," turning to Malcolm. "Cedric will have it that we are not sufficiently up-to-date. We are mediæval or in the Dark Ages, according to him, but how is one to alter one's nature or to talk unknown languages? My sister and I are very conservative, and we cling to the beliefs and loves of the past."

"I don't believe Cedric wants to change you in the least, Miss Templeton; he is only posing a bit for your edification, and trying to make you think that he is as clever as he looks."

"Come now, draw it mild," growled Cedric. And then he looked discontentedly round the room. "Where's Dick and the rest of the fellows? I bet you anything you like, Die, that they are down with Elizabeth at the Pool."

Dinah smiled as she rose from the table. "You are right, dear," she returned composedly, "I saw the whole train following her as usual. Dick wanted to go with the dog-cart,—he knew his master was expected, but Forbes said it was too hot for the run. If you are ready, Cedric, we might go down to the Pool now." And as Cedric graciously intimated his readiness, Dinah led the way through the flower-garden, only pausing on the rustic bridge to let Malcolm lean over and admire the hanging gardens below, the sides of the little ravine being clothed from the top to the bottom with wild-flowers and plants of every description. The traveller's joy had even gained a footing on the bridge itself. To add to the beauty, a tiny rivulet, which seemed to take its rise from some invisible source, flowed through the flowery ravine like a silver thread.

"What a charming spot!" observed Malcolm in a tone of such sincere admiration that Miss Templeton looked quite gratified.

"It was my sister's idea," she said softly; "she originates most of our improvements. Now, as you see, we have come to the end of our garden and are going down that little woodland path. We are both passionately fond of flowers, and like to see them from the house, but in our hearts I believe we love our wild garden best."

"And you are right—one could never be tired of this," and Malcolm glanced at the slender stems of the firs and the soft green light between the tree-boles. Just here the ground was bare except for the carpet of brown needles, but the next moment the path became more tangled and sloped rather steeply. They could distinctly hear a dog bark. "Take him to the peep-hole," whispered Cedric in his sister's ear, and Miss Templeton nodded and stepped off the path; then she beckoned Malcolm to look through some interlacing branches which formed a natural arch.

It was a charming little sylvan scene that met his eyes. The spot had been fitly called Ophelia's Pool. The small pond was shut in with rowans and thickets of alder and blackberry bushes, and on the pond itself some water-lilies and other aquatic plants were growing. Two or three rough boulders, cushioned with moss, made comfortable seats, and were at the present moment occupied by two people—one of them evidently the second Miss Templeton, and the other a young man in a rough serge suit, whom at first sight Malcolm certainly did not take for a clergyman; and round them, in various attitudes of waiting and expectancy, dogs of all sorts and conditions—from a handsome brown retriever to Cedric's little fox-terrier, Dick.

"My word, there's Carlyon," observed Cedric in rather an aggrieved tone; "why, the fellow lives here;" and then he put his hands to his mouth and gave a view-hallo so lustily that all the dogs began barking like mad. Only Dick—who was a knowing fellow and up to tricks—rushed up the path and began dancing excitedly round his master.

"What barbarians boys are!" observed the other Miss Templeton somewhat coolly to her companion, and then she rose from the boulder and walked rather majestically towards her sister and their guest.

Her manner was friendly, and she greeted Malcolm kindly enough, but it was less soft and winning than her sister's, and did not impress him so favourably. Then she introduced Mr. Carlyon, and the two young men shook hands; and afterwards the dogs passed in review, and Elizabeth gravely named each one, ending up with her sister's little dachshund Mike.

Malcolm, who was a dog-lover, although he had none of his own, was soon making friends with all the animals; but as he praised and caressed them, he was telling himself over and over again that the second Miss Templeton could not hold a candle to her sister.

Malcolm was terribly critical with regard to women; Anna had often blamed him for his severity.

"It is a mistake to expect perfection," she would say; "it is so easy to find fault and pick holes in people;" but though Malcolm agreed with her, he still remained fastidious and hard to please. So he at once decided that Miss Elizabeth Templeton was not to his taste. In the first place, he did not admire big women—and she was tall, and decidedly massive. Her dress, too, was singularly unbecoming—a big woman in a cotton blouse and a battered old hat was a spectacle to make him shudder. Miss Templeton's blue muslin and dainty ruffles were a pleasing contrast.

"It is a woman's duty to set herself off as much as possible," he would say to the long-suffering Anna, and then he transposed a certain saying, "If you can't be handsome, be as handsome as you can;" and he would hold forth on the immorality of slovenliness.

"I daresay Miss Elizabeth Templeton would not be bad-looking if she only took a little pains with herself," he thought, as they all grouped themselves comfortably on the boulders. After a moment's hesitation, Elizabeth placed herself beside him and begun to talk to him. Somehow her voice pleased him. It was not so sweet as her sister's, and there was a sort of burr in it, and when he knew her better he discovered that when she was eager or excited about anything there was a slight hesitation, as though her words tripped each other up; but with all its defects it was a voice to linger in the memory. She was so close to him now that he could judge of her better. She was certainly not handsome, her features were irregular and her mouth decidedly too wide for beauty; but the gleam of faultlessly white teeth and a certain brightness in the dark Irish-gray eyes redeemed her face from plainness; her skin, too, was clear and naturally fair, but was evidently embrowned by air and sunshine.

Nature had formed her in a generous mould, for even her hands and feet were large; and then Malcolm thought of Anna's pretty little hands, and again he said to himself that in his opinion Elizabeth Templeton was not an attractive woman.

CHAPTER X

WHAT THE FERN-OWL HEARD

There is but one thing that can never turn into suffering, and that is the good we have done.—MAETERLINCK.

It takes two to speak truth—one to speak and another to hear. —THOREAU.

WHILE Malcolm was trying to make himself agreeable to the second Miss Templeton, and not succeeding as well as he could wish, he more than once broke off the conversation to listen with some amusement to the bantering by-play going on between Cedric and the young clergyman, Mr. Carlyon.

They were evidently on intimate terms, for Cedric addressed him as David or Davie in the most unceremonious manner. Mr. Carlyon appeared to be quite young, certainly not more than six- or seven-and-twenty, and had an odd, characteristic, but most pleasant face, that somehow took Malcolm's fancy at once. It was rather thin and pale, and the mouth a little receding, but the broad forehead and kindly, frank-looking eyes somewhat redeemed this defect. There was so much life and animation in his expression; and a boyish eagerness in his manner, a curious abruptness in his speech, a certain quick clipping of words and sentences, only added to his marked individuality, and was by no means disagreeable when one had become accustomed to it.

Malcolm soon found out that he was the curate belonging to Rotherwood, the church attended by the Templeton family; and it was soon evident to him that the sisters, Miss Elizabeth especially, took a great interest in parochial matters.

100

"How is old Dr. Dryasdust?" asked Cedric presently, but he spoke in a jeering tone. Then Elizabeth laughed, but Dinah looked shocked, and Mr. Carlyon threw a dry clod at him.

"It really is not such a bad name," observed Elizabeth softly, as though to herself, and then her eyes encountered Mr. Carlyon's—it was evident that he agreed with her.

"The vicar is not a lively person, certainly," he rejoined, "but all the same I have a great respect for him. He is a trifle too mediæval for these days, and his environment does not suit him a bit."

"He ought to be a fellow of his college—spending his days in disinterring dusty old folios in the Bodleian," pursued Cedric, "instead of being vicar of Rotherwood."

"I think very highly of Mr. Charrington," and Dinah spoke rather gravely. "He is not only a very learned man, but he is such a thorough gentleman. Poor man, it is a blessing that he has you near him, Mr. Carlyon, for his life is very lonely."

"Why does he not get married then?" growled Cedric. "I bet you he is not much over fifty." Then again Elizabeth and Mr. Carlyon exchanged glances.

"I don't think the vicar ever intends to enter the holy estate of matrimony," returned Mr. Carlyon. "He is an old bachelor by choice, and in my humble opinion is likely to remain so; and then his worthy housekeeper, Mrs. Finch, makes him so thoroughly comfortable."

"I heard something once from one of our fellows," observed Cedric, with a mischievous glance at Dinah— he knew well her objection to gossip. "He was not always a woman-hater. Palgrave of Lincoln told me that he had been engaged to a lady, and that just before the wedding-day the engagement was broken off; no one seemed to know the rights of it, but ever since he has been a little shy of petticoats."

"Cedric, I am sure it is time for us to dress for dinner,

the gong must have sounded long ago. Will you show Mr. Herrick his room?" Dinah spoke with gentle decision, and as she evidently expected Malcolm to join her, he rose from his seat. As he did so he heard Elizabeth say in a low voice to Mr. Carlyon, "I wonder if Cedric's story is a true one." "Very possibly—why not?" was the answer; "he looks like a man with a past," and then they dropped behind and he heard no more.

It is never well to form an opinion too soon; before the next half-hour had passed Malcolm had been compelled to readjust his ideas on the subject of Miss Elizabeth Templeton. When he saw her again he would hardly have recognised her. Her massive but well-proportioned figure looked to its best advantage in the black evening dress; the transparent material only set off the round white throat and finely-moulded arms to perfection. The coils of brown hair were effectively arranged, and the shape of the head was beautiful. Before the evening was over Malcolm, in sheer honesty, was obliged to confess to himself that Miss Elizabeth Templeton was a very attractive woman, and would cast many prettier and younger faces into the shade. "I wonder where her charm lies," he soliloquised when he had retired to his bedroom that evening; "her sister is really almost beautiful, but, with the exception of a pair of very bright and expressive eyes, Miss Elizabeth has not a single good feature, and yet one is compelled to admire her. She is a little dignified and reserved with a stranger, and yet she is not shy; even while she talked to Mr. Carlyon, who certainly seems a sort of tame cat at the Wood House, I could see her looking at me as though she regarded me with interest, but we have broken the ice now with a vengeance.

"One thing I have discovered," he went on, as he looked dreamily down into the scented darkness of the garden, " she is a woman of large sympathies, with an excellent sense of humour, which her good heart and kindly nature keeps in good control; and if I do not mistake, she is the leading spirit of the house. The sisters seem to be devoted to each other; and the way they spoil that boy——" and here Malcolm shook his head in strong disapproval, without being in the least aware that he was not free from that fault himself. He had just sent the lad away proud and happy by his delicately implied praise of the Wood House and its inmates.

"I am quite sure that I shall get on with your sisters, Cedric," he had said with good-natured condescension; "they seem to me such thoroughly good, kind-hearted women, and very superior to the generality of folk. How beautifully your sister Elizabeth sings! I have seldom heard a voice that pleased me better."

"They both like you," returned Cedric shyly. "Dinah told me so at once; and though Elizabeth did not actually say so, I could see by her manner how she enjoyed talking to you;" and indeed Malcolm had never been in better form.

It had been a very pleasant evening; the small oval dinner-table, with its flowers exquisitely arranged, the open windows, with the dogs lying out on the terrace, were all to Malcolm's taste. Everything was so well-appointed and so well-managed. The servants were evidently old retainers, and took a warm interest in their mistress's guests.

After dinner they had their coffee on the terrace, and watched the sun setting behind the fir woods, and when the last yellow gleam had faded away from the sky, at Dinah's suggestion Elizabeth went into the drawing-room, where two pink-shaded lamps were already lighted, and seated herself at the piano.

"There is no occasion for us to go in," observed Dinah, who had noticed Malcolm's evident enjoyment of his cigarette; "we shall hear her perfectly out here, and Mr. Carlyon will turn over for her."

Such is human nature, for one instant Malcolm felt strongly impelled to throw away his cigarette and oust Mr. Carlyon from his snug corner, if only to teach him his place; but indolence prevailed: his cigarette was too delicious, the air was so refreshing and balmy, and the pale globes of the evening primroses and the milky whiteness of the nicotianas gleamed so entrancingly in the soft dusk, that he felt himself unwilling to move. Even the curious notes of the night-jar seeking its prey in the dim light had a strange fascination for him, and he spoke of it more than once to Dinah. "It is like the humming of a spinning-wheel," he remarked; "it is very weird and uncanny."

"So people always say," she returned. "It is the goat-sucker, you know; they are very fond of feeding on that sort of beetle called the gnat-chafer; in fact, it is their favourite food. It has another name, the fern-owl."

"So I have heard;" and then, as a rich strong voice broke suddenly on his startled ears, he leant back in his hammock chair and composed himself to listen.

It was a wonderful voice, so sweet and true and full of expression; there was such tenderness and depth in it, that it seemed in some mysterious way to touch the very recesses of the heart, and to play on the whole gamut of human feeling. Malcolm found himself thinking of his lonely childhood, and of his father, then he recalled his youthful aspirations and his old ideals. "The thoughts of youth are long, long thoughts," he said to himself, "and the wind's will is a boy's will;" and then, as the last lingering notes died away, he flung his cigarette aside and rose abruptly from his seat.

"You have given us a great treat," he said in a low voice as Elizabeth stepped through the window. Mr. Carlyon was laying aside the pile of songs in the music cabinet as neatly as though it were an accustomed duty. Malcolm gave him an impatient glance. "One would think he belonged to the house," he said to himself rather crossly.

"Please do not thank me," returned Elizabeth smiling; her eyes were very bright, and there was a warm flush on her face, which made her look young and handsome. "It is my greatest pleasure to sing; I believe if I had nothing else to do I should waste hours at the piano."

"The hours would not be wasted," replied Malcolm. "It is a great gift, and like all other great gifts it should be utilised as much as possible. I could find it in my heart to envy you, Miss Templeton."

"Oh, how often I have said that!" chimed in Dinah. "I think I enjoy my sister's voice as much as she does herself; in the evening she always sings to me."

"Mr. Herrick and Dinah are trying to make me vainer than I am by nature," observed Elizabeth with her happy, childlike laugh, as Mr. Carlyon came to her side. "Cedric, it is such a lovely evening that we might have our usual stroll. Would you care to come with us?" to Malcolm.

"You may as well go my way," remarked Mr. Carlyon, and Elizabeth nodded; and then Dinah fetched her a light gossamer scarf, which she tied over her head.

"Dinah does not care for moonlight rambles, she thinks them frivolous," she observed, as they walked slowly through the dark woodlands, "but Cedric and I love them. I like the silence and emptiness; the villages are asleep, and the whole world seems given up to fern-owls and bats and night-moths. Take care of the branch, Mr. Herrick, or you will knock your head. It will be lighter on the road outside. I am so used to this path that I think I could find my way blindfold."

The two young men were before them, but Elizabeth, to Malcolm's relief, showed no inclination to join them;

even at this early stage of their acquaintance he experienced an odd desire to monopolise her society. He never felt more content with his surroundings. The tranquillity of the hour, the soft half-lights, the mystery of the long wide road, with two dark specks moving before them —all appealed to Malcolm's artistic and romantic sense. "It is a study in black and white," he half murmured to himself; but at that moment he was not thinking of the tall, black-robed woman beside him, with the shimmering white veil over her head. Nevertheless, when Elizabeth laughed, he understood her and laughed too.

"Mr. Herrick," she said suddenly, and her voice became grave, "I am so glad to have this opportunity of speaking to you alone—without my sister, I mean. For months—for nearly two years—I have longed to see you and thank you for what you have done for Cedric. No —do not stop"—for in his surprise Malcolm had paused in the act of crossing the road; "they are looking back, and I do not want them just now," and here she waved her hand a little impatiently. "We must follow them through that gate into the woodland path that leads to Rotherwood. It is so pretty in daylight. The moon will soon be rising, and then you will see it better."

Malcolm followed her meekly. When he stumbled over a concealed root, Elizabeth quietly put her hand on his arm to guide him. The firm, soft touch, the spontaneous kindness of the action, and her utter unconsciousness, gave him a positive thrill of pleasure.

"When one's heart is full of gratitude to a person," went on Elizabeth in the same grave, low tone, "it is so difficult to find words. Mr. Herrick, I know all you did for our dear boy—I know everything." Malcolm started. "Cedric told me; but of course we kept it from my sister."

"My dear Miss Templeton," began Malcolm in an embarrassed voice, for he was not prepared for this. But Elizabeth would not let him speak.

"You must let me have my innings," she said, with a delicious laugh. "I have pent up my feelings for nearly two years, and they must find vent. Mr. Herrick, you have been our benefactor—Dinah's and mine as well as Cedric's. When you held out your generous hand to a stranger—when you saved our poor boy from disgrace and a ruined career, you did far more than you thought——"

"Miss Templeton, for pity's sake——"

"Please, please, let me finish," a pressure of his arm emphasised her words; "it is so difficult for a woman to hold her tongue. Dinah knows nothing of all this; we dare not tell her—it would break her heart. My sister is too good for this world; you know what I mean Mr. Herrick—she believes too much in other people's goodness, and then when they disappoint her she is quite crushed."

"I should have thought Miss Templeton's nature an exceptionally happy one," returned Malcolm.

"You are right," and Elizabeth spoke with evident feeling; "but these bright, sunshiny natures have their hours of eclipse. Cedric is her special darling, the object of her tenderest care; if she only knew——" but here she paused, as though her emotions were too strong.

"My dear Miss Templeton"—Malcolm was determined to be heard now, he should not be suppressed and silenced any more—"you are making far too much of the trifling service I was able to render to your brother. What was a small loan?"

"What was it?" here Elizabeth struck in again; "it was, humanly speaking, life and salvation to a poor weak boy who was on the brink of despair; who was so desperate, with trouble and misery, that he might have fallen deeper and deeper if a Good Samaritan had not passed that way. He has told me since that the thought of Dinah's unhappiness almost drove him crazy, and that he could not have answered for himself. Cedric is a dear lad, but he is not strong."

"He has had his lesson. We all enter our kingdom of manhood through some tribulation, Miss Templeton."

"Ah, true, but we would gladly spare our belongings such a painful experience. Mr. Herrick, they are waiting for us at the little gate, and I have only time to say one thing more. I offered to help Cedric repay his debt, but he refused. I am glad to say he absolutely refused; he wishes to do it all himself."

"I think all the more of him," was Malcolm's answer; "a little self-denial will be good for Cedric. He has already paid the first instalment. Miss Templeton, in return for your confidence, I will be quite frank with you: I do not need the money, as far as that goes he is welcome to every penny, but for Cedric's sake I thought it best to take it. I hope you will understand this."

"I understand you perfectly, and I thank you from my heart for dealing so wisely with him; but not another word—voices travel far in this clear silence—and they are just by." Indeed, the next moment a voice hailed them.

"Hallo, you people," shouted Cedric, "have you been looking for glowworms or hunting moths? David is quite tired of waiting."

"I am afraid we have dawdled," observed Elizabeth briskly. "Mr. Herrick and I were deep in conversation. I think we will not come any farther; I have done my lady's mile, or thereabouts. Good-night, Mr. Carlyon, I shall be over at the school to-morrow morning——" but here Elizabeth dropped her voice, and Malcolm heard no more.

She was rather silent when she joined them, and left the conversation to Cedric. More than once Malcolm

·wondered what made her so thoughtful; but when they reached the house, and she bade him good-night in the hall, there was no coldness or abstraction in her beaming smile.

"If you sleep as well as you deserve——" she said; but he chose to misunderstand her.

"I should be hag-ridden and tormented, I fear."

"Oh no, you would have rosy visions of celestial bowers," returned Elizabeth merrily. "Now, Mike," to the little dachshund, "let us make tracks for the upper regions. Good-night, Cedric."

As Elizabeth paused at the foot of the staircase, Malcolm thought what a splendid subject she would make for a picture. The soft draperies gave her a queenly aspect, and the white scarf that she still wore over her head lent her a mystic look; in her hand she carried a curious brass lamp of some antique design, and at her bosom were fastened, negligently, a great spray of crimson roses. "She looks like a St. Elizabeth in this dim lamplight," he thought. "Those red roses look like a dark stain on her breast. The figure, the turn of the head, is superb. If only Goliath could see her. Ah, now she has moved, and the illusion has gone—faded into thin air," and then Malcolm smiled at his own conceit and fancy as he took up his chamber candlestick.

CHAPTER XI

" A LITTLE EGOTISTICAL, PERHAPS"

We always like those who admire us, but do not always like those whom we admire.—LA ROCHEFOUCAULD.

Trifles make perfection, and perfection is no trifle.—MICHAEL ANGELO.

THE bedrooms at the Wood House opened on a wide corridor which extended the whole length of the house. It was known by the name of the Red Gallery, probably from the great stained-glass window through which the sunset glow filtered on summer evenings, and reflected purple and crimson stains on the tessellated pavement of the hall below. By some odd coincidence, a figure of the Thuringian queen St. Elizabeth was the subject of the window. Something in the figure and the pose of the crowned head of the saint reminded Malcolm of Elizabeth Templeton; but the meek beauty of the upturned face resembled Dinah.

The gallery was carpeted, and comfortably furnished with easy-chairs and one or two oak settles; the walls were covered with pictures. On winter afternoons, when a great beech log burnt cheerily in the fireplace, it must have been a pleasant place for a twilight gossip before dressing for dinner. As the family was small, several of the bedrooms had never been used; they were twelve in number, and an artist friend of the sisters had suggested that each chamber should bear the name of a month of the year. By a happy conceit which had greatly delighted them, he had with his own hand not only illuminated the name, but had with exquisite taste painted a spray of flowers that were typical of each month. For example, over Elizabeth's door—June—hung a lovely cluster of crimson and white roses; while Dinah, who had appropriated September, had a cluster of blackberries and traveller's joy.

When Malcolm had taken possession of the guest-room —April—he had gazed admiringly at a festoon of pink apple-blossoms over his door, but when he had praised the novel adornment with his wonted enthusiasm, the sisters modestly disclaimed all credit.

"It was not our idea," observed Elizabeth regretfully; "neither Dinah nor I had the genius to evolve it. It was our friend, Mr. Leon Power. You will know his name; his 'Andromache' was so much talked about last year.'"

"Of course, every one knows Leon Power," returned Malcolm quickly. "A friend of mine, Mr. Keston, quite swears by him."

"We know Mr. Keston's pictures well," observed Dinah in her placid way. "I hear he is to have Mr. Logan's house for the summer, and then we shall have the pleasure of making his acquaintance. I assure you, Mr. Herrick, that it was all Mr. Power's idea. He used to come down for a few days and paint a door at a time. We loved to sit in the gallery and watch him. You have no idea how it interested us."

When Elizabeth, still carrying her antique lamp, passed swiftly down the gallery, she paused as usual at her sister's door. Dinah was sitting in a carved oak chair by the open window with a reading-lamp beside her. Her evening dress was replaced by a white muslin wrapper, which made her look younger than ever. The red edges of the St. Thomas à Kempis that she had been reading was the only spot of colour about her.

"You are later than usual, dear," she said gently. "Did you go all the way to Rotherwood?"

"In this garb! My dear child, supposing I had met

the vicar! Oh no, we only walked to the usual trysting-place. Well, Dinah"—seating herself in a comfortable easy-chair beside her—"what do you think of our new friend?"

"I was going to ask you that question," returned her sister in a disappointed voice. "I did so want to know your opinion; but you are so dreadfully quick, Betty. Of course I like him; he is very gentlemanly and agreeable, and I think clever."

"Oh, I should say there was no doubt of his cleverness." Then Dinah brightened up as though she had received a personal compliment.

"I am so glad you think so. The society of a clever, cultured man like Mr. Herrick must be so good for Cedric; and then he is so pleasant, and has so much to say on every subject, and he has such original ideas. Really, poor dear Mr. Carlyon was quite cast into the shade this evening."

"Oh, there I differ from you. Mr. Carlyon is original too, and can hold his own with any one;" and Elizabeth spoke with some warmth, almost with asperity, and her sister looked at her rather anxiously.

"Dear Betty, I meant no disparagement of Mr. Carlyon. He is such a favourite with all of us that we are not likely to undervalue him. It struck me once or twice that he was not quite in his usual spirits."

"He is a little worried about his father," returned Elizabeth. "He thinks Theo does not look after him properly. But we were talking about Mr. Herrick, were we not?"

Elizabeth was not quite herself. Something in Dinah's speech had ruffled her. She was a little quick-tempered and impulsive; but she soon recovered herself.

"Does it strike you, Die, that Mr. Herrick is quite aware of his own cleverness, and that he rather prides himself on being original and out of the common. Oh,

I mean nothing unkind," as Dinah looked rather grave at this. "I like him exceedingly. I should be an ungrateful wretch if I did not," she added to herself. "He is a good man, I am sure of that; and," with a merry laugh, "I am also sure that to know him will be a liberal education."

Though Dinah joined in the laugh, she was evidently discomposed by her sister's observation. "I am afraid you think him conceited," she said regretfully.

"Oh dear, no; a little egotistical, perhaps—I might even say a little opinionative; but then we all have our faults, and I fancy he will improve greatly on acquaintance. When I know him better, Die, I shall delight in arguing with him. There is no use arguing with Mr. Carlyon, he always gives in to me at once; but Mr. Herrick would fight it out to the bitter end."

Dinah shook her head at this lukewarm praise. Elizabeth's opinion was of the utmost moment to her. She relied on it with a simple faith that astonished strangers. Malcolm was right in suspecting that the younger sister was the moving spirit of the house. Elizabeth's vigorous mind, her clear insight, and strong common-sense, made her quick to judge and discriminate. As Dinah knew, she very seldom made a mistake in her opinion of a person. Dinah's charitable nature was rather prone to overestimate her friends and acquaintances—"all her geese were swans." As Elizabeth often said, when she cared for any one she simply could not see their faults. "If we were all as blind as Dinah," her sister would say, "the world would be a happier place;" but all the same she loved and reverenced the simple goodness and sweetness that by a divine alchemy transmuted base metal into gold.

Elizabeth was quite aware why Dinah shook her head so disapprovingly. Cedric's hero had found favour in her eyes, and she wished her other self—for so she tenderly termed Elizabeth—to do homage to him likewise;

8

but Elizabeth's gratitude and her wholesome liking were not disposed to hero-worship. " Mr. Herrick was very nice, and a great acquisition, and she was quite sure they would soon be good friends;" and as Elizabeth always meant what she said, Dinah felt tolerably satisfied with this verdict.

" And now let me hear about Mr. Carlyon, Betty," she observed cheerfully. " I do hope his holiday was not spoiled by Theo's shiftless ways."

" Oh, as to that," returned Elizabeth impatiently, " Theo will be Theo to the end of her days. It is a mystery to me how good people can be so aggravating. Her brother always declares that she is really a good woman."

" I should certainly think he was right, dear."

" Her goodness is rather microscopic then," returned Elizabeth drily. " Mr. Carlyon—our Mr. Carlyon, you know—told me that it fretted him sadly to see how his father's little comforts were neglected. Theo puts her parochial work before her home duties. He said the meals were badly served and badly cooked; that Theo often came in late for dinner and took a hasty meal in her bonnet; that in the evening there was no sociality—his father wrote his sermons or buried himself in his books, and Theo worked at her accounts or dropped asleep from sheer fatigue on the couch."

" Poor Mr. Carlyon, he deserves a better daughter; but Theo has always been a restless, bustling sort of mortal. I suppose David—we really must call him David between ourselves, Betty, to distinguish him—I suppose he will have his father as usual in August?"

" Oh dear, yes; and Mrs. Pratt will lead them both a life. She always does; I never saw such a woman. I mean to give her a bit of my mind one of these days."

" She is almost as trying as Theo," returned Dinah with a smile. " I think David gives in to her too much for the sake of peace."

" So I often tell him."

" I wish Mr. Charrington would invite Mr. Carlyon to the vicarage. Mrs. Finch is such a comfortable soul: she thinks nothing a trouble. But I suppose such an idea would never enter the vicar's head."

" Oh dear, no. But after all it does not matter, Die; nothing would induce Mr. Carlyon to leave his son's roof. I do not believe that any amount of creature comforts or learned conversations would tempt him away from his boy. I think their affection for each other is one of the most touching things I know."

" Indeed it is, Betty," and Dinah looked at her sister rather wistfully; but Elizabeth was too much engrossed with her subject to notice her.

" David's attachment to his father is quite beautiful," she went on; " but I cannot help wondering over it sometimes. He seems as proud of that shabby, mild-spoken little man as though he were a bishop in lawn sleeves, and not a broken-down, hard-working curate-in-charge, who preaches dull, dry little sermons."

" But his life is his best sermon, Betty!"

" Ah, you are right there," and Elizabeth's beaming look was good to see. " David sometimes tells me that his father's patience with Theo is almost angelic. ' I don't know how he bears it,' he said once. ' I am not particular about food myself, and would dine cheerfully on bread and cheese any day; but I hate a smoky chimney and dust; and really that Bridget of theirs is a terrible female, and one of the worst specimens of a maid-of-all-work that I ever knew. I took to dusting the place myself, but Theo never noticed it.' Well, well, it's a queer world, Die. Now it is late and I am keeping you up," and then the sisters kissed each other affectionately, and Elizabeth withdrew to her own room.

Dinah sat still in her chair, and there was a thoughtful, almost a perplexed look on her face.

"I wish I could understand it," she said to herself; "but in some things Betty is so reserved. People who only know her a little would never find it out. They persist that she is frankness itself, but there are limits that no one can overstep—even I dare not." Here Dinah paused. "But she knows very well that I should never ask her the question.

"All the same," a moment later, "I am sorely puzzled. Is it only a friendship between those two, or is it something else on David Carlyon's part? Once or twice I have seen him looking at her as a man only looks at one woman.

"If I could venture to give her a hint, to beg her to be careful! Elizabeth is so careless. She has no idea of her own attractions, and how irresistible she can be. It is all very well for her to say she is older than David, and that she takes a sisterly interest in him because Theo is so unsatisfactory; but there is no need to give him so much of her company. Oh, no need at all, and it will only make people talk." And here the careful elder sister sighed as though she were oppressed with her responsibilities.

"Elizabeth is only thirty," she went on. "Why, that is quite young nowadays, and after all David is not more than three or four years younger. It is not the age that matters, or David's poverty, for Betty has plenty of money of her own. But he is not good enough for her. She is such a grand creature—when she marries she ought to have a husband worthy of her—one whom she could honour and obey as well as love—a man of intellect and power." Had a name suddenly occurred to Dinah, for as she rose hastily a girlish blush came to her cheek? "I am quite ashamed of myself," she whispered. "If there is one thing or person I detest it is a match-maker. How could such an idea come into my head!" But whatever idea it was, Dinah soon banished it, and before long both the sisters were sleeping sweetly on their lavender-scented pillows.

Malcolm saw little of his hostesses the next day. Elizabeth spent the greater part of the day at Rotherwood, and Dinah was busy with her household duties. He and Cedric played tennis the most of the morning. Then they lounged about the garden and woodlands in their flannels, and chatted and smoked endless cigarettes, and after luncheon Cedric ordered out the dog-cart and showed his friend some of the beauties of the surrounding neighbourhood. They drove back through Rotherwood, and as they turned the corner by the church they came upon Mr. Carlyon. Malcolm did not recognise him at first in his straw hat, until he hailed them in a cheery voice.

"Hallo, Cedric, are you going to cut me? Look here, my dear fellow, you and Mr. Herrick must have some tea at my digging. It is a few steps farther. The mare looks hot. Why don't you put her up at 'The Plough' and let her have a feed and a rub down?" And as Cedric approved of this arrangement, Malcolm was obliged to acquiesce, though he was inwardly bored by the delay.

They had been out for hours, and he was rather weary of the lad's chatter. Some new acquaintances of the name of Jacobi had been the subject of Cedric's talk—a brother and sister living in Gresham Gardens. It was in vain that Malcolm had repeated more than once that he knew nothing of them. Cedric would not take the hint, and he held forth on the brother's cleverness and the sister's beauty. To listen to the boy one might have thought the Jacobis were much above the average of human beings—that there must be something idyllic, angelic, and altogether seraphic in their persons and dispositions; but Malcolm, who knew his man, discounted largely from this, and kept his amusement and incredulity to himself.

But the name of Jacobi palled on him at last, and he was counting the milestones between him and the Wood

House rather anxiously, when they saw Mr. Carlyon
standing on the curb with his straw hat very much tilted
over his eyes.

No maiden lady of uncertain age loved her tea better
than Malcolm. Nevertheless, the curate's invitation did
not please him.

As he got down from the dog-cart he thought regretfully of the cool, shady drawing-room at the Wood
House, and the pretty tea-table with its silver urn and
old-fashioned china. Cedric was so thoughtless. Of
course his sisters would be expecting them. Carlyon
seemed a pleasant fellow, but he was not sure that he
desired a closer acquaintance with him. Malcolm was
inclined to be a little distant, but neither of his companions seemed to notice it. A low white cottage, standing back in a shady little garden, was their destination.
As Mr. Carlyon unlatched the gate, Cedric said in an
audible aside—

" It is not washing-day, is it, David? I hope Mother
Pratt has her kettle boiling, for Herrick and I are as
thirsty as fish."

" My dear fellow, I have no idea," and Mr. Carlyon
looked a little alarmed. " Just look after Mr. Herrick
for a few minutes while I tackle the good lady."

" I don't believe Mrs. Pratt will bring the tea-things
for another half-hour," observed Cedric cheerfully.
" Poor old Davie, it is awful hard lines for him to have
such a landlady. She imposes on him shamefully."

" Why does he put up with it?" returned Malcolm
drily. He was not in the humour to discuss Mr. Carlyon's
household arrangements. The room into which Cedric
had ushered him was a very pleasant one. It was rather
low, but a side window with a cushioned recess looked
out on a small lawn, with beautifully-kept flower-beds
and long borders filled with old-fashioned herbaceous
flowers, where brown bees were humming in the sunshine.

"Mrs. Pratt evidently keeps a good gardener," he said, as he took note of the neatly-shaven and carefully-swept paths.

"David is the gardener," returned Cedric laughing. "The garden is his hobby. He is at work sometimes at six o'clock in the morning. It is rather a good garden. as you see; but when David first came to the White Cottage it was a perfect wilderness. A lone widder woman cannot be expected to attend to house and garden too," he continued in a lackadaisical voice. "Hallo, Davy, what cheer, my lad? Are the fates propitious?"

"Not exactly," in a depressed tone. "I am afraid it is washing-day, and that Mrs. Pratt will keep us waiting. I filled the kettle for her myself, but it has got to boil; but if you don't mind waiting——" in a still more embarrassed manner.

"What's the matter, good friends?" observed a cheery voice. "Can I be of any use and assistance? I am not afraid of a dozen Mrs. Pratts. May I join your tea-party, Mr. Carlyon? I was just going to ask Mrs. Finch for a cup. but as I passed I saw Cedric at the window," and before any could answer Elizabeth had advanced into the room with a smile that seemed to evoke responsive smiles on every face.

"Thank goodness! Bet," exclaimed her brother devoutly; "we shall get along now."

"Oh yes, we shall get along." and Elizabeth took off her hat and hastily smoothed her hair. "Now for the Pratt woman and tea. Au revoir, gentlemen." And then she vanished, and after a moment's hesitation Mr. Carlyon followed her.

CHAPTER XII

MR. CARLYON'S TEA-PARTY

If there be a smile on our lips, those around us will soon smile; and our happiness will become the truer and deeper as we see that these others are happy.—MAETERLINCK.

Smiles are as catching as tears.—MAETERLINCK.

WHAT a sudden change in the atmosphere! If a fresh moorland breeze had swept through the little sitting-room at the White Cottage it could not have effected a more beneficial change.

A few words from a brisk, cheerful young woman had acted like magic; Mr. Carlyon lost his harassed look, Malcolm's bored expression had vanished, while Cedric's fervent " Thank goodness! Bet, we shall get along now," was inwardly echoed by his friends.

Malcolm's good-humour returned, and he gave his undivided attention to the flower-borders, and enlarged in his poetical way on the beauties of the Iceland and Shirley poppies.

" They are like fine court ladies," he observed to Cedric, " they are so smart and dainty and graceful. What a charming combination of colour! Your friend Carlyon must have an artistic eye."

" I expect it was Elizabeth's idea," returned Cedric lazily; " she is quite gone on poppies. She and David are rival gardeners, and have no end of discussions. My word, to listen to them one would think they were a later edition of Adam and Eve."

Now, why did Malcolm frown at this boyish speech, and drop the subject hastily? But Cedric only stretched himself with a yawn and went on—

120

"It is my private opinion that David knows very little about it, except what he gets from gardening books. But he is so full of hobbies, and so energetic, and so determined not to be beaten, and takes such a lot of trouble, that even Elizabeth is astonished at the results. She comes down here and gives him ideas, and then he works them out, or he potters about our place and talks to Johnson, and gets hints that way.

"I never saw such a fellow for picking other people's brains," continued Cedric enthusiastically. "Why, he got a splendid degree at Oxford; I remember how surprised his own father was."

"Carlyon has a father then?" Though Malcolm was so lukewarm on the subject of the young curate's merits, he felt some degree of curiosity about him.

"To be sure he has," replied Cedric. "Carlyon senior is a dry, chippy sort of little man, as meek as a mouse and as good as gold. He is curate-in-charge of an iron church at Stokeley; it is in the Black Country, you know—a regular inferno of a place—nothing but tall chimneys and blasting furnaces, heaps of slag and rows of miners' cottages. Stokeley town is a mile or two farther on; it is a beastly sort of hole."

"It does not sound an inviting spot certainly."

"Well, it is not exactly a Garden of Eden," returned Cedric with a grin. "But, as David says, it has its advantages, for one can wear out one's old clothes quite comfortably. I believe there is really beautiful country two or three miles away."

"I suppose Mr. Carlyon's mother is living too?" But here Cedric shook his head.

"No, she died when David was a youngster—consumption, I believe—and two or three of the children died too. But there is one daughter, Theo they call her —for Theodora, I expect—and a precious uncomfortable piece of goods she is."

Malcolm raised his eyebrows in a questioning manner, but Cedric needed no encouragement to rattle on.

"She is a young woman with a mission—a sort of female Moody and Sankey rolled in one—and she calls herself the Miner's Friend. She is so full of good works, don't you know, that she has not time for domestic duties; and so Carlyon père and Carlyon frère have a roughish time of it."

Malcolm's thoughts instinctively reverted to his mother. With all her work and philanthropic schemes, she was never too busy to see to her household. She might neglect her own personal comfort and overtask her willing helper Anna, but her servants did their duty, and were well fed and well managed; and they worked all the better for the knowledge that their mistress's keen eyes would detect the slightest laxity. "My mother is a good woman," he said to himself; "she is true and just in all her dealings," and he felt with a sudden pang of remorse as though he had never valued her enough.

"Is Miss Carlyon like her brother in appearance?" he asked the next minute.

"Not a bit; she would make two of David. She is a big, red-haired woman, not exactly bad-looking—if she would only set herself off. But the Carlyons have a family failing, they cling to their old clothes and eschew fashion. Hush, here comes Mother Pratt with the tea-tray. Look at her well, Herrick, she is a good imitation of the immortal Mrs. Gummidge, and bears a mortified exterior, out of compliment to the late Samuel Pratt, sexton and grave-digger and parochial Jack-of-all-trades."

The bumping sounds in the distance that Cedric had heard had drawn nearer, and the next moment a tall, angular woman in a black hat, and a suspicion of soap-suds freshly dried about her bare arms, entered the room and set down the tea-tray with a heavy sigh, as though the burden of life were too hard to bear.

Mr. Carlyon followed her with a crusty loaf and the butter, while Elizabeth brought up the rear triumphantly with a plate of raspberries and a little brown jug of cream.

"Is there anything more you'll be needing, sir?" asked Mrs. Pratt lugubriously—she spoke in an injured manner. "If it had not been washing-day I would have baked you a currant-loaf, or some scones; but having only two hands, and no chick or child to help me, and——"

"Oh, we shall do very nicely," returned Elizabeth cheerfully. "Please do not let us hinder you, Mrs. Pratt; if you will keep the water boiling we can easily replenish the teapot. Mr. Carlyon," looking at him severely, "you have left the sifted sugar on the kitchen table; please go and fetch it. Mr. Herrick, are you fond of raspberries? These are from our own garden—Johnson gathered them this morning."

"They are just prime!" exclaimed Cedric—"food for the Olympian gods, ambrosia and nectar too. Come along, David, or there will be none left for you. Sit down, man, no one wants you to be waiting on us."

"Yes, do sit down, please," observed Elizabeth softly; and Mr. Carlyon slipped at once into the empty chair beside her.

It really was a pleasant little tea-party, and Malcolm quite forgot his longing to be back in the drawing-room at the Wood House. Indeed, he was in high good-humour, and told his best stories, quite convulsing Mr. Carlyon with his comic ones; indeed, he made himself so agreeable and entertaining—he so threw himself into the spirit of their informal picnic—that Elizabeth's bright eyes rested on his dark face more than once with marked approval. And when they went out into the front garden to wait for the dog-cart, Mr. Carlyon said to her confidentially, "Your friend improves on acquaintance; I thought him a bit stand-offish and highty-tighty yesterday, but I see now it was only mannerism."

"Some people are difficult to know at first," returned Elizabeth thoughtfully, but she also spoke in a lowered tone. "Mr. Herrick is not one of those people who keep all their goods in their shop window; there is plenty more of good stuff inside, if you only take the trouble to search for it. Dinah likes him immensely; she is getting an empty pedestal ready for him—you know my dear old Dinah's way, bless her." And as David knew it well, his answer was a merry laugh.

Never had Malcolm enjoyed himself more; never had he felt less disposed to criticise and find fault; and yet Miss Elizabeth Templeton wore the very striped blouse that had excited his ire on the previous evening; and her hat was certainly bent in the brim, perhaps in her frantic efforts to put up a straggling lock of brown hair that had escaped from the coil, and which would perpetually get loose again. Malcolm noticed at once the ripe, rich tint of the brown. "It is the real thing," he said to himself, "it is the burnished brown of the horse-chestnut; one seldom sees it, it is quite out of the common." And then he told himself that he had never seen a face so capable of expression. Perhaps this was why he watched her so closely when she talked to Mr. Carlyon.

It was arranged that Elizabeth should drive back with them in the dog-cart. And as Malcolm took the reins, which Cedric had relinquished in his favour, she mounted to the place beside him, while Cedric clambered up behind. Mr. Carlyon looked after them regretfully as Elizabeth waved gaily to him. The next moment she was pointing out the vicarage to Malcolm, a gray, picturesque-looking house, standing in a pleasant garden.

"It is not really the vicarage," she explained, "although it goes by the name. It used to belong to old Colonel Trelawney; but when he died and Mrs. Trelawney left Rotherwood, Mr. Charrington took it. It is not large, but quite the right size for an old bachelor.

He has really a grand library, and a very good dining-room, though the drawing-room is rather a dull room. Ah, there is the vicar," and Elizabeth smiled and bowed to a tall, gray-haired man who was just letting himself in at the gate.

"Wait a moment, please, Mr. Herrick," she exclaimed hurriedly. "I quite forgot I had a message from Dinah;" and then, as she sprang lightly to the ground, Mr. Charrington turned back to meet her, and they stood talking for a few minutes.

"Hurry up, Bet, or we shall be late for dinner," called out Cedric, impatient at this delay. Then Elizabeth looked up and nodded.

"Just one moment more," she said breathlessly. "Dinah will not mind our being late."

Malcolm did not mind it either. He sat contentedly flicking the flies from Brown Becky's glossy sides and listening to the distant cawing of rooks.

What a peaceful, drowsy sort of place Rotherwood was! The wide village street seemed empty, with the exception of a black collie lying asleep in the middle of the road, and a patient donkey belonging to a travelling tinker. The clean, sleek country sparrows were enjoying a dust bath, and a long-legged chicken—evidently a straggler from the brood—was pecking fitfully at a cabbage stalk, unmindful of the alarmed clucking of the maternal hen.

When Elizabeth rejoined them the vicar was with her, and she introduced him to Malcolm.

Mr. Charrington had been a handsome man in his youth; but a sedentary life and a somewhat injudicious burning of the midnight oil had tried his constitution. He had grown pale and thin, and his shoulders were slightly round, so that he looked older than his years. Malcolm thought Cedric's name of Dr. Dryasdust was not an inapt title. His eyes were a little sunken, though very bright and keen, and his manner was extremely courteous. He spoke very civilly to Malcolm.

"Mr. Charrington is hardly my idea of a country vicar," he observed as they drove away.

"Perhaps not," returned Elizabeth quickly, "but he is a very conscientious clergyman, and his people's welfare is very near his heart. He is a great etymologist and archæologist, and at times he is so immersed in his studies that but for the care of his excellent housekeeper, Mrs. Finch, he would often forget to eat his dinner. Mr. Carlyon often tells us amusing stories of the vicar's absence of mind."

"Could you not remember one of them, Betty?" suggested Cedric. But Elizabeth was not to be cajoled into repeating them. She respected Mr. Charrington far too highly, she remarked, to make merry at his expense. "My friends' oddities are always sacred to me," she said quite seriously. "Most people have their own little failings and idiosyncrasies, but one need not make copy out of them. Don't you agree with me, Mr. Herrick, that there is too little sense of honour in these matters? To raise a laugh, or to sharpen their own wit, many people will expose their best friend to ridicule."

"Oh, shut up, Betty," remonstrated her brother, "it is too bad to moralise; and after all old Dr. Dryasdust is a capital subject for sport."

"Perhaps so, but all the same your sister is right," returned Malcolm. "We are a little thoughtless, as she says. We ought to refuse to give our tongue such licence when a friend's crochets and whimsies are in question. It is the easiest thing in the world to satirise and caricature. You could poke fun at Milton or Shakespeare if you liked, and make them utterly ridiculous. Don't you hate parodies, Miss Templeton? To me they are utterly profane and detestable, and the cleverer they are the more I abhor them."

"We think alike there," returned Elizabeth eagerly.
"I remember that Cedric read such capital parodies once
on 'Excelsior' and 'Locksley Hall,' and I have never
been able to enjoy those poems since. I have utterly
refused to listen to any more. Oh," interrupting herself,
"there is Dinah on the look-out for us."

They caught sight of the trim little figure in gray silk
waiting for them in the porch. But if they had been
an hour late Dinah would have greeted them with the
same kind smile, and hoped that they were not tired.

That evening they sat out on the terrace again; but
to Malcolm's chagrin and disappointment, Elizabeth declared that her long day at Rotherwood had deprived her
of all voice for singing. "I have been shouting to the
children all the morning," she observed, "and reading
to deaf old women all the afternoon, and my vocal chord
has suffered," and then she challenged Cedric to take a
stroll with her; but to Malcolm's vexation the invitation
was not extended to him. "Dinah has been alone, we
must not all leave her," she said so pointedly that he had
no choice in the matter. But he was secretly chafed by
this treatment, for Malcolm was one of those men who
object to be managed. "I wonder, if Carlyon had been
in my place, if my Lady Elizabeth would have ordered
him to remain behind," he thought. But Dinah's first
words healed this soreness.

"My sister has kindly made this opportunity for me
by taking Cedric off our hands," she said gently. "She
knew that I wanted a little talk with you about him."
Then Malcolm's brief sullenness vanished.

"You shall talk to me as much as you like," he said in
the most cordial manner, and indeed he felt very kindly
towards this gentle, simple-minded creature. "I am
ready for any amount of conversation on any subject from
'cabbages to kings.'" Then she smiled well pleased at
his little joke.

"I wanted to ask you about these new friends of Cedric's," she began. "He seems so full of them, and neither Elizabeth nor I know anything about them. My sister, who is certainly not at all a narrow-minded person, has taken a most singular prejudice against them."

"Do you mean the Jacobis? My dear Miss Templeton, I am sorry to say that I have never met them." Then Dinah's face fell. "It is not surprising, of course, that many of Cedric's friends are unknown to me, for we move in very different circles. He has been raving about the Jacobis all the afternoon; but all the same I don't seem to focus them properly."

"Cedric is going to stay with them next month," observed Dinah. "They have taken a house at Henley for some weeks. He is very much excited about it; he is so fond of boating. And he declares they will have such a pleasant house-party; but," rather anxiously, "I do wish we could find some one who knew them."

"I should not be surprised if Mrs. Godfrey had come across them. She knows everybody." Dinah looked at him in surprise.

"Do you mean Mrs. Godfrey of the Manor House, near Cookham?" she asked—"Colonel Godfrey's wife?" Malcolm nodded assent.

"Do you know her too? What a small world this is after all! Mrs. Godfrey is a great friend of mine. We hit it off capitally on most subjects. In my opinion she is the cleverest and pleasantest woman in London." Then Dinah fairly beamed.

"I am so glad you like her. She is a great favourite of ours. Elizabeth often stays at the Manor House. They get on splendidly together. And the Colonel is so charming. Oh, Mr. Herrick, I am relieved that you mentioned them. Henley is not far from Cookham, and I should think they must know something of the Jacobis."

"I will ask Mrs. Godfrey directly I see her," he returned. "I am going to the Manor House next week."

"Next week!" in surprise; "I hoped you would have stayed with us for ten days at least."

"You are very kind," in a tone of regret, "but, my dear lady, I fear it is utterly impossible. My engagement with the Godfreys is of long standing, but I shall only remain at the Manor House three or four days. My regular holiday comes later."

"I suppose you have already made your plans?" in a friendly tone.

"Yes, I have decided not to go abroad this year. I have some literary work I do not wish to lay aside, and I think of taking up my quarters at the Crow's Nest, where I can combine country air and work."

"Then you will be our neighbour," and Dinah's voice expressed such satisfaction at the prospect that Malcolm felt quite pleased. "What a pity Cedric will be away most of August—the dear boy has so many engagements." But Malcolm, who was extremely truthful, did not endorse this regret. Cedric was a nice enough fellow, he thought, but he did not always know when he was not wanted, and at times his lively chatter was a weariness to the flesh.

"I expect I shall see something of him," was all he could bring himself to say. "But you may depend on me for getting information about the Jacobis. I am a little curious myself on the subject," he added with the frankness that was natural to him; and then, as the sound of approaching footsteps reached them, they mutually dropped the subject.

CHAPTER XIII

THE CROW'S NEST

Take the little pleasures of life, watch the sunsets and the clouds, the shadows in the streets and the misty light over our great cities. These bring joy by the way, and thankfulness to our Heavenly Father.—ANNE T. CLOUGH.

In a certain sense all are historians.—CARLYLE.

PERHAPS Elizabeth's conscience pricked her that night, or more probably, being rather a casual and careless young woman, a gentle hint from Dinah may have had its effect.

Dinah had merely remarked in her quiet way, when she was bidding her sister good-night in the Red Gallery, that she feared they were not doing enough for their guest's amusement, and that she thought they had better ask the vicar to dinner.

"Mr. Herrick is a literary man, and they will get on very well together," she observed. "Don't you think so, Betty?" And as Elizabeth did think so, and had no objection to offer, Dinah said that Johnson should take a note round the following morning.

Elizabeth felt a twinge of compunction as she closed her bedroom door; she was by no means given to introspection, but " conscience, that makes cowards of us all," told her that she had not been quite gracious to Mr. Herrick that evening.

" It was too bad of me not to sing to him." she said to herself, as she recalled his disappointed look. " I was not so very tired after all; it was just a fit of laziness, and——" but here Elizabeth checked herself abruptly—self-examination is sometimes embarrassing.

" I will try and make up for it to-morrow," she

thought; " he is such a good fellow, and we owe him so much;" and she was still in this complaisant mood when she came down to breakfast.

Even her outward garb was improved: she wore a fresh and extremely becoming morning dress, which set off her fine figure to advantage; and before Malcolm had tasted his coffee or looked at his letters she was challenging him gaily to a game of tennis.

Malcolm was charmed—he had no idea that she played tennis; but her next proposition rather took off the edge of his enjoyment.

" I know you are a good player, Mr. Herrick," she remarked coolly, " but it would be too great an exertion this warm weather for you to beat Cedric and me. Would it not be a good plan," turning to her brother, " for you to go over to the White Cottage on your bicycle and ask Mr. Carlyon to make the fourth? We should have a much better game."

" But we decided to ask Mr. Charrington to dinner, Betty," remonstrated her sister. Then Cedric looked disgusted, and muttered something under his breath about old Dr. Dryasdust spoiling the fun, but Elizabeth put him down with a strong hand.

" People's notions of fun differ." she said severely. " I am quite sure that the vicar and Mr. Herrick will have many interests in common. As for Mr. Carlyon," with a sudden change of tone, " he and Mr. Charrington are such good friends that they dine together two or three times a week, so there is no objection on that score. Well, Cedric," with an amused look at his bored expression. " do you feel equal to the exertion of bicycling over to Rotherwood, or shall Johnson go?"

" I suppose I can do the job," returned Cedric in a grumbling tone. " You may as well give me the vicarage note too, Die." But Dinah, distressed by her darling's ill-humour, followed him out into the hall to explain matters more fully.

" You must not be cross about it, dear," she said, with tender anxiety in her tone. " You see we are bound to entertain a visitor like Mr. Herrick; he is not just an insignificant person." Cedric's brow cleared. " He is a clever man, and it will be a compliment to ask a distinguished scholar like Mr. Charrington to meet him. If the Logans had been here we should have invited them."

Cedric felt a little ashamed of himself. " I daresay you are right," he said grudgingly, " but it will be so precious slow. Well, I'm off. Look after Herrick while I am gone," with a fine assumption of manly dignity. But he need not have troubled himself; Malcolm was not disposed to miss him in the least.

As for Elizabeth, her flow of benevolence was not dry yet. " I heard you tell Dinah last night that you wanted to look over the Crow's Nest," she observed to Malcolm as they rose from the breakfast table, " if you have no letters to write we might stroll down there now."

" Oh, my letters will keep," he returned, with such evident pleasure at the proposition that Elizabeth went off in search of her hat; not the hat with the battered brim, mark you, but a charming hat with cream-coloured lace and delicious yellow poppies, that seemed to match the dewy freshness of the morning, and which would not disgrace the gentleman from London; and although she wore no gloves—Elizabeth always drew the line at gloves—her Indian silk sunshade was worthy of Bond Street. As the Crow's Nest was within sight of the gates of the Wood House, they very soon accomplished the distance.

It was a homely little place enough, and the Kestons had described it pretty accurately. It was a mere cottage, and not a picturesque one either, for the architecture left much to be desired; but the row of trees that divided it from the road, amongst which shone the red berries of the rowans, and the trim, shady lawn, gave it a secluded and pleasant aspect.

The sitting-room was small but cosy, and there was a

fair-sized dining-room; but Malcolm at once took a fancy to a small upper room with a window overlooking the road; it had evidently been used as a dressing-room, for there was a gentleman's wardrobe in it, and a writing-table and easy-chair.

"I must coax Verity into giving me this room," he said half to himself; but Elizabeth heard him.

"Verity! is that Mrs. Keston?" she asked. "What a very original name! I do not believe I ever heard it before."

"I daresay not, but it just suits her. Yea-Verily, as her husband calls her." Then Elizabeth looked extremely amused.

"What a droll idea! Your friends seem rather out of the common, Mr. Herrick. I am quite impatient to make their acquaintance. We have a large circle of friends—an inner and an outer circle—but I am always glad to add to the number."

"I think you will like Verity," he returned seriously; "she is such a genuine little soul, and so fresh and original. Oh, I am quite sure you will take to her." Malcolm spoke in such a decided manner, as though it were a foregone conclusion that Verity would be admitted to the privileged inner circle, that Elizabeth's curiosity was strongly excited.

"You seem rather certain of the fact," she said perversely; "but, as my sister would tell you, I am not so easily pleased after all."

"Nevertheless you will like Verity," he returned quickly. "Like attracts like—a transparent, truthful nature, which is absolutely without guile, will not fail to appeal to you; I already know you well enough to predict that with certainty."

Elizabeth turned this speech off with a laugh, but her colour rose at the implied compliment; if like attracts like, as Mr. Herrick said, he must think her original and guileless too. Something in Malcolm's tone—in the expression of his dark eyes—confirmed this impression, and in spite of her stateliness and thirty years the second Miss Templeton felt a little shy.

"We have not seen the garden-room yet," she said hastily, and then she led the way downstairs.

The garden lay on the side of the house, and was well kept and full of flowers; but the temporary building erected by Mr. Logan rather spoiled the view from the back of the house, though a gay flower-border surrounded it.

Elizabeth, who had procured the key from the servant, now opened the door.

It was rather a bare-looking place, as Verity had said; more of a workshop than a studio, though it was used for both purposes, and, as both of them knew, good work had been done there; but Mr. Logan, who had a fine studio in town, was content with rather a primitive state of things in his country cottage.

It was sufficiently large, though part of it was partitioned off as a bedroom; the partition, for the sake of airiness, was only eight or nine feet high, and the furniture was of the plainest description; a white Indian matting covered the floor, and there were pink Madras curtains at the window. As Elizabeth pointed out, it could not have been closed for months, for actually beautiful clusters of roses had not only festooned the casement, but had found their way into the room, and hung their sweet heads over the sill, as though they were trying to reach the floor.

Malcolm declared himself quite enchanted; he had never seen any place he liked better. There was room for his big bath—his tub he called it mentally—and a comfortable chair or two, and when he had concluded these little arrangements to his own satisfaction, he joined Elizabeth, who was making friends with a great sandy cat, who rejoiced in the doubtful name of Old Tom.

"I am glad you are so pleased," she said in quite an interested tone, as they walked down the road again. "I hardly expected that you would be so easily satisfied. Cedric calls the Crow's Nest a wretched little hole."

"Oh, he is so young, Miss Templeton—he is at the age when one has great expectations; we learn to moderate and alter our ideas as we grow older. Don't you remember Carmen Sylva's charming description of youth and age? I like it so much."

Elizabeth shook her head. "I am afraid I do not read enough," she said rather sadly. But he looked at her very kindly.

"She is one of the wisest and wittiest of women," he returned; "and she is your namesake too."

"Oh yes, I know that."

"When I go back to town may I send you her little book—*Thoughts of a Queen* it is called?"

Elizabeth, after a moment's hesitation, thanked him and said she would be glad to see it.

"It is well worth your perusal," he went on, too much engrossed by his subject to notice her hesitating manner. "But I have not given you her definition of youth."

"'In youth,' she remarks, 'one is a mediæval castle, with hidden nooks, secret chambers, mysterious galleries, trenches, and ramparts; one becomes afterwards a modern mansion, rich, morocco-leathered, elegant, stylish, and only open to the select; and ultimately a great hall open to the whole world, a market, a museum, or a cathedral.'"

"I think I know what she means," returned Elizabeth thoughtfully. "Youth is so fond of mysteries, and all its castles have endless winding galleries, that lead to all sorts of curious nooks and corners. When we grow older our horizon widens—we care more for utility and less for subterranean passages. What could be better than a market, where one sells one's best and most durable goods *pro bono publico!*"

Malcolm was delighted with this answer. Miss Elizabeth Templeton might not be a profound student of books,
but she was certainly an intelligent and sympathetic
woman. They had turned into the woodlands by this
time, and Elizabeth, who was determined to entertain
their guest to the best of her ability, proposed that they
should stroll down to the Pool.

" If you will go on, I will just fetch my work," she ob-
served, " and tell Dinah where we are going, and then
Cedric will join us. He ought to have been back by now."
Then Malcolm, in high good-humour, sauntered over the
rustic bridge and amused himself by looking down on
Elizabeth's wild garden.

" Oh, Betty, what a pity to wear your pretty new hat !"
exclaimed Dinah, looking up from her accounts. She
was rather a martinet on the subject of dress, and had
funny little old-fashioned notions of her own ; but Elizabeth, who was ten years younger, was more up-to-date.

" It was part of the programme," she returned
solemnly ; " and the sunshade too. I was determined to
make myself as nice as possible. Remember, I trimmed
it myself, Die, and as I had the materials it only cost me
five shillings." Here she took it off and looked at it
admiringly, for Elizabeth was rather fond of dress in her
way. " My sailor hat will do for the Pool. I wish you
could come with us, dear." Then, as Dinah shook her
head, " Yes, I see, you are busy, so I will not bother you.
Please tell Cedric where we have gone."

Malcolm was still on the little bridge when Elizabeth
rejoined him. He looked regretfully at the sailor hat.

" It does not suit her a bit," he thought. " I wonder
a sensible woman like Miss Templeton does not know
what becomes her. Anna would never have made such
a mistake." But Elizabeth, unconscious of this criticism
of her offending head-gear, walked on serenely.

Some of the dogs had followed them, and while Elizabeth worked at a piece of beautiful embroidery, Malcolm

amused himself with throwing sticks into the pond for their delectation; and as soon as he was weary of the sport, he stretched himself comfortably on the ground beside her and began to talk. How it came about neither of them knew, but all at once Malcolm fell to speaking of his father, and of his lonely boyhood, and by-and-bye, Elizabeth grew so interested that she laid down her work, and propping her chin on her hand, gave him her undivided attention.

Malcolm was very unreserved about his mother. " She is perfectly unique," he said; " a grand worker, with brains and energy that, if she had been a man, would have qualified her for a legislator. She has a gift for organisation. Oh, you would admire her immensely. You are a worker yourself, Miss Templeton, and that would be a bond of union."

" Would it?" she returned quietly. " I am not quite so sure of that. I think your mother would rather look down on my small efforts. Please do not call me a worker, Mr. Herrick. I potter about the village two days in the week, and teach the children needlework, and tell them stories, and read to a bedridden old woman or two. but I am afraid on the whole I waste my time dreadfully," and here she looked at him with one of her beaming smiles. " I do so enjoy my life, especially in summer— the world is so beautiful, and one has the birds and flowers, and it is just lovely to wake to another new day."

" I wish Anna could hear you," he returned; and as she looked a little puzzled at this, he explained that his mother had an adopted daughter—a dear, lovable girl, whom he regarded as a sister. And when he said this Elizabeth's bright eyes glanced at him a little keenly.

" She is your adopted sister," she said dubiously; " is that not rather a difficult relationship, Mr. Herrick?"

" Not at all," he returned quickly, for somehow this remark did not quite please him. " Anna was so young when she came to us, I think sometimes that she quite forgets that she is not really my mother's daughter."

"She must be a great comfort to Mrs. Herrick," observed Elizabeth, "especially as you are not always with her." There was nothing in this speech to offend Malcolm's *amour propre*, nevertheless a dull flush mounted to his brow.

"Of course I should not have left my mother alone," he said so stiffly that Elizabeth opened her eyes rather widely; but her keen woman's wits soon grasped the situation.

"My dear Mr. Herrick, you must not misunderstand me," she said quite gently. "I am quite sure that you are backward in no filial duty. To tell you the truth," colouring a little, "I hardly liked to show you how thoroughly I comprehended things—your home has never been a real home to you, and though you love each other dearly, you and your mother are really happier apart. How can two walk together unless they are agreed?"

"Thank you for saying this," he returned gratefully; "I am sure you mean what you say."

"Most certainly I do."

"I know it—I am sure of it; you are not one of those people who are afraid to speak the truth. Forgive me if I seemed put out for a moment, but something in your manner made me think that you disapproved of the step I had taken."

"Mr. Herrick, I disapprove—a mere acquaintance who has not even seen your mother!"

"Ah, it is you who misunderstand now," in a reproachful voice. "Even a mere acquaintance," dwelling on the word rather pointedly, "can judge pretty correctly of a man's circumstances. I thought you were saying to yourself, 'Mr. Herrick must be a selfish sort of man; he is the only son of a widowed mother, and he has left her roof because her charitable works bore him to extinction.'"

"No—oh, no!" in a shocked voice. "How can you say

such dreadful things? I shall begin to be afraid of you; and I have never been afraid of man, woman, or child in my life. Shall I tell you of what I was really thinking when you turned on me in that crushing manner? I was thinking of that poor dear girl, and how dull and moped she must be. Mr. Herrick," rather shyly—Elizabeth never looked more charming or more irresistible than when she put on this soft, appealing manner—" do you suppose Miss Sheldon would care to stay with us while you are at the Crow's Nest. We should so like to have her. You see," her voice softening still more, " you have done so much for us that we want to make some return, and it would be such a pleasure."

" You are very kind," he returned, and indeed he was so surprised and touched by this unexpected speech that he hardly knew how to express his sense of her thoughtfulness. " It is good of you to think of it, and nothing would have given Anna greater pleasure, but——"

" You mean she has some other engagement this summer?"

" Yes; it is a great pity. My mother has taken rooms at Whitby for the middle of next month, and she never goes anywhere without Anna."

" Then it cannot be helped; another time perhaps we shall be more fortunate." And then, as though she were desirous of changing the subject, Elizabeth began talking of her own and Dinah's movements, how they never went away in the spring and summer except for a week or so in town for shopping and picture-galleries, but filled the Wood House with relays of guests.

" For the last three years we have gone abroad in the middle of October, and returned for Christmas and the New Year," she finished, " but we have made up our minds to remain in England this year. Why, here comes the truant, and it is actually nearly luncheon time."

Cedric, flushed and panting, flung himself down beside her.

CHAPTER XIV

"YOU DO SAY SUCH ODD THINGS"

Womanhood should be the consecration of earth.—U. A. TAYLOR.

In the region of domestic affections a new and ennobling motive came from Bethlehem—"that I may please God."—KNOX LITTLE.

ELIZABETH put on an air of great severity as she regarded the culprit.

"Rotherwood is about a mile and a quarter from our gate," she observed, apostrophising some midges that were dancing in a sunbeam overhead. "You could walk there easily in twenty minutes. It is now one o'clock, and you have been away exactly three hours and a half," and here she consulted the miniature watch that she wore as an ornament as well as for utility. "If it be not impertinent, may we inquire why you have absented yourself the whole morning?"

"Oh, shut up, Bet," returned her brother impatiently. "Sarcasm is not your style at all. It is like killing a grasshopper with a pair of iron-heeled clogs. It is precious heavy, I can tell you."

"You rude, unmannerly boy," and here Elizabeth attempted to pull his hair, but she might as well have tried her prentice hand on a young convict freshly shorn by the prison barber.

"Hands off, Betty, I tell you," returned the graceless lad. "I have had rather a good time of it. I knew Herrick was getting pretty sick of me." Here Cedric rolled over on his back, and tilted his straw hat over his eyes. "Familiarity breeds contempt and all that sort of thing.

140

Conversation is like a salad, isn't it, Herrick?—you may have plenty of green stuff and oil, but it wants pepper and a dash of vinegar too."

"Why don't you box his ears, Miss Templeton? He is getting positively abusive."

"I prefer pepper to oil," she returned calmly. "Well, Cedric, perhaps you will kindly inform me if your mission has been successful."

"Oh, it is all right. David will be here to tea, but he says it will not be cool enough to play until nearly five. Now, don't go tugging at my coat-collar, or I won't say another word." Elizabeth, with a resigned expression, folded up her work. "I left the vicarage note," continued Cedric, mollified by this submission. "Mr. Charrington was engaged, but Mrs. Finch brought me his message—his kind regards to Miss Templeton, and he would have much pleasure in dining at the Wood House to-night."

"Did you tell Dinah?"

"Do I not always do my duty?" rather sententiously. "Well, before I could get to the White Cottage I met old David. He was going to the church to practise on the organ, and he was a bit bothered because he could not get any one to blow, so, being a good-natured chap, I volunteered."

"Good boy," observed Elizabeth softly.

"Well, there we were for pretty nearly an hour and a half—David perched up like a glorified cherubim, and rolling out music by the yard; and there was I grinding away like a saintly nigger in a beastly hole till I could stand it no longer, and told him I must chuck it. He declared he had quite forgotten me."

"I expect he had. Mr. Carlyon plays the organ so beautifully"—Elizabeth was addressing Malcolm now. "My sister and I often go into the church to listen to him."

" It must be a great resource," he returned regretfully, " and I am inclined to envy Carlyon. I am passionately fond of music myself, but the power of expression has been denied me."

" I would back David against most organists," went on Cedric. " Well, as I was pretty much used up by my exertions, he proposed we should go into the vicarage garden and help ourselves to fruit. The greengages were ripe and so were the mulberries, and you bet I did not need pressing.

" Mrs. Finch saw us from the porch room, and sent us out some cider and home-make cake, so we had a rattling good feed. David said he was in a loafing mood, and would not hear of my hurrying away."

" Mr. Carlyon does not seem overworked," remarked Malcolm; but he regretted his speech when he saw Elizabeth's heightened colour.

" Thursday is a slack day with him," she said rather gravely. " I assure you he works harder than most clergymen, and is very conscientious and painstaking. He is not at all strong, but he never spares himself."

" My hasty speech meant nothing," returned Malcolm smiling. " Mr. Carlyon is certainly no loafer—he looks the incarnation of energy."

" How doth the little busy D——
Improve each shining hour,"

chanted Cedric. But Elizabeth would stand no more nonsense. She called to the dogs, and warned their guest that the gong would sound in five minutes, and then marched off with her sailor hat slung on her arm, which she filled on her way to the house with Canterbury bells and blue larkspur.

The game of tennis was a great success. Dinah sat in the shade and watched them.

There was some little difficulty in choosing partners,

so Cedric said they must toss up for it, and Elizabeth fell to Mr. Carlyon.

If Malcolm felt secretly disappointed, no one guessed it. To his surprise he and Cedric were ruthlessly beaten.

Mr. Carlyon played a masterly game, and Elizabeth ably seconded him. Malcolm, who had always held his own on the tennis green, and was an excellent golf player, was much chagrined at his defeat. They had lost three successive games, when Cedric flung up his racket and declared he could play no more.

" They have given us a regular beating, mate," he said cheerfully. " You were in capital form, Herrick, and I did not do so badly myself, though I say it as shouldn't; but David has taken the shine out of us. I say, old fellow, you ought to be champion player."

" I think Miss Templeton played a good game," returned David modestly, and then he and Cedric went off to hunt for missing balls, and Elizabeth sauntered to the house. Half an hour later she was just putting the finishing touches to her dress when Dinah tapped at the door, and, as Elizabeth gave her a welcoming smile, sat down by the toilet table. It was one of Dinah's homely, pleasant little ways, but these few minutes of sisterly chat would have been sorely missed by both of them.

" How nice you look, dear!" in an admiring voice. Then Elizabeth glanced at herself with her head a little on one side.

" Do I?" she said simply. " I was afraid I should never regain my normal colour. Are you sure I don't look rather blowsy, and like a milkmaid?" But Dinah indignantly repudiated this; it was Dinah's private belief that Elizabeth was a very beautiful woman. " She has such lovely eyes, and then her face has so much expression," she would say; but Dinah had the good sense to keep this opinion to herself.

Elizabeth, who was not at all vain, and was quite conscious of her own defects, continued to gaze at her own reflection rather critically.

" I suppose on the whole I am passable, Die," she said rather philosophically. " When people like me they seem to like my looks; and really when you think of all the plain and downright ugly people in the world, there is surely room for thankfulness."

" Have you just found that out, Betty?"

" My dear Die, I am rather in a humble frame of mind just now. Don't you recollect my telling you Mrs. Robinson's speech last Monday. I have never thought quite so much of myself since."

" If I remember rightly, Mrs. Robinson paid you a compliment. She told Miss Clarkson that she wished Selina were as fine a woman as Elizabeth Templeton."

" And you call that compliment!" and Elizabeth arched her long full throat in rather a haughty and swanlike manner. " Fancy that goose of a Miss Clarkson repeating such a speech. A fine woman is my abhorrence. It always seems to me to rank in the same category with a prime turkey or a prize bullock, or something ready for the market."

" My dear Betty, you do say such odd things!"

" Of course I do. Elizabeth is nothing if she is not original. Don't you remember dear old dad's speech? But I am really serious, Die—you know I never coveted beauty."

" No, nor I, dear," and Dinah spoke quite earnestly.

" Oh, you," returned Elizabeth with playful tenderness. " I should hope not. I expect many women would be glad to change with you, you sweet thing." Then Dinah smiled and patted her sister's hand.

" No, Betty, you must not say that. I have often thought that even our poor faces, with all their defects, ought to be sacred to us. If we are a thought of God, as some one has beautifully put it, surely the stamp of His handiwork must be precious to us."

" But how about the marred and ugly faces, Die?" and Elizabeth looked at her dubiously.

" It is their cross," returned Dinah simply—" a heavy cross perhaps, but when I see a very plain, unattractive woman I do so long to whisper in her ear—

" 'Don't trouble about it, poor thing. What does it matter? You will be beautiful one day, and even now, if you are good and patient, the angels will think you lovely.' Dear me, Betty," interrupting herself, " why are you creasing my pretty silk dress."

" Lord love you, miss, I am only a-feeling for your wings," returned Elizabeth in a droll voice, and then they both laughed, for this was a standing joke between them ever since Dinah had repeated poor old Becky Brent's speech, when the wrinkled hand of the blind and doited old creature had fumbled about her shapely shoulders.

Dinah had been right in thinking that the vicar and Mr. Herrick would have much in common, and the conversation at the dinner-table that evening was unusually animated.

She and Elizabeth were attentive listeners, and on comparing notes afterwards both of them owned that they had been struck with Mr. Herrick's intelligence and broad-minded views.

The slight egotism that Elizabeth had detected seemed to drop from him like a veil, and he showed his true nature; he was evidently a patient and reverent searcher after knowledge, and his marked deference to the elder scholar became him greatly. Dinah quite glowed with innocent pleasure as she listened to them. " It is so seldom the dear vicar gets any one to talk on his favourite subjects, but one could see that Mr. Herrick is after his own heart," she remarked, as they sat on the terrace drinking their coffee and waiting for the gentlemen to join them.

"He is certainly very clever," observed Elizabeth thoughtfully.

"David was unusually quiet," went on Dinah; but her sister apparently did not hear this, for she went on talking about the advantage of a more varied reading.

"I am such an ignoramus," she continued, "when those men were talking about the MSS. in that old unknown monastery, I felt like a little goggle-eyed charity-school girl. When I get Mr. Herrick alone I mean to ask him about the Behistun Inscription;" and then Mr. Carlyon strolled towards them, followed by Cedric, and Elizabeth, who had finished her coffee, advanced towards them.

"They are still at it tooth and nail," observed David in an amused tone. "I should have stopped to listen to them, only this fellow was so sick of the discussion. What a well-informed chap Herrick is!"

"So Dinah and I were saying," remarked Elizabeth, as they paced slowly down the terrace. "Why were you so silent?" she continued; "you know a good deal about these subjects too."

"Who? I! My dear Miss Elizabeth, you are quite mistaken. Ask the vicar, and he will tell you that I am really a duffer in these matters. It is a wise child who knows his own father, and I am wise enough to know my own ignorance. Don't you know," with a smile, "it is easier to hold one's tongue and listen in an intelligent manner than flounder about out of one's depth among the billows of cuneiform inscriptions and the insurmountable precipice of the Behistun Rock."

"Why do you undervalue yourself so?" returned Elizabeth gently; "don't you know people take us at our own value? I have got it into my head that you and Mr. Herrick do not quite take to each other—woman's eyes are rather sharp, you know." But Mr. Carlyon turned this off with a laugh.

"Oh, we hit it off all right," he replied; "please don't

go and take fancies in your head. He has his innings now, but we got the best of him this afternoon." Elizabeth's merry answering laugh reached Malcolm's ears, and made him lose the drift of the vicar's argument.

But he lost it still more, and became increasingly absent-minded, when a few minutes later he heard her rich, full tones in his favourite song, "Loving, yet leaving." Mr. Charrington noticed it at last. "The siren is too much for you, Mr. Herrick," he said pleasantly; "we will resume our discussion another time," and to this Malcolm cheerfully assented.

Did Elizabeth perceive the dark figure that glided in at the open window and settled itself so comfortably in the easy-chair? If she were conscious of the silent auditor, she made no sign.

Never had her voice been sweeter and truer; never had she sung with such birdlike clearness, with such abandon and pleasure. Now and then a whispered word from David made her exchange one song for another, or a low-toned "bravo" from the same source greeted some special favourite.

Elizabeth was in the mood for singing. She was a creature of moods and tenses, and would probably have gone on carolling blissfully for another hour if the vicar had not interrupted them.

"It is getting late, Carlyon, and we may as well walk back together," he remarked in his leisurely manner, for being an old bachelor he was rather precise in his ways. David jumped up at once.

"I will go with you, sir, of course," he replied quickly. Then in a lower voice, "It is a lovely evening—will you do your lady's mile?" He spoke so low that Malcolm could only guess at what he said; but Elizabeth's answer was quite clear and audible.

"No, not to-night; I think I have exerted myself sufficiently. But I daresay Mr. Herrick and Cedric will go."

And Malcolm, who felt himself dismissed and had no excuse to offer, was soon plunged into an argument again that lasted all the way to Rotherwood.

"Betty, did you notice that Mr. Herrick did not want to go?" asked Dinah, who was always keenly alive to the likes and dislikes of her neighbours. "It was naughty of you to put him in such a position. How could he refuse to go when the vicar was waiting for him?"

"I thought a walk would do him good," returned Elizabeth demurely; "he was almost asleep when Mr. Charrington spoke to us. A comfortable chair, and moonlight, and a German lullaby are soporific influences."

"Nonsense, Betty," replied Dinah in her practical, downright way, "he was as wide-awake as I was; but," with a little sigh of sympathy, "he looked rather sad. Are you sure he is quite happy, dear?"

"I expect he is quite as happy as he deserves to be," returned Elizabeth in rather a hard-hearted way; and then she went off, singing to herself in a low tone a line or two from her last song:

> "It may be in the Land above—
> The Land beyond our ken;
> Yet we shall meet again, my love,
> Though none can answer when."

And as Dinah stood listening in the moonlight her face looked like the face of a radiant infant.

"That is so true," she whispered, "and what does it matter—when!"

CHAPTER XV

"BETTY IS A TRUMP!"

A character is like an acrostic or Alexandrian stanza: read it forward, backward, or across, it still spells the same thing. . . . We pass for what we are: character teaches above our wills.—
EMERSON.

It had been Malcolm's intention to go back to town on the ensuing Monday, but on Dinah's pressing invitation he promised to remain another day.

"You know I am due at the Manor House on Thursday," he observed, as they sat at breakfast the next morning, "and I must have a couple of days in town first."

"It is a very short visit," she returned regretfully, "and you are to dine at the vicarage to-morrow evening."

"I could not get out of it," he replied quickly, but he glanced at Elizabeth as he spoke. "Mr. Charrington never gave me the option of refusing. He seemed to look on it as a foregone conclusion that his invitation would be accepted. He was so very kind and cordial. He wants me to see his library, and to show me some rare books he has got."

"Oh yes, he is a collector of curious books and first editions. He has a very valuable library. It is his hobby—is it not, Dinah? Old books, old wine, and plenty of learned talk—you will be in luck's way, Mr. Herrick," and Elizabeth flashed an amused look at him.

"I suppose Mr. Carlyon will be there," observed Dinah composedly, as she replenished Malcolm's cup. Cedric had not yet made his appearance, but they could hear him whistling in the distance. But before Malcolm could answer in the negative, Elizabeth broke in again.

"You are wrong there, Die; Mr. Carlyon never goes

out on Saturday evenings. It is his day for writing his sermon, and I have never known him break his rule. Mr. Charrington wishes to have Mr. Herrick to himself. He," with another smile, "knows two are company and three are none. Well, good people, I must not dawdle this morning, as there is so much to do;" and as Elizabeth rose from the table she gave her sister a meaning glance, and Dinah, who was like wax in Elizabeth's hands, took the hint at once.

"We are so glad you have made up your mind to stay until Tuesday," she said cordially, "for we are asking some people to come over for tennis on Monday afternoon. Elizabeth has gone off to write the notes now." "Why on earth could she not have said so?" thought Malcolm, with secret irritation. But Dinah went on cheerfully—

"It will be only an informal affair; there is no time to arrange a regular garden-party. We will keep that until you take up your quarters at the Crow's Nest. We generally have one big affair before the summer is over, and then our friends come down from town, and we have to commandeer all the carriages in the place to meet the train. Elizabeth calls it 'The Templeton's Bean-feast.'"

"Yes, I see," and Malcolm forced a smile at the little joke.

"This will be a very different function," continued Dinah. "We are only asking about five-and-twenty people. We shall have tea in the hall—it is the coolest place in this weather—and there will be two or three sets of tennis, and croquet for those who like it. It was all Elizabeth's plan. You have no idea what a talent she has for organisation—she almost takes my breath away sometimes. She planned everything last night and had the list ready for me when I went to bid her good-night."

"That accounts for the light in the Red Gallery when Cedric and I came in," remarked Malcolm.

"Yes, we were dreadfully late; but Elizabeth was so wide-awake that I was quite ashamed of my own drowsiness. I think we shall get a pleasant party together." And as Cedric came in at that moment, Dinah retailed their little plan for his benefit. Cedric was delighted, and voted Betty a brick. Any form of sociability was welcome to him—an impromptu garden-party in Malcolm's honour met with his decided approval.

"David must give us our revenge," he said, chuckling with glee at the idea. But Malcolm did not respond to this.

He felt inwardly provoked at the whole affair, and regretted that he had promised to remain another day. Could not Miss Elizabeth have guessed—pshaw! what an ass he was, how was she to know?—that a motley and miscellaneous collection of people was his distinct aversion! A rustic *Olla podrida,* an *Omnium-gatherum* was not to his taste. It was his last evening too, and he would have to make himself pleasant to strangers.

He knew what these impromptu garden-parties meant. People drove over from distant villages and expected to remain late. There would be no dinner, no coffee on the terrace, no songs in the dimly-lighted drawing-room. Ah, just so, was not Cedric endorsing his thought at this very moment?

"Betty is a trump, Die! She has thought of just the right people. I suppose we shall have a scratch meal when the rush has gone. But we must ask the Brent girls to have a snack with us."

"Oh, of course, Elizabeth said so at once, and she mentioned the Ross party too. Tina and Patty will expect to remain—they always do, and they think the drive back by moonlight the best part of the fun. Very well, Cedric dear, you will go over on your bicycle and leave the notes?"

"Well, I don't mind taking trouble in a good cause,"

he returned in a virtuous tone; and then Dinah, with an air of great satisfaction, addressed herself to her guest.

"I wonder if you would care to drive Elizabeth over to Earlsfield this afternoon; she has a good many commissions to execute. Brookes has to wait for the vet, as one of our carriage horses is lame, and I do not like her to go alone with James." But Malcolm carefully disguised his pleasure at this unexpected request.

"Is this Miss Elizabeth's idea too?" His tone rather puzzled Dinah.

"Oh dear, no—at least, I think not. I rather fancy I suggested it to her."

"And she made no objection?"

"My dear Mr. Herrick, of course not. She will be only too grateful to you. James is a good lad, but we dare not trust him with Brown Becky, and though Elizabeth drives very well, she wants to be free for her business."

"Then in that case I shall be delighted to go," and there was no fault to be found with Malcolm's tone now. His satisfaction was hardly diminished by a hair's-breath when Cedric suggested that they might go round by Rotherwood on their way home and give David a verbal invitation. "He might be engaged if we waited until to-morrow," he said seriously; "the busy D—— is rather a popular person, and the young ladies of Earlsfield and Staplegrove are always on the look-out for him."

"You would not dare to say that if Elizabeth were in the room," but Dinah spoke quite innocently and had no *arrière pensée*.

"I know that Betty monopolises him to any extent," retorted Cedric, "and it is a shame when that poor little Tina——"

Then Dinah quite flushed up and said quickly, "Hush, how can you be so silly, Cedric. Tina is a perfect baby. Who cares what a foolish little flirting thing says about Elizabeth! You ought not to repeat such speeches."

"There is always so much gossip in a village," observed Malcolm, with a laudable intention of casting oil on the troubled waters, for he saw that Dinah was really vexed at Cedric's careless speech; "and an unmarried curate is always rather an attraction to some genus of young ladies."

"Mr. Carlyon never encouraged them," returned Dinah quietly. "The fact is, Mr. Herrick, Tina Ross is rather a mischievous little person. She is very pretty and very much spoilt, and she cares far too much for admiration. My sister used to be very fond of her—she was quite a favourite at one time; but the other day she owned that she was greatly disappointed in her, and that she was afraid Tina was rather an empty-headed little thing."

"Oh yes, we understand that, don't we, Betty?" retorted Cedric, nodding at Elizabeth knowingly as she entered the room. "Tina is in your black books now." But Elizabeth received this with perfect serenity.

"Oh, she is an amusing child," she returned carelessly, "but she makes a very common mistake. She thinks a pretty face and a flippant tongue and a childish manner are perfectly irresistible, but in her study of mankind she is certainly an unlessoned girl."

"I think old David admires her," observed Cedric casually. He spoke in such a matter-of-fact way that Elizabeth was quite taken in.

"To be sure he admires her," she said seriously. "How can he help it? Even Mr. Herrick—who, I have been told, is really a severe critic on female beauty—will admire her too when he sees her on Monday. You shall have an introduction," with a mischievous look. "We will not allow Mr. Carlyon to monopolise her." Here they both stared at her. "Tina is an old friend of his. Now then, Cedric lad, if you have finished your breakfast, I want you in the morning-room."

"One moment, please," and Malcolm barred her way. "I believe I am to drive you over to Earlsfield this afternoon."

"Dinah has arranged it then," with rather an inscrutable little smile. "Thank you, it will be very kind, and I know it will be a relief to her mind." But she added hastily, "There is no use in our going round by Rotherwood. We can post Mr. Carlyon's note. If there is time we might go on the Downs—you will like that much better," and then Elizabeth gave him a friendly little nod.

Malcolm enjoyed his afternoon. Brown Becky was in excellent form, and it gave him a great deal of pleasure to drive her; and then Elizabeth was so sociable and so altogether charming. He had glanced more than once at the paper she held in her hands. "Are you going to order all these things?" he asked, and she had laughed in his face.

"Five-and-twenty to thirty people to entertain is rather a large order. We have plenty of cider and fruit, and of course there will be claret cup, but we have no time to make cakes—besides, there must be a cold collation for at least a dozen."

"Oh yes, I understand," he returned good-humouredly; but he was secretly surprised by the quickness with which her commissions were executed. Evidently the ladies of the Wood House were people of consideration to the tradesmen of Earlsfield, for obsequious shopmen stood bowing and smiling on the threshold; and was it his fancy, or was there an added stateliness in the second Miss Templeton's step and carriage as she threaded the pretty little market-place, exchanging greetings with every other person she met?

"Now I have finished," she observed presently, "and you and Brown Becky have behaved like a couple of angels." Then she chanted merrily, "Oh, who will o'er the downs with me?" and Malcolm turned the mare's head in the direction she pointed out.

It had been very hot in the market-place, but when they had gained the open down a honey-sweet wind blew refreshingly in their faces, and not only the moorland but the roadside was clothed with the purpling heather. Malcolm checked the mare involuntarily, and sat silently feasting his eyes on the glorious colouring before him.

"No Tyrian garment could equal that," he said half to himself.

Elizabeth looked at him curiously.

"I thought you would like it," she returned, well pleased by his rapt admiration of her favourite view.

"Like it! I only wish I had Keston here; but if I am a living man I will bring him and Verity too. What a grand old world it is after all, Miss Templeton, though we do our best to spoil it."

"Ah, you are right there," and Elizabeth's voice was a little sad.

"Don't you remember what Clough says?" continued Malcolm quietly:

> 'The work-day burden of dull life
> About the footsore flags of a weary world.'

We all have our pedlar's pack to carry through Vanity Fair; but how good for us to turn aside into some of Nature's holy places which she keeps so fair and sweet and untainted, and to take a long draught of the elixir of life!"

"Mr. Herrick, do you ever write poetry?" Malcolm shook his head.

"No," he said regretfully. "One day, if you care to hear it, I will tell you the story of an impotent genius."

"An impotent genius?" It was evident that Elizabeth was puzzled, but then she had only known Malcolm Herrick five days.

Malcolm nodded gravely. "The story of a man who was halt and maimed and crippled from his birth—a tongue-tied poet and a paralysed artist. The story is a sad one, Miss Templeton, but it will keep."

Elizabeth's eyes danced with amusement. She began to have an idea of his meaning.

"I rather think you are a humourist, Mr. Herrick." And then Malcolm laughed, and after that they fell into quite an interesting conversation. Elizabeth turned the subject to her own ignorance, and begged Malcolm to tell her what books she ought to read.

"Dinah puts me to shame," she observed frankly. "She reads all the best books, and she often tries to persuade me to follow her example. The fact is, I am rather a desultory sort of person, and I have so many interesting occupations that I never know what to do first."

"One must always have a little method in one's daily life," returned Malcolm indulgently. "How would you like me to make you out a list? You might slip any books you did not want to read."

Then Elizabeth thanked him quite gratefully.

"I mean to turn over a new leaf on my thirty-first birthday," she continued serenely. "Isn't it a great age, Mr. Herrick?"

But Malcolm only smiled in answer. He was thinking how strange it seemed that she was actually his senior by two years; but he soon grasped the idea that Elizabeth Templeton was one of those women who grow old slowly, and who are sweetest in their ripened prime.

The evening at the vicarage passed very pleasantly, and when Malcolm took his leave he was much surprised at the lateness of the hour, and sorely disturbed when he found Dinah sitting up for him. But she would not listen to his excuses.

"An hour later does not matter to me, and I was reading and quite forgot the time. I am so glad you have enjoyed yourself," and Dinah dismissed him with her gentle smile.

Malcolm was rather disappointed with the vicar's sermon the next day. It was learned, and full of quotations from the Fathers, but he could not but perceive that it was perfectly unsuited to a village congregation. "Can these dry bones live?" he thought, as they came out into the sunny churchyard.

Mr. Carlyon had read the service. His manner had been extremely reverent and devout, but Malcolm found his delivery unpleasing. The peculiarity in his speech was very noticeable in the reading-desk, and there was no clearness of articulation.

"I am not versed in phonology," he said reluctantly, when Elizabeth asked him a little anxiously about Mr. Carlyon's reading, "but I know you would not have questioned me if you did not want to know my real opinion. I think it is rather a pity that Mr. Carlyon has not taken elocution lessons."

"You are quite right," she returned quietly. "I can assure you that he is fully aware of his deficiencies."

"I am not sure that he has not some physical difficulties to surmount," went on Malcolm; "but however that may be, a course of elocution and some sound advice about the management of the voice would have been of immense value. I have always thought that every young man who intends to take holy orders should be compelled to attend elocution classes as part of the training. You will not think me too critical in saying all this?"

But Elizabeth, with evident sincerity, assured him that she perfectly agreed with him.

They all spent the afternoon down at the Pool, and Malcolm read aloud to the sisters, while Cedric and the dogs enjoyed a nap. When he had finished the poem— it was Browning's *Christmas and Easter Eve* he had been reading—Dinah thanked him with tears in her eyes. "I never heard any one read so beautifully," she said. But Elizabeth was silent; only as they were crossing the little bridge she turned for a moment to Malcolm, who was following her closely.

" You have a right to be critical," she said meaningly; " I should think you must have been top of the class," and a flush of gratification came to his face.

They all went to church again in the evening, and this time Mr. Charrington read the prayers and the lessons, in a mellow, cultured voice that was very agreeable to Malcolm's ear. Mr. Carlyon preached.

Malcolm settled himself in his corner and prepared himself for twenty minutes' endurance, but to his surprise he soon found himself roused and interested.

If the preacher's articulation was imperfect—if he took hurried breaths and stumbled here and there over a sentence—Malcolm soon ceased to notice it.

The treasure might be in an earthen vessel, but it was goodly treasure for all that; the priest might be young and inexperienced, but he had his Evangel, his message to deliver, and the earnestness of his purpose was reflected in his face. " Rejoice, oh young man, in thy youth," was the text; but before the short sermon was over, the row of ploughboys near them had roused from their drowsiness and stroked down their sleek heads with embarrassed fingers, as David Carlyon's voice rang through the darkening church with the concluding words, " but know thou, that for all these things God will bring thee into judgment."

Involuntarily Malcolm glanced at Elizabeth as they rose, but she did not see him; her large bright eyes were fixed on the preacher for a moment, then her head bent meekly to receive the blessing, and to Malcolm's disappointment she made no allusion to the sermon on their way home.

CHAPTER XVI

"IT REALLY IS A GOOD IDEA, DIE"

It is most certain that woman's most womanly affections are the likeness of affections which have their pure and perfect fountain in the nature of God.—PULSFORD.

AFTER supper that evening Malcolm found himself alone with Dinah. Elizabeth and Cedric had gone down to the Pool to find a book she had left there in the afternoon, and he had been on the point of following them when he saw a wistful look in Miss Templeton's eyes, and immediately sat down again.

"You want to speak to me," he said pleasantly. He was quite aware that Elizabeth had carried off her brother with intent and purpose, and smiled to himself over her little ruse.

"She is very clever. I wonder if the missing book is a figment of her imagination," he thought; but in this he wronged her, for that little red-edged copy of Keble's *Christian Year* was very dear to Elizabeth.

"Yes, I want to speak to you," returned Dinah, and her tone was rather anxious and flurried. "The time is growing so short now, and to-morrow there will not be a moment, and so Elizabeth said——" and here again a flickering smile played over Malcolm's face.

"And she has carried Cedric off because you wanted to speak to me about him." Dinah was so hesitating in her manner that he thought it best to finish her sentence for her. "I hope nothing is troubling you on his account. In my opinion he is very much improved."

"Oh, I am so glad you think so," and all Dinah's mother-soul shone out of her mild eyes. "Elizabeth was only saying last night how strong and manly he has grown. But, Mr. Herrick, I am rather anxious about one thing. You know Cedric is to row in the Oxford and Cambridge race."

"I am certainly aware of the fact," replied Malcolm drily. The Jacobis and the University race had been the two standing dishes with which Cedric had regaled him. "I have heard of little else, I can assure you. Well, he is a lucky fellow; it is not every one who gets the desire of his heart."

"Then you approve of it?" questioned Dinah; but her tone was so dubious that he looked at her with unfeigned astonishment.

"My dear Miss Templeton, how could I do otherwise? It will be valuable training for Cedric; the discipline and self-denial that it entails will be the making of him. Of course his head is rather turned at present, and he is crowing like a bantam cock who wants to challenge the world, but he will soon be all right."

"You and Elizabeth think alike, then," replied Dinah; "she only laughs at me and calls me old-fashioned. I suppose I am not up-to-date," with a touching little smile; "it seems to me such waste of time and energy. And then there is the Civil Service Examination."

"Oh, we need not trouble our heads about that for another eighteen months."

"You think not?" still more anxiously. "Both Mr. Charrington and Mr. Carlyon tell me that it is a terribly hard examination."

"Well, it is pretty stiff, of course, and Cedric will have to work hard. You must give him his head for the present, Miss Templeton," he continued. "When he has taken his beating like an Englishman—for perhaps you are not aware there is a very poor chance for Oxford next year; their best men have left, and they have to lick a lot of raw recruits into shape. Well, what was I saying?—when Cedric has taken his beating and cooled down a bit, he will settle to work like a navvy."

Dinah looked a little comforted. "Then you think he will pass?"

Malcolm almost laughed outright at her simplicity.

"Miss Templeton, am I to prophecy smooth things to you, or am I to answer in the spirit of Micaiah the son of Imlah?"

"Oh, please tell me exactly what you think."

"Well, then," with obvious reluctance, "in my opinion Cedric stands a very poor chance." Here Dinah's face fell. "He has plenty of abilities, but I doubt his staying power; he works too much by fits and starts—there is no method or application. But of course he may turn over a new leaf. It is just possible that he may pass by some lucky fluke. It is not always the best workers who get through. You will give him a coach, of course. Oh, I see," reading Dinah's expression correctly, "he may have a dozen coaches if he needs them; but if you care to consult me when the time comes, I think I know the right man for cramming."

"Oh, thank you—thank you!" in a fervent tone of gratitude; "how good you are to listen to me so patiently!"

"My dear lady——" in a friendly tone of remonstrance. "But there is something else you want to say."

"Only this: if Cedric does not pass, what are we to do with him? You know he has utterly refused to enter the Church or to study for the law. He has no taste for engineering or architecture, and we should not care for him to be a business man."

"Need we consider the point at present?" returned Malcolm gently. "There is a limited number of professions, certainly. What do you say to a mastership in a public school? I fancy the life would suit Cedric; his love of boating would score there." Then Dinah brightened visibly.

"We never thought of that; even Elizabeth, who is so full of ideas, only suggested his going to an agricultural college to learn farming."

"Oh, that would never suit him," replied Malcolm in an off-hand manner. "He likes to have his bread ready buttered for him; cornfields and flour-mills are not in his line at all. Ah, here comes the search-party," and Malcolm looked a little curiously at the book in Elizabeth's hand.

"Oh, we have had such a hunt for it." Elizabeth looked quite hot and tired. "Cedric found it at last wedged between two boulders. I wonder he did not fall into the Pool while he was trying to get it out."

"Oh, Cedric, you ought to be more careful."

"Why on earth did you say that, Betty?" rather crossly. "Don't you see Die is wearing her grannie face?"

"But the Pool is so deep," in a terrified tone.

"Of course it is deep. Well, what of that; can't I swim like a fish? Oh, these women, Herrick!" and Cedric shrugged his shoulders. "I wonder how often I have taken a header into the Pool before breakfast!"

"You would have been sorry to lose the book," remarked Malcolm sympathetically, as they went into the house.

"Yes," returned Elizabeth hurriedly, "it was given to me by a friend." And then she bade him good-night.

Dinah followed her into her room. "I am so glad you found it, Betty dear," she said kindly. "It was the copy David gave you at Christmas, was it not?" Elizabeth nodded.

"I do so love it," she said frankly; "and the limp leather binding and red edges are just to my taste. I always care so much more for books that are given me than for those I buy myself." Elizabeth spoke with such complete unconsciousness that Dinah thought she had made a mistake in imagining that she specially prized the book.

"Oh, I want to tell you, dear, how very kind Mr. Herrick has been." And then with many little feminine interpolations Dinah related the substance of their conversation. She was almost childishly pleased when Elizabeth graciously approved of Malcolm's suggestion.

"It really is a good idea, Die."

"And to think it never entered our heads! Don't you wonder Mr. Carlyon never thought of it?"

"Well, you see he has never taken Cedric's future into serious consideration. But what fun it would be! We would furnish his rooms so beautifully, and we could stay with him sometimes. And when he married we could build him a house that would be the envy of all the masters. Fancy Cedric marrying and our having a dear little sister-in-law of our own."

"Oh, how I shall love her!" murmured Dinah with a happy little coo of satisfaction. This was not the first time they had talked on the subject. That her darling would marry, and that she would dearly love his wife, was a foregone conclusion to Dinah.

The little fair-haired girl of her dreams was not Tina Ross, nor even pretty Nora Brent—no one that Dinah knew was quite good enough for her boy.

"You ridiculous grannie," Elizabeth once said to her, for she and Cedric often called her grannie, probably from her careful, loving, old-womanish ways, "do you suppose such a *rara avis* exists in Earlsfield or Rotherwood? Let me see," ticking off each qualification on her fingers, "young Mrs. Cedric Templeton must be pretty—oh, very pretty; fair, because Cedric has a fancy for fair women with blue eyes; not tall—oh, decidedly not tall; *petite*, graceful, and *je ne sais quoi*——"

"Now, Betty——"

"Betty has not finished, and does not like to be interrupted. This Blanche—shall we call her Blanche? it is short and handy—Blanche is also full of gentle animation; she is docile, yielding, and has nice caressing ways that grannie loves. Indeed, she is such a guileless, simple little creature that it is difficult to believe that she is grown up—just eighteen, I think you said, Dinah, or was it nineteen, dear?" But Dinah refused to hear any more.

Elizabeth might laugh at her and call her grannie, but in her secret thoughts Dinah cherished a fond idea of a little fair-haired girl whom she would mother for Cedric's sake.

And now first Malcolm and then Elizabeth had given her this charming new idea.

" I am afraid you will be shocked," she said presently, " but I do not think I shall be so dreadfully disappointed if Cedric does fail in his Civil Service Examination. He might have to go to India, you see, and it would be so much nicer to keep him in England."

" The heart of man, and woman too, is deceitful and desperately wicked," and Elizabeth heaved a deep sigh. " To think that you can be so selfish, Die, as to build up your happiness on the poor lad's ruined hopes," and then she burst out laughing and took her sister by the shoulders. " Grannie," she said solemnly, " you just idolise that boy. If it would do him any good you would lie down and let him trample on you. Have I not often warned you that if you go on like this you will turn him out a full-fledged tyrant? Human nature—masculine human nature I mean," correcting herself—" will not stand it. An *enfant gâté* is always odious to sensible people. Now, if you were to try and spoil me," expanding herself until she looked twice her size, " I should only bloom out into fresh beauty—approbation, commendation, blindfold admiration would be meat and drink to me. I have the digestion of a young ostrich," continued Elizabeth blandly—" nothing would be too difficult for me to swallow. As for satiety, my dear creature, you need never expect to hear me call out, '*Eheu, jam satis.*'"

"Dear Betty, how you do talk," Dinah's usual formula; "and how I do love to hear you," she inwardly added. "But it is very late, and we shall have a tiring day to-morrow."

Dinah spoke in her cheery way, but when she was in her own room her sweet face grew pensive and a little sad. Was there not an element of truth under Elizabeth's jokes? Did she not make an idol of her young brother? Was she altogether reasonable on the subject?

"If I am weak, I trust such weakness will be forgiven me," she whispered as she stood in the perfumed darkness, with a wandering summer wind playing refreshingly round her, and tears from some hidden fount of sadness stole down her cheeks. "If he were my own child he could not be dearer to me. I remember my stepmother once told me so. 'My boy has two mothers, Dinah,' these were her very words. Well, he is my Son of Consolation," and Dinah heaved a gentle sigh, as though the motherhood within her, the divine maternal instinct inherent in all true women, felt itself satisfied.

At breakfast the next morning Malcolm proffered his services; but Elizabeth assured him that Cedric and Johnson would do all that was required, so he spent his morning indolently down by the Pool—reading and indulging in his favourite daydreams—until Cedric joined him.

Cedric looked heated and tired.

"I never saw such a person as Betty for getting work out of a fellow," he grumbled. "She would do splendidly on a rice plantation—wouldn't the niggers fly just! Why, she set me rolling the tennis lawn, because she wanted Johnson; and then I had to bicycle over to Rotherwood for something that had been forgotten. I took it out in cool drinks though, I can tell you. My word, Bet does

know how to make prime claret cup"—and Cedric
smacked his lips with the air of a veteran gourmand; and
then he sparred at Malcolm, and called him an absent-
minded beggar, and asked if he had finished his ode to the
naiad of the Pool, and made sundry other aggravating
remarks, which proved that he was in excellent spirits
and only wanted to find a safety-valve.

Just before the first carriage drove up, Malcolm, who
was standing by Elizabeth on the terrace, suggested that
she and Mr. Carlyon should give him and Cedric their
revenge; but she told him quite seriously that they must
not think of it for the present.

" The sets are all arranged, and Dinah and I must devote ourselves to our guests," she remarked; and as this
was only reasonable, Malcolm said no more.

" I am going to introduce you to Tina Ross," she continued. " There she and her sister Patty are just coming
up the drive now. She is a very good player, and your
opponents will be Nora Brent and Mr. Carlyon."

" We are under orders, Herrick," observed David with
mock humility; and then the introduction was made, and
the little white and blue fairy walked off demurely enough
with Malcolm.

Tina Ross was certainly a very pretty girl; she had
one of those babyish sort of faces that appeal so strongly
to some men; her manners were kittenish and full of
vivacity, and she had a way of glancing at a person from
under her long curling lashes that was considered very
alluring. " Do please be good and kind to a poor little
harmless thing like me," they seemed to say to each fresh
comer, " for you are such a nice man;" but Malcolm, who
saw plenty of girls in town, took no notice of a little
country chit's airs and graces; indeed, he thought Nora
Brent far more attractive—human kittens not being to
his taste.

" I don't think much of the fine gentleman from London," whispered Tina rather venomously to Nora when the game was finished. "I hate a town prig like poison."

"Anyhow he .played splendidly, and has given us a regular beating," returned her friend, who would willingly have exchanged partners. There was nothing exciting in playing with an old friend like David Carlyon, who was a sort of connection of the Brents, indeed, a distant, a very distant cousin; but Malcolm's dark intellectual face and rather melancholy eyes somewhat at-

Nora had her wish presently, and again Mr. Carlyon was Malcolm's opponent; this time a Miss Douglas was his partner. It was a well-contested game, but again Malcolm was the victor; but he wore his honours meekly. tracted Nora.

"Bravo, Mr. Herrick, and you too, Nora," exclaimed Elizabeth, clapping her hands, "you both played splendidly; now come into the hall and let me give you some claret cup;" but she lingered a moment until Mr. Carlyon came up with his partner.

"I am not in good form to-day," he said, sinking into an easy-chair as though he were tired. "I feel Mondayish—do you know what I mean, Herrick?"

"I can guess. It is a purely clerical term. You have taken it out of yourself, and then you feel a sort of reaction—or rather, to speak more correctly, a sort of depression;" but as he spoke, he realised for the first time the truth of Elizabeth's assertion that Mr. Carlyon was not strong.

Elizabeth had never looked better in Malcolm's opinion than she did that afternoon; if he had not admired her before, he must have owned then that she was a disguished-looking woman.

She wore a gray dress of some soft material, which Malcolm, who was rather a connoisseur on feminine attire, decided in his own mind was a Paris gown,—strange to say, he was right,—and the black Gainsborough hat and feathers suited her exactly. It was evident Mr. Carlyon agreed with him, for Malcolm saw him once looking at her intently under his hand.

A little while afterwards Malcolm, who was too hot to play any more, strolled off by himself down one of the woodland paths to get cool, but to his chagrin he heard voices which told him the speakers were parallel with him, and the next minute he heard Tina Ross say pettishly—

" Did you ever see any one so ridiculous as Elizabeth Templeton; just fancy wearing her Paris gown at a trumpery little home affair like this! Talk of coquetry," in a disgusted voice, " do you suppose she did not know what she was doing when she pinned those La France roses in her dress! It is not as though she were our age; she is thirty—thirty; why, that is quite an old maid!"

" How can you be so absurd, Tiny?" It was Nora Brent who spoke. " Fancy calling Miss Elizabeth Templeton an old maid. Mamma was only saying how handsome she looked." Here Malcolm coughed rather loudly, but no one took any notice.

" Handsome is as handsome does," returned Tina, in rather a vixenish tone. " I hope you noticed, Nora, that I was never allowed to have Mr. Carlyon for a partner. Talk of Queen Elizabeth indeed—we have Queen Elizabeth the second at Staplegrove. If one spoke to the poor man it was ' hands off—don't poach on my preserves,' just as though she thought him her own property, which he is not, and never will be."

" Really, Tina, you are too bad; you ought not to say such things of our dear Miss Elizabeth. You had Mr. Herrick for your partner."

" Oh, he is a town prig," began Tina recklessly; but here Malcolm, who had cleared his voice in vain, now began to whistle with such unmistakable purpose that a dead silence ensued.

" What a spiteful little toad!" thought Malcolm, who

cared nothing for fluffy hair and curling eyelashes if a shrewish tongue accompanied them.

He thought both the girls avoided him in rather a guilty fashion when he passed them on the terrace; and he was inwardly disgusted when, most of the guests having taken their leave, and supper being announced, Elizabeth asked him to take Miss Tina Ross into the dining-room; Nora followed with Mr. Carlyon, but the width of the table separated him. Malcolm paid the young lady proper attention; that is to say, he kept her plate supplied with good things, but otherwise he took very little notice of her, and talked to gentle-looking Mrs. Brent, who was on his other side.

But Tina was not used to being ignored, and by this time she had made up her mind that Malcolm could only have heard a fragment of their talk in the woodlands, so she addressed him pointedly, and obliged him to break off something he was saying to the elder lady.

"So you dined at the vicarage on Saturday, I hear. How dreadfully bored you must have been! Mr. Charrington is an old dear, but he is rather a prig. I mean"— transfixed by the sudden gleam in Malcolm's eyes—"I mean, that is—that he is so learned."

"Oh, I am quite aware of your meaning, Miss Ross," returned Malcolm quietly, "but I am rather an embryo prig myself." Then for the remainder of the meal Tina was absolutely dumb.

CHAPTER XVII

" ADIEU—AU REVOIR"

If there is power in me to help,
It goeth forth beyond the present will,
Clothing itself in very common deeds
Of any humble day's necessity.

MacDonald.

THE pleasantest part of the whole evening to Malcolm was the hour spent on the terrace when the last guests were gone. The Brents had undertaken to drive Mr. Carlyon to the White Cottage, much to the chagrin of the Ross girls, whose homeward route took them through Rotherwood, and who also had a seat to spare. Malcolm had a dim suspicion that Elizabeth had connived at this arrangement.

"You had better go with the Brents if they ask you," she had said earlier in the evening, but he had not heard Mr. Carlyon's reply.

"Well, what do you think of little Tina?" asked Elizabeth. They were standing by the drawing-room window; Malcolm could see the mischievous look in her eyes, and refused to be drawn.

"Most people would admire her," he returned coolly.

"But unfortunately you are the exception—is that what you mean, Mr. Herrick? What a shame not to admire our pretty little blue-eyed kitten!"

"Kittens can scratch," he returned quietly; and then Elizabeth looked more amused than ever.

"What, has Tina shown her claws to you? I thought she always wore her velvet gloves for strangers. I fancied I was doing you a good turn to introduce you to

170

the prettiest girl in Rotherwood. She and Patty will be rich too, for there is no son, and Mr. Ross is very wealthy."

"Made his fortune on the Stock Exchange," explained Cedric. "Clever old chap—shouldn't mind if he would give me the straight tip. I tell you what, Die," and here Cedric lit himself another cigarette, "if I come a cropper in the exam, the Stock Exchange would not be a bad place for me to make my little pile."

It was impossible not to laugh at Dinah's horrified face.

"Don't believe him, Die," observed Elizabeth calmly. "Cedric has no vocation for a business man—he is only teasing you. Yes, Tina and Patty will have plenty of money," but as Malcolm did not seem to warm up to any interest, Elizabeth with much tact changed the subject, and they were soon discussing the other guests.

When Malcolm woke the next morning his first feeling was regret that his visit was over. He had accepted Cedric's invitation with reluctance, and had put him off again and again. He had a remorseful consciousness that he might have been a guest at the Wood House eighteen months ago. By this time he would have been intimate with the sisters. He might——but here Malcolm leapt rather impatiently from his couch. What was the good of thinking over past mistakes! He had been a fool, and stood in his own light—that was all. During breakfast he was very cheerful, and seemed in such excellent spirits that the passing thought occurred to Elizabeth that Mr. Herrick was not sorry that his visit had ended.

"We are not clever enough for him," she said to herself regretfully; but Malcolm's next speech dispelled this idea.

Dinah had just expressed her regret at losing him.

"I have no wish to go, I assure you," was his reply; "I have never spent a happier week in my life. But you know in another two or three weeks I hope to be settled at the Crow's Nest. We shall be near neighbours then." He looked at Elizabeth as he spoke. It struck him that she was a little embarrassed. Her colour rose, and there was a slight pucker in her brow, as though something perplexed her; but the next minute it was gone.

"In that case we must fix the date for the Templeton Bean-feast," she remarked briskly. "Mr. Herrick," her voice changing to earnestness, "will it be quite impossible for Miss Sheldon to come to our garden-party. We could put her up easily—and it is really rather a pretty sight. We had two hundred people last year, and the Hungarian band."

"It was rattling good sport," chimed in Cedric. "There were fifteen of our fellows sleeping at 'The Plough,' because we had a dance in the evening; not only our house, but Hazel Beach, the Ross's house, and Brentwood Place, where Colonel Brent lives, were crammed with guests. People talked about it for a month afterwards."

"It cost a great deal of money," observed Dinah, in rather an alarmed voice. "We could not do that sort of thing again. You see, Mr. Herrick, it was really to make up to Cedric because he had no party when he came of age. I was ill just then, and we had to go away."

"No, no, you are quite right, Die, we must keep our Bean-feast within limits," returned Elizabeth soothingly. "We thought of fixing the twentieth of August," she continued, addressing Malcolm. "That is nearly a month later than last year. I expect most of our inner circle friends will be away, but we shall have a good house-party; and with some of Cedric's Oxford friends we shall be able to infuse sufficient new life into our country clique. Well, Mr. Herrick, is that likely to suit Miss Sheldon?"

"I am afraid not," he returned regretfully, for he was

really quite touched at this thoughtfulness on her part. And how Anna would have loved it! "They will be at Whitby by that time. But I will tell her of your kind thought for her." And then, as it was getting late, for they had lingered pleasantly over the meal, he went off to make his preparations, and half an hour afterwards the dog-cart was brought to the door.

"Good-bye, we shall miss you so much," observed Dinah almost affectionately; "but we shall see plenty of you when you are at the Crow's Nest."

"I hope so. Thank you, dear Miss Templeton, for all your kind hospitality," and then it was Elizabeth's turn.

"Adieu—au revoir, Mr. Herrick," but she pressed his hand very kindly as she spoke, and her eyes had a friendly beam in them.

"Au revoir, and thanks to you too," returned Malcolm; but the smile on his face was a little forced.

As the dog-cart turned the corner he looked back. The sisters were still standing side by side. Elizabeth waved her hand. She was no longer the stately-looking woman in the Paris gown and picture hat, who had moved with such a queenly step among her guests. This was a far homelier Elizabeth, in the old striped blouse and battered garden hat, only this morning Malcolm found no fault with it. He was very silent for some time, but as he leant back in the dog-cart with folded arms and closely compressed lips, there was a glow in his dark eyes that somewhat contradicted his outward calmness.

"And you are going down to the Manor House on Thursday," observed Cedric, as they came in sight of the station. "What a pity my Henley visit is put off till the following week, or we might have had a good old time together."

"Oh, I don't know," rather absently; "you will be too much taken up with your new friends to want an old stager like me."

" You are wrong there," returned the lad eagerly. " I should be glad to have your opinion of"—he hesitated, and then finished lamely, " of the Jacobis, I mean. You are such a judge of character, and all that sort of thing."

" Am I?" with a smile; but they had no time to say more, as the London train was signalled.

An hour and a half later Malcolm was in his chambers in Lincoln's Inn, opening his letters and dashing off replies, to be posted in due time by the obsequious Malachi. Malcolm found so much to occupy him that he decided not to go to Queen's Gate until the following evening, and sent Anna a line to that effect. He felt a quiet evening at Cheyne Walk would be more in harmony with his feelings.

As he crossed the broad space at the foot of the steps in Lincoln's Inn, he overtook Caleb Martin wheeling the perambulator. Kit had her new doll hugged in her thin little arms.

" Oh, dad, do stop," she exclaimed eagerly; " it is the gentleman what gave me my baby;" and then Malcolm stepped up to the perambulator.

" Kit has been looking out for you the last week, sir," observed Caleb in his humble, flurried way. " She won't even take notice of the pigeons; her heart is so set on thanking you for the doll. It is my belief that she thinks it is alive the way she goes on with it."

" My baby's asleep—should you like to see her open her eyes?" asked Kit with maternal pride. " She has blue eyes, she has, like dad's and mine—only prettier. She is just the beautifullest thing I ever saw, ain't she, dad? and Ma'am says she must have cost a lot."

Malcolm smiled, but there was a pitiful look in his eyes. Even in these few days Kit's face had grown thinner and more pinched, and the shrill voice was weaker. There was no longer a stiff halo of curls under the sun-bonnet; they hung in limp wisps about her face.

"Has the child been ill?" he asked, and then Caleb looked at him in a dazed, nervous fashion.

"Not to call ill, sir, but just a bit piny and dwiny from the heat. Our place is like the Black Hole of Calcutta for stuffiness. She is that languid and fretty that we can't get her to eat, so my wife made me take her out for an airing."

Malcolm pondered for a moment. Then a sudden inspiration came to him. There was a fruiterer in the Strand, and he was just thinking of carrying a basket of fruit to Verity. He bade Caleb follow him slowly, and a few minutes later a great bunch of roses and a paper bag of white-heart cherries and another of greengages were packed into the perambulator; some sponge-cakes and a crisp little brown loaf were also purchased for Kit's tea, and then they went rejoicing on their way. As Malcolm walked on he made up his mind that his first act when he arrived at the Crow's Nest would be to take counsel with Elizabeth. "The child will die if something is not done for her," he said to himself; "perhaps she will be able to suggest something;" but it never occurred to him to confide in his mother. "Individual cases do not appeal to her," he had once said to Anna. "She prefers to work on a more extended scale," and though Anna contradicted this with unusual warmth, Malcolm had some grounds for his sweeping assertion.

Malcolm spent the evening very pleasantly discussing future arrangements with his friends. To his satisfaction the room he coveted was at once allotted to him, with the title of "The Prophet's Chamber;" and, as he professed himself quite content with the bedroom in the garden-house, matters were soon settled, and both Verity and Amias looked pleased when Malcolm announced his intention of spending most of his summer vacation at the Crow's Nest. They talked a good deal about the Wood House. Malcolm gave graphic descriptions of the house and the garden and the Pool, and he also drew rather a charming picture of the elder Miss Templeton.

"She is lovely in my opinion," he said in his enthusiastic way. "I quite long for you to see her, Verity. She is just a gray-haired girl. She has the secret of perpetual youth. She is as guileless and simple as a child—any one could deceive her, and yet she is wise too."

"And her sister?" asked Verity, as Malcolm paused.

"Oh, Miss Elizabeth Templeton is quite different," returned Malcolm hurriedly, as he filled his pipe; "it is not easy to describe her—you must judge of her yourself."

"Then she is not as nice as this wonderful Dinah?" observed Verity in a disappointed tone.

"Oh, yes, she is quite as nice," he returned briefly; "but the sisters are utterly dissimilar." And not another word could Verity, with all her teasing, extract from Malcolm.

"I should like you to be perfectly unbiassed in your opinion," he remarked sententiously. Verity made a naughty little face in the darkness.

"I wonder if it is the Crow's Nest, our society, or Miss Elizabeth Templeton that is the attraction," she thought. But, being a loyal little soul, she never hinted at a certain suspicion that had taken possession of her mind, even to her husband.

Malcolm received a warm welcome from his mother and Anna the next evening. He found them sitting by one of the open windows in the large drawing-room. Mrs. Herrick was working, and Anna was reading to her. The sun-blinds had just been raised, and the fresh evening air blew refreshingly through the wide room. The tall green palms behind them made a pleasant background to Anna's white dress. It struck Malcolm that she looked paler and more tired, and her eyes had a heavy, languid look. To his surprise Mrs. Herrick spoke of it at once.

"Anna is not looking her best this evening, Malcolm," she said as he sat down between them; "this great heat tries her. Dr. Armstrong thinks we ought to leave town as soon as possible, so we are going to Whitby a week earlier."

"Mother has cancelled a lot of her engagements," observed Anna, looking at her affectionately. "I am so sorry to give her all this trouble." But Mrs. Herrick would not allow her to finish.

"Mothers are only too glad to take trouble for their children," she said kindly. "Anna has been behaving badly, Malcolm; she fainted at church on Sunday, and had one of her worst sick headaches afterwards."

There was unmistakable anxiety in Malcolm's eyes when he heard this, but Anna only laughed it off. The church was hot, she said, any one might have fainted. But the sea-breezes would soon set her up; they had beautiful rooms quite close to the sea, with a wide balcony where they could spend their evenings.

"I hope you will come down to us for a week or two," observed his mother presently. Malcolm felt rather a twinge of conscience as he replied that he feared this was impossible; he had some literary work on hand, which he intended to do at Staplegrove. Mrs. Keston was able to spare him a nice room, which he could use as a study; and so he had made his arrangements. And then he added rather regretfully that, as he was going to the Manor House the following afternoon, he feared that he should not see them again. Mrs. Herrick said no more, she was not a woman to waste words unnecessarily; but she was undoubtedly much disappointed, and even a little hurt, and for the moment Anna looked grave. At dinner-time she made an effort to recover her spirits, and questioned Malcolm about his new acquaintances at the Wood House; and on this occasion he was less reticent.

But it was not until his mother had left them alone

together that he told Anna of Elizabeth's kind invitation.

A surprised flush came to the girl's face.

"Do you think you could possibly manage it, dear?" he asked with brotherly solicitude. But he was sorry to see how her lips trembled.

"Oh no—no, you must not tempt me," very hurriedly; "it is quite—quite impossible. I must not think of it for a moment, Malcolm," trying to speak calmly. "I am so grateful to you for not speaking of this before mother; it would trouble her so, and quite spoil her pleasure; mother is so sharp, she always finds out things, and she would know at once that I should like to go to the Wood House."

"Then I was right when I told Miss Elizabeth so," returned Malcolm. "It is just the place you would like, Anna; I know you would be happy with those kind women."

"I do not doubt it for a moment," and Anna's voice was rather melancholy. "I should so love to know your friends, Malcolm; it all sounds so lovely, and you would be near, and—and it was so dear of Miss Elizabeth to think of it. Will you thank her for me, Malcolm, and tell her that mother needs me so much, and that she has no one else."

"Did you mean that for a hit at me, Anna dear?" and Malcolm's voice was rather reproachful.

"For you," looking at him tenderly, "oh no—no, Malcolm;" and then to his dismay she suddenly burst into tears.

"Don't mind me, I am silly to-night," she said, struggling to regain her composure. "Mother is right, and I am not quite well, and—and things will go crooked in this world." But though Malcolm petted her, and called her a foolish child, and his dear little sister, Anna did not regain her former cheerfulness. And when Mrs. Herrick joined them she said her head had begun aching again, and that she would go to bed.

Malcolm wished her good-night at the foot of the staircase, and watched her until she was out of sight. His mother looked at him a little keenly when he rejoined her.

" What have you and Anna been talking about?" she asked rather abruptly; " the child does not look quite happy."

" We were only talking about the ladies of the Wood House," he returned quietly. " Anna thinks she would like to make their acquaintance some day." But Mrs. Herrick made no reply to this; she was regarding her son thoughtfully, and her strong, sensible face wore an expression almost of sadness. But she gave him no clue to her feelings, and when the time came for him to take his leave her manner was more affectionate than usual.

She was still on the balcony as he passed out, and a cheery " Good-night, my son," floated down to him. But as she stood listening to his departing footsteps she said to herself, " He is changed somehow, he is not quite himself, and Anna has noticed it. I wonder"—and here she sighed rather heavily—" I wonder what sort of woman this Miss Elizabeth Templeton can be."

CHAPTER XVIII

"YES, SHE GAVE HIM UP"

Thou art so good,
So calm!—If thou shouldst wear a brow less light
For some wild thought which, but for me, were kept
From out thy soul as from a sacred star!
                                        BROWNING.

To every living soul that same He saith,
"Be faithful;" whatsoever else we be,
Let us be faithful, challenging His faith.
                                CHRISTINA ROSSETTI.

THE Manor House where the Godfreys lived was a fine old red-brick Elizabethan house, standing about a quarter of a mile from the river.

A delightful garden surrounded it, but the chief point of attraction to visitors was a terrace walk, shaded by old chestnut trees, which formed its extreme boundary, and which, on the hottest summer's day, offered a cool and shady retreat.

The terrace was broad, and at one end was a sort of loggia or alcove built of grayish-white stone, with a wide stone bench running round it. From this point there was a charming view of the river between the trees, and it was here that Malcolm found his hostess on his arrival at the Manor House.

Mrs. Godfrey was reading in the loggia, with her husband's magnificent deer-hounds lying at her feet. She laid aside her book and welcomed her visitor with a warmth and cordiality that were evidently sincere. Strangers who saw Mrs. Godfrey for the first time were generally apt to remark that she was one of the plainest women they had ever seen; and they would add in a parenthesis, "It is such a pity, for the Colonel is so hand-

180

some." But even the most critical agreed that no woman could be more charming. She had spent a great deal of her life abroad, and her easy, well-bred manner, her *savoir-faire* and broad, sagacious views on every subject, had been gained in the world's academy. In spite of her goodness of heart and real unselfishness, she was essentially a woman of the world. Little as Malcolm guessed it at that time, she was Elizabeth Templeton's greatest friend; indeed, both the sisters were devoted to her, and some of Elizabeth's happiest and gayest hours had been spent in the Manor House.

"I certainly never hoped to find you alone," were Malcolm's first words. Mrs. Godfrey smiled.

"It is almost an unprecedented fact in the Manor House annals," she returned gaily; "but we shall be absolutely alone until Tuesday, and then every room will be filled. If you had consented to stay for a week, I could have promised you a big affair on a steam-launch, a picnic, and a tennis tournament; but now our solitary function will be a garden-party on Monday."

"Please do not speak in such an apologetic tone," replied Malcolm. "If you knew how my soul abhors picnics and water-parties! It is really too delightful to know that I may enjoy your society in peace for three whole days. By the bye, where is the Colonel?"

"Oh, Alick has gone to Henley to see an old chum of his, but he will be back in good time for dinner. Is it not lovely down here, Mr. Herrick? I thought it would be such a pity to go indoors that I told Deacon that we would have tea here." Then, as Malcolm signified his approval of this arrangement, they sauntered slowly down the terrace, that Malcolm might take in all points of the extensive view. When they retraced their steps to the loggia, the butler and footman were setting out a rustic tea-table.

"And so you have been staying at the Wood House?"

began Mrs. Godfrey as she handed Malcolm his tea. "Elizabeth Templeton's letter this morning almost took my breath away. What a small world it is after all, Mr. Herrick!"

"Life treads on life," murmured Malcolm, "and heart on heart;

"We press too close in church or mart
To keep a dream or grave apart."

"How true!" was the quiet rejoinder. "Mrs. Browning said that. Well, do you know, I was quite childishly surprised when I heard you had been a guest at the Wood House. 'Mr. Herrick has only just left us,' were Elizabeth's words; 'Cedric is driving him to the station; we have greatly enjoyed his visit,' etcetera, etcetera."

Then a slight flush came to Malcolm's dark face.

"I had a very pleasant time," he returned; "they were most kind and hospitable. Miss Templeton is one of the most charming women I have ever met."

"Dear Dinah—yes, she is very sweet. I do not think I have ever seen her ruffled. She is just lovely. But it is Elizabeth who is my friend."

"Indeed!"

"Our friendship is a very real one," continued Mrs. Godfrey thoughtfully; "and next to my husband there is no one whom I could trust as I could Elizabeth Templeton. She is very strong."

"Oh yes, she is very strong," in a ruminative manner.

"Have you found that out already?" in a surprised tone. "But I remember you are a student of human nature, Mr. Herrick, and rather a keen observer. Most people would not be able to diagnose Elizabeth Templeton's character correctly at the end of one short week. When I was first introduced to her, thirteen or fourteen years ago, I told Alick that I should never get on with any one who was so reserved and so stand-offish, but I soon changed my opinion. I found out that a great deal

of her reserve was in reality shyness, and that her frankness and openness of disposition were her chief charms."

"And then you became friends?"

"Yes; but not for a long time. We are neither of us
at all gushing, and I was an old married woman, you
know. But there came a time when she needed my help
—when she was in anxiety—and a woman's counsel and
woman's sympathy were a comfort to her." Here Mrs.
Godfrey paused as she became aware of the concentrated
keenness in Malcolm's eyes, and added hastily, "The
trouble was not her own; but it is Elizabeth's nature to
take the burdens of others on her own shoulders. I never
knew any one capable of such intense sympathy. It is a
rare gift, Mr. Herrick, but it brings its possessor great
suffering."

"You are right," in a low tone.

"I knew then that she was a woman in a thousand,
and we have been close and dear friends ever since. Not
that we often meet. She is a busy woman and so am I,
but we generally stay at the Wood House once a year, and
Elizabeth comes to me for a few days' rest and refreshment whenever she can spare the time. Alick teases me
sometimes about my lady-love, but I assure you that he
is very fond of her, and is always delighted to hear she
is coming to the Manor House."

Malcolm listened to this with deep interest. It seemed
to him that every one who spoke to him of Elizabeth
Templeton praised her without stint or limit; she was
evidently much beloved, and the very fact that a person
like Mrs. Godfrey should choose her for her most trusted
friend was no mean title of honour; never was there a
woman more fastidious and discriminating in her ideas
of female friendship.

Malcolm would willingly have heard more, but a curious sort of embarrassment and a fear of betraying too
deep an interest made him speak of her sister.

" Miss Templeton seems to have a happy nature," he said a little abruptly. " I never saw any one so perfectly peaceful and serene; it makes one better only to look at her. Her hair is gray, and yet when she smiles one is reminded of an innocent child, it is such a perfectly radiant expression."

" Yes, I know. Dear Dinah, she has the secret of perpetual youth. She is one of ' the little ones'—you know what I mean. When I talk to her, as I tell Elizabeth sometimes, I feel such a worldly, frivolous creature. Her sister perfectly realises this, for she has the prettiest names for her. ' That angel-woman,' I have heard her say that; very often she calls her ' das Engelkind;' and without exaggeration she has a rare and beautiful nature."

Malcolm assented to this, then he said slowly, " Has it ever struck you that there are no lines on Miss Templeton's face? I should think her life-story must be a happy one. I mean, that she has not known any very great trouble." Then rather a peculiar expression crossed Mrs. Godfrey's face. " Ah, I see I have made a mistake," observed Malcolm quickly.

" Yes, you have made a mistake," she replied a little sadly. " Did you really think that even Dinah Templeton could have her forty years in the wilderness without her share of pain and difficulty? Well, it is ancient history, and there is no harm in telling you what every one knows, that in the bloom of her fresh young womanhood she had a sore trial and a great sorrow."

" You say every one knows about it?" returned Malcolm eagerly.

" Yes, every one in Staplegrove and Earlsfield. Oh, I can read your face; you would like to hear about it. Well, there is no harm in my telling you. When Dinah Templeton was about three- or four-and-twenty she was engaged to Douglas Fraser, a doctor just beginning practice in Earlsfield.

"Mr. Templeton was living at that time, and approved of the engagement. Dr. Fraser was devoted to his profession. He was a rising man, and people predicted that before many years were over he would make his mark."

"Douglas Fraser, the great authority on neurotic diseases in Harley Street!" exclaimed Malcolm in a tone of intense surprise. Mrs. Godfrey nodded.

"As a young man I have been told that he was perfectly irresistible. Even now he is a grand-looking man of commanding presence, with a fine intellectual head and face. And as for Dinah, she must have been one of the sweetest-looking creatures on God's earth.

"Well, they were engaged, and if ever a young pair of human lovers walked in the Garden of Eden, Dinah and Douglas Fraser were that couple—until the cloud came that was to eclipse their happiness in this world. There is no need for me to enter into the matter very fully, though I know everything. One unhappy day Dinah discovered that Dr. Fraser was an agnostic—that for some time he had had grave doubts on the subject of revealed religion, which he had kept to himself for fear of distressing her; but now a sense of honour compelled him to tell her the truth. He had lost his faith, and he no longer believed in anything but science."

"Good heavens, what a shock!" ejaculated Malcolm.

"You may well say so," returned Mrs. Godfrey sadly. "It was no light cross that Dinah had to bear. Even in her youth she was intensely religious. Religion was not a portion of her life, it was her life itself. To such a nature the idea of marrying an agnostic was practically impossible. 'If I marry Douglas I shall be committing a great sin,' she said to her sister; 'I shall be denying my Lord and Master;' and in the semi-delirium in the illness that ensued, Elizabeth could hear her say over and over again, 'Whoso loveth father and mother more than Me is not worthy of Me.'"

" And she actually gave him up."

" Yes, she gave him up, though it broke her heart and his to do so. I believe that he suffered terribly, and that he used every argument in his power to shake her resolution, but in vain.

" She had a long illness after that. Elizabeth took her abroad. It was at Rome that I met them, and after a time we became intimate. Poor Dinah had a relapse, and I assisted Elizabeth in nursing her. Well, Mr. Herrick, I can read a question in your eyes."

" Yes, there is one thing I want to know—has not Dr. Fraser married?"

" To be sure he has; but he did not marry for some years. He left Earlsfield and took a London practice, and his career has been a brilliant one.

" I believe Mrs. Fraser is a lovely woman, and they have three beautiful children. But the strangest part of my story is still to be told—Douglas Fraser is no longer an agnostic."

Malcolm looked at her silently; but Mrs. Godfrey said no more, and not for worlds would he have asked another question. He could see that she was deeply moved, for her lip quivered a little. He rose from the bench and paced up and down the terrace, listening to the faint soughing of the dark chestnut leaves and looking at the cool, silvery gleam of the river between the tree-boles.

Malcolm was a man of intensely imaginative and sympathetic nature. His mother had once told him that he had something of the woman in him. And certainly no one was more capable of filling up the outlines of the story he had just heard and giving it life and colouring.

" I admired her before," he said to himself, " but I shall look upon her as a saint now. She has had her martyrdom, if ever woman had, and has fought her fight nobly;" and then, with that clear insight that seemed natural to him, he added, " She knows that he has come right, and this is the secret of her serenity," which was indeed the truth, though not the whole truth; for Dinah Templeton had indeed realised her Master's words, that through much tribulation we must enter into the kingdom of heaven.

When Mrs. Godfrey rejoined Malcolm her husband was with her. Malcolm always declared that Colonel Godfrey was his typical and ideal Englishman. He was a well-built, soldierly-looking man of unusually fine presence. As he was over fifty, his golden-brown moustache was slightly grizzled, and the hair had worn off his forehead; but he was still strikingly handsome. He and his wife were alone. Both their sons were in the Indian army, and their only daughter was married and lived in Yorkshire.

"We are just an old Darby and Joan," Mrs. Godfrey would say; but though she was only a year or two younger than her husband, she wore remarkably well, and still looked a comparatively young woman.

Colonel Godfrey and Malcolm were excellent friends, and in a few minutes they were strolling through the fields towards the river-bank, talking on various topics of social and political interest, while Mrs. Godfrey returned to the house to write letters and dress for dinner.

It was not until the following afternoon that Malcolm found an opportunity of sounding Mrs. Godfrey on the subject of the Jacobis.

They were sitting in the loggia again, and the row of dark chestnut trees looked almost black against the intense blue of the sky.

A faint breeze was just stirring the leaves, and every now and then a sort of ripple of sunlight seemed to streak the sombre foliage with gold. On the terrace there was a wealth of sunshine, and the stones felt hot to the feet. Only under the chestnuts tiny flickering shadows seemed to dance in and out among the tree-boles.

Colonel Godfrey had just been summoned to a business interview, and for the first time that day Malcolm found himself alone with his hostess.

"Oh, by the bye," he observed rather abruptly, "there is something I want to ask you. There are some people of the name of Jacobi who have taken a house at Henley. I wonder if you have come across them."

"To be sure I have," in rather a surprised tone. "Miss Jacobi called here on Tuesday. Mrs. Sinclair drove her over."

"Well, I want you to tell me what you think of them," asked Malcolm. An amused look came into Mrs. Godfrey's eyes, and she held up her finger in chiding fashion.

"Oh, fie, for shame, Mr. Herrick! You are deep—deep. So the handsome siren has attracted you too."

"Handsome siren," repeated Malcolm with unnecessary energy. "Why, what nonsense you are talking, my dear lady. I never saw Miss Jacobi in my life. It is Miss Templeton who desires information, and I promised her that I would sound you on the subject." Then the mischievous spark died out of Mrs. Godfrey's eyes.

"Miss Templeton! Do you mean Dinah? What on earth can be the connection between her and the Jacobis. They were certainly not on hers or Elizabeth's visiting-list when I was last at the Wood House."

"No, they are complete strangers to them," was Malcolm's reply; "but Cedric has come across them and seems rather thick with them. He is going to stay at Beechcroft—is that not the name of the place they have taken for the season?"

"Yes, I believe so," returned Mrs. Godfrey in rather a perturbed tone. "Cedric, that boy, going to stay with the Jacobis!" And then she broke off and said abruptly, "I am sorry to hear it. I should not care for one of my boys to be thrown much into the society of Saul Jacobi and his sister."

CHAPTER XIX

"A TOUCH OF THE TARTAR"

Here comes the lady: O, so light a foot
Will ne'er wear out the everlasting flint.
Romeo and Juliet.

When you doubt, abstain.—ZOROASTER.

MALCOLM gave a slight start of dismay. Mrs. Godfrey's manner conveyed more than her words; in spite of
his secret prejudice, he was not prepared for so strong
an expression of disapproval. She was a woman of sound
judgment, and very charitable in her estimate of people,
and he knew that he could rely on her opinion. Her
intuitions were seldom at fault. Whether she blamed or
praised it was always with rare discrimination and perfect justice, and she was never impulsive or rash in her
verdicts.

There was a moment's silence. A blackbird, evidently
attracted by Mrs. Godfrey's clear, resonant voice, had
perched on the stone parapet beside them and watched
them in bright-eyed curiosity. Then, as Malcolm moved
his arm, it flew off, with clucking notes of warning, to
rejoin its mate.

"I am rather troubled to hear you say this," began
Malcolm. "Will you tell me all you know about these
people?"

"That is just the difficulty," returned Mrs. Godfrey
slowly. "No one seems to know much about them.
Even Mrs. Sinclair, who has taken them up so lately,
knows scarcely anything of their antecedents. As far as
I remember, Mrs. Sinclair asked me one day if I were

189

not going to call on the Jacobis. 'They are perfectly charming,' were her words. 'They are a brother and a sister who have taken Beechcroft for the season. They seem wealthy people and live in good style, and Miss Jacobi is one of the handsomest women I have ever seen.'"

"And this was all?" as Mrs. Godfrey paused.

"It was all I could gather. Mr. Sinclair certainly told Alick that he understood that Mr. Jacobi had made his money in business—something connected with a mining company, he believed. But no one seemed to know exactly, and the Jacobis are rather reticent about their own concerns. They seem to have a large visiting-list, and to know some big people."

"And Miss Jacobi called here?"

"Yes, Mrs. Sinclair brought her; but I confess I was somewhat embarrassed by the visit—it has placed me in an awkward predicament. I have no wish to make their acquaintance, but I cannot well be unneighbourly; one meets them everywhere, so Alick tells me that I must get rid of my insular prejudices and leave our cards at Beechcroft."

"It must be an awful nuisance," replied Malcolm sympathetically.

"Oh, I don't know; Miss Jacobi is very civil and pleasant. She is rather a reserved sort of woman, but remarkably good-looking, and she dresses beautifully. I am afraid," with a laugh, "all you gentlemen will lose your hearts to her. Even Alick raves about her. He declares they must be Italian Jews, although they have lived in England and America all their lives. Miss Jacobi has certainly rather a Jewish type of face, and she has the clear olive complexion of the Italian. Well, you will see them for yourself on Sunday, for they are regular church-goers, though Mr. Jacobi's behaviour during service is not always edifying. They have seats near us, and it irritates me dreadfully to see him lounging and yawning while other people are saying their prayers."

"Does Miss Jacobi lounge too?" in an amused tone.

"No, she behaves far better than her brother. I must confess to you, Mr. Herrick, that I am rather prejudiced against Mr. Jacobi. I do not like either his face or his manners; his eyes are too close together, and this, in my opinion, gives him rather a crafty look; and in manner he is self-assertive and ostentatious."

"I know what you mean," returned Malcolm with a laugh; "he spells me and mine with a capital M." Mrs. Godfrey nodded.

"Mrs. Sinclair tells me that the brother and sister are devoted to each other, but that Miss Jacobi seems to defer to her brother's opinion in everything. But there, I have told you all I know, and you must find out the rest for yourself."

"I shall keep my eyes open, I assure you," was Malcolm's reply. And then he continued in a perplexed tone. "How on earth did Cedric get hold of them?" But as Mrs. Godfrey could not answer this, Malcolm allowed the subject to drop. In his case forewarned was forearmed, and but for his promise to Dinah and his very real concern for Cedric, he would have given the Jacobis a wide berth.

It was only natural, however, that his curiosity should be strongly excited by this conversation, and when on the following morning they took their seats in church, his attention wandered at the sound of every footstep in the aisle.

The service had commenced before the vacant seats near them were occupied. Malcolm had a momentary glimpse of a tall, graceful-looking figure, in soft, diaphanous raiment, that seemed to pass them very swiftly; he even caught a strange, subtle fragrance that seemed to linger in the air; and then they all knelt down and

Miss Jacobi buried her face in her hands, and her brother removed his lavender kid gloves with elaborate care as though Saul Jacobi had nothing in common with the rest of the miserable sinners. During the rest of the service Malcolm had plenty of opportunity for studying his physiognomy, for he turned round more than once and encountered Malcolm's eyes.

He was certainly handsome in his way. His features were good, though of the pronounced Jewish type; but his dark, brilliant eyes had a shifty look in them—probably, as Mrs. Godfrey suggested, from their being set a little closely together. In age he appeared to be between thirty and forty.

He could see little of Miss Jacobi except the dark, glossy coil of hair under her hat; for during the entire service she was as motionless as a statue, and never once turned her face in Malcolm's direction—even when her brother spoke to her she answered without looking at him. Whether Miss Jacobi was a devout worshipper or a mere automaton was not for him to judge; she might have her own reasons for not joining in the singing.

Colonel Godfrey was always a little fussy about his hat in church, and so it was that Malcolm and Mrs. Godfrey were still in their places when the Jacobis passed their pew. Malcolm seized his opportunity and looked well at Miss Jacobi, but she did not appear to notice him.

She was certainly a most striking-looking woman. Indeed, Malcolm's trained eye was obliged to confess that she was really beautiful. The features were perfect, and the clear olive complexion, just flushed with heat, was wonderfully effective, while the large, melancholy eyes were full of a strange, flashing light.

"What a superb creature!" was Malcolm's first unuttered thought. His second showed his keen insight—"But it is not a happy face, and with all its beauty, there is no restfulness of expression."

Colonel Godfrey was still brushing his hat in the anxious manner peculiar to the well-dressed Englishman when they reached the porch. To Malcolm's surprise he saw Miss Jacobi and her brother in animated conversation with a little group of ladies, made up of Etheridges and Sinclairs. Malcolm, who knew them all, was at once greeted as an old acquaintance, and, to Mrs. Godfrey's secret amusement, the Jacobis were introduced to him. Miss Jacobi bowed to him in rather a grave, reserved manner, but her brother shook hands with real or assumed cordiality.

"I am delighted to make your acquaintance, Mr. Herrick," he observed volubly. "We have a mutual friend, I believe. What a capital fellow Templeton is—charming—charming! We are going to put him up at our diggings for a few days;" and then before Malcolm could answer, some one tapped Mr. Jacobi on the shoulder and asked him a question, and Malcolm found himself beside Miss Jacobi.

"Mr. Templeton is an intimate friend of yours, is he not?" she asked carelessly. Her voice was very full and rich, but she spoke slowly, as though she were accustomed to weigh each word. It struck Malcolm that she listened with some intentness to his answer.

"Oh yes, we are very good friends," he returned with studied indifference.

"Mr. Templeton is more demonstrative," she said with a curiously grave smile that seemed habitual to her. "He sings your praises, Mr. Herrick; you would be amused to hear him. It is so refreshing to find any one natural and unconventional in this world; but he is so nice and frank—a nice boy," with a low laugh that showed her white teeth. Mr. Jacobi turned round at the sound.

"Come, Leah," he said impatiently; "the horses are tired of standing, and I want my luncheon." Miss Jacobi bowed in rather a hurried fashion and at once rejoined

13

her brother. Malcolm looked after the mail phaeton as it dashed down the road, but he made no response as Mr. Jacobi waved his whip to him in an airy fashion.

"Well, Mr. Herrick," said Mrs. Godfrey quietly, "I suppose I may ask your opinion now?"

"I do not think I am anxious for a further acquaintance," returned Malcolm grimly. "The big M's are too much in evidence for my taste. I suppose I am a bit of a misanthrope, but I hate to be hail-fellow-well-met with every one. Why, that fellow Jacobi actually patronised me, patted me on the back, don't you know. He might have known me for six months."

"I call that sort of thing bad form," observed Colonel Godfrey. "Jacobi is too smooth and plausible. My wife will have it that he is not a gentleman."

"Oh, Alick, you ought not to have repeated that."

"Why not, my dear lady?" observed Malcolm. "You are perfectly safe with me. I expect we think alike there. Somehow Jacobi has not the right cut."

"But his sister is very ladylike," murmured Mrs. Godfrey, her kindly heart accusing her of censoriousness and want of charity. Both the gentlemen agreed to this. Then Malcolm, true to his character as a lover of the picturesque, launched into unrestrained praise of Miss Jacobi's beauty.

"If my friend Keston were to see her," he remarked, "he would be wild to paint her as Rebekah at the well— or Ruth in the harvest-fields. One does not often see a face like Miss Jacobi's." And then after a little more talk they reached the Manor House.

The following morning Malcolm spent on the river, and late in the afternoon they drove to Glebelands— where the Etheridges lived.

The beautiful grounds sloping to the river presented a most animated scene. A band was playing, and a gaily-dressed crowd streamed from the house on to the lawn. Canoes, punts, and a tiny steam-launch were ready for any guests who wished to enjoy the river; and the croquet, archery, and tennis grounds were well filled.

Tea and refreshments were served in a huge marquee just below the house. Malcolm, who met several people whom he knew, soon began to enjoy himself, and he was deep in conversation with a young artist when Miss Jacobi and her brother passed them; she bowed to Malcolm with rather a pleased smile of recognition.

"What, do you know la belle Jacobi?" observed his friend enviously. "What a lucky fellow you are! Look here, couldn't you do a good turn for a chap and introduce me?"

"My dear Rodney, I have not spoken a dozen words to Miss Jacobi myself. Get one of the Etheridge girls to do the job for you. You had better look sharp," he continued, "for there is quite a small crowd of men round her now;" and as Mr. Rodney speedily acted on this hint, Malcolm joined some more of his friends.

Later in the afternoon, as he was listening to the band, he saw Miss Jacobi opposite to him; she had still a little court round her, and seemed talking with great animation. She looked far handsomer than on the previous day, and her dress became her perfectly. She wore a cream-coloured transparent stuff over yellow silk, her Gainsborough hat was cream-colour and yellow too, and she carried a loosely-dropping posy of tea-roses, and two or three rosebuds of the same warm hue were nestled at her throat. The contrast of her dark eyes and hair and warm olive complexion was simply superb, and Malcolm secretly clapped his hands and murmured "bravo" under his breath. "She has the soul of the coquette and the artist too," he said to himself. "Oh, woman, woman, surely Solomon had you in his thoughts when he declared 'All is vanity;'" and then he remembered Elizabeth Templeton and felt ashamed of his cynicism.

The next moment he noticed the coast was clear, and obeying an involuntary impulse he crossed the lawn.

Miss Jacobi welcomed him with a soft, flickering smile, but did not speak.

"Your court has deserted you, Miss Jacobi?"

"Not entirely," she returned. "Captain Fawcett has gone to fetch me an ice—it is so hot in the tent—and Mr. Dysart is looking for my fan; they will be back presently." She spoke in rather a weary tone.

"Why do you stand here?" he remonstrated. "There is a vacant seat under that acacia, and you will hear the music quite well. There, let me take you to it; the afternoon is unusually warm, in spite of the river breeze." Rather to his surprise, she bent her head in assent, in her queenly way, and he guided her to the cool retreat.

"Will you not sit down too?" she asked in rather a hesitating manner, but there was no coquetry in her glance. Malcolm shook his head.

"I must look out for Dysart and the other man," he observed, "or they will think I have spirited you away. I am not the least tired. What a pretty scene it is, Miss Jacobi! Look at those children dancing under the elm trees."

"They seem very happy," was her reply; but there was a sad expression in her eyes. "Certainly childhood is the happiest time in one's life. If it could only last for ever!"

"Are you sure you mean what you say?" replied Malcolm in a grave, argumentative tone. "Remember it is the age of ignorance as well as innocence; with knowledge comes responsibility and the pains and penalties of life, nevertheless few of us desire to remain children."

"I am one of the few," she returned curtly.

"I cannot believe that," and Malcolm smiled; "but I grant you that the best and highest natures have something of the child in them. As Mencius says, ' The great man is he who does not lose his child's heart.' "

Miss Jacobi looked impressed.

" That is well said," she replied softly. " Mr. Herrick, I think your friend Mr. Templeton is rather like that: he is so young and fresh, it is delightful to listen to him. He is two-and-twenty, is he not? and he is such a boy." She laughed an odd, constrained little laugh as she said this, and added in a curious undertone, " And I am only nine-and-twenty, and I feel as though I were seventy. See what responsibilities and the pains and penalties of life do for a woman !"

It was a strange speech, and a strange flash of the eye accompanied it; then her tone and manner suddenly changed, as a footstep in their vicinity reached her ear.

" Saul, were you looking for me?" she said, starting from her seat. " I was tired, so Mr. Herrick found me this nice shady place. I suppose it is time for us to go."

" Well, we have a dinner-party on to-night," returned her brother blandly, " and it will hardly do for the hostess to be late. Wait a moment, Leah," as she was about to take leave of Malcolm, " I found Dysart hunting for your fan, so I told him I had it. It cost ten guineas, you remember," in a meaning tone. Then Miss Jacobi flushed a little as she took it from his hand.

" I must have dropped it in the tent—there was such a crush," she murmured. " Good-bye, Mr. Herrick, I am much rested now."

" Good-bye, Herrick," observed Mr. Jacobi in a familiar tone that grated on Malcolm; " we shall be very glad to see you at Beechcroft when young Templeton is with us. It is Telemachus and Mentor over again, is it not?" and here he broke into a little cackling laugh. " Well, ta-ta. Come along, Leah;" and taking his sister by the arm, Mr. Jacobi quickly crossed the lawn with her.

" He is a cad if ever a man was," mused Malcolm as

he followed them slowly; " and if I do not mistake there is a touch of the Tartar about him. She may be a devoted sister, as Mrs. Sinclair observes, but she is afraid of him all the same.

" What a strange girl she seems," he continued— " woman rather, I should say; for there is little of the girl about her. Somehow she interests me, and she puzzles me too. She is so beautiful—why is she still Miss Jacobi?" He stood still for a minute to ponder over this mystery; then he walked on very thoughtfully. " I am a bit bothered about it all—I wish Cedric had never made their acquaintance;" and Malcolm looked so grave when he rejoined his friends that Mrs. Godfrey thought he was bored and hastened her adieux.

Malcolm did not undeceive her, neither did he speak of the Jacobis again to her; but he made himself very pleasant all that evening, and the next day he left the Manor House.

CHAPTER XX

A WHITE SUN-BONNET

My soul its secret hath, my life too hath its mystery:
A love eternal in a moment's space conceived.

AROERS.

ONE lovely morning in August, about a fortnight after the garden-party at Glebelands, Malcolm Herrick sauntered slowly down the woodland path which the Templetons always called "the lady's mile." His face was set towards Rotherwood, and in spite of his loitering pace there was an intent and watchful look in his eyes; but what his purpose or design might be was best known to himself; for wonderful and devious are the ways of man, and who can fathom them? Presently a tempting tangle of honeysuckle attracted him, and he clambered up the bank in search of it. The bank was dry and slippery, and the honeysuckle was difficult to reach, but Malcolm was not to be conquered. He had just caught hold of the branch, when the far-off click of a gate attracted his attention, and still holding the branch he peeped cautiously through the brambles.

The next minute a tall, massive young woman in a white sun-bonnet came into view—actually a white sun-bonnet, such as a milkmaid or farming wench might have worn; but this was no rustic lass who walked so briskly through the woodlands—none but Elizabeth Templeton moved with that free, graceful step, or carried her head in that queenly fashion.

In his hiding-place Malcolm had a good view of her face. Her eyes were bright, and she had a soft smile

on her lips, as though some thought pleased her—
some dream's dream that seemed fair to her inward
vision.

"Miss Templeton——" then Elizabeth gave a great
start, and stood still and looked up at him. "Wait a
moment, please," he continued hurriedly; "this branch
is so tough and my knife is small. There, I have secured
it;" and then, waving the festoon of honeysuckle triumphantly, he scrambled down the bank and stood beside
her.

Elizabeth shook hands with him rather gravely.

"So you have taken up your quarters at the Crow's
Nest," she observed as they walked on together.

"Yes, I came down last evening, and settled in with
all my goods and chattels. I thought I was in the Garden of Eden when I woke this morning and saw all those
pink and white roses nid-nodding their beautiful heads
at me."

"Oh, I remember how the roses clambered into the
room," returned Elizabeth in an interested tone.

"Yes, and the birds seemed as though they wanted to
get up a sort of Handel Festival, only the prima donnas
and the big guns were missing. But there was plenty of
twittering and bird chatter—I think they were settling
the solos."

Elizabeth laughed—she was always amused at Mr.
Herrick's nonsense.

"I have begun by enjoying myself immensely," he
went on. "I have eaten a record breakfast and smoked
two pipes, and now I have picked all this honeysuckle and
met you"—a slight emphasis on the last word. "To tell
you the truth, Miss Templeton"—and here he looked at
her with a pleasant smile—"the meeting was not purely
accidental, I knew it was your morning for the schools."

"And you came to meet me?" Elizabeth's manner
stiffened; if Malcolm had been thin-skinned he might

have suspected that she was not quite pleased at this avowal.

"Yes, I was anxious to meet you." Malcolm spoke with quiet assurance. "There is something I wanted to tell you—if I had waited to call at the Wood House this afternoon your sister would have been with you."

"And it is something you do not wish her to hear?" and Elizabeth's slight frown vanished.

"Well, I thought it would be better to talk it over with you first. I have seen the Jacobis, Miss Templeton, and I must confess that I am not favourably impressed by them."

"Cedric is with them now," exclaimed Elizabeth in rather a distressed voice. "Dinah heard from him this morning; he is very happy, having a good old time, as he expresses it. He saw the Godfreys before they left for Scotland."

"They have gone then—what a pity!" observed Malcolm. Then Elizabeth looked at him inquiringly.

"You mean on Cedric's account. Yes, I am sorry too. Will you tell me all you can about the Jacobis?" And then Malcolm, with masculine brevity and great distinctness, retailed his impressions of the brother and sister. Elizabeth's face grew grave as she listened.

"Oh, I am sorry!" she exclaimed. "What will poor Dinah say when I tell her; she is so anxious for Cedric to choose his friends well, and by your account Mr. Jacobi is certainly not a gentleman."

"I thought perhaps you would keep this to yourself;" but Elizabeth shook her head.

"I dare not; Cedric is her own boy, and I must hide nothing from her. There was only one thing I kept to myself, but then Cedric told it me in the strictest confidence. Mr. Herrick, it is an absurd question, for Cedric is such a boy—but is not Miss Jacobi likely to be the attraction? You say she is so handsome."

"I might go farther and say she is a beautiful woman," returned Malcolm. "But tastes differ, you know; I admire Miss Jacobi as I should a picture or a statue, but I could not imagine falling in love with her."

"Indeed! I am rather surprised to hear you say that; I thought you were a lover of the picturesque." Elizabeth's tone was a little teasing.

"I do not deny the soft impeachment," replied Malcolm somewhat seriously; "but moral beauty and the loveliness of a well-balanced character outweigh, in my estimation, mere outward beauty. Miss Jacobi is a stranger to me certainly, but in my opinion there is something complex and mysterious in her personality; there are hard lines in her face, and her expression is at once cynical and unhappy. One could pity such a woman," continued Malcolm to himself, "but one would never, never yearn to take her to one's heart."

Elizabeth looked at him curiously, as though she understood this unspoken speech; and when she spoke again it was with a new and added friendliness.

"You are a good judge of character, Mr. Herrick, and I feel I can rely on your opinion. If only the Godfreys were at the Manor House!"

"You forget that Beechcroft is at Henley," he observed with a smile.

"Oh no, I have not forgotten, but I was thinking that I might have gone down to spy out the land for myself. Of course it would have vexed Cedric, but I should have done it all the same. Well, there is nothing for it but patience. By the bye, Mr. Herrick, we have fixed the date of the Templeton Bean-feast; Cedric will have to come back for that."

"Do you think he would care to bring his friends?" he asked in rather a meaning tone. Then at this daring suggestion Elizabeth's eyes opened widely.

"Do you think that would be wise, that it might not

complicate matters and increase the intimacy?" Elizabeth put this question with manifest anxiety. "We have no desire to have the Jacobis on our visiting-list."

"Of course not," was Malcolm's answer, "you know I never meant that; but it would give you and Miss Templeton an opportunity of studying them, and it could be managed without difficulty."

"I wish you would tell me how. I suppose we should have to send Miss Jacobi a card of invitation?"

"No, I think not—at least not at first. Tell Cedric that he may have *carte blanche* for his friends, and leave him to follow up the hint. He will answer by return, and tell you that he has asked the Jacobis, and then the card can be sent."

"Yes, I see; it is a good idea. I will talk to Dinah, but thank you all the same for your suggestion. I am quite ashamed of bothering you about our concerns; I fear we trespass on your good-nature."

"Not at all," returned Malcolm easily. "I was going to ask your advice about a little protégée of my own;" and then Elizabeth lent a willing ear while Malcolm, in his best style, told the story of little Kit.

They had turned in at the gate of the Wood House by this time, and the dark firs stretched on either side. Elizabeth had taken off her sun-bonnet, and it dangled from her arm; her eyes were soft with womanly sympathy; never had the charm of her personality appealed so strongly to Malcolm, he scarcely dared to look at her for fear she should discover the truth. "It is too soon, she would not believe it," he said to himself. But as he talked his voice was strangely vibrant and full of feeling; and when the sun-bonnet brushed lightly against him he was conscious that his arm trembled.

But Elizabeth was too much occupied with little Kit to notice Malcolm's slight discomposure.

"Oh, I am so glad you told me," she said in her eager

way. " I really think I shall be able to help you. There is the dearest old woman in the village, Mrs. Sullivan. She lives in a pretty cottage quite close to ' The Plough,' and she was only telling me the other day that she wished that she had another child to mother. " Sometimes my sister and I have a little East-end waif and stray down for a few weeks in the summer," continued Elizabeth modestly—" some sick child, or occasionally some over-burdened worker, and we always lodge them at Mrs. Sullivan's. It is not much of a place, but we call it ' The Providence House;' the cottage is really our own property, and Mrs. Sullivan has it rent-free."

" Do you think that she would take care of Kit?"

" I am sure of it. But, Mr. Herrick, Kit must be our guest, please remember that. Hush," peremptorily, " I will not hear a word to the contrary. And there is something else I want to say. Would not Caleb Martin like to come too? Kit would be strange without him, and there is plenty of room for them both. Think what a month of this sweet country air would mean to him after Todmorden's Lane. You must write to him at once, and tell him to hurry Kit down."

" I think it would be better to go up and speak to him myself to-morrow morning," returned Malcolm. He spoke rather reluctantly, but the beaming look of approval that followed this speech rewarded him for the little sacrifice.

" Now I call that kind," returned Elizabeth warmly. " Very few people would take so much trouble for a shabby little cobbler and an ailing child," she thought. " How pleased Dinah will be when she hears about it."

" The kindness is on your part, Miss Templeton," returned Malcolm. But he was much gratified by her manner. " If Kit and her father are to be your guests there is little enough for me to do; when I spoke to you just now I had quite decided to take lodgings for them at Rotherwood."

"Kit is my guest," replied Elizabeth obstinately. "Now, will you come in, Mr. Herrick, and have luncheon with us?" But Malcolm declined this; he would look in later in the day and pay his respects to Miss Templeton; and then he lifted his hat and turned away. Elizabeth stood in the porch and watched him. "He is a good man," she said softly, "and I like him—I like him very much;" but she sighed a little heavily as she turned away.

Meanwhile Malcolm was saying to himself in his whimsical way, "It is my destiny—is it not written in the book of fate? The Parcæ Sisters three have willed it so. Good heavens, what an enigma life is! Some winged insect whirling in a cyclone would have as much chance of escaping its doom as a human being under such circumstances." Then he stopped, and looked with blank, unseeing eyes down the slanting fir avenue. "It is a mystery," he went on—"the very mystery of mysteries; the Sphinx is nothing to it. A month ago we were strangers—I neither knew nor cared that such a person as Elizabeth Templeton existed; and a week—a little cycle of seven or eight nights and days—has wrought this wondrous change. Am I the same man? Is this the solid earth on which I am walking?" And then he gave an odd sort of laugh, which seemed to hurt him. "My God," he muttered, "how I love this woman!" and his head was bowed as he walked on.

The following afternoon, when Malcolm returned from his charitable errand to Todmorden's Lane, he saw the Keston family grouped on the shady patch of lawn in the front garden. Verity, who had Babs in her arms, flew to meet him; but Amias merely waved his pipe and grunted in an amicable fashion.

"Oh, how tired and dusty you look!" exclaimed Verity, in the pretty, maternal way that always sat so quaintly on her. "Look at him, Amias; I do believe he has walked all those miles from Earlsfield."

"Yea-Verily, you are right, child," returned the giant placidly; and then Verity put down Babs on the grass to sprawl among the daisies.

"Sit down," she said, pushing Malcolm with her tiny hands into a big hammock chair; "I am going to make you some fresh tea—iced lemonade is out of the question;" and then she flitted into the house on her usual errand of "hunting the Snark."

Malcolm was certainly tired; he had been unable to get a fly at Earlsfield, and the long climb in the heat had rather taken it out of him, so he was well content to lie back in his lounge and let Verity wait on him.

"We have had visitors," she observed presently; then Malcolm looked up quickly.

"The ladies from the Wood House," she continued. "They were here for quite an hour. You are right, Mr. Herrick, the eldest Miss Templeton is a perfect darling. Amias was just saying as you turned the corner that he would like to paint her as a Puritan lady; the dress would exactly suit her."

"She has a very sweet face," endorsed Amias, "and her manners are remarkably pleasing. Yea-Verily fell in love with her because she admired Babs. 'Love me, love my Babs,' don't you know!"

"Don't be a goose, Amias! He was as much pleased as I was, Mr. Herrick, when Miss Templeton kissed Baby and made much of her; she said the sweetest things to her, and Babs was so charmed that she actually put up her face and kissed her of her own accord."

"The other Miss Templeton is a striking-looking woman of rather uncommon type," observed Amias, blowing away a cloud of smoke rather lazily. "She made herself very pleasant too, and said all sorts of civil things."

"I thought her rather formidable at first," annotated Verity, "but I soon discovered that she was interesting; she is very bright and original, and we soon got on very nicely together.

"By the bye, Mr. Herrick, they want us all to dine at the Wood House to-morrow; it is to be a comfortable, informal sort of meal. I told Miss Templeton that I had no company manners, as I had lived all my life in Bohemia; and then Miss Elizabeth laughed, and said she was rather unconventional herself, and that she thought I should exactly suit them."

"I told you so," responded Malcolm in a low voice. "I suppose there will be no other guests?"

"Only the Carlyons," returned Verity. "Mr. Carlyon is the curate at Rotherwood, Miss Templeton told us, and just now his father is staying with him."

"Oh, Carlyon junior seems always on the premises," replied Malcolm carelessly; "he is a sort of tame cat. Well, I am off to the Garden of Eden now." But as he stood by his window the nodding roses turned their pink cheeks to him in vain, and wasted their sweetness on the desert air.

"He is always there," he muttered; "one is never free from him. Perhaps it is her goodness of heart, she is so kind to every one, and he is her clergyman. Of course it must be that." He frowned and sighed impatiently; but as he turned away he saw the sprays of honeysuckle that he had gathered the previous day lay on the window-sill forgotten and neglected, with all the beautiful creamy blossoms withered and dead.

CHAPTER XXI

" IF I WERE ONLY LIKE YOU !"

Who, seeking for himself alone, ever entered heaven? In blessing we are blest.—C. SEYMOUR.

There is no separation—no Past; Eternity, the Now is continuous. . . . The continuity of Now is for ever.—RICHARD JEFFERIES.

THE party from the Crow's Nest were somewhat late in arriving the following evening. Verity made her excuses very prettily.

"It was all darling Babs's fault," she said to Miss Templeton; "she would play instead of going to sleep. Mr. Herrick lost patience at last, and declared he would go on alone."

"I must take my god-daughter in hand, or she will be ruined body and soul," observed Malcolm severely. "Babs is already a domestic tyrant, and screams the house down if any of her fads and fancies are resisted. I am thinking of writing a series of essays on degenerate and irresponsible parents, and the cruelty of modern education in the nursery, which out-Herods Herod." Of course they all laughed at this idea, and then David Carlyon crossed the room to shake hands with Malcolm and to introduce his father.

The two men were curiously alike. The Rev. Rupert Carlyon was an older, shabbier, and more careworn David; but there was the same broad, intellectual brow, the same bright intelligence of expression, and their voices were so strangely similar that if Malcolm had closed his eyes he could not have distinguished between them; they both spoke with the same quickness, and in the same clipping fashion.

Malcolm noticed before the evening was over that David Carlyon looked unusually pale and tired, though he seemed in excellent spirits. Dinah made the same remark to his father.

"Oh, I have been giving that boy of mine a lecture," he said quickly; "he is a perfect spendthrift and prodigal with regard to the midnight oil, and burns both ends of his candle in the most reckless fashion."

"I should not have thought a sleepy little place like Rotherwood would have overtaxed his energies," observed Malcolm in rather a surprised tone.

The elder man shook his head.

"There is always work enough if one looks for it. My son is a sort of medical missionary in his way, and concerns himself with the bodies as well as the souls of his people. The last two nights he has been up until nearly dawn with a stranger—a sort of commercial traveller who has been taken ill at 'The Plough.' It is a sad case; he is quite a young man, and our doctor fears that he will not pull through." But Mr. Carlyon forbore to state the fact that each night he had relieved his son, rising from his bed in the gray pearly dawn, before the first bird-twitter was heard, to take his watch beside the fever-stricken stranger. The Carlyons were men whose left hand did not know what their right hand did, and the Rev. Rupert Carlyon's ministry had been a record of humble, unobtrusive acts of good-will and kindness to man, woman, and child; nay, the very dumb animals knew their friend, and would come to him for protection.

The Carlyons took their leave soon after this. Elizabeth walked down to the gate with them. Malcolm thought she looked rather grave when she returned, as though something troubled her, but she would not hear of the party breaking up, and promised Malcolm that she would sing all his favourite songs to his friends, and

14

she kept her word. Malcolm sat in a trance of beatitude while the beautiful voice floated out into the darkness, startling some night-bird in the copse; and Verity's eyes were wet, and she stole closer to her husband, for it seemed to her as though the shadows from the old life were creeping round her; and unseen by any one but Dinah, she leant her cheek against Amias's hand.

"Oh, how can you sing like that!" exclaimed Verity in her naïve way, when Elizabeth joined them on the terrace. "You sing right down into people's hearts. Oh, I felt so sad, and then so happy, and the world did not seem wide enough to contain me."

"You must not flatter me," returned Elizabeth, but she was evidently gratified. Then she turned her head to Malcolm, who was behind her, and said in an undertone, "You were quite right, the Jacobis are coming to our party. I have sent them a card this afternoon."

"I hope Miss Templeton approved of my suggestion?"

"Yes, she thought with you that it would be an excellent opportunity of taking stock of the enemy. And Cedric was so pleased. Mr. Herrick," she continued, as they walked down the terrace, "I must tell you that we are charmed with Mrs. Keston. She is a dear little thing, and so fascinating and original, and she looks really pretty to-night."

"No, she is not pretty," returned Malcolm, "but her dress becomes her. We call it Keston's *chef d'œuvre*. He always designs her gowns. He is very æsthetic in his tastes, and he knows exactly what suits her. If Verity were left to her own devices, she would be very crude and unfinished."

"He is very proud of her," observed Elizabeth. "It is good to see two such happy people. We like them immensely, and shall hope to see a great deal of them;" and Malcolm was so elated by these encomiums on his friends, and by Elizabeth's gracious friendliness, that he actually suggested that she should walk down the drive with them; but to his secret chagrin she made some excuse.

Half an hour later she entered her sister's room. Dinah was reading as usual, with her little green lamp beside her; but she closed her book and looked up at her inquiringly.

"What is it, Betty?" she said gently. "Something has been troubling you to-night." Then Elizabeth turned aside her face for a moment, but she was not regarding herself in the great mirror. "It concerns David," continued Dinah calmly. Then Elizabeth gave vent to a heavy sigh.

"Yes, it concerns David," she returned. "I have been talking to him, oh so seriously, and to his father too; but it is no use. They will let me do nothing to help them. I wanted to send in a night nurse, but they will have it that it is not necessary. Old Mrs. Roper takes care of the patient by day, and it is only the night."

"But, Betty dear, surely David Carlyon is not going there again to-night?"

"Indeed he is," very sadly. "I heard them arranging it this afternoon. Mr. Carlyon is to relieve him at three. He was so tired that he could scarcely eat his dinner, and he told me that he dared not stay for the music, as I should certainly sing him to sleep. Die," in rather a choked voice, "it is not right. He will kill himself if he goes on like this."

It was evident that Elizabeth was in a depressed mood; perhaps she was tired too. Dinah, who knew her well, quite understood her.

"Don't worry, Betty," she said kindly. "David Carlyon is young enough and strong enough to bear the loss of a few nights' rest, and the fever is not infectious. By all accounts the poor fellow cannot last many days. To-morrow I will go over to the White Cottage and talk to them both. I shall tell David that he has no right to let his father work so hard during his holiday."

"Tell him we know such a nice woman, Die," and Dinah promised that she would do her very best. But Elizabeth had not wholly eased her mind; she stood looking at her sister rather doubtfully, and then she said abruptly—

"Die, there is something I want to ask you. You heard from Douglas Fraser this morning, did you not?" Then a faint colour came to Dinah's pale cheeks.

"Were you afraid to ask me that before, my dear?" she said with a smile. "But it was my fault; I ought to have told you—this sort of question is not easy even for a sister to ask. Yes, Douglas wrote and Agnes too. Dear little Lettice is so much better. He thinks she will pull through now, thank God! but they nearly lost her."

"Was it so bad as that, Die?" in an awed tone.

"Yes, it has been a terrible illness. They have nurses, of course, but poor Agnes is almost worn out. She is their only girl, and Douglas does so doat on her. He has suffered so—one can read it in every word," and Dinah's voice shook a little.

Perhaps it needed only that to bring Elizabeth's emotion to a culminating point, for to Dinah's surprise she suddenly knelt down and put her arms round her and the tears were running down her face.

"Oh, Die, stop! I cannot bear to hear you—it pains me so—it pains me all over!"

"My darling Bet! Oh, you foolish, foolish Betty!" But Elizabeth was not to be soothed so easily.

"That is why I never mention his name. I try to pretend sometimes that I do not see his handwriting. Oh, Die," caressing her, "how can any woman be such an angel! It is not natural. In your place, under your circumstances, I would never have seen him again."

"Dear Elizabeth," returned Dinah quietly, but her face

had grown very white, " you must surely remember that we never met—never thought of meeting—until dear Agnes herself brought us together. Don't you recollect how sweetly she wrote and begged me to be their friend. She said that it would make him happier, and herself too —that she never wished him to forget me; that it was through my influence that he had been brought right and that they were no longer divided in faith. Oh, Betty, I was a happy woman the day I got that letter, and I have been a happy woman since. ' Through pain to peace,' " she went on softly, " I should like those words to be inscribed on my tombstone. To think of the terror and the struggle, the buffeting of all those cruel waves and billows, and then to see land at last! Dearest, how you cry! You will make me cry too, and I have been singing a Te Deum in my heart all day for dear Lettice's sake." Then Elizabeth tried to control her sobs.

" Die, I am quite ashamed of myself. I cannot think what has come to me. Think of a woman of thirty blubbering like a little school-girl! It is not like me, is it, dear? but my heart feels as heavy as lead to-night. Things are going wrong somehow, or is it my fancy?" And then she said a little wildly, " Oh, my darling, if I were only like you!"

" Like me! Oh no, Elizabeth," for Dinah's humility could ill brook this speech.

" But it is no use—I could never reach you. I am so human—a passionate, self-willed woman, who wants her own way in everything; and you, oh, Die, you are miles above me. That is why I love you so—I love you so!"

" Not more than I love you," returned her sister tenderly. " Dear Elizabeth, it is only your generosity that makes you say this, but it is not true. I wish I knew what has upset you so to-night." But Elizabeth made no reply to this; the friendship between the sisters was so perfect that speech did not always seem necessary. When

Elizabeth remained silent, Dinah did not repeat her question.

Elizabeth had seated herself on the cushioned window-seat close to Dinah's chair. The little green lamp had been extinguished, and the room was bathed in moonlight. Down below were the dark woodlands. "Let me stay for a little while," Elizabeth had whispered, and then they had both remained silent.

Dinah felt perplexed and troubled by her sister's unusual emotion. Elizabeth's strong, healthy nature was never morbid; her temperament was even and sunshiny, and a depressed mood was a rare thing with her.

Dinah's sweet serenity was vaguely disturbed, and the quiet tears gathered in her eyes. Silence was good for both of them, she thought. When one has lived through a great pain, and by God's grace has conquered, it is better to bury the dead past. Elizabeth's passionate incredulity, the difficulty she felt in understanding her sister's motives, her exaggerated praise, made Dinah wince in positive pain. How could human love misjudge her so! Did not even her nearest and dearest—her own sister-friend—know how often she had striven and failed and fainted under that hard cross that had been laid upon her?

And in truth few women had suffered as Dinah had in the sweet blossom of her early womanhood, and more than once she had been very near the gates of the dark valley whose shadow is the shadow of death.

How she had gloried in her lover—her "Douglas—Douglas, tender and true," as she had called him to herself—in his great intellect and his strong man's heart, in the plan and purpose of his life, with its scientific research and its passionate love of truth!

And then that awful struggle between her affection and her sense of right, the doubts and terrors, the wakeful nights and joyless days, the vast blank of life that stretched before her poor eyes, half-blind with their woman's weeping.

"O Galilæan, Thou hast conquered," were the words that came to her when the crucial test had been passed, and she had parted with her beloved.

Those were sad days at the Wood House, and there were sadder days still at Rome; but she lived through them, and Elizabeth helped her; and so by and bye the light of a new dawn—a little gray and misty perhaps, but still dawn—opened before Dinah's tired eyes.

"I loved much and I prayed much, and God answered my prayers," she said long afterwards.

But the wound was wide and deep and healed slowly, and it was not until Douglas Fraser had married a noble-hearted and beautiful woman, whom he called his Lady of Consolation, that Dinah recovered a measure of her former cheerfulness. But the day she heard that he was no longer an agnostic was always kept by her as a festival. Then indeed the cup of her pure joy seemed full to the very brim.

He had come right, and now all was well with him and with her too. Pain and loss had been his teachers, and great indeed was her reward.

"It was your renunciation and sacrifice that first opened my eyes," he wrote. "I know now how rightly you acted. If I had married you then—if my entreaties had prevailed—I should never have made you happy. My dear Agnes has taught me this." And this cherished letter was Dinah's treasure.

She and Dr. Fraser seldom met—not more than once a year—but from time to time he wrote to her, and his wife and children were very dear to her.

"I cannot understand it," Elizabeth had more than once said. But Dinah could furnish no explanation: she only knew that it was so—that her life was a happy one, and that she asked for nothing more.

Douglas and his wife were her dearest friends, and Lettice, her sweet god-daughter, ranked next to Cedric in her heart.

With so many to love, how could life fail to satisfy her! "And it so short—so short," she would say to herself. "One sees so little of one's friends here; but one will have plenty of time to enjoy them in Paradise."

Continuity of life—continuity of love, this was Dinah's simple creed, but it kept her young and happy.

"Dinah has the secret of perpetual youth," Elizabeth would say to her friend Mrs. Godfrey; but she generally ended with a sigh, "If only I were like her!"

CHAPTER XXII

"TWO MAIDEN LADIES OF UNCERTAIN AGE"

How poor a thing is man! Alas, 'tis true;
I'd half forget it when I chanced on you!
SCHILLER.

Thy clothes are all the soul thou hast.—BEAUMONT AND
FLETCHER.

THE day of the Templeton's garden fête was as bright
and cloudless as the heart of man or woman could desire.
Verity, who had dressed herself at an unconscionably
early hour, sat at an upper window with Babs in her arms,
watching brakes and carriages drive past, filled with gaily
attired people. Malcolm had issued his sovereign man-
date that they must not be amongst the earliest arrivals,
and Verity panted with impatience long before she could
induce her household tyrants to lay aside pipe and cigarette.

Malcolm was not in a festive mood. He had spent his
morning restlessly, pacing up and down the woodlands,
with an unread book under his arm. He was secretly
chafed and even a little hurt that neither of the sisters
had needed his help. He had dropped more than one hint
on the previous day, when some errand took him to the
Wood House, and he found Elizabeth looking heated and
tired, superintending the removal of some furniture.

"You might make use of an idle man," he had said
half-jestingly. "I assure you that I am a complete Jack-
of-all-trades, and I don't mind 'a scrow,' as old Nurse
Dawson calls it." But though Elizabeth smiled, she did
not avail herself of this friendly offer; but it was Dinah
who gave him the real explanation.

"Oh, thank you, Mr. Herrick," she had returned gratefully; "we should have been so glad of your help, only David Carlyon and his father are doing all we want. Mr. Carlyon is so useful, and David spends all his spare time with us."

"David"—in a pondering voice. And Dinah blushed as if she had been guilty of an indiscretion.

"Oh, we only call him that in order to distinguish him from his father—the two Carlyons are so puzzling; but he is an old and a very dear friend, and at my age it does not matter," finished Dinah with her charming smile.

Malcolm had to content himself with this explanation. They were old friends. Yes, of course, and he was a comparatively new one. He expected too much; his demands were unreasonable. Nevertheless Malcolm felt a pang of envy when he saw David Carlyon tearing breathlessly through the woodlands with his arms full of greenery from the vicarage garden, and whistling like a schoolboy.

When at last Malcolm and his friends turned in at the gates of the Wood House that afternoon, they could hear the band playing in the distance. A group of village children were gathered in the road; empty carriages passed them; a smart dog-cart, with four young men, rattled down the drive; and through the openings in the trees the gleam of white dresses looked silvery in the sunlight.

Miss Templeton was standing in the porch to receive her guests. Elizabeth had only just left her, she said, to arrange the tennis tournament. And then, as more guests were arriving, Malcolm left her. The next moment he came upon Cedric; he was looking rather bored and disconsolate. He lighted up, however, at the sight of his friend.

"Here you are at last," he grumbled. "I have been looking all over the place for you. I came down with a lot of our fellows, but Betty has paired them all off for tennis. There are the Kestons, I must go and speak to them." But Malcolm had him by the arm.

"Wait a moment; '" no hurry!" said the Carpenter.' I suppose you brought the Jacobis with you." Then Cedric's face clouded again.

"Oh, Jacobi came right enough—there he is, talking to David—but Miss Jacobi had a bad sick headache, and he would not let her come."

"I am sorry to hear that," returned Malcolm; and he was sorry, for his cleverly-devised plan had been frustrated.

"She was sorry too, poor girl," went on Cedric in a vexed voice. "She had been so looking forward to the Bean-feast ever since Betty's invitation arrived. It is my belief that Jacobi is to blame for the whole thing, for he was rowing her in her room like anything last night. I could hear them through the ceiling going it like hammer and tongs."

"Do you mean to tell me that Miss Jacobi and her brother quarrel?" asked Malcolm in a disgusted voice. Then Cedric looked as if he had said more than he intended.

"No, not quarrel," rather hesitatingly. "It takes two to do that, you know, and Leah—Miss Jacobi, I mean," biting his lip—" is much too fond of her brother to quarrel with him; but Jacobi has a temper, you see."

"Oh, he has a temper, has he?"

"Well, lots of people have, if you come to that," returned Cedric, who evidently repented his frankness. "Jacobi is a decent fellow, but he is hot and peppery, and when things go crooked he lashes out a bit. Something must have vexed him last night, for he came into the drawing-room looking very much put out. Miss Jacobi had just gone upstairs, and he went after her at once."

"And then they quarrelled?"

"Well, not quarrelled exactly; but there was a good

deal of talking, don't you know. He kept her up late, and bothered her, and then she got a headache." But Cedric forbore to tell his friend that he had been so perturbed by the sound of Saul Jacobi's angry voice that he had stolen down the stairs to the passage below. How long he stood there transfixed with fear and pity it was impossible to say. No words reached him—only the harsh, vibrant tones of Saul Jacobi's voice and Leah's low, piteous sobbing.

He might have stood there until morning, but the door suddenly unlatched, and he had only just time to steal away; but before he could enter his room a few words did reach him.

"Oh, Saul, please do not leave me like this. Don't I always do as you wish; only—only I thought you approved; that—that——" but here sobs choked her voice.

"What is the use of turning on the waterworks like this?" muttered her brother angrily. "What fools you women are! A boy like that too!"

"But, Saul, Saul——"

"Yes, I know," sulkily. "I have not changed my mind, but I mean to have my way about to-morrow all the same. If you had been sensible I would have told you my reasons; but you chose to aggravate me, and I said a precious lot more than I meant. There, go to sleep and forget it"—evidently a rough attempt to be conciliatory; but Leah's sad and weary face told its own tale the next morning.

Malcolm did not ask any more questions, and after a few more casual remarks Cedric went off in search of the Kestons, and Malcolm sauntered across the lawn, looking at the various groups in the hope of seeing Elizabeth's tall figure.

Presently he came upon Mr. Jacobi. He was standing by the sun-dial, looking smart and well-groomed in his frock-coat, and a rare orchid in his button-hole. He was contemplating the house with fixed attention. A sudden impulse made Malcolm join him. Mr. Jacobi greeted him with his usual affability, and then, as though by mutual consent, they strolled together in the direction of the rustic bridge.

"Nice sleepy old place this," observed Mr. Jacobi condescendingly. "Seems as though it had been in existence for a hundred years at least. Do you know how long it has belonged to the Templetons?"

"No, I have no idea," returned Malcolm stiffly, for he resented the question. "What a perfect day it is! I am sorry to hear from Templeton that your sister is indisposed."

Mr. Jacobi's eyes narrowed a little; he looked rather sharply at Malcolm.

"Oh, Templeton told you that. Nice fellow—as good a specimen of a young Briton as ever I wish to see; sensible too, and a good companion. Yes, my sister is a bit seedy—a bad sick headache, nothing more. It is in our family; my mother had them, and Leah takes after her. It is hard lines, poor old girl," continued Mr. Jacobi in a feeling tone, "for she was longing to make the Misses Templeton's acquaintance."

Malcolm returned a civil answer, and Mr. Jacobi continued—

"Templeton is a lucky fellow, between you and me and the post," in a jocular tone. "It must be a good thing for him that his sisters have set their faces against matrimony. Nice-looking women, both of them, but in my humble opinion Miss Elizabeth is the most attractive. Templeton let out to Leah the other day that she could have married a dozen times over if she had wished to do so, only she vowed she was cut out for an old maid."

"I don't suppose he knows anything about it," returned Malcolm, feeling this speech was in the worst possible form. It revolted him to hear this man even mention

Elizabeth's name—he would give him no encouragement;
but Saul Jacobi, who could be dense when he chose, did
not drop the subject.

"It is rather a big place for two maiden ladies of uncertain age," he remarked blandly; but this speech irritated Malcolm beyond endurance.

"There is nothing uncertain about the second Miss
Templeton's age," he said impatiently; "she is still a
young woman." Then it struck him that Mr. Jacobi
looked a trifle crestfallen.

"Young, do you call her? Oh no, very mature and
sedate, like a middle-aged woman. Gyp Campion told
me as a fact—do you know Gyp? he is in the Hussars,
and a tiptop swell in the bargain—well, Gyp let out that
his brother Owen had proposed to Miss Elizabeth Templeton years ago at Alassio."

"Oh, I daresay," indifferently. "I think I must go back
to the house now;" it cost Malcolm an effort to be civil.

"I will walk back with you. What was I saying?
Oh, she refused the poor chap, and told him that the
holy estate of matrimony had no attraction for her, or
some such rubbish. That is why I call Templeton a lucky
fellow. There is not a creature belonging to them, except
a distant cousin or two in New Zealand, so of course he
will come in for everything;" a pause here, and a furtive
glance of inquiry; but Malcolm remained mute, and his
face might have been a blank wall as far as expression
was concerned.

"They have got a pretty penny saved too," went on
Mr. Jacobi, not in the least silenced by Malcolm's lack of
interest. "Gyp told me a thing or two about that. It
seems they had a farm in Cornwall"—here he sniffed at
his scentless orchid with an air of enjoyment, a habit of
his when his subject interested him. "It was a rotten
concern—farm buildings out of repair, and a few scrubby
fields with more stones than grass. Miss Templeton was

just going to sell it for a mere song when some one discovered tin. My word, those few acres rose in value! Gyp declared they realised quite a small fortune on it. That was only three or four years ago."

"Indeed," returned Malcolm drily; "if you will pardon my speaking plainly, Mr. Jacobi, I do not think the Misses Templeton's business affairs are any concern of ours, and I would prefer to talk on any other subject."

This was too manifest a hint to be disregarded even by the irrepressible Jacobi; but the next minute Malcolm added, "Will you excuse my leaving you, I see some old friends of mine on their way to the Pool, and they will expect me to join them;" but if Malcolm intended to do so, he chose a most circuitous route.

"Rum chap that," observed Saul Jacobi, turning on his heel—"not easy to get any information out of him; looks as though he had swallowed the poker first, and then the tongs as a sort of relish afterwards, and neither of them agreed with him. I wonder what young Templeton saw in him. He lays it on pretty thick too: it is Herrick this and Herrick that, as though he were Solomon in all his glory. Confound his airs and impudence! Let me tell you, my young gentleman," with a sly smile, "that the Misses Templeton's private business is a matter that concerns Saul Jacobi pretty closely."

Meanwhile Malcolm was in a white heat of righteous indignation.

"That wretched little cad, how dare he meddle and pry into the Misses Templeton's family affairs! There is something I mistrust in the man; he is smooth and plausible, but he is crafty too; he is deep—deep—and if I do not mistake, he is clever too."

Then he added, "I must get hold of Cedric; I am not comfortable at his associating with this man. Cedric is as weak as water; he is so easily led, he would be the dupe of any designing person; but the Jacobis will have to reckon with me;" and here Malcolm, who had uttered the last words aloud, stopped and looked rather foolish, as a merry laugh greeted his ear, and Elizabeth, in all the glory of her Paris gown and picture hat, barred the way, and regarded him with her beaming smile.

"Mr. Herrick, you are quite dramatic; Hamlet or the melancholy Jacques could not have been more lost in gloomy meditation. If I may presume to ask the question, why will the Jacobis have to reckon with you?"

"Did I say so?" returned Malcolm, with an uneasy laugh. "I suppose I was thinking aloud. That fellow Jacobi has been rubbing me up the wrong way; he stuck to me like a burr, and I could not get rid of him."

"I had some trouble in shaking him off myself," she owned. "You were quite right, Mr. Herrick, he is not a gentleman, and I dislike his manner excessively; it is too subservient, and he is too soft-tongued. Poor dear Die, I wish you could have seen her face when he paid her a compliment; she looked quite bewildered."

Elizabeth's eyes were dancing with amusement at the recollection, but Malcolm did not respond to her merriment; he felt things were too serious.

"I am not at all easy in my mind," he said, and then Elizabeth looked at him inquiringly. "Jacobi seems to have got a hold on Cedric. He goes back with him to-night, does he not? Ah, I thought so," as Elizabeth nodded. "I must have some talk with him; I shall tell him that I disapprove of the Jacobis, and shall beg him to break off the acquaintance."

"Oh, thank you—thank you!" returned Elizabeth earnestly, and there was a beautiful colour in her face; she even held out her hand impulsively to him, as though her gratitude carried her away. "How good you are to us—a real friend to two lone, lorn women!" and here something twinkled in Elizabeth's eyes; but perhaps she was a little taken aback when Malcolm very quietly and reverently raised the hand to his lips, as though he were vowing knightly service to his liege lady.

"I should ask nothing better than to be your friend," he said in a low voice; but perhaps something in her manner checked him, for he added hastily, "and your sister's too."

It was rather a lame conclusion, but Elizabeth accepted it graciously. "I shall rely on you to help us," she said very seriously; "get him to break with the Jacobis, and Dinah and I will owe you a debt of gratitude."

"Hush! please do not mention names," whispered Malcolm; "some one might overhear us;" but he was too late, Elizabeth's incautious speech had reached an unseen auditor.

Malcolm felt a little ashamed of himself when he remembered his impulsive action. "She will think it so strange," he thought; "she will not understand that it was only the outward and visible sign of my inward reverence." But he was wrong, Elizabeth did understand, and she did not misjudge him.

"He is a high-minded gentleman," she said to herself; and then she sighed and her face grew troubled, "but I wish—I wish he had not done that."

Malcolm found his work cut out for him; for the remainder of the afternoon he was hunting his quarry. But Cedric was never alone. He was either surrounded by a bevy of girls or else Jacobi was beside him. Even Cedric seemed surprised at the tenacity with which his friend and host stuck to him.

"Herrick wants me," he said once; "I will come back to you right enough, old fellow;" but Jacobi still pinioned him.

"We will go together, my dear boy," he said pleasantly. "I have taken a fancy to your Mentor. He seems a clever chap. He is a barrister, isn't he, and literary, and all that sort of thing?"

15

"I have told you about him often enough," returned Cedric, in rather a surly tone, as though the iron hand under the velvet glove made itself evident. Cedric felt he was being managed and coerced, and he waxed indignant; but Saul Jacobi was more than a match for him, and in spite of all Malcolm's efforts, Cedric went back to Henley without a word of warning.

Malcolm was quite troubled and crestfallen over his failure.

"I did my best," he said to Elizabeth; "I followed him about the whole afternoon, but that fellow stuck to him like a leech."

"So I saw," she returned rather sadly; "it was no fault of yours, Mr. Herrick, I am quite sure of that. Well, we must find some other opportunity." And then Elizabeth smiled at him very kindly, and Malcolm went back to the Crow's Nest feeling somewhat comforted.

CHAPTER XXIII

SAINT ELIZABETH!

Love lies deeper than all words;
And not the spoken but the speechless love
Waits answer, ere I rise and go my way.
                                        BROWNING.

WHEN in after-years Malcolm Herrick reviewed this portion of his life, he owned to himself that during the five weeks that followed the Templeton Bean-feast he had lived in a fool's paradise—in a state of beatitude that was as unsubstantial and fleeting as the sunset clouds that piled themselves behind the fir woods.

He was very happy, almost pathetically so, and the new wine of youth seemed coursing through his veins. "This is life," he would say to himself; "I have only existed before, but now I am reborn into a new world, and I have learned the secret of all the ages."

Every day his passion for Elizabeth Templeton increased, and the charm and sweetness of her personality attracted him more powerfully. He had never seen any one like her; she was so full of surprises, her nature was so rich, so original, and yet so womanly, that the man whom she blessed with her love could never have grown weary of her society. Without an effort, simply by being herself, a truthful, noble-hearted woman, she had dominated his strong nature and brought him to her feet. Was she conscious of his devotion? This was a question that Malcolm vainly tried to answer, but her manner perplexed and baffled him. She was always kind and friendly, and her cordial welcome never varied, but Malcolm could not flatter himself that he received any special

227

encouragement, or that she regarded him in any other light than a trusted and valued friend. Now and then, when he found himself alone with her, he fancied her manner had changed—that she had become quiet and re-served, as though she were not at her ease with him. Was it only his imagination, he wondered, that she seemed trying to keep him at a distance, as though she were afraid of him? But such was his blindness and infatuation that he drew encouragement even from this.

To Malcolm those summer days were simply perfect. His morning hours were devoted to his literary work, and the essays were taking shape and form under his hand. Never had his brain been clearer; he worked with a facility that surprised himself. " I am inspired," he would whisper; " I have a patron saint of my own now," and he would tell himself that no name could be so sweet to him as Elizabeth. He would murmur it half-aloud as he wandered in the woodlands in the gloaming—" Eliza-beth, Elizabeth"—and once as he said it, something seemed to rise in his throat and choke him.

He had not forgotten Anna; he had never forgotten her in his life, for his adopted sister was very dear to him.

Every week he wrote to his mother and also to her—pleasant, chatty letters, full of affection and warm with brotherly kindness. If Anna ever shed tears over them he never knew it.

With what touching humility she acknowledged his thoughtfulness!

" Another letter—how good you are to me!" she would say in her reply. " Mother declares that you spoil me. I read her all your description of the Bean-feast. Oh, if I had only been there! But it is wicked of me to say that."

But later on there was a touch of curiosity, almost a shadow of doubt.

" You say so little about Miss Elizabeth Templeton,"

she wrote, "and yet you are at the Wood House every day. It is always Miss Templeton. Is it heresy, dear? but I fancy I should like Miss Elizabeth best. Tell me more about her next time you write. I want to see her with your eyes." But Anna pleaded in vain—on the subject of Elizabeth's merits he kept silence.

But it was quite true that he was at the Wood House nearly every day, and that the sisters always welcomed him most kindly. Sometimes he dined there, either alone or with the Kestons; or he would stroll across at tea-time, or oftener in the evening, when they were sitting on the terrace. David Carlyon was often with them; his father had left him by this time. The young men used to look askance at each other in the dim light, and Malcolm would shake hands with the curate rather stiffly.

"Carlyon was there again," he would say to Amias, when he found his friend smoking in the porch. "I don't dislike the fellow, but one may have too much even of a good thing." Then Amias looked at him rather queerly but made no answer.

Caleb Martin and Kit were established comfortably at the cottage under Mrs. Sullivan's motherly wing, and Kit's white pinched little face filled out in the sweet country air.

"She is a different creature," Caleb assured Malcolm. "I wish Ma'am could see her. She is just as happy as the day is long. We are in the woods from morning to night, picking up fir-cones and building with them, and making believe that we are gypsies. She's ready to drop with fatigue before she lets me take her home, and then our good lady scolds us a bit."

"And poor Mrs. Martin is alone in Todmorden's Lane?" remarked Malcolm.

"Lord love you, sir," returned Caleb, "you don't need to be pitying Ma'am; she's glad to be rid of the pair of us. She is whitewashing and papering the rooms. She is a handy woman, is Ma'am, and she says we shall not know the place when we go back. I never knew such a woman for scrubbing and cleaning—it seems to make her happy somehow."

Malcolm made frequent visits to Rotherwood to see Caleb and Kit, and he generally paid them on the days when Elizabeth was at the schools, so that he could walk back with her through the woodlands.

The first time he did this Elizabeth seemed rather surprised, though she offered no objection; but after that she took it as a matter of course, and chatted with him on all manner of subjects. She listened very kindly when Malcolm sounded her on the subject of Kit, and made all sorts of impossible plans for the child's future; and though she laughed at him good-humouredly, and told him that he was a visionary, impracticable person, she soon became serious and brought her shrewd commonsense and feminine wits to his assistance. And so it was that one day he made a proposition that nearly took Caleb's breath away.

Kit must certainly not go back to Todmorden's Lane until she was stronger, he remarked. Miss Templeton and he were fully agreed on this point; the fogs and low-lying mists from the river were harmful to her poor little chest.

Caleb must leave her under Mrs. Sullivan's care. Miss Templeton had made all arrangements, and he would be responsible for the expense. There had been a pitched battle over this point; but for once Elizabeth had been forced to give in, Malcolm had been so stern and masterful.

Caleb should come down for the week-end every three weeks or so, he could promise him that, and a whole week at Christmas. But Caleb looked too much dazed to answer, and there was a misty look in the transparent, light-blue eyes.

"I'm took all of a heap!" he ejaculated at last. "It is not that I don't thank you kindly, sir, for I am pretty nigh choking with gratitude; but you see there is Ma'am to reckon with—if Kit were her own little 'un she couldn't be fonder of her."

"I daresay not," remarked Malcolm, and there was a trace of impatience in his tone; "but, after all, Mr. Martin, you are Kit's father." But Caleb only shook his head doubtfully, and went on in his slow, ruminating way.

"Most folk think that Ma'am is a bad-natured woman because she gives them the rough side of her tongue; but, Lord bless you, her bark's worse than her bite. Her heart is just set on Kit, and she would not hurt a hair of her head in her most contrary moods, when even the black cat won't stay in the place she is making such a scrimmage with the pots and pans. But Kit only laughs. 'It is Ma'am at her music,' she says; 'but it t'aint the sort of music I like.' Yes, indeed, sir, I have heered her say that a score of times."

"Very well, then, you had better go and have a talk with your wife," returned Malcolm.

And Caleb went, and came back to Rotherwood the next day a sadder and a wiser man.

"Well, and what did Mrs. Martin say?" asked Malcolm when he saw Caleb again.

The little cobbler drew his hand across his eyes in an embarrassed fashion; he was evidently trying to recollect something.

"Ma'am sends her humble duty," he answered presently in a sing-song voice, "and she is greatly obliged to you and the kind lady, and Kit may stay along of Mrs. Sullivan—those were her very words, sir."

"Mrs. Martin is a sensible woman then."

"Oh, she is that, sir. She was scolding me all supper-time for not thinking of the child's good. 'You can bring her back if you like, Caleb,' she says, 'and poison her with the filthy fogs, and get her ready for her coffin, poor lamb. And you call yourself a father, Caleb Martin? Drat all such fathers, I say!' She made me clean ashamed of myself, did Ma'am;" and here the little man looked ready to cry.

"Well, Mr. Martin, I do think the child will be better here, and you can come down every three weeks or so to see her—you know we have arranged that—and now and then you can bring your wife too;" and Caleb brightened up at this.

But the day he left Rotherwood he was so lugubrious and tearful that Malcolm felt quite sorry for him; but Kit took a less depressing view.

"I don't want you to go, dad," she said feelingly; "but I like staying along with this good lady," with a friendly nod of her head to Mrs. Sullivan. "I have got a black kitten of my own and a yellow chick, and they are better than dolls because they can love me back. And the ladies from the Wood House are going to take me out for drives —my, won't that be 'eavenly!" Nevertheless Kit shed a few tears when Caleb closed the little gate behind him. "I want to stay here, and I want daddy too," she said rather pitifully.

All these weeks Malcolm had seen nothing of Cedric. His visit to the Jacobis had been prolonged for another ten days, and then he wrote, in high spirits, to tell his sisters that Dick Wallace had invited him to go down to his father's place in Scotland.

"I expect I shall have rare sport there, and stalk a deer or two," he continued. "Dick and I are to go down by the night mail on Thursday, but I will run over to Staple-grove for a few hours. Tell Herrick I will look him up at his diggings."

By some oversight Elizabeth forgot to give Malcolm this message, and Malcolm, who had to go up to town on business, was much chagrined to find that Cedric had called during his absence, and had been greatly disappointed at missing him.

He went across to the Wood House directly after supper, and found the ladies sitting out on the terrace.

Elizabeth was very contrite.

"It was dreadfully careless of me," she confessed; "I meant to have sent you a note last night, but some one called—who was it, Dinah?—and put it out of my head." But Dinah could not recollect that any one had called except David Carlyon, and seemed rather surprised at the question.

"Oh, it must have been Mr. Carlyon," returned Elizabeth; but she coloured slightly. "It was really very stupid of me; Cedric was quite put out about it."

"Oh, well, it cannot be helped," observed Malcolm, philosophically. "Did he say much about the Jacobis?"

"No, he only remarked that they had been very kind, and that he had had a rattling good time. Those were his words, were they not, Die?" and Dinah smiled assent.

"We both asked him a heap of questions, but they seemed to bore him; he was full of his Scotch visit, and would scarcely talk of anything else."

Malcolm was not quite satisfied, but he kept his doubts to himself. Elizabeth, who was as sharp as a needle, looked up at him quickly. "We did our best, I assure you, Mr. Herrick, but he refused to be drawn; he seemed very much excited."

"The Wallaces are a good sort of people, are they not?" was Malcolm's next question.

"Oh yes, they are thoroughly nice;" it was Dinah who answered him. "Sir Richard is charming, and so is Lady Wallace; and of course Dick is an old acquaintance of ours."

"There are some daughters, I believe?"

"Yes, but they are not very young or attractive, poor things," replied Elizabeth—"heavy, podgy sort of girls,

but very kind-hearted. By the bye, Die, I wonder if
Cedric will come across the Godfreys, they are somewhere in the neighbourhood." And then she explained
to Malcolm that Fettercairn Hall, where Sir Richard
Wallace lived, was only a few miles from the shooting
lodge where the Godfreys were staying; and this fact
appeared to give the sisters a good deal of satisfaction.

It was the middle of September now, and Malcolm
reflected with some uneasiness that more than half his
holiday was over. The Kestons had decided to return
to Cheyne Walk in another three weeks or so, and of
course he must accompany them; his mother and Anna
would be back in town by that time, and his presence
would be needed in Lincoln's Inn.

"The shadows of the prison-house," as he called it,
began to haunt him, and he counted up his days as jeal-
ously as a miser counts his gold.

Every day he saw Elizabeth; and each hour he was
alone with her he found it more difficult to keep silence;
but as yet he had had himself well in hand. Perhaps
something in her manner had sealed his lips, or he feared
that the spell of this happy dream would be broken. But
during those wakeful summer nights, when that sweet
pain kept him restless, he would tell himself that the time
had not yet come, that she did not know him well enough.

"She is not a young girl," he would say to himself;
"she is a mature woman who knows the world and has
thought deeply—why, even to know her is a liberal education." And then he repeated to himself in the darkness
those lines of Shelley—

> "Her voice was like the voice of his own soul,
>   Heard in the calm of thought,"

for all the sweet influences of summer and nature had
only fed the passion, and every day it seemed to grow
stronger and stronger.

"She is my other self, she thinks my thoughts, we have a thousand things in common, how can she help loving me!" he would say when his mood was jubilant and sanguine; but at other times a chill doubt would cross his mind.

"She is different from other women, she will not be easily won, that is why I fear to speak;" but all the same Malcolm registered a mental vow that he would not leave Staplegrove until the decisive words had been spoken.

CHAPTER XXIV

DOWN BY THE POOL

The heaven
Of thy mild brows hath given
Grace to all things I see;
And in thy life I live, and lose myself in thee.
                                    J. ADDINGTON SYMONDS.

I would love infinitely, and be loved.—BROWNING.

MALCOLM was no hot-headed boy to be moved by mere impulse, nevertheless the day came when all his prudent resolutions were forgotten, when silence and self-repression were absolute torture to him, when he felt he must speak or for ever hold his peace.

It was Elizabeth's birthday; he only heard that afterwards, or he would have brought her some choice offering in the shape of flowers or books, in honour of his patron Saint's fête-day; but happily Elizabeth was unconscious of this.

"I am thirty-one to-day," she said to him gaily; "is not that a great age? Oh, no wonder Cedric calls me an old maid." And then she laughed with an air of enjoyment, as though her new title amused her. "Old maids can be very nice, can they not, Mr. Herrick?"

They were sitting down by the Pool, and Dinah had just left them at Elizabeth's suggestion to tell the servants that they would have tea there, and to answer a business note. The afternoon was sultry, more like August than September; but down by the Pool there was a pleasant shade and coolness. As usual, all the dogs were grouped round them; and Elizabeth, in spite of her thirty-one years, looked quite youthful in her white gown. A dark

236

velvety Cramoisie rose nestled against her full throat.
Malcolm remembered suddenly that he had noticed that
special rose in the garden of the White Cottage when he
last dined at the vicarage; he wondered with a sudden
fierce prick of jealousy if that fellow Carlyon knew it
was her birthday, and had brought it to her. At the idea
there was a dangerous throbbing of his pulses.

The previous evening he had strolled across to the
Wood House in the hope that Elizabeth would be in one
of her gracious moods, and then he could coax her to
sing to him. But to his disappointment his visit had
seemed less welcome than usual; and though Dinah received him with her wonted gentle courtesy, he had a
vague suspicion that something was amiss. Dinah looked
as though she had been shedding tears, and Elizabeth's
face was flushed, and she was very silent; if he had
not known them so well, and their intense love for each
other, he would almost have suspected that there had
been a warm altercation between them, but this was mani-
festly impossible.

No, they had never quarrelled even in their childish
days, he remembered Elizabeth had once told him that,
and assuredly they never quarrelled now. Nevertheless,
there was something troubled in the atmosphere, and even
Dinah seemed to find it difficult to talk.

Malcolm raged inwardly over his disappointment, but
he had too much tact to prolong his visit. He was rewarded for his forbearance when Dinah said in her gentle
way, " I am afraid we are rather stupid to-night, Mr.
Herrick; Elizabeth is tired, and—and—we have been
talking for hours; if you look in to-morrow afternoon
we will promise to behave better." But though Elizabeth
did not endorse this, Malcolm accepted this invitation
with undisguised pleasure.

But his satisfaction would have been sadly damped
if he had overheard Elizabeth's speech. " Why did you

ask him, Die? You know"—hesitating a moment—" that I like to be quiet on my birthday."

"He looked so dull," returned Dinah apologetically; "I think we depressed him. I am very sorry, dear; I ought to have found out your wishes first. But he will not stay long unless we ask him." Elizabeth made no answer to this; she looked thoughtful and a little troubled, and Dinah felt she had done the wrong thing. But this afternoon Elizabeth was in her old sunshiny mood, and she made her little speech about being an old maid in a way that charmed Malcolm.

How still it was down by the Pool! Only a dry leaf dropping into the water, or the sleepy snapping of one of the dogs at the midges, or the faint twitter of a far-off bird broke the silence. The air was sweet with the warm, resinous smell of the firs; the strong perfume seemed to pervade his senses.

He was alone with her—not a human creature was near them; and he was so close that if he had stretched out his hand he could have touched her dress. Malcolm's heart began beating dangerously, and there was a curious throbbing at his temples; when he tried to speak his voice was thick and indistinct; then with a great effort he steadied himself, for his time had come and he knew it.

"There is something I want to say to you—that for weeks I have been trying to say—will you let me speak now?" Did he really say those words, or did he whisper them inwardly? But no, he could see the sudden startled look in Elizabeth's eyes when she saw his face.

"May I speak?"

"No—no," in a frightened tone. "Mr. Herrick, for my sake—for both our sakes—I implore you to be silent; I cannot—I will not listen"—her agitation increasing with every word. But she might as well have tried to control the wind.

"You cannot mean that," he returned gently but firmly;

" forgive me if I do not obey you—if it is not possible for me to keep silence any longer. Elizabeth, surely all these weeks you must have known that you were the one woman in the world for me?"

" No—no," she returned, covering her face with her hands, " I never knew it; how could I—how could I?" But he mistook the cause of her emotion.

" I think no woman was ever loved so well! All these weeks that I have been dumb, I have been living for you —only for you." Then she put up her trembling hand to stop him, but he caught it in his own.

" Elizabeth, will you try to love me a little?"

" Hush—hush," endeavouring to free herself. " Indeed—indeed you must not say such things, Mr. Herrick; you are deceiving yourself. We are friends, and I like you, and I am very, very grateful to you for all your goodness to Cedric, but I never meant it to come to this."

" How do you mean?" he asked, and his face was white with emotion. " Surely you must have seen how things were with me;" and Malcolm's voice was a little hard.

" I think I tried not to see," she answered truthfully. " Once or twice I was afraid, and then I told myself I was mistaken. Mr. Herrick, I do not want to hurt you, I would not add to your trouble for the world, but at least you will do me the justice of owning that I never gave you any encouragement."

" No," he returned, in a tone of forced composure, " you never encouraged me in my presumption. I loved you because I could not help myself—because you were Elizabeth Templeton and I was Malcolm Herrick." Then her eyes grew very sad.

" Dear friend, it was no presumption—any woman would have felt honoured by such devotion; but," and here a burning flush came to her face, " it is too late—I am not free."

Malcolm stared at her. Surely he was in some hideous nightmare, but he would wake directly. What an awful stillness seemed round them!—as though a storm were impending: the water-lilies on the Pool looked like dead things, and even the dragon-fly hung motionless in mid-air; only the dogs panted and snored round them. Elizabeth pressed her hands together as though something pained her.

"I am not free," she repeated in a low voice; but she did not look at Malcolm as she spoke. "Last evening Mr. Carlyon spoke to me, and—and we are engaged."

"Good God!" but Malcolm did not say the words aloud, for his tongue felt suddenly dry and palsied,—it was only the cry of his soul to his Maker in the hour of his agony. But Elizabeth dared not look at him, or her heart would have been wrung with pity at the sight of his drawn, haggard face.

"We have cared for each other for a long time," she whispered, "but he was poor and did not like to speak. Only Dinah knows. I had just told her when you came in last evening. We did not want any one else to know just yet."

"But I forced your hand." Malcolm had pulled himself together now. "Thank you for telling me the truth; but you were always a brave woman," and he tried to smile.

"Oh no, I have not been brave;" and then her eyes suddenly filled with tears. "Mr. Herrick, I am so unhappy; this—this—has spoiled everything."

"No—no, you must not say that. If I have been a blind fool, it is no fault of yours, and I have no one to thank but myself for the misery that has come upon me. Elizabeth"—oh, how sad his voice was! it thrilled her to hear it—"before I leave you, let me wish you every happiness—you and Mr. Carlyon too;" and then he rose to his feet.

" Must you go?" she pleaded.

" Yes, I must go," he returned hurriedly; " will you excuse me to your sister?" Then Elizabeth stretched out her hand to him in silence, and he saw that she could not trust herself to speak.

" You must not be too sorry for me," he said rather brokenly; " I am not the only man who has been denied his heart's desire;" and he turned away and plunged into the little fir wood. Elizabeth sat listening to his retreating footsteps. The tears were running down her cheeks. She was still weeping when Dinah rejoined her.

" Have I been long?" she observed cheerfully. " That tiresome Mrs. Carrick called about the mothers' meetings. Where is Mr. Herrick?" Then, as she caught sight of Elizabeth's face, " Oh, my dear Betty, what is it?—what has gone wrong?—and on your birthday too!"—Elizabeth wept afresh.

" Hush, don't ask me—not now. David will be here directly, and he must not see me like this. You were right, Die, you saw how it was, and I would not believe you—I did not want to believe you. Now let me go away and recover myself." But Dinah held her fast.

" You shall go in a moment, dear; but just tell me one thing—did Mr. Herrick ask you to be his wife?"

" Not exactly—I would not let him go as far as that; but, Die, he loves me so, and he is so unhappy." Then Dinah sighed, and her hand dropped from her sister's arm.

" You had better go," she returned. " I see Mullins crossing the bridge. If David comes I will make an excuse for your absence;" and Elizabeth nodded and turned away. Dinah's heart was very heavy as she stood looking down upon the pool. It is the looker-on who sees most of the game, and weeks ago she had vainly tried to open Elizabeth's eyes to a sense of her danger.

" He has never said a word to me that the whole world

16

might not hear—I don't believe he ever will," Elizabeth had replied obstinately; but Dinah knew that she was wilfully deceiving herself—that her intuition was truer than her words, and that in Malcolm Herrick's presence she was always on guard, as if she feared an invasion of her woman's kingdom.

Dinah could have wept too in her grievous disappointment and passionate pity, for Elizabeth's choice seemed to her a great mistake. David Carlyon was a dear fellow, and as good as gold, but he was not equal to Malcolm.

"If only they had met a year ago," she thought, "before David's influence grew so strong, she would surely have discovered then that they were made for each other. Mr. Herrick is just the sort of man she would have admired. There is something striking and original about him, and then in spite of his cleverness he is so simple and good. "Oh, Betty, my darling," she went on, "why could you not have given me such a brother! I should have been so proud of him!" And then Dinah checked herself in very shame, for she remembered how she had promised Elizabeth the previous evening that she would take David Carlyon to her sisterly heart.

It was not a very cheerful birthday tea, though each one of the trio tried to do his or her best to promote innocent hilarity. Elizabeth talked a great deal, but her face was still flushed, and she rather avoided her lover's eyes, and as for David he talked principally to Dinah. He told funny little parish stories which made her laugh, and to which Elizabeth listened with a manifest effort, and he took no notice when she chimed in with some irrelevant remark. Dinah wondered to herself more than once if he really had not noticed that Elizabeth's eyelids were still reddened, in spite of cold water and eau de Cologne. David was certainly a little dense in his happiness, she thought, and then she sighed involuntarily as she thought of the lonely man who had left them.

"He will take it hardly," she said to herself. "His nature is intense, and he will suffer more than most men;" and as this thought passed through her mind, she looked up and found David's keen, bright eyes fixed on her, and coloured a little as though he had read her thoughts.

When tea was over, Dinah made some transparent little excuse to go back to the house, for in these sweet, early days of their happiness she knew well that the lovers would have much to say to each other. And she was not wrong: before she was out of sight David had flung himself down at Elizabeth's feet, and had taken her hands.

"What is it, dearest?" he said tenderly. "You have been shedding tears—do you think I did not know that?" Then Elizabeth blushed as though she were a child discovered in a fault. "Tell me all about it, darling," he whispered; but she shook her head.

"I cannot, David—indeed I cannot; you must not ask me to tell you this." Elizabeth's voice quivered a little, but she was very much in earnest.

"Must I not?" he returned with a smile. "Don't look so frightened, sweetheart; perhaps there is no need to ask, perhaps I know all you are trying to keep from me." And then in a low voice full of meaning, "So Herrick has spoken at last."

"At last!" It was evident those two words had startled Elizabeth. David with some difficulty suppressed an irresistible smile.

"Do you mean," he asked incredulously, "that you never noticed, what every one else saw so plainly, that that poor fellow fairly worshipped the ground you trod on?" Then again a painful flush came to Elizabeth's face.

"I was not sure," she stammered, for her conscience did not wholly acquit her—"I would not let myself see or notice things; besides, I was thinking of you." Then

David kissed the hands he held; but there was a troubled look in his eyes.

"Poor beggar!" he muttered to himself. Then aloud, "Do you know, my darling, what people will say when they hear you have thrown over a man like Herrick for me—for a mere curate, with empty pockets and not too many brains."

"Do you suppose I care what they say!" throwing her head back in rather a regal fashion.

"They will say you are mad; and upon my word," and here David knit his brows in a puzzled manner, "I am not sure that they will be wrong. Look at the difference between us. Herrick is my superior in every way. I used to shake in my shoes to hear him talk to the vicar. Elizabeth, my heart aches for that poor fellow, but even you do not know what I have suffered on his account all these weeks. There were times when I was tempted to throw up the sponge."

"Oh, David, when you knew—when you must have known my feelings!"

"Yes, I knew; but there were days when my courage failed me, and I felt I had no right to stand in your light. Dearest," and here he was kneeling beside her with all a man's worship in his honest eyes, "you are too good for me—do you think I do not know that it is your goodness and generosity that make you stoop to me!" But Elizabeth laid her hand upon his lips.

"Hush, you shall not talk so. It is I who am not worthy of you. I love you, David—I love you, oh so dearly; that is enough for you—and me too," and Elizabeth looked at him with an adorable smile. Then for a little while Malcolm Herrick was forgotten.

CHAPTER XXV

"IT HAS GONE VERY DEEP"

When you depart from me, sorrow abides and happiness takes his leave.—SHAKESPEARE.

Fulfil the perfection of long-suffering—be thou patient.— *Teaching of Buddha.*

ALL his life long Malcolm never spoke of the hours that followed that fateful interview down by the Pool, when he was as one who had just received his baptism of fire—when he was scorched through and through with that new and terrible agony.

"He will take it hardly," Dinah had said to herself. "His nature is intense, and he will suffer more than most men;" and she was right. Malcolm did suffer cruelly.

He had spoken his parting words to Elizabeth with outward calmness, though his lips were blanched and his features drawn with pain; for he was a gentleman, and *noblesse oblige,* and why should he make her suffer when she had done him no wrong? "I am not the only man who has been denied his heart's desire," he had said to her in a dull, lifeless voice, and in this he was certainly right. All are not winners in the race; many fail to attain their goal, and retire baffled and disheartened from the contest; but few suffer as Malcolm Herrick did, and though he did not curse the day he was born, as Job did, the whole plan and purpose of his life seemed frustrated and the future a hopeless blank.

And the fault was his own! Even in his most despairing moments he never ceased to tell himself that she had never encouraged him—never held out her woman's

245

sceptre for him to touch; and even when she had been most sweet and winsome, she had not abridged the distance between them, nor, in her noble sincerity and friendship, attempted to draw him closer.

No, it was he who had been a blind fool, and he must pay the penalty of his madness. The gates of his earthly paradise had closed behind him for ever. He could hear them clanging in the distance; and the golden bells of his city of dreams were chiming " Nevermore—oh, nevermore !"

" His City of dreams—what a good name !" thought he; and through the long summer days he had dwelt there like a king. And now the gates had closed, and the golden pinnacles were no longer visible, and the breath of the roses and the fragrance of the spices of Araby the blessed would no longer steep his senses in sweetness. Nevermore—oh, nevermore would those blissful dreams be his !

Malcolm never quite recollected what he did with himself that evening. The idea of going back to the Crow's Nest in his present state of mind was simply intolerable. How could he have joined in the simple meal and listened to Goliath's talk !

No, it would be better to have a good long walk and look things in the face, and if he tired himself so much the better. But Malcolm never retained any clear recollection of that walk. He had a vague idea that he passed Earlsfield station, and presently he found himself on the open moor, where he had driven with Elizabeth the day when she had so naïvely confessed her ignorance to him. " I am rather a desultory sort of person," she had said to him, and he had offered to make out a list of books for her to read.

He had done so, and she had thanked him very sweetly, and had sent for some of the books, but he had never seen her read them. Perhaps Carlyon—and at this thought he ground his teeth hard—perhaps Carlyon had discouraged her. Horticulture seemed his chief hobby, and he was always talking to her about a new fern-house they were making at the Wood House, and Malcolm's poor books were neglected.

He flung himself down on the heather. He would battle it out with himself, he thought, and when he was in a quieter frame of mind he would go home. Home, pooh! he would never have a home now!

It was a glorious evening. A fresh, soft breeze had risen and blew refreshingly in his face, but he never heeded it, for in some moods we take the gifts and graces of Nature as a matter of course, and yield her no thanks or acknowledgment for her gentle benison. Even the glowing crimson tints of the sunset clouds could not move him to admiration. A line of Browning came involuntarily to his mind:

I will not soil thy purple with my dust;

but he was thinking of Elizabeth and not of the sunset.

"I must battle it out with myself," he repeated. But hours passed, and the moon had risen, and he still lay there, plucking up the heather and flinging it aside in a stupefaction of misery. It was only when the September darkness stole over the moor that he recollected himself and stumbled to his feet.

He was almost worn out when he unlatched the little gate at the Crow's Nest. Amias was smoking as usual in the porch, and Verity was with him. The lamplight from within fell full on Malcolm's face as he approached them. Verity gave a start.

"Oh, how tired you look!" she said in quite a shocked voice. Malcolm gave her a weary smile.

"I have had a long walk," he returned. "It was such a lovely evening, so I resolved to miss supper for once." He tried to speak in a jaunty fashion, but it was a ghastly failure, and he knew it. He was so sick and faint with inanition that he felt as though he could not utter another word. " I am tired, I think I will go to bed. Good-night you two;" and he groped his way to the garden-house.

Amias took his pipe from his mouth and looked at his wife inquiringly.

" What's come to Herrick?" he said in a concerned tone; " he looks dead beat. We thought he was dining at the Wood House; at least you said so, Yea-Verily, my child, and I believed you."

" Yes, I know, dear; but we were both wrong, and he has eaten nothing, that is evident." And then she got up quickly. " The kitchen fire is still alight, and the kettle will soon boil; I told Martha to leave it. I will make him some coffee, and you shall take it to him. And, Amias, you dear old thing, don't talk to him; he is not fit for it to-night."

And so it was that a quarter of an hour later Amias knocked at Malcolm's door, and was reluctantly bidden to enter.

Malcolm was sitting still fully dressed by the open window, and the moonlight made him look still more ghastly. Amias, without a word, lighted the lamp and placed the tray beside him. " Verity sends her love, and says you must eat your supper," was all he ventured to say, but his large hand rested kindly on Malcolm's shoulder for a moment. Malcolm tried to thank him, but the words would not come. But when his friend had left the room he suddenly covered his face with his hands and cried like a child. " Elizabeth—Elizabeth!" but there was no response; only a sleepy bird stirred in the shrubbery. In spite of his great intimacy with the Kestons and his very real friendship, Malcolm did not confide in either of them. He was undemonstrative and self-reliant by nature, and, as he said himself afterwards, " There are some things that a man ought to keep to himself." But

neither Amias nor Verity expected any such confidence.

If Amias seemed puzzled by the change in Malcolm,
Verity needed no explanation. She had seen how things
were from the first. She had once caught sight of Malcolm's face when Elizabeth Templeton had passed him
so closely that her dress brushed against him. She had
seen that look in Amias's eyes in the dear auld lang syne.

Verity was a loyal little soul, and she never even hinted
her suspicions to her husband. Neither did she attempt
to find out what was amiss. When, the next evening,
Malcolm told them hurriedly that he would be obliged to
return to town earlier than he thought, she interrupted
Amias's clumsy exclamations of regret. "Mr. Herrick
has been very good to give us so much of his company,"
she said cheerfully. "Of course we shall miss him, and
so will Babs;" and then in her pretty, housewifely way
she set about making arrangements for his comfort, and
Malcolm felt inwardly grateful for this unspoken sympathy.

He went over to the vicarage to bid Mr. Charrington
good-bye. On the way back he met David Carlyon. The
young curate looked rather nervous and discomposed, but
Malcolm was quite calm.

"As I am leaving Staplegrove to-morrow," he said
quietly, "I am glad to have this opportunity of offering
my congratulations and bidding you good-bye." The lie
came glibly to his lips. Glad, when he would have gone
a dozen miles to avoid his rival—his successful rival!
Nevertheless—such hypocrites are the best of men—the
words flowed smoothly from his lips.

"Thanks awfully," replied David, prodding the dust
with his stick. "Are you going up to the Wood House
now? I think—that is, I am sure the ladies are out;"
which was certainly the fact, as he had just seen them
driving in the direction of Earlsfield.

" No, not this afternoon, I think," replied Malcolm. " Well, good-bye, I am a bit pressed for time;" and then the young men shook hands, and David's grip was almost painful.

" Poor beggar!" he muttered to himself as he turned away; but Malcolm could not give expression, if he tried, to those bitter thoughts of his.

" David Carlyon her husband—the husband of Elizabeth Templeton—why, the very birds knew how to mate more fitly!" he thought. " He is good and true, but he is not worthy of her;" and David in his sad humility was saying the same thing of himself.

That evening Dinah received a note; Amias Keston left it.

" My dear Miss Templeton," wrote Malcolm, " tomorrow I am leaving Staplegrove, and I know you will understand the reason why I do not call to bid you good-bye, and that you will not think me ungrateful after all the kindness and hospitality I have received from you. Your sister has often told me that you have no secrets from each other; so you will know why it is better for me to return to town. I have been to the vicarage this afternoon, and have seen Carlyon. With kindest regards to you and your sister, yours very sincerely and gratefully,

" MALCOLM HERRICK."

Elizabeth grew a little pale and bit her lip when Dinah showed her the note.

" It has gone very deep," she said to herself. " David said so, and he was right—it has gone very deep."

So Malcolm shook off the dust of Staplegrove, and the gates of his City of dreams clanged behind him.

" He must dree his weird," he said to himself, as he sat down to his work in the gloomy room in Lincoln's Inn, and in spite of heart-sickness he worked on stolidly and well. The evenings were his worst time, when he went back to the empty house at Cheyne Walk and sat on the balcony brooding over his troubles, until the light faded and an eerie darkness crept over the river.

"I suppose many men have to go through this sort of thing," he would say to himself, trying to philosophise in his old way, but if any one had seen his face! "What does our glorious Will say?—'Men have died from time to time and worms have eaten them, but not for love.' Ah, but he also says, 'How bitter a thing it is to look into happiness through another man's eyes!'" And sometimes, when the silence and solitude oppressed him terribly, he would picture to himself the dreary future. "I shall never marry," he would say. "There is only one woman in the whole world that I want, and she will have nothing to do with me and my love, and no other woman shall ever be my wife." And then he would wonder sadly what life would be like when he was an old bachelor; would he be living on here with Amias and Verity, or would he go back to his mother and do his duty to her in her old age? But with all his bitter ruminations he never let himself go again, but battled manfully with his pain, though as the days went on he grew paler and thinner, and looked wretchedly ill.

Malcolm knew that his mother and Anna were back at Queen's Gate, but it was quite ten days before he saw them. He dreaded the ordeal of his mother's searching glances; but at last one evening he plucked up his courage and went.

Anna, who saw him coming, flew down the staircase to meet him. She looked younger than ever, and quite pretty, with the soft pink colour in her cheeks and her fair hair; but her smile faded when she saw Malcolm's face.

"Oh, Malcolm, have you been ill?" she asked in an alarmed voice.

"No, dear, not ill—only a trifle seedy and out of sorts. Come, let me look at you, lady fair?" and he pinioned her lightly. "Good child," he continued approvingly, "I shall tell the mater you do her credit."

"Yes, I am quite well, and quite rested; and oh, Malcolm, I am so glad to see you again!" Then he smiled at her kindly, and they went upstairs hand in hand. Mrs. Herrick, hearing their voices, came out on the landing to greet her son. Her manner was more than usually affectionate.

"My dear boy," she said, "what an age it is since we saw you! It is more than a fortnight since you even wrote. When did you come back to town?"

Malcolm had dreaded this question, but he was compelled to answer it truthfully.

"About ten days ago," he returned coolly; he knew his mother never tolerated excuses.

"Ten days, and you have never been near us!" Then her tone changed. "Have you been ill, Malcolm?" and she regarded him with undisguised anxiety.

"Anna asked me the same question," he replied, impatiently. "I have only been out of sorts, as I tell her—rather off my feed and that kind of thing." Then Mrs. Herrick said no more on that subject, but as they sat at dinner the keen gray eyes were often fixed on his face. Malcolm did his part manfully: he talked and questioned Anna about her doings; he would not brook an instant's silence. Anna must tell him this and that about her water-party and the picnic, and those wonderful people who tried to force an acquaintance on them; he would not let her off, though more than once the girl looked wistfully at him. Why did he not tell them about Staplegrove? He had not once mentioned the Wood House and the Templetons. Was anything wrong with him? He did not look himself; and she had never before noticed those lines on his forehead. He looked different somehow in these two months. When he went on to the balcony to smoke his cigarette she followed, and stood silently beside him, until he turned and saw her anxious face.

"Well, Annachen," one of his pet names for her, "what is it, little woman?" Then her soft hand smoothed his coat-sleeve.

"Malcolm dear, I don't like to ask, but I am sure something has gone wrong between you and your friends at the Wood House; you have not once mentioned their name, and there is such a sad, sad look in your eyes." Malcolm took the girl's slender wrists and held them firmly.

"Anna, you are my dear little sister, are you not?"

"Oh yes," in a shrinking voice, for he was evidently waiting for an answer.

"A faithful little sister, who will not misunderstand her brother, even if he doesn't confide in her?

"Anna, you are right, and something is troubling me —something that can never be set straight in this world; but not even to you can I speak of it." Then she knew, and in her innocent love she would fain have comforted him.

"I am very sorry—very, very sorry," was all she could find to say.

"I am sorry too," he returned gently, and then he kissed her cheek, and Anna stole away sadly to her own room. If she shed tears they were for him, and not for herself. Anna's affection for her adopted brother was perfectly unconscious and selfless; she never indulged in unwholesome introspection; she never asked herself why her heart ached that night, and a sense of loneliness and desolation stole over her.

Malcolm was unhappy, that was her one thought— things had gone wrong with him. Oh, if she could only give him his heart's desire! This wonderful unknown Elizabeth—had she refused him? Was there some one

else? Alas, these questions were not to be answered.
She must play her part of a faithful little sister, who must
ask nothing, refuse nothing.

Malcolm's ordeal was not yet over. When he threw
away his cigarette and went back to the drawing-room,
he found his mother alone.

"I thought Anna was with you," he said apologetically,
"or I would not have stayed out there so long. I am
afraid I must be going now."

"You have your latch-key," she returned quietly; "sit
down a moment, I want to speak to you, Malcolm. You
are not yourself this evening, something has gone wrong."
Again Anna's very words. He was silent. Why had his
womankind such sharp eyes?

"I am a bit flattened out," he acknowledged, "but I
shall be all right in a day or two;" but she passed this
by almost contemptuously.

"Something is troubling you," she continued, "and to
judge by your looks it is no light thing. You have
grown thinner, Malcolm."

"Oh, I was always one of the lean kine," he returned
lightly; but she seemed almost affronted at the little
joke.

"Does that mean you do not intend to tell me your
trouble?" and here her eyes grew very wistful. "You
are my only son, Malcolm;" she never called him her
only child, her adopted daughter was too dear to her.
"Is there anything that I can do to help you?"

"Nothing—nothing," and he kissed her hand gratefully, for her motherly tone touched his heart. "Mother
dear, forgive me if I cannot speak to you or Anna about
this."

"Not even to poor little Anna?"

"No, not even to her. Mother, please do not misunderstand me, or think me ungrateful, but there are
some things of which a man does not find it easy to

speak." Then Mrs. Herrick said no more; she must bide her time, and until then she could only pray for him.

And up in her pretty room Anna was praying her guileless, innocent prayers, and watering every petition with her tears.

"How could she—how could she?" she cried more than once; "how could any woman refuse my dear Malcolm?"

Can such prayers help? Yea—a thousand times yea! Only He who reads human hearts knows the value of such prayers! When the son—the brother—the lover— has gone into the battle of life, when his strength is failing and the Philistines are upon him, it may be that the pure petition of some loving heart may be as an invisible shield to withstand the darts of the evil one, or haply that "arrow drawn at a venture" which else had pierced between the joints of his armour. "I said little, but I prayed much for you, my son," Mrs. Herrick once said to Malcolm in after-years when they understood each other better, and he knew that she spoke the truth.

CHAPTER XXVI

"I SEE LIGHT NOW"

Every man's task is his life-preserver.—EMERSON.

Life is an opportunity for service.—DR. WESTCOTT.

It is in the silence that follows the storm, and not in the silence before it, that we should search for the budding flower.—*Hindu Proverb.*

ONE gray October afternoon, a fortnight later, Malcolm was walking down Victoria Street, when he came face to face with Colonel Godfrey. The Colonel, who was full of business as usual, seemed unfeignedly pleased at the meeting.

"This is a stroke of good luck!" he exclaimed in his hearty way. "You are just the man I want, Herrick. I was rather in a fix, and was going to Victoria for one of those boy messengers; but you will do my business for me, like a good fellow? Have you anything particular to do?"

"Nothing special. I was only going to the Army and Navy Stores for some stationery." Then the Colonel looked still more delighted.

"There, I was sure of it! My wife is in the tea-room at this very minute expecting me to join her. I should have been punctual to the minute, only I came across Erskine of ours; he wants my advice about a mare he is thinking of buying, and he was so pressing that I felt I must send Catherine a message."

"And I am to do the job for you? All right: Barkis is willin'." And then they both laughed at the familiar words, for Colonel Godfrey loved and studied his Dickens as some men study their classics.

256

"Tell her to be at the entrance at a quarter to six, and I will be there. Well, I must be off, Erskine will be waiting for me." And the Colonel saluted Malcolm and marched off with his head in the air, while more than one fashionable lounger turned round to look at the fine soldierly figure.

At this hour the refreshment-rooms at the Army and Navy Stores were generally crowded, and for two or three minutes Malcolm searched them vainly, before he discovered Mrs. Godfrey sitting alone at a table at the other end of the long room.

She gave an exclamation when she saw him. "Life is full of surprises," she said with the bright, vivid smile that always welcomed her favourite—"Alick promised to join me here!" And Malcolm sat down beside her and gave her the Colonel's message.

Mrs. Godfrey was evidently well used to these messages, for she received it with becoming resignation.

"I have ten minutes to spare," she observed serenely, "so you had better order yourself some tea, and we can tell each other our news. By the bye, how long have you been in town?" And when Malcolm told her nearly a month, she seemed surprised.

"I made up my mind you were still at Staplegrove," she replied; "though, now I come to think of it, there has certainly been no mention of you in Elizabeth's last two letters. By the bye," turning to him with her customary quickness—but Malcolm was just then studying the menu—"what do you think of this engagement?"

"I think it is for me to put the question to you," he returned with admirable *sang-froid;* but one hand clenched itself so tightly under the table that the marks of the nails were in the palm.

"Then I may as well be frank and tell you that I would forbid the banns if I could. Elizabeth ought to have married better—she is far too fine a creature to throw herself away on David Carlyon."

"He is a very good fellow," observed Malcolm rather feebly; it was hard lines that he should be expected to discuss this.

"Oh yes, he is a good fellow," a little contemptuously. "I remember I liked him very well when we were down at the Wood House this spring; there is nothing to say against the young man, he is as good as gold, and an excellent clergyman; and he is gentlemanly too—both the Carlyons are that; but," very decidedly, "he is not good enough for Elizabeth."

Malcolm agreed with every word, but he dared not trust himself to say so; he waited a moment, and then said quietly—

"It seems that Miss Templeton holds a different opinion; she appears quite satisfied with her choice."

"Satisfied"—and here Mrs. Godfrey gave a little laugh. "To judge from her letters—and we have been corresponding pretty freely lately—one would think she was a girl in her teens; she is absurdly happy—even Dinah says so. But between you and me I don't believe Dinah is a bit better pleased than the rest of us."

"What does the Colonel think?" asked Malcolm, feeling as though he ought to say something.

"Oh, Alick always agrees with me, though he expresses his ideas rather differently. He took quite a fancy to Mr. Carlyon, and they were always together last spring; so of course he will not say much—only he will have it that he is not big enough or strong enough for Elizabeth. 'She will master him, and make him look small,' that was what Alick said. They are not to be married until Easter, I hear, and Dinah wishes them to live at the Wood House."

Malcolm had never felt anything like the sudden throb of pain that shot through him when Mrs. Godfrey said this; he grew so pale that she rose hastily, thinking the room was too hot for him.

"Shall we go downstairs?" she said kindly; "the atmosphere of this place is quite suffocating." And Malcolm agreed to this; he was just thinking that he would make some excuse to leave her, when to his chagrin she led the way to the little waiting-place by the entrance, and, seating herself, beckoned to him to follow her example. "There is something I ought to tell you," she said rather seriously; "it is nice and quiet here, and there is plenty of fresh air. You are not looking the thing, Mr. Herrick; you are thinner—much thinner; I am afraid you have been working too hard."

"Oh, no, I cannot lay that flattering unction to my soul," he returned. "Is this what you have to tell me? for in that case I must remark that I have about a ton of stationery on my mind."

"No, do be quiet a moment," and her faultlessly gloved hand rested on his arm. "There is really something I want to say. You know we saw Cedric when he was staying at Fettercairn?" Malcolm's forced rigidity relaxed.

"Oh, yes, Cedric told me that in one of his letters."

"The Wallaces are nice people, and in our cramped quarters the Hall was rather a find. Sir Richard and my husband took to each other, and Lady Wallace and I followed suit."

"That must have been a pleasant sort of arrangement," observed Malcolm.

"I liked the girls too, they were so honestly, frankly ugly; and they were so good-natured, and so delightfully aware of their shortcomings, that they were quite refreshing. Fancy Martha, the eldest girl, saying to me seriously, 'Dick is the only one who takes after mother and father; he is really nice-looking, you know, but Ailie and I are a couple of squat little toads. Now, please don't laugh, Mrs. Godfrey,' she went on, ' for we are very fond of toads, and they have such bright, projecting eyes.' What on earth could I say! for indeed poor Martha is almost grotesque-looking, and yet one can't help loving her. I know I had a fit of laughing, and both of them laughed with me."

" Cedric always said they were good sort of girls."

" Cedric—oh, he is their hero. By the bye, Mr. Herrick, did you know the Jacobis were staying a mile and a half from Fettercairn? Ah I thought so"—as Malcolm started and frowned—" I was sure that bad boy never let any of you know."

" Were they there all the time?"

" Yes, they all travelled together. Mr. Jacobi had taken the cottage they call Shepherd's Hut, because at one time Sir Richard's shepherd lived there; but a room or two has been added, and people take it for the fishing. Alick rather thought of it himself, only the rooms are so small, and one of the chimneys smoked; we were far more comfortable at the shooting-lodge."

" I suppose Miss Jacobi was there too?"

" Of course she was there," in a significant tone, " and Cedric and Dick Wallace spent most of their time with them. I believe they fished, and wandered over the moors, and when they were not at Shepherd's Hut the Jacobis were at the Hall. Mr. Herrick, I am afraid—I am really afraid that that foolish boy Cedric is head over ears in love with Leah Jacobi."

" It looks rather shady," acknowledged Malcolm; " he is not the sort of fellow to keep things to himself." Then with a sudden change of tone—" Did you tell his sisters?"

" I just mentioned the fact of their being there; and then Elizabeth's engagement occupied my attention. Young Dick was half in love too. Miss Jacobi is really very handsome, but, as Alick says, she ought to marry a man at least ten years older."

"My dear lady, she will never marry Cedric; she is only fooling him a bit."

"Don't be too sure of that," returned Mrs. Godfrey quietly; "you know I am rather observant, and it struck me more than once that Mr. Jacobi was playing a double game. He seemed at one time to take a great deal of notice of Dick Wallace, and Cedric was rather shunted. But one Sunday afternoon, when Mr. Jacobi and Sir Richard had been having a long walk together, he suddenly changed, and Cedric was in favour again."

"I am afraid I don't quite follow you," returned Malcolm, who certainly did not understand what she meant to convey to him.

Mrs. Godfrey arched her eyebrows in surprise.

"My dear friend, you are not generally so dense. Don't you see the poor man had never heard of the existence of Ralph Wallace, and so he thought Master Dick was heir to the baronetcy—*voilà tout*."

"Oh, I see light now."

"Sir Richard, who is immensely proud of his eldest son, entertained his companion with graphic descriptions of Ralph, Mrs. Ralph, and all the Ralph olive branches; and of course Mr. Jacobi was immensely interested. But he was rather cool to poor Dick that evening, and now Cedric is in the ascendant again."

Malcolm reflected for a moment; then he said in rather a puzzled tone—

"Of course I see my bearings now, but all the same I am not out of the fog. At the garden-party at the Wood House Jacobi was evidently fishing for information; but he got precious little, I can tell you. But I remember he seemed to know far more than I did about the Templetons"—here Malcolm's voice unconsciously changed; "he even told me about the tin mine that had been discovered on a Cornish farm that belonged to them."

"I wonder where he got his information," observed

Mrs. Godfrey thoughtfully. "But he was quite correct. Mr. Templeton was not a rich man by any means; he was just a country squire, with a moderate income, which his first wife brought him, and of course her money was left to her daughters. Cedric is absolutely dependent on his sisters."

"Oh, Jacobi quite understands that."

"So much the better. Well, then, three or four years ago this mine was discovered, and that beggarly little farm has brought them quite a fortune. Elizabeth told me that their income was nearly doubled."

"Oh, then Jacobi was right when he said they were rich." And then Malcolm smiled bitterly as he remembered the two maiden ladies of uncertain age.

"Of course he was right. Dinah was talking to me on this very subject last May. She said then that she felt that Elizabeth would marry, and that in that case she would like her to have the Wood House. Of course, I am telling you this in confidence. 'Cedric will be my heir,' she continued; 'but I do not wish him to know this at present. It will be better for him to work, and not eat the bread of idleness;' and of course I approved of this. Now, Mr. Herrick, I must not wait a moment longer. Why do you not come down to the Manor House for a quiet Sunday?" But Malcolm excused himself. He was busy; he had been away so much, he could not take any more holidays, and so on. Mrs. Godfrey looked as though she hardly believed him.

"It would do you good," she persisted, looking at him very kindly. "This week we have a young American coming to us for two or three nights—Hugh Rossiter, the famous bear-hunter. I have often mentioned him to you. Alick is devoted to him; he says of all the acute Yankees he is the acutest, and that he could see through any number of brick walls. No, I will not ask you to meet him. Bears are not in your line. Come the week after." But Malcolm shook his head.

Much as he valued his friends, and dearly as he loved to be with them, the Manor House was the last place for him just then. Elizabeth's name would be frequently mentioned, and there would be constant references to the Wood House, and he fancied that at some unguarded moment he might betray himself. At present Mrs. Godfrey had no suspicion. She very naturally attributed his jaded looks to overwork, and he had been able to mask his feelings, except at that one dreadful moment. When she spoke of the intended marriage the sudden sickening pain at his heart told him that he could not trust himself. As he walked towards the station, when he had done his business, he pondered over all Mrs. Godfrey had told him.

Was it possible that the sisters had known all these weeks that Cedric had been thrown into daily and hourly contact with Leah Jacobi and her brother? Was it likely that Cedric had told them that there was even such a place as Shepherd's Hut?

Perhaps he did not mean to wilfully deceive them. Very probably he had his excuse ready. Malcolm could almost hear his words. " I said nothing about the Jacobis because I knew your prejudice, and I did not want to fluster you. I thought Mrs. Godfrey would spin her yarn, and I left it to her. It was not my fault if the Wallaces took to them, and that they were often up at Fettercairn." Some such words Cedric would say when he saw his sisters.

What a blessing term had begun and he was back at Oxford! He was safe from the Jacobis there. They would be in town probably; and then the fancy came into his head that he would find that out for himself before he went home. His evening hours always hung heavily on his hands, and a walk more or less would not hurt him,

That was the best of living with Bohemians. No one questioned his movements, or took it amiss if he were an hour or two late for meals.

He knew where the Jacobis lived—Cedric had told him —at 12 Gresham Gardens; so he went on to Queen's Road by train.

It was quite dark by that time, but he would just pass by the house and see if it were lighted up. His curiosity to know if they were there rather surprised himself. When he came in sight of No. 12 the door opened, and, unwilling to be seen, he stole into the portico of the next house, which was dark and uninhabited, and waited there for a moment.

He could hear Saul Jacobi's voice distinctly, smooth and unctuous as usual, and Leah's deep, flute-like tones chiming in. Somebody, a young man he guessed, was answering her. "You will not be late on Monday. I always like to be in good time for a new piece."

"That is so like a woman," interrupted her brother in a jeering voice. "Don't attend to her, old fellow; we have seats in the stalls, and you can please yourself."

"You bet, I always do that!" was the answer, in a slightly nasal tone. "Ta-ta, Jacobi;" and then a muscular, active-looking young man ran down the steps. Malcolm had just a glimpse of a lean brown face and deeply-set eyes, and then the door closed.

"Another string to the Jacobi bow," he thought as he followed him slowly. "I wonder how many he has." And then, as he walked back to the station, he made up his mind that as soon as possible he would run down to Oxford and have a talk with Cedric. "I think I could manage it on Friday or Saturday," he thought. "I should soon find out for myself if those people have done him any mischief."

Malcolm felt his conscience easier when he had planned this. Mrs. Godfrey had really made him very anxious about the boy. That evening he was less self-centred; the conversation had roused him; it gave him a dreary sort of satisfaction to know that there was still something that he could do for her.

He ate his supper with something of his old appetite, and the next evening he went to Queen's Gate and made himself very pleasant to his mother and Anna. " I think I shall run down to Oxford to-morrow or the next day," he said casually as he bade them good-night, " and look up Cedric Templeton," and he was still in the same mind when he woke the next morning. He would go to Lincoln's Inn and open his letters and see if he could get away that afternoon. But as he entered his chambers Malachi handed him a telegram that had just come. It was from the Manor House. " Please come at once. Hugh Rossiter here. Important news about Jacobi.— GODFREY."

CHAPTER XXVII

HUGH ROSSITER SPINS HIS YARN

Speak to me as to thy thinkings,
As thou dost ruminate, and give thy worst of thoughts
The worst of words.
Othello.

The reward of one duty is the power to fulfil another.—
GEORGE ELIOT.

MALCOLM read the telegram twice. Then he took up his time-table. A quarter of an hour later he was in a hansom on his way to the station. With all his impracticable fads and fancies, he was not one to let the grass grow under his feet. It was quite early, barely noon, when he walked up the hill leading to the Manor House; nevertheless Mrs. Godfrey was evidently on the watch for him.

"Good man," she said approvingly; "I knew you would not fail me;" and then she led him into the morning room, her own special sanctum, which opened into her husband's study.

Colonel Godfrey always called it his study, though it may be doubted if he ever studied anything but his *Times*, *Spectator*, and his three favourite authors, Thackeray, Dickens, and Kingsley; but his wife was a great reader, and there were few modern books that she could not discuss and criticise.

"And now, my dear lady, what is wrong?" asked Malcolm. He spoke with the coolness of the well-bred Englishman, who refuses to give himself away. In reality the telegram had made him very anxious—his old friend would not have summoned him without a good reason; but this was not apparent in his manner.

266

"Wrong!" she replied; "I think everything is wrong. Mr. Rossiter has been making us so uncomfortable; by his account Mr. Jacobi is a mere vulgar adventurer, if not worse."

"And Mr. Rossiter knows him?"

"Yes, in a sort of way. Miss Jacobi is evidently the attraction there. As he says himself, he knocks up against lots of shady characters in his nomadic existence. But you must question him yourself. It was Alick who made me send you the telegram, as Mr. Rossiter goes back to town this evening."

"You were quite right to send for me," returned Malcolm, and then he followed her into a pleasant room with a bay window overlooking the front drive.

Malcolm gave a slight start of recognition when he saw the American. It was not the first time he had seen the lean brown face and deep-set eyes, but he kept this to himself. In spite of his nasal twang and a little surface roughness, Hugh Rossiter was decidedly a gentleman: the mere fact of his presence at the Manor House was a sufficient proof of this. But he was evidently a very eccentric and unconventional being. In age he was about seven-and-thirty.

Malcolm, who felt his position was somewhat delicate, hardly knew how to begin the conversation; but Colonel Godfrey soon put things on a comfortable footing.

"Look here, Rossiter," he said frankly, "we are all friends here, and you may speak out. Mr. Herrick is very much interested in this young fellow, Cedric Templeton, and acts as a sort of guide, philosopher, and friend to him. He has always put his foot down as far as the Jacobis were concerned; he and my wife were dead against them."

"I never believed in the man," observed Malcolm; "there was no ring of true metal about him."

"You are about right there," returned the American;

"but I have come across worse fellows than Saul Jacobi. He is a clever chap—about as cute as they make 'em, and knows a trick or two; he is not too nice, does not stick at trifles, and the almighty dollar is his only deity."

"Do you mind telling my friend Herrick all you said to us?" asked Colonel Godfrey.

"Not the least, if you have a taste for chestnuts," and Hugh Rossiter laughed in a genial way. "I owe you a good turn, Colonel——" but here Colonel Godfrey held up a warning hand. "Well, I suppose I must spare your blushes, so I will take up my parable."

"May I ask you one question first?" interrupted Malcolm. "How long have you known these people?"

"About six or seven years, I should say," was the answer. "Jacobi was a billiard-marker in San Francisco when I first came across his trail, and his sister had just married an Italian count."

"Married! Leah Jacobi married! What on earth do you mean?"

"That's so," returned the American coolly. "Count Antonio Ferrari—that was the name; a hoary old sinner with a pedigree that nearly reached to Adam, and as rich and miserly as Shylock. He bid high for the girl, I can tell you that, but I believe our friend Saul had a tough job to get her to marry him."

"He is a greater brute than I thought him," returned Malcolm in a disgusted tone. "That poor girl!" Then Hugh Rossiter looked grave.

"It was a bit rough on her, but Jacobi was in Queer Street just then, and the old fellow gave him a helping hand."

"Jacobi is an Italian Jew, is he not?" Mr. Rossiter nodded.

"Yes, his father was an artist model in Rome—a fine-looking old fellow, I believe—and his mother sold flowers in the market. Some one told me she had been a model

too, and that they were rather a shady couple; but peace
to their manes! They have joined the majority long ago."

" And Saul Jacobi was a billiard-marker?"

" Yes, till they turned him out; and then he became
valet to a young millionaire who had more dollars than
brains. I was shooting grizzlies in the Rockies then, and
did not come across him again until eighteen months ago.
The millionaire was dead then; he never had any constitution worth mentioning, and he was evidently gradu-
ating for the idiot asylum. You bet, he would have taken
a first class there, for he had fits, poor beggar; so it was
a mercy that he went where the good niggers go."

" May I ask where you met Jacobi, Mr. Rossiter?"

" To be sure you may, and I have no objection to
answer. It was the Hôtel de Belleville at Paris. He was
sitting opposite to me at table-d'hôte, and his clothes were
so new and glossy that I contemplated them with admiration, not unmixed with awe. He had a valuable ring on
his finger, and a superb orchid in his buttonhole, and
looked like a millionaire himself; things had improved
with him, and the billiard-marker and valet were safely
shunted. Miss Jacobi was with him"—and here Hugh
paused a moment—" and she was handsomer than ever."

" Miss Jacobi—I suppose you mean the Contessa Ferrari?"

" No, Mr. Herrick, the marriage had worked badly.
Count Antonio was an infernal brute—excuse my strong
language. After a few months his behaviour was so
ɛ cious that the poor thing left him and fled to her
brother for protection. It would have been difficult, nay
impossible, for her to obtain a divorce. Count Antonio
was a wily old rascal, and he had too much influence at
court. There had been no proper settlements; he had
cheated them all through. Some people say he was mad,
that his father had been in a lunatic asylum; but when he
died he left all his money to charitable institutions."

"When did he die?"

Hugh Rossiter hesitated a moment. "Some time in September—I do not know the exact date. But he had been failing for months. I know a cousin of his, Count Orsino, and he was asking me what had become of the woman he married; but I did not give him much information."

"But why does she call herself Miss Jacobi when she is really the Contessa Ferrari?"

"Oh, that is just her craze. I believe she was a bit queer and unhinged when Jacobi got her back. Anyhow, he was obliged to pacify her a bit. She threw away her wedding-ring and never again alluded to her wretched marriage, and he is obliged to give in to her. I believe Jacobi was properly frightened that time. When I saw them in Paris Jacobi had just had a run of good luck. It is my private opinion he gambles. I once lost a good bit of money to him; but a burnt child dreads the fire—eh, Colonel? No more baccarat for me."

"And Miss Jacobi seemed in fairly good spirits?"

"Yes," hesitatingly; "but I fancied she had a fit of the blues sometimes, as though Count Antonio's ghost haunted her—oh, by the bye, he was still in the land of the living then. She and Jacobi seemed good friends, though she was evidently afraid of him. He told me one day, when he had been rather too free with the Burgundy, that she was in his way; that he wanted her to marry, and that he intended marrying himself; but he had promised her that her next husband should be young and an Englishman. I remember that this greatly surprised me. 'I understood that Count Antonio was living,' I observed; but Jacobi only winked at me in a stupid sort of way. 'Oh, we know all about that, my boy, but the gout will soon finish him; and there is no hurry—Leah is not thirty yet, and she is handsomer than she ever was in her life;' and he filled himself another bumper."

Malcolm was silent. Hugh Rossiter had apparently finished his recital, for he took up his meerschaum and polished it tenderly, an action that was full of suggestion. But Colonel Godfrey put his hand on his arm.

"One moment, my dear fellow, and then we will go out and have a smoke before luncheon. I can see Herrick has something else to ask you. Hurry up, my boy, or our friend here will lose patience."

"I shall be sorry to tax Mr. Rossiter's patience," replied Malcolm; "but I hope he will be good enough to satisfy me on one point. Is it your opinion," turning to him, "that Saul Jacobi and his sister have any designs on my friend Cedric Templeton?"

Hugh Rossiter opened his eyes rather widely at this. "Well, I suppose so—at least, Jacobi means her to marry him. Whew," with a droll gesture, "this is getting a trifle hot—you will be telling me next that you did not know they are engaged."

"Engaged! My good sir, excuse me, but this is no joke."

Mrs. Godfrey's face grew anxious. "You never told us that, Mr. Rossiter," she said rather reproachfully.

"I am not sure that I should have let the cat out of the bag now," he replied with a laugh, "if Mr. Herrick had not asked such a direct question. I am not one for meddling in other folks' business; but as this seems a grave matter, and my friend Saul is evidently playing the dark horse, I will tell you the little I know."

"I shall be obliged to you if you will do so," returned Malcolm, and Hugh Rossiter nodded good-humouredly.

"Well, then, I was dining at Gresham Gardens about a fortnight ago, and Jacobi told me in the course of conversation that his sister had never been to Oxford, and that they meant to run down for a day or two, and that a friend of theirs had offered to be showman and pilot them about the place."

Malcolm muttered something, and Mr. Rossiter stopped and looked at him inquiringly; but as he remained silent he resumed his narrative.

"They put up at the 'Ranelagh,' and had a good old time, and I believe, from a word Jacobi dropped, that the job was done then. I wanted to congratulate the lady, but Jacobi said that would do later on; his sister wished the engagement to be kept quiet, she had not been a widow for many weeks, and so on; so of course I took my cue. I am bound to say that Miss Jacobi seemed in unusually good spirits."

"And this is all you have to tell me?" asked Malcolm hurriedly.

"Well, now, I call that ungrateful, Colonel," with a droll look at his host; "here I have been talking myself dry for the last hour."

"And I am infinitely obliged to you," returned Malcolm, trying to smile. "The question is what are we to do next—there seems no time to be lost." And then, before any one could speak, he added, "I think it would be best for me to go down to Oxford at once." And as they all agreed that this would be the wisest course to pursue, Malcolm settled to go down by an early afternoon train.

They went out on the terrace after this, and Hugh Rossiter entertained them with a description of his adventures in Colorado, to which Malcolm listened somewhat absently; but once, when Colonel Godfrey had left them for a moment together, the American broke off his story rather suddenly.

"Look here, Mr. Herrick," he said quickly, "I want to give you a straight tip. If the youngster will not listen to reason, and you find yourself in a fix, just talk to the girl herself."

"To Miss Jacobi?" for he was naturally surprised at this piece of advice.

"Yes, to the fair Leah herself. Oh, the girl is not so

bad, considering her antecedents and the way she has been educated. Think of her own flesh and blood selling her to that son of Belial! Old Beelzebub, I call him. No wonder she got a bit queer. Jacobi knows how to manage her: she is fond of him, but she is afraid of him too. You will have to get her alone, remember that."

"Oh, that's the difficulty. Besides, I am not on visiting terms with the Jacobis."

"My good sir, what does that matter! I am to give you a straight tip, am I not? Well, then, to the best of my knowledge Miss Jacobi is in Kensington Gardens soon after ten every morning. She takes the dog for an airing before her brother is up. Saul is a lazy beast," continued Hugh Rossiter, "and is seldom down before mid-day. He takes his beauty sleep when the rest of the world is at work."

Malcolm thanked Mr. Rossiter cordially for this advice, and then the Colonel came back to them; but as they walked back to the house he stole more than one glance at the young American. The thin brown face was both intelligent and sagacious, and there was a keen, searching look in the brown eyes.

Why was this stranger so anxious to help him, he wondered. Was it mere good-humour and a wish to please, or had he any private reason of his own for desiring to break off this engagement? Had Leah Jacobi's strange beauty ensnared him too? He seemed to know her habits as though he were a constant visitor in Gresham Gardens. But his cool, impassive manner gave no clue to his feelings, and at this stage of the proceedings Malcolm was not to be enlightened. They parted in the friendliest manner. "Good luck to you, Mr. Herrick," he said cordially; "don't forget my straight tip."

Mrs. Godfrey walked with Malcolm to the station. She wanted a few last words, she said, and her mankind had had their innings.

18

"There is one thing you must do, if Cedric refuses to listen to reason," she said very seriously to him; "you must go down to Staplegrove and tell his sisters everything."

"I suppose I must," he returned; but he spoke under his breath, for this new duty filled him with dismay. He had shaken off the dust of Staplegrove, as he believed, for ever, and the thought that he must stand face to face with Elizabeth again turned him giddy. "I suppose in that case I must do it," he went on. His hesitating manner made Mrs. Godfrey look at him.

"It is the only thing to be done," she repeated firmly. "You must see them both and tell them all Hugh Rossiter said. Dinah will be very much upset, but Elizabeth never loses her wits; she will grasp everything in a minute—Elizabeth has such a clear head, and she never muddles things—and then you can hold a friendly council."

"Of course I will do what I can to help them," he replied quietly, for he had been fully aware of Mrs. Godfrey's look; but as he sat in the first-class compartment he told himself with some irritation that his position was a cruel one.

"It is Carlyon who ought to be the family adviser now," he thought. "If I could only wash my hands of this business! What a fool Cedric is to get himself into this mess. Good lack, to think he has fallen among thieves for the second time! The young jackanapes seems to have a natural affinity for sharpers and swindlers. That infernal cad Jacobi!" and here Malcolm boiled with impotent wrath as he thought of that dastardly conspiracy to entrap a young and innocent girl. "I should like to horsewhip him," he went on; "how is one to keep one's hands off such a fellow! He may be a dark horse, as Rossiter says, but he will have to reckon with me." And Malcolm straightened his shoulders with quite a martial air, as though he were ready to fight to the death.

CHAPTER XXVIII

"THE LADY CALLING HERSELF MISS JACOBI"

Master, master! news, old news, and such news as you never heard of!—*Taming of the Shrew.*

The first and worst of all frauds is to cheat oneself.—BAILEY, *Festus.*

MALCOLM had telegraphed to Verity to pack his Gladstone bag and send it by special messenger to Paddington. Verity, who was accustomed to these commissions, had fulfilled her orders with neatness and despatch, and he found it waiting for him on his arrival at the station. It was nearly half-past six when the spires and pinnacles of the old collegiate city came in sight, so he drove straight to the "Randolph," ordered his room, then dined and refreshed himself after his journey; and it was not until after eight that he went across to St. John's and found his way to Cedric's rooms.

Cedric's sisters had taken great pride and pleasure in furnishing them, and they were the envy of all his friends. A rather impatient "Come in," answered Malcolm's knock.

Cedric was at his writing-table, but he was evidently not at work. He gave a surprised exclamation when he saw his visitor's face; but Malcolm at once perceived that he was not welcome. Cedric frowned slightly and closed his blotting-case, but not before Malcolm's sharp eyes had caught sight of a cabinet photograph of Leah Jacobi.

"What on earth has brought you to Oxford?" asked Cedric in rather an uneasy tone. "I thought it was one of our fellows, and was just swearing to myself for forgetting to sport the oak. I suppose you are staying with Dr. Medcalf as usual?"

"No, I had no time to let him know; I am sleeping at the 'Randolph,'" returned Malcolm quietly. "I am sorry to interrupt you, my boy," with another glance at the blotting-case; "but I have only a few hours, so I have no time to lose. May I take this comfortable chair?" —sinking into it as he spoke. "I have just dined, so we might as well smoke a friendly weed together."

"You can help yourself—there are some excellent cigars in that drawer—but I do not feel like smoking myself." Cedric spoke rather sulkily and with none of his accustomed amiability. "Shall I give you some whiskey and soda?" But Malcolm refused this refreshment—no man was more abstemious than he.

"If you want to finish your letter I can look at the paper for half an hour;" but this suggestion seemed only to irritate Cedric.

"Oh, there is no hurry," he returned hastily; "I could not write a sentence decently, feeling you were waiting for me to finish. Well," struggling with his ill-humour, "what have you been doing with yourself since you left Staplegrove? You look rather seedy and a bit pale about the gills—do you and the giant smoke too much?"

"Oh, I am well enough," replied Malcolm hurriedly. "If we come to that, you have rather a weedy appearance yourself;" for Cedric looked decidedly thinner, and his eyes were almost unnaturally bright. He seemed older, too, and changed in some undefinable way; but he had never looked handsomer. Malcolm forgot his own troubles in his anxiety to prevent his protégé falling into the hands of the adventurer, Saul Jacobi. For the moment his own soul seemed to yearn over the boy who was his sisters' darling and the object of their thoughts and prayers.

"Look here, old fellow," he went on, as Cedric seemed

relapsing into moody silence, " there is no use beating about the bush. I have come down to-night to have a talk with you, because a report has reached my ears. Is it true that you have been mad enough to engage yourself to the lady calling herself Miss Jacobi?" Then Cedric flushed up, and his eyes blazed with anger.

" May I ask if the report be true?" went on Malcolm, taking no notice of Cedric's fiery looks.

" I object to the manner in which you frame your question," returned Cedric proudly. Strange to say, at that moment he reminded Malcolm of Elizabeth. " Granted that such a report were true, I fail to see where the madness comes in. Any man might consider himself fortunate in winning the affections of a woman like Leah Jacobi."

" And you are engaged to her? Speak out, man; I suppose you don't intend to keep your engagement dark?"

" Of course not," angrily; but Cedric's manner was decidedly embarrassed, and he seemed unwilling to look Malcolm in the face. " But I must tell you, Herrick, that I strongly object to the way you are questioning me. I don't want to quarrel with you, but what the deuce can it matter to you if I choose to keep my private affairs to myself for a week or two! I have reasons of my own for not wishing my sisters to hear of my engagement for a fortnight or so. I—I," hesitating and floundering in his sentence, " meant to tell them myself, and to introduce Leah to them. It is a confounded shame," lashing himself up to great wrath, " that it should have leaked out in this underhand fashion. May I ask how you got your information?"

Malcolm considered for a moment; then he made up his mind that it was best to be perfectly open.

" I had it from a man who knows the Jacobis. His name is Hugh Rossiter. He is a friend of the Godfreys."

Cedric started. " I had quite forgotten that," he mut-

tered; "the fat's in the fire with a vengeance." Then
aloud, "Why, the fellow's in love with Leah himself. He
made up to her, only Jacobi would not hear of it. He said
he could not bear the idea of the roving, uncomfortable
life she would have to lead as his wife."

"Mr. Rossiter is not well off, is he?" asked Malcolm
tentatively. Then Cedric looked at him as if he suspected
some *arrière pensée*.

"No, he has lost a good bit of money lately—invested
it in some rotten concern or other. Jacobi says he can't
afford to have a wife."

"I should have thought he would have said the same
of you," rather pointedly. "He must be aware that you
have only an allowance from your sisters?" And at this
plain speaking Cedric reddened again with annoyance.

"I suppose I shall have a profession some day," he
returned with a lordly air; "and as my sisters are rich,
and Dinah is certainly not likely to marry, I think I may
safely count on a pretty handsome allowance."

"If you marry in accordance with your sister's wish,
I should think you are right," returned Malcolm coolly.
"My dear fellow, would it not have been as well to find
this out before you pledged yourself to the lady?"

"There was no necessity for that," replied Cedric;
"Jacobi seemed quite satisfied with my prospects. He
is not a bit grasping. He told me that he wished his
sister to marry a gentleman; that he had been to the
Wood House and seen my sisters, and he was quite willing to give his sanction to the engagement; and as Leah
and I understood each other perfectly, I had no difficulty
with her. Why don't you congratulate me, Herrick," exclaimed the lad excitedly, "instead of badgering and
cross-examining me like an Old Bailey witness? I am
the happiest fellow in existence! Leah's a darling—there
is not such a woman in the world!"

"Is there not?" returned Malcolm quietly. His face

looked a little haggard as he spoke, and there was a wistful, pining look in his eyes. Oh, why was the boy so
like Elizabeth? There was no real similarity—it was
only a trick of expression, a turn of the head, a sudden
impulsive movement that recalled her. "May I ask one
more question, old fellow? Is it by your own or Mr.
Jacobi's wish that the engagement is kept a secret?" But
Cedric refused to answer this. He said with a good
deal of dignity that there were limits to everything. He
had a great respect for Herrick, and always looked upon
him as his best friend, but he must excuse him answering
this.

"Well—well, we will talk of that again," returned
Malcolm; but in his own mind he was certain that Saul
Jacobi had his own reasons for preventing the news of
Cedric's engagement from reaching his sisters' ears.
"There is another question I must ask you. Why do
you call your *fiancée* Miss Jacobi?"

Cedric stared at him.

"I suppose because it is her name," he replied rather
impatiently. "What a fellow you are, Herrick! I think
your wits must be wool-gathering."

"Oh dear, nothing of the kind; I am not mad, most
noble Felix, but in my sane, sober senses. I am quite
aware the lady you wish to marry was at one time Leah
Jacobi, but her married name is the Countess Antonio
Ferrari."

"What!" exclaimed Cedric, springing to his feet; but
he added something rather stronger. "Confound you,
Herrick, what do you mean by talking such infernal rot?"

"Sit down," returned Malcolm calmly; "I can't talk
while you are walking to and fro like the old gentleman.
My dear boy, I am sorry to give you this shock, but do
you actually mean to tell me that you do not know that
Leah Jacobi is a widow—that neither she nor her brother
have informed you of her previous marriage?"

"No," broke from Cedric's lips; he seemed quite stunned. Then he exclaimed indignantly, "But it is a lie—a cursed lie!"

"You would hardly dare to say that to Hugh Rossiter's face, Cedric," returned Malcolm somewhat sternly. "He was my informant; he knew the Jacobis when Saul Jacobi was a billiard-marker in San Francisco, and his sister living with her husband in Verona. You have been badly treated, my dear boy—how badly you little know. You have been encouraged to make love to a married woman. When you were at Fettercairn, Count Antonio was still alive; he only died last month."

Cedric seemed too dazed to take it in. He got up from his chair, in spite of his friend's remonstrance, and began to pace the room again. "Impossible," he muttered; "I will not believe it. She knew then that I loved her, and she promised to marry me if Saul gave his consent. For some reason he seemed to hold off a bit, but we were as good as engaged then."

"Ah, I thought so," returned Malcolm drily; and then, like a skilful surgeon, he did his work thoroughly; to be kind it was necessary to be cruel, so he spared Cedric no particulars. He told him all he knew himself; he saw him wince when he spoke of the Roman models and the billiard-marker turned into a valet.

"Saul Jacobi told me his father was a banker and his mother of noble blood, one of the Orsinos; I suppose he was ashamed of it all, and wanted to keep it back. He might have trusted me and told the truth," faltered the lad.

"Instead of which he told you this pack of lies. And his sister is no better, for she has lied to you too; and this is the sister-in-law you propose to introduce at the Wood House—a woman who has allowed you to make love to her in her husband's lifetime!"

"Look here, Herrick," returned Cedric hoarsely—his

fresh young face looked quite gray—" not a word against her—not a word against my Leah. You may be right about Jacobi—I have had my doubts about him once or twice myself; he is not always kind to Leah, he bullies her dreadfully and she is afraid of him, and he is too fond of getting his own way. But I won't believe that she is to blame. Anyhow, she is more sinned against than sinning. I will go to her to-morrow and make her tell me everything. No one shall come between us—not even Saul Jacobi. Leah shall account to me for this deception. I will get to the bottom of it as sure as my name is Cedric Templeton."

Cedric spoke with an air of resolution that secretly surprised Malcolm. " It will make a man of him," he said to himself—" it will make a man of him." Then he put his hand on his shoulder.

" My dear boy," he said kindly, " I feel for you from the bottom of my heart, but you must be very firm. There can be no compromise or vacillation in a case like this; you must give her up, Cedric—you must break off this unlucky engagement." But Cedric would not be induced to promise this; he would decide nothing until he had seen Leah and heard the whole story from her lips. " No one shall come between us," cried the poor lad; " she is my promised wife." Then Malcolm's manner changed and became more resolute.

" It will be a wrench, of course," he returned; " desperate diseases require desperate remedies. But, Cedric, listen to me. If you refuse to take my advice you will repent it all your life. If you go to Gresham Gardens to-morrow you will be a lost man. The Jacobis will talk you over and persuade you that black is white. At least let me accompany you?" But Cedric absolutely refused this, and Malcolm could not press it.

" You mean kindly, Herrick," he observed hurriedly, " but a man must manage his own business. I shall have to leave you now, if I am to see the Dean to-night and get permission for a few hours' absence; and as I shall probably go up by the early train to-morrow, I shall not see you again."

"I shall be in my rooms at Lincoln's Inn by mid-day," returned Malcolm, "will you come to me there?" But Cedric hesitated.

"I shall have to go back to Oxford," he returned; "I think I had better write to you." But this proposal by no means satisfied Malcolm.

"That will not do," he said decidedly. "I would rather you wired to me from Paddington—the letter can follow. Surely you can have no objection," he continued, as Cedric seemed reluctant to do this; "it will set my mind at rest, and I shall have a better night;" and then Cedric rather ungraciously promised that a telegram should be sent.

"You must be very firm," were Malcolm's parting words, and Cedric nodded impatiently as he put on his cap and gown.

Malcolm slept restlessly; he was tired and anxious, and had done a hard day's work. His failure to influence Cedric troubled him greatly.

"They will talk him over," he repeated, "and that woman will lure him into her wiles again;" and Malcolm felt there was grave cause for fear, as he remembered Leah's rare beauty, and the strange brilliancy of her dark, melancholy eyes. Oh, what would Dinah Templeton say if she knew of the danger that threatened her cherished boy!

Malcolm tossed restlessly on his bed as he tried to formulate plans, which he rejected one by one. "If it comes to the worst, I must do as Mrs. Godfrey suggests," he thought—"I must go down to the Wood House and take counsel with them;" and in all probability it was this thought that kept him wakeful.

The next morning Malcolm learnt from Cedric's scout that his master had left by an early train; and as he himself had one or two appointments that morning, he only waited to swallow a hasty breakfast before he followed him.

For the next few hours he was very busy, and could hardly give Cedric a thought; but as work slackened and the afternoon wore on, he wondered at the non-arrival of the telegram. It was half-past four before Malachi brought in the yellow envelope. Malcolm frowned as he read it.

" Know all—have forgiven all—engagement holds good—sorry cannot take advice.—TEMPLETON."

" Unhappy boy," he groaned, " the fowler has him in his net again." Then he scrunched the thin paper in his hand, and set his teeth hard like a man who sees the dentist coming towards him with the forceps.

" I must go down to them; there is nothing else for me to do. I dare not take the responsibility of keeping this to myself an hour longer. It is all in the day's work, as the lion-tamer said when the lion prepared to bite off his head." And after this grim jest Malcolm summoned Malachi and confided the Gladstone bag to his care, and they sallied forth together. At Waterloo he sent off a telegram to Verity; a few minutes later he was in the train and on his way to Earlsfield.

CHAPTER XXIX

"SHE IS A WICKED WOMAN"

Am I cold—
Ungrateful—that for these most manifold
High gifts, I render nothing back at all?
Not so! not cold, but very poor instead.
E. BARRETT BROWNING.

To love, is to be made up of faith and service.—SHAKESPEARE.

IT was half-past six when Malcolm reached the well-known station, and taking a fly bade the man drive him to the "King's Arms," an old-fashioned inn of good repute about half a mile distant from the Wood House. Here he secured a room for the night; ordered supper, of which he partook without appetite; then sallied forth to pay his call. It was late in October, and the darkness of the country roads surprised him, accustomed as he was to the well-lighted London streets; he could scarcely find out his bearings until a welcome light streamed out from the windows of the Crow's Nest. Malcolm lingered a moment at the little gate. "It was there I dwelt in my fool's paradise," he muttered, "and tried to eat of the forbidden fruit. Now I know good and evil, and am a sadder and wiser man." And then he went on doggedly; but he stopped again before he reached the gate of the Wood House, for he knew intuitively that he had stumbled into the little path leading to the woodlands. He strained his eyes through the darkness, but could see nothing—only the chill, damp October wind played round him, and the smell of moist earth and decaying vegetation filled his nostrils. "Change and decay in all around I

284

see," he thought heavily; but as he turned away and crossed the road a sudden remembrance came to him and made him giddy.

It was morning or early afternoon, he forgot which, and the sunshine was filtering through the firs, and steeping his senses with the warm, resinous perfume—"spices of Araby," he had called it to himself, for he loved the scent above all things. He had clambered up the bank to pick some honeysuckle, and then the little gate had clanged on its hinges, and he had peeped through the brambles to see who was coming.

And of course he knew who it was—that tall, robust young woman in the white sun-bonnet who came down the path swinging her arms slightly, but with the free proud step of an empress. "Elizabeth, Elizabeth!" he had whispered even then, and all the manhood within him seemed to welcome her gracious presence. Poor fool—poor blind fool that he was!

Perhaps it was as well that Malcolm stumbled over the root of a tree at that moment; the rude shock roused him. "It is a blessing I have not sprained my ankle," he said to himself; but he had struck his foot rather severely and limped on with difficulty. The pain sobered him, and he thought how Elizabeth had told him that they always used lanterns in the grounds; and he made up his mind to borrow one for his return journey.

"I wonder if Carlyon will be there," he muttered, as he went up to the front door. He had never seen it closed before, for in summer it was always open from morning to night. Somehow the sight chilled him: he was outside in the darkness and the cold, and for him no household fires would burn warm and bright, and a bitter sigh came to his lips.

He had raised his hand to the bell, when the door opened suddenly, and the rosy-cheeked housemaid he remembered peered out into the darkness. She was evidently very much startled when she saw Malcolm.

"Did you ring, sir?" she asked in some confusion, "for no one heard a bell. The ladies are still in the dining-room, but I will tell Mullins."

"Please do not bring them, I can well wait. I know my way to the drawing-room." And Malcolm put down his hat and crossed the hall, which looked warm and cheery with its bright fire.

The lamps had been lighted in the drawing-room, and the fireplace was heaped with pine logs that spluttered and blazed merrily, and diffused a sort of aromatic fragrance. There were pleasant tokens of feminine occupation on the round table: an open book and a knitting basket that he knew belonged to Dinah, and a piece of embroidery of an ecclesiastical pattern, over which he had often seen Elizabeth bending. There were the very gold scissors and thimble that she had once left down by the Pool, which cost him and Cedric an hour's search before they could find them. How pleased she had been when he had brought them back to her! Malcolm felt an irresistible desire to hold them in his hand a moment—then he turned quickly away.

There was a little side window in the drawing-room that formed a sort of alcove; it was fitted up very prettily with palms and flowering plants, and amongst the foliage stood a beautiful marble figure of a Roman peasant with her pitcher on her shoulder.

Malcolm had often admired it. It was the work of a young German sculptor, whom the sisters found in somewhat distressing circumstances in Rome, with a sick wife and hampered with debt. Arnim Freiligrath always regarded the dear ladies, as he called them, as his benefactresses, for, strange to say, from that time orders flowed in upon him, and he was soon looked upon as a rising and successful sculptor.

Dinah had once told Malcolm that the woman's features reminded her of Elizabeth, and Malcolm had agreed with her.

"I think it is the figure that most resembles your sister," he had said; "but you were wise to buy it, it is very beautiful, and Arnim Freiligrath is becoming quite the fashion."

Malcolm stepped up to the alcove; he would look at his favourite water-carrier again. He put aside the heavy plush curtains that half-veiled the recess, but the next moment he recoiled—for Elizabeth herself was standing there, almost as motionless as the marble woman beside her.

She was lost in thought, and had evidently not heard his footfall on the soft carpet, and she was gazing out into the darkness. Something in her expression arrested Malcolm's attention: he had never seen her look like that before, her lips were pressed tightly together, and her eyes were full of sadness. One hand was resting lightly on the statue, and Malcolm could see the gleam of the opal ring on her finger.

He feared to startle her, and yet it was impossible for him to stand there any longer. He pronounced her name almost timidly; and as Elizabeth started violently and turned round, he could see the tears glistening in the large gray eyes.

"Mr. Herrick," in an astonished tone, as she gave him her hand—it was very cold, and trembled a little in his grasp—"what makes you steal upon us like a ghost in the darkness? Why did you not tell us you were coming?"

"I thought it would be better not," he returned quietly. "I wanted to speak to you and your sister about something that seemed to me important." Then Elizabeth gave him one of her quick, searching glances.

"It is about Cedric," she said abruptly—"that boy has got into trouble again?" Then Malcolm bowed his head. They were standing on the rug before the fire now, and at Malcolm's mute answer Elizabeth shivered slightly and held out her hands to the blaze as though she were physically cold. Malcolm leant for support against the mantelpiece, and watched her for a moment under his shading hand—if she had only seen that hungry, eloquent look! But Elizabeth's eyes were fixed on the fire. Poor Malcolm! never had she looked more beautiful to him: the black velvet gown suited her to perfection, and the antique Roman necklace she wore just fitted the full white throat. This was not the rustic owner of the white sunbonnet, but a grand, imperial-looking Elizabeth. Malcolm felt as though he were fast losing self-control: his forehead grew clammy, and though he tried to speak—to break the embarrassing silence—no words would come; but Elizabeth, lost in her own sad thoughts, was oblivious of his emotion.

"Dinah will be here directly," she observed presently; "she is engaged just now with a woman from the village, but she will not be long, I hope. I trust"—and here she looked at him anxiously—"that you have no bad news for us."

"I am afraid it is not good," he replied evasively.

"It has something to do with those odious Jacobis?" Again Malcolm bowed his head.

"Cedric seems infatuated about them," she returned, with something of her old impetuosity, the words tripping each other up in the usual Elizabethan way. "We thought the man detestable—even Dinah could not tolerate him. Oh," interrupting herself, "what am I thinking about? you have come all this distance on our account, and I have never thought of your comfort—you have not dined, of course;" and Elizabeth's hand was on the bell, but he stopped her.

"I have just had supper at the 'King's Arms,' where I have taken a bed; I want nothing, I assure you."

"At the 'King's Arms'!" exclaimed Elizabeth. Then she suddenly flushed and bit her lip. She had forgotten —how could she suppose that anything would induce him to sleep under their roof again! Malcolm's manner, his painful air of consciousness, the deep melancholy in his eyes, told her plainly that his trouble was as fresh as ever.

Elizabeth began to feel nervous; it was a relief to both of them when Mullins entered the room with the coffee. "At least, you will have a cup of coffee," she said with a little effort. "Mullins, will you put the tray down, and tell my sister that Mr. Herrick has come down to speak to us on business, and ask her not to keep him waiting."

Malcolm did not refuse the coffee. As he took the cup in his hand he said in a low voice, "I hope Mr. Carlyon is well."

"Thank you, he is far from well," she returned gravely. "Mr. Charrington has been away for the last six weeks, and he has had far too much to do; he has taken a bad cold, and his cough is troublesome. I have been speaking to Dr. Randolph to-day, and he thinks the vicar ought to come back." Then she stopped as Dinah came hurriedly into the room. Malcolm's unexpected visit had evidently alarmed her.

"Oh, Mr. Herrick, what is it?" she said in such a troubled voice that Malcolm felt almost afraid to tell his news. Evidently Elizabeth read his thoughts.

"You must tell us everything," she said rather abruptly; "it will be wrong to keep anything back." And thus admonished, Malcolm began his long story—his summons to the Manor House, and Hugh Rossiter's revelation concerning the Jacobi family. The sisters listened in breathless silence, only when Malcolm mentioned the words billiard-marker and valet Elizabeth uttered a quick exclamation, and threw up her head with a

19

proud gesture, while poor Dinah grew white when she heard that her boy was actually engaged. "It is impossible—there must be some mistake," she whispered, as though to herself—"our dear boy would never keep such a thing from his sisters. Cedric is so frank and open, he would never have secrets from us."

"Cedric is under a bad influence," replied Malcolm; "these people have got hold of him and will not let him go." And then he went on to tell of his interview with Cedric, and his total want of success. "I could do nothing," he went on despondently; "I seem to have lost my influence with him. I did my best, Miss Templeton," with an appealing look at Dinah's sad, sweet face; but it was Elizabeth who answered him.

"Do you think we do not know that," she returned impulsively—"that Dinah and I are not grateful to you! You have taken all this trouble for us—you have been to Cookham and Oxford, and now you have come here, and you are quite tired and worn out with the worry of it all, and we can do nothing for you in return!" and Elizabeth quivered with emotion. But Malcolm, suppressing his own agitation, tried to turn off her speech with a laugh. She was grateful to him—good heavens! she might as well have offered a cupful of earth to a man dying of thirst!

"Let him finish, Betty dear," observed Dinah faintly; "he has more to tell us." And then Malcolm produced the telegram and laid it before them. The sisters glanced at each other with dismay, and Dinah's forehead was furrowed like an old woman's.

"What is to be done, Mr. Herrick, to save my poor boy from this iniquitous marriage?" she inquired in a tremulous tone, and Elizabeth's eyes were asking him the same question.

"That is just the difficulty, my dear lady," he replied slowly. "If I can only see my way clear—Mr. Rossiter advised me to speak to Miss Jacobi; he seems to think she is more amenable to reason than her brother, and probably he is right." But to Malcolm's surprise Dinah's mild eyes began to flush angrily.

"I have a worse opinion of her than I have of her brother," she said hurriedly; "she is a wicked woman—she let men make love to her when she knew her husband was alive! If she marries Cedric, I will never see her or him either;" and here Dinah trembled from head to foot.

Elizabeth, startled by the excitement of one generally so gentle, knelt down by her sister and put her arms round her. "Dear Die," she implored, "don't make it worse for us all. Mr. Herrick is trying to help us, and we must not make things more difficult for him. What do you advise?" she continued, turning to Malcolm. "You have seen this Leah—would it be better to bribe or frighten her?"

"That is impossible for me to say," returned Malcolm, averting his eyes quickly from the earnest, troubled face. "I have only exchanged a few words with Miss Jacobi, and know little about her."

"You mean the Contessa Ferrari," interrupted Dinah almost harshly; "for heaven's sake let the woman be called by her right name!"

"It is a name she refuses to own," he returned quietly. "Will you let me say what I really think?—you know I have only seen her twice. I think she is a wronged and unhappy woman, and that her troubles have hardened her nature and made her reckless. Her brother tyrannises over her, and she has never been free to lead her own life or follow her own better impulses, and her beauty and wonderful fascination have only been used to further Saul Jacobi's ambitious aims. In my opinion Cedric was right when he declared to me that she was more sinned against than sinning."

"Then in that case you will be able to influence her,"

returned Dinah quickly. "Tell her from me, Mr. Herrick, that if she persists in marrying my poor boy, she will be marrying a pauper; that on the day the marriage takes place I shall alter my will, and that my sister Elizabeth will be my heir. Tell her this, and I will write to Cedric and let him know what he has to expect."

"Do you really mean this?" asked Malcolm, much impressed by this unexpected resolution on the part of one usually so yielding and gentle.

"I mean every word," returned Dinah firmly. "Yes, Betty dear," as she saw her sister's astonished face, "I am perfectly serious. You know what Cedric is to me"— and here her sweet voice quavered for a moment—"if it would do him good, I would give him half my fortune at this moment, and would never grudge it; but no money of mine shall be used for his undoing. Let him give up this woman and come back to me, and there is nothing I will not do for him. Am I right, Elizabeth? Do you agree with me?"

"I agree with you, and you are always right, darling. Mr. Herrick, will you do as she says, and make this Leah understand that she has nothing to expect from us. Oh, what trouble we are giving you, and we have no right!" and here Elizabeth turned her head away in pained confusion. She had said the wrong thing. Why did not Dinah come to her assistance and say some word of grateful acknowledgment?

"You have every right to use me as you will," returned Malcolm in a low voice, "for I have done nothing to forfeit your friendship." And with a dreary attempt at a smile—"A friend is born for adversity." Then Elizabeth rose from her kneeling position, but she did not answer—perhaps she could not, for Malcolm's worn face and sad, kind eyes seemed to bring a sudden lump to her throat. How good he was—how generous and forgiving and unselfish! She longed to take his hand

and bid God bless him; but she could not trust herself
or him. "It has gone too deep," she said with inward
wonder, for Elizabeth was truly humble in her estimation
of herself. Dinah was too much wrapped up in her own
troubled thoughts to notice Elizabeth's emotion.

"Will you tell me what you mean to do?" she asked
anxiously, for Malcolm had risen too as though he intended to take his leave. He explained briefly that he
intended to act on Hugh Rossiter's suggestion. He would
waylay Leah Jacobi in Kensington Gardens and do his
best to induce her to give Cedric up.

"I shall tell her you have written to him and advise
her to talk things over with her brother. 'When he
knows Cedric Templeton is not his sister's heir, he will
be the first to insist that your projected marriage should
be broken off'—I shall say some such words to her."

"And you will come down again, and let us know the
result of your interview?" and Dinah looked at him im-
ploringly. "Your room shall be ready for you at any
time."

"You are very kind," he returned hesitating. "My
room at the 'King's Arms' seems very comfortable."
Then Dinah understood and changed colour slightly.

"It will be giving you trouble," she observed regretfully.

"No—no, it is not that," he returned hurriedly; "but
it is impossible to say how things may be—what circumstances, or what complications may arise to keep me in
town. I will write—you shall not be kept in suspense an
hour longer than I can help; and you may depend on me
that I will do my utmost to break off this wretched engagement."

"I trust you implicitly," returned Dinah gravely.
"You will forgive me if I cannot thank you properly to-
night."

"You need not move, Die; I will light Mr. Herrick's

lantern for him"—Elizabeth spoke in her old natural way. Malcolm stood beside her silently as she performed her hospitable task. Then she placed it in his hand. "I wonder how you groped your way through the plantation," she said smiling; "but this little glimmer will guide you safely. Good-night, Mr. Herrick; we shall look eagerly for your promised letter. Poor Dinah will have one of her bad sick headaches to-morrow—worry always brings them on."

"She looks far from well," replied Malcolm; "I fear this has been a great shock to her, and to you too;" and then he shook hands and went out into the darkness. When he was half-way down the drive he turned round— the door was still open, and the cheerful light streamed out into the blackness. Elizabeth was standing on the threshold looking after him. When she saw him stop she waved her hand with a friendly ' good-night;' then the door closed, and there was only the October darkness, and an eerie, wandering wind moaning through the woodlands.

CHAPTER XXX

IN KENSINGTON GARDENS

If you would fall into any extreme, let it be on the side of gentleness. The human mind is so constructed that it resists vigour and yields to softness.—St. Francis de Sales.

Malcolm went up by an early train the next morning. He had a long day's work before him—a mass of correspondence to sift, several business interviews, and some proofs to revise. It was later than usual when he went back to Cheyne Walk, but Verity had put aside his dinner for him, and sat beside him while he ate it. She even brought him coffee with her own hands. Perhaps these little womanly attentions soothed him insensibly—though he was so used to them by this time that he was almost tempted to take them as a matter of course—for his face lost its strained, weary look.

" There is a beautiful fire in your room, Mr. Herrick," she observed cheerfully before she left him. " I shall tell Amias that you are tired, and that he must not expect you in the studio to-night."

Malcolm smiled gratefully. " What a good little soul you are, Verity—you always say just the right thing! Tell Goliath, with my love, that I am busy, so there must be no pipe and no palaver to-night. I shall have to be up betimes too;" and then he took counsel with Verity as to the hour when his breakfast should be served.

It was quite true that he had business waiting to be done; nevertheless, as he lay back in his easy-chair by the fire, he could not bring himself to take up his pen. At this very hour on the previous evening he had been with

295

Elizabeth; the dear face—dearer, alas! than ever—had
been before him; the changing, characteristic voice, so
musical yet so uneven, had been in his ears! He recalled
her look as she stood so wrapt in thought in the alcove
before she perceived his presence. Its deep sadness had
surprised him. What could be troubling her? In a few
months she would marry the man she loved. Truly God's
best gifts were hers—health, wealth, and love—and yet
the shadowed brow and the eyes misty with unshed tears
seemed to speak of some hidden sorrow. What could it
be? That was his last waking thought that night, and
the question still troubled him when he walked the next
morning in the direction of Kensington Gardens to keep
his self-made tryst with Leah Jacobi.

He knew the gate that was nearest to Gresham Gardens; but it was long before the hour that Hugh Rossiter had mentioned when he reached it, and began pacing
up and down like a sentinel on duty.

Fortunately the morning was fine, and a faint gleam of
sunshine tried to penetrate the thin haze brooding over
the Gardens. Although it was the last day of October,
the air was mild; but, contrary to his usual custom, Malcolm failed to notice the effect of the clinging mist round
the leafless trees, the nebulous distances, and the faint
golden streaks of sunshine; his mind was full of the approaching interview and the difficult work that lay before
him.

It was so early that the place seemed quite deserted;
but presently he heard dogs barking, and the next moment two little fox-terriers, curiously alike, rushed past
him intent on their play. He recognised them at once
from Cedric's description—they were Tim and Tartar,
belonging to Saul Jacobi; and he knew their mistress
was at hand.

He looked at her intently as she came slowly towards
him. She wore a dark red dress and jacket, that set off

her graceful figure, and her close velvet hat was a darker shade of the same colour.

On any one else the effect might have been too striking, but it exactly suited her; and as Malcolm noticed the exquisite colour of her face and the wonderful coils of black hair, he was obliged to acknowledge that Cedric's temptation had been strong, and that many an older man might have lost his heart to so beautiful a creature.

Leah's eyes had been fixed on the ground, and she did not see Malcolm until she was quite close to him; but, though she was evidently surprised to meet him, she only bowed gravely, and would have passed on. But Malcolm placed himself at her side.

"You are an early riser, Miss Jacobi," he observed in a friendly tone. "Are you always so energetic?"

"I like an early morning walk," she replied quietly; but there was an uneasy flush on her face, as though she found Malcolm's society embarrassing. "I generally have the Gardens to myself at this hour. My brother is a late riser, and this is my leisure time. I have never met you here before, Mr. Herrick;" and here Leah gave him a quick, furtive glance from under her long lashes.

"I daresay not," he retured coolly, "this is hardly my beat. To tell you the truth, Miss Jacobi, my errand is to you this morning." A quick, undefinable expression almost resembling fear came over her face; but she answered him quietly.

"You have come here to talk to me?" with an air of well-simulated surprise. "How could you know my habits? I think," a little stiffly, "we have only met twice."

"You are quite right, Miss Jacobi. I spoke to you first in the porch at Cookham church, and the second time at the Etheridges—as far as that goes we are little acquainted with each other; but we have a mutual friend, you and I." Then he saw her eyes suddenly droop.

"Forgive me if I am abrupt," he went on, "but the matter concerns me intimately. I am informed that you are engaged to my friend Cedric Templeton."

It was evident that she was prepared for this—the bolt out of the blue had not startled her. She stood still and looked at him with an air of proud displeasure.

"May I ask the name of your informant, Mr. Herrick?" she asked coldly; but he saw that she knew.

"Why should I not have heard it from Cedric himself —we are close friends?" but he watched her narrowly as he said this.

"Because he would be the last person to tell you." Then she checked herself, as she saw the snare he had laid for her. "What if I am engaged to him?" as though determined to brave it out; "it can surely be no business of yours, Mr. Herrick." There was rising temper in Leah's voice.

"You must forgive me if I say that I differ from you there—my friend's interests are my own. Miss Jacobi, how can you reconcile it to your conscience to injure that poor boy's prospects by entering into a clandestine engagement with him?"

He could see her eyes flash with anger, but she made no reply.

"You know his position. He is utterly dependent on his sisters—his father left him nothing; he has no profession; he has not even finished his university training; he is far too young to think of marrying."

She opened her lips to speak, and then closed them resolutely again.

"Pardon me if I am obliged to speak plainly, but I have no option. This engagement cannot go on—you must set him free."

"Who says so—you, or Hugh Rossiter?" stopping and regarding him with a frown that made her look for the moment like a beautiful Medusa. Then she walked on again. "Excuse me, Mr. Herrick," very haughtily, "if I say that I regard your interference with my private concerns as unjustifiable impertinence. I refuse to discuss the matter with you; I am going home. Tartar—Tim!" raising her voice. And she turned and walked back so swiftly that he had some trouble in overtaking her.

"Miss Jacobi," in an urgent voice, "I must speak to you. I am an accredited ambassador from Miss Templeton and her sister—they have asked me to speak to you."

"They must choose another ambassador then," and Leah walked on faster.

Malcolm was at his wits' end. How could he compel this haughty and obstinate young woman to listen to him? Then an idea came to him.

"If Miss Jacobi is so unapproachable," he said quietly, "perhaps the Countess Ferrari will not refuse to listen to me?" Leah stopped suddenly as though she had been shot, and her face grew white.

"What do you mean? How dare you call me that—do you want to kill me!" But the expression in her eyes was not pleasant to see. For a moment she seemed almost distraught.

"Hush—hush!" he said soothingly; "I would not have called you that if I could have helped it; but you would not hear me. Let us go down that little path; there is a seat there, and we will talk this out quietly;" and taking her arm, he gently guided her to the bench. "Sit down and recover yourself," he continued kindly; for she was drawing deep breaths as though she were on the verge of an hysterical attack. Malcolm felt secretly frightened at the result of his experiment. It was clear to him that the mere utterance of her married name almost maddened her—that for some occult reason it was not safe to use it. Up to this moment she had played her cards well: she had guessed his errand and had evaded and kept him at bay—first by pretended ignorance, and next by refusing to discuss the engagement with him. That he was Miss Templeton's mouthpiece and messenger mattered little or nothing to her. No wonder Malcolm found himself nonplussed. A moment later he heard his name called. Leah's manner had changed; she was still very pale, but she had regained outward calmness. "I will hear you now," she said in a low voice; "but you must be more careful—if you mention that name again I must leave you. What is the message you have for me from Miss Templeton?"

"You shall know directly; but there is one thing I must say first. Miss Templeton and her sister are fully acquainted with your past life—your parentage, your brother's occupations, and above all, the fact that you have only recently become a widow—hardly more than six or seven weeks ago."

He was standing before her as he spoke, and she tried to look at him; but some sudden sense of womanly shame made her cover her face with her hands.

"It was not my fault," she almost whispered; "I am not good, but I am not so bad as that. Saul said it did not matter; and after that, when I began to get uncomfortable, he told me a lie."

"You mean that he told you that your husband was dead?"

Leah shivered, and bowed her head in assent. Then as she saw Malcolm's kind and pitying look, she continued in a low, constrained voice, as though something compelled her to speak—"It was not all Saul's fault. I ought not to have believed him, for he does not always tell the truth. After a time I found out that it was a lie, and then it was too late—Cedric knew I cared for him."

"You really care for him?" Malcolm was not aware

how gently he spoke, but his tone thrilled through Leah; her manner softened still more, and her dark, unfathomable eyes were full of womanly tenderness.

"Is that such a strange thing?" she asked in a dreary tone. "Could not any woman love him?—so young, so fresh, so true—so different from any one I have ever met in my unhappy life! What does it matter that I am older —what has age to do with it, when two people care for each other!"

"Ah, I will grant you that," returned Malcolm slowly.

"I shall make him a good wife," she went on, "and in the years to come the old wounds will be healed, and I shall forget the terrible past. Oh," recalling herself with difficulty, "why am I talking to you like this, and I have never even heard Miss Templeton's message." Then Malcolm sat down beside her and gently repeated Dinah's words.

"'Tell her from me that if she persists in marrying my poor boy, she will be marrying a pauper; that on the day the marriage takes place I shall alter my will, and that my sister Elizabeth will be my heir. Tell her this, and I will write to Cedric.'"

There was no answer to this; but he could feel the tremor that passed through her. "She has written," he went on, "and by this time Cedric has her letter. Miss Jacobi, if you love this poor lad, how can you have the heart to ruin him? Be generous, be merciful, and set him free!" Then she turned upon him almost fiercely.

"Generous! merciful!—and who has ever shown me mercy! When my own flesh and blood have traded on my beauty—my hateful beauty—and sold me without pity or remorse. And now," still more passionately, "you and his people want to come between me and happiness. You wish me to give him up, but I cannot—I will not. I am not marrying him for Miss Templeton's money," she continued indignantly, "but for himself, and because we

love each other. It is Saul who thinks of the money; but
he will not believe that message—he knows she will not
do it. Her sister Elizabeth is rich—rich, and we should
be so poor."

"You are wrong, Miss Jacobi, she will do it. Miss
Templeton is gentle and loving, but she is very firm. It
is possible—nay, probable—that she would continue Cedric's allowance, but in the event of this marriage he will
have nothing more from her."

"Do you mean that she would let him starve?"

"I mean that he would have to work for his bread as
other men have to work, and that his whole life, and
yours too, will probably be a failure. Miss Jacobi, I
entreat you to listen to me for a few moments—I am
speaking for your good as well as his. May I tell you
what I think?" She made a movement of assent. Malcolm never could recollect afterwards what he said to her;
but his words, strong, eloquent, convincing, seemed to
overwhelm her like a torrent, and yet his manner was
perfectly quiet and calm.

He told her, without attempting to soften or palliate
the fact, that nothing would reconcile Miss Templeton
and her sister to such a marriage; that her brother's
character was regarded by them with abhorrence; that
their cherished brother should marry the sister of a
billiard-marker—a mere adventurer and gambler—was
utterly impossible; and Leah's head was bowed low as
she listened. He touched delicately on her own past;
but his few words were terribly convincing. "You have
spoken to me of Cedric's youth and freshness," he observed—"do you think that your past life with its sad
experiences make you a fit mate for him? You may tell
me you are only a few years older; but in knowledge of
life he is a mere child compared to you. It is in the name
of his youth—his fresh, unsullied youth—that I implore
you to be generous and set him free."

Malcolm said more than this—for his own love for Elizabeth made him eloquent. He must do her this one service: he must deliver her young brother out of the contaminating hands of these Philistines; and so he reasoned and pleaded with Leah as he had never pleaded in his life before.

Soon she was weeping; he could see the tears dropping into her lap. Then suddenly, as a clock struck, she started up. "It is late—I must go now or Saul will question me. Indeed—indeed I must go."

"But you will think over all I have said, and let me see you again?" asked Malcolm anxiously.

"Yes, I will think over it; and if possible I will be here to-morrow. But I cannot answer you now. You have made me very unhappy, Mr. Herrick. What is it that the Bible says?—'There is no peace for the wicked.' I must be wicked, for there is no peace for me."

"No—no, you must not say that," he returned kindly; "let me give you my card, that you may know where to find me. Miss Jacobi, if you will only bring yourself to do this thing, you will be a brave woman, and I shall be your friend for life." But she only smiled faintly as she took the card and asked him as a special favour not to come any farther with her.

"Have I done any good?" thought Malcolm sorrowfully, as he walked away. "Poor soul, how she loves him! Cedric was right, as I told Miss Templeton: Leah Jacobi is more sinned against than sinning. Nature intended her for a noble woman, but Saul Jacobi and Count Antonio Ferrari have marred her handiwork." And all the rest of the day Malcolm thought of Leah with strange kindness and pity.

CHAPTER XXXI

PLOT AND COUNTERPLOT

Many a one, by being thought better than he was, has become better.—JOWETT.

Not as little as we dare, but as much as we can.—BISHOP OF WESTCOTT.

MALCOLM wrote to Dinah that afternoon, giving her a full account of his interview with Leah Jacobi; then he spent the rest of the day making up arrears of work. The last post brought him a reproachful little note from Anna.

"Mother thinks you have forgotten us. Why are you staying away in this unmannerly fashion, you naughty boy?" she wrote. "It is ten whole days since you were here, and we both feel lone and lorn without you"—and so on. But under the playful words he could detect a shade of earnestness.

Tired as he was, and needing rest sorely, he answered the letter and posted it before he slept.

Anna read it aloud to Mrs. Herrick the next morning, and they both agreed that it was a charming letter. The dear home people must forgive his seeming neglect, it said, for it was not possible for him to put in an appearance just yet. He was arranging a troublesome affair for a friend that gave him a great deal of anxiety and worry. He had been to Oxford, and might have to go down again, and he could not spare an hour for social duties.

"Oxford—I wonder if the business concerns his friend Cedric Templeton," observed Anna thoughtfully. But Mrs. Herrick only looked grave and said she did not know, and that evidently Malcolm did not wish to enlighten them. She spoke dispassionately and not in the least as though his reserve troubled her; but Anna was rather absent and distrait the rest of the day. She had watched Malcolm narrowly and had come to the conclusion that he had something on his mind. All his attempts at gaiety, his little jokes, his badinage, did not deceive her for a moment. Trouble had come to him. In some ways he was a changed man: he looked older, graver, and in repose his features had a care-worn expression, as of one who has worked hard in turmoil of soul. And this trouble—could it be connected in any way with this mysterious Elizabeth, of whom he never spoke? Ah, that was the question over which Anna pondered so heavily as her fair head bent over her typewriter.

Malcolm had ordered an early breakfast again in his own room, but as he sat down to it Hepsy brought him a note. A slip of a lad had delivered it, she said, and was waiting for an answer.

Malcolm had never seen the handwriting before, but he at once guessed it was from Leah—and he was right. It was written in pencil, and was without any conventional beginning or end.

"I am not going out this morning—will you come straight to 12 Gresham Gardens? If you come early you will find me alone. Saul went to Oxford last night, and will be back by mid-day. Send answer by bearer."

Malcolm wrote a few words—" Many thanks. Will be with you as early as possible;" then he made a hasty meal, for he felt there was no time to be lost; and as he walked to Sloane Square station his thoughts were full of perplexity. Why had Saul Jacobi gone down to Oxford—on what new mischief was he bent? Malcolm felt he had good reason for his fears. Cedric's weak, impressionable nature would be like wax in the hands of this unscrupulous adventurer; he would simply mould him

to his will; the poor lad's passionate love for his sister
would be turned to account and made to further his own
wily purposes. Malcolm groaned inwardly, as he realised
that their sole chance lay with Leah herself. Her mes--
sage had given him a shade of hope, but he would not
allow himself to be sanguine; he knew too well that
women of Leah's calibre were not always to be depended
on; in such cases one must reckon with moods and impulses. Her brother dominated her; he was the evil
genius of her life. How could any one hope to influence
her, when she, poor soul, lived under a reign of terror?
One might as well ask some wretched prisoner to break
off the fetters that bound him, as to expect Leah Jacobi to
walk out of that house of bondage a free woman.

Malcolm found it impossible to rid himself of these
gloomy forebodings; nevertheless he made such good
speed that it was barely half-past nine when he stood in
the stone porch of 12 Gresham Gardens. It was evident
that he was expected, for though the maid who admitted
him regarded him somewhat curiously, she did not ask
his name, but conducted him at once upstairs to a handsome drawing-room where a fire was burning.

The little fox-terriers, Tim and Tartar, began barking
furiously at the sight of a stranger; but before Malcolm
could quiet them the plush curtains that veiled the archway were thrown back and Leah entered from an inner
room.

Malcolm was quite shocked when he saw her face. She
looked as though she had spent a night of weeping, that
had dimmed her beauty; the hand she gave him was icy
cold. Perhaps she read the silent pity in Malcolm's eyes,
for her lips quivered.

"I am not ill—not really ill," she said quickly; "only
I have not slept, and the night was so terrible. You were
right to come early, Mr. Herrick; sometimes Saul takes
an earlier train than he says. He has done that two or

three times; he declares he never really trusts me. He made me promise not to go in the Gardens this morning, so I was obliged to stay at home."

"Will you tell me why your brother has gone to Oxford?" asked Malcolm, with a keen, steady glance, under which she grew still paler.

"Yes, I will tell you: he has gone to see Cedric. He was waiting for me when I got back yesterday, and he saw at once by my face that something had happened. Oh, you don't know Saul—when he means to find a thing out he is like a gimlet, one has no chance at all. He held my wrists until I told him everything—you can see how bruised they are," and she showed him the purple marks. "Oh, how angry he was! I never saw him in such a rage before, but it only made him more determined to hurry on the marriage."

"He has no objection then to your marrying a pauper?" asked Malcolm coolly, but inwardly he was boiling with impotent wrath.

"Oh, he will not believe that Cedric is poor," she returned sadly; "he only laughs at the idea of Miss Templeton disinheriting him. 'She wants to frighten him, and to choke us off, but I know a trick worth two of that,' was all he said; and then he cooled down, and called me a little fool, and bade me bring him the time-table, and ten minutes later he told me he was going to Oxford to arrange things with Cedric."

"You mean about your marriage?"

"Yes; it was fixed for next week, but last evening I received this telegram," and Leah put it in his hand. She had said all this in a weary, mechanical voice, as though she were reciting a lesson she had learnt by heart.

"Make preparations at once—Cedric returns with me —function day after to-morrow, nine sharp—all arranged —hang results." Malcolm's lip curled with disgust as he gave it back to her.

"Do you understand it?" she asked, as though distrustful of his quiet bearing. "Saul has hurried things on because he is afraid. He does not trust Cedric: he thinks he is weak and easily influenced, and fears that you may get hold of him again; his one idea is to have the marriage ceremony performed before Miss Templeton knows of it."

"Ah, just so;" but Malcolm muttered "the villain!" between his teeth.

"That is why I sent for you," continued Leah in the same dull, inward voice; "because he and Cedric have fixed it for to-morrow, and there is no time to lose. If he comes, and I were to see him again," and here her voice broke and her eyes grew piteous, "I should not have the strength to do it—to do what you want."

"What I want?" And then he added breathlessly, "Do you mean that you will give him up?"

"Yes, I mean that," in a choked voice. "I must give him up—the only creature I ever loved, and who was good to me. All night long I was thinking of it, fighting and struggling for my poor little bit of happiness; but you were right, Mr. Herrick, I love him too well to drag him down to poverty and ruin, for Saul would ruin him, I know that too well."

"I know it too. God bless you for this noble resolve," returned Malcolm quickly; but she stopped him.

"Hush! not a word of praise; you do not know—I have been to blame as well as Saul. But now what am I to do? they must not find me here."

"No, of course not. Is there any friend to whom I could take you?" But Leah shook her head.

"We have no friends, only a few acquaintances at Henley; but I could not go to them. I might take a lodging somewhere, only"—here her poor face grew crimson—"Saul never gives me any money, except a few shillings at a time; he pays my bills or leaves them unpaid, but it always makes him angry when I ask him for money."

"That need be no difficulty," returned Malcolm kindly. "Will you allow me to settle things for you?" Then she looked at him inquiringly, yet with an air of trust that moved him profoundly.

"Will you put on your walking things at once, while I make my plans?" he went on. "Be as quick as possible; we must not lose time." And she went off with the ready obedience of a child.

Malcolm hastily reviewed the situation. It was full of difficulties. Where could he take her? He thought of his mother; then he remembered that she was a woman of strong prejudices—she had her own opinions and would decline to see with other people's eyes. Leah would be to her merely an extremely dangerous and objectionable young woman, and she would dislike the idea of Anna being brought into contact with her.

The Kestons would help him, he knew that, and Verity would be a trusty and faithful little counsellor; but Cheyne Walk was hardly the place for her, and he would not be safe from Cedric.

For a moment he thought of the Wood House—they would never look for her there; but he dismissed this idea the next moment. No; the Manor House was their only resource. He would put her in Mrs. Godfrey's care, and ask her to keep her safe until they had made their plans. Mrs. Godfrey was a woman of the world; she would make allowances for any human creature so broken and buffeted in the battle of life, whose womanhood had been so tempted and crushed. His mother was kind-hearted, but her sympathies were less broad, and she often failed in tact. Leah would be to her a puzzling enigma. He felt with shrewd intuition that it would be impossible for them to understand each other.

"No, it must be my dear Mrs. Godfrey," he said to

himself.' " She is more human; it is not her way to use a sledge-hammer when a lighter weapon will serve her purpose; and then she never forces confidence, she is the most tactful woman I know." Malcolm broke off abruptly here as Leah entered the room. She wore the same dark red dress she had worn the previous day, and had a travelling wrap over her arm. She carried a small Gladstone bag, of which Malcolm at once relieved her.

" I packed this last night," she said in a low voice, " and I wrote this letter. Will you give it to him?" Then Malcolm glanced at the address; it was to Cedric, and he put it carefully in his breast-pocket.

" He shall have it," was his answer. " Now, if you are ready, we may as well go."

" If we are quiet no one will hear us," she observed in the same subdued voice. " The servants are in the back kitchen; I heard them laughing and talking as I came downstairs."

Then she led the way, and Malcolm followed her closely. Leah's remark about an earlier train had made him supremely uncomfortable. What if they should come face to face with Saul Jacobi· and Cedric as they turned out of Gresham Gardens! The idea was unpleasant. Fortunately, at that moment he saw an empty cab crawling towards them, after the manner of growlers when a fare is wanted, and he at once hailed it. Leah looked somewhat surprised when she heard him direct the man to a pastry-cook's shop in the near vicinity of Paddington station. She gave him a questioning glance.

" We cannot go straight to our destination until I am sure the coast is clear," he explained. " There is an upstairs room at Falconer's, and I am going to order you some luncheon, and you must do your best to eat it. I shall have to leave you for a quarter of an hour or so, until the Oxford train is in."

" You mean to go to the station?" she asked nervously.

"Oh, Mr. Herrick, is that wise? Saul is so sharp-sighted, if he sees you he will guess that you have been to Gresham Gardens."

"He will not see me," returned Malcolm confidently; "there is a corner where I can secrete myself and watch the passengers go by. When we are really off I will tell you our destination, but at present I must ask you to have faith that I am doing my best for you."

She smiled faintly and said no more. Five minutes later the cab stopped, and Malcolm took her upstairs and found a quiet corner for her. "You must take a few spoonfuls of soup," he pleaded, "for the sake of appearances. Falconer is rather famed for mock-turtle." Then he put down the bag beside her and went on his quest. It was more than twenty minutes before he returned.

"It is all right," he observed. "They passed me quite close. We shall be in the train before they reach Gresham Gardens. I think I heard your brother say that they had better do their business first." Leah shivered; she knew too well what that business was. A quarter of an hour later they were on their way to Cookham.

Leah seemed very much startled and even alarmed when she learnt their destination, and at first Malcolm found it difficult to reassure her. "Mrs. Godfrey!" she exclaimed. "Oh, I scarcely know her. Somehow she frightens me; her eyes seem to read one through and through. And then the Etheridges will be so near."

"I believe they are abroad," replied Malcolm, "and not expected home until the middle of December, so you need not trouble your head about them. But indeed you are wrong about Mrs. Godfrey; she is a dear woman, and the greatest friend I have. She is so warm-hearted and true that she would go through fire and water for any one she loved."

"Oh yes, no doubt."

" And not only for her friends," he went on, " for her
sympathies are world-wide. Trust her, my dear Miss
Jacobi, and you will see how good she is to you. She
is not hard and censorious in her judgments, she is far
too well-balanced for that; if you can only secure Mrs.
Godfrey for a friend, you will need no other." But it
was plain to him that Leah was only half convinced;
under her veil he could see she was vainly trying to
repress her tears, and his heart ached for her.

During their short walk to the Manor House he kept
silence; he was wondering what he should say to Mrs.
Godfrey, and how he could best explain matters. But just
as they turned into the drive he saw her coming round
from the garden with a basket of late blowing flowers in
her hand; she stood still as though petrified with astonishment when she saw Malcolm's companion.

" What is it—what does it mean?" she asked in her
clear voice. " Has anything happened?"

" Much has happened, my dear lady," he returned
quietly. " I am going to confide Miss Jacobi to your care
for a few days;" and then very briefly but distinctly he
gave her an account of Saul Jacobi's scheme—the intended marriage and Cedric's arrival at Gresham Gardens. " But for Miss Jacobi's noble behaviour," he continued, " this disgraceful plot would have been carried
out. She has generously given him up, and I for one am
deeply indebted to her."

" Will you hide me for a few days, until I know what
to do?" asked Leah, fixing her great troubled eyes on the
other woman's face. Mrs. Godfrey's manner changed.

" Hide you from your brother do you mean, or Cedric,
or both? My dear, you will be perfectly safe with us.
No one will molest you at the Manor House, and we will
both do all we can for you." She took the girl's hand
kindly and kissed her cheek. " We will have such a talk
presently—you and I; but just now you are worn out,

and must lie down.   Your head aches, does it not?"   Then
Leah owned that she was right.

"Alick is about the grounds somewhere," Mrs. Godfrey continued; "when I have made Miss Jacobi comfortable I will join you both."   But when she rejoined
them half an hour later, Malcolm was quite sure she had
been shedding tears.   "Poor thing," she said to him in
an undertone, "how she must have suffered; she is terribly exhausted, she has had no sleep, and has eaten
nothing for four-and-twenty hours.   I made her swallow
some warm brandy and milk, and have covered her up
snugly.   Now I mean to send the servant away at
luncheon, and we will wait on ourselves, and then you can
tell us everything."

"You must promise not to interrupt me then," was
Malcolm's answer, "for I shall have to be off in an hour
or so.   I mean to go down to Staplegrove by a late afternoon train, and tell Miss Templeton all we have done."

Malcolm certainly had the art of narration.   Not only
Mrs. Godfrey but the Colonel hung on his words with
the deepest attention.   Neither did they interrupt him by
comment or question until he had finished.   Then Mrs.
Godfrey said softly—"You have done a good work there,
Mr. Herrick."

"Who, I?—pooh—nonsense," but Malcolm flushed a
little at her appreciative look.   "I have done nothing—
it is all Miss Jacobi's generosity."

"I think we should hear a different version from her,"
returned Mrs. Godfrey with a smile, "and I can see Alick
agrees with me," nodding to her husband.   "Must you
really go to Staplegrove to-night?   Suppose Cedric goes
to Cheyne Walk?"

"That is quite possible," returned Malcolm; "nay,
more, it is extremely probable; and I pencilled a line to
Verity in the train.   She is to tell him where I have gone:
but my only fear is that he will not follow me—Saul

Jacobi will keep too tight a hold of him. By the bye, Colonel, I wonder what infernal lies that fellow has induced him to tell the authorities. If he has taken French leave of absence, they will rusticate him."

" I think he had better leave the university," returned Colonel Godfrey grimly, " for he is only bent on mischief, and will never pass his examination. Let him go abroad a bit with some reliable person and get over his folly, and then see if he will not settle down better. Dinah could afford to give him a year's travelling, and I know she would never begrudge the money."

" No, indeed, she is only too generous by nature," returned his wife; and then after a little more conversation Malcolm took leave of Mrs. Godfrey, and he and the Colonel walked down to the station.

CHAPTER XXXII

STORM AND STRESS

And yet, because I love thee, I obtain
From that same love this vindicating grace—
To live on still in love, and yet in vain;
To bless thee, yet renounce thee to thy face.
ELIZABETH BARRETT BROWNING.

" C'EST le premier pas qui coûte," and Malcolm proved the truth of the old French proverb, as he dismissed his fly and walked up the dark drive towards the Wood House.

He no longer felt the hot and cold fits that had shaken him as though with inward ague on his previous visit. He had seen Elizabeth again, had at least retained his outward calmness, and now he felt more sure of himself.

" The pains and penalties of life," Leah had said to him once, and he had thought the expression a strange one on the lips of so beautiful a woman; but he knew better now, and how such pains and penalties fall to the share of many men. " It is all in the day's work," he muttered as he rang the bell, for it was Malcolm's nature to philosophise even in trouble.

It was only six o'clock, and the two sisters were sitting together in the fire-lit twilight. Dinah was lying back in her easy-chair with her eyes closed, but Elizabeth had drawn her chair opposite the fire, and sat with her chin supported by her hands, gazing fixedly at the blazing logs with an absorbed gravity that again surprised Malcolm.

When they heard the visitor announced they both started to their feet and came towards him, but it was Elizabeth who spoke first. " Mr. Herrick, this is too good of you. I hope—I trust," in an anxious tone, " that your news is also good."

" You may rest assured of that," he returned, with an unconscious pressure of her hand. Dinah heaved a deep sigh of relief, and pointed silently to the chair that stood between them. She did not speak, perhaps because she could not: her face looked as though she had passed through an illness. Elizabeth, with her wonted quickness, answered Malcolm's unspoken question.

" Dinah has had one of her bad sick headaches, and has only just come downstairs. All this sad business has upset her greatly, but you will be her best physician," with the old beaming smile which Malcolm dared not meet. " Now," with a housewifely air, " shall I give you some tea? You will dine with us, of course?" But Malcolm declined the offered refreshment.

" I will dine with you if you wish it," he said rather formally, " and if you and Miss Templeton will excuse the absence of war-paint; but I am going back to town to-night."

" Oh no, not to-night!" she exclaimed in quite a shocked voice; " you will be so tired." But Malcolm assured her with absolute truth that he had never been less tired in his life. The storm and stress and excitement of the day had acted on him like a tonic as well as an anodyne; in thinking and planning for others he had found relief from the intolerable ache of ever-present pain that had made his life so purgatorial of late, and the unhealed wound throbbed less cruelly.

" I have so much to tell you that I think I had better begin at once," he observed in a business-like tone, and then both the sisters composed themselves to listen. But this time they heard him less calmly. The shock of learning Saul Jacobi's disgraceful plot, and Cedric's infatuation and weakness, was too much for Dinah, and she sobbed audibly.

"Oh, Betty!" she exclaimed piteously, "to think that our dear boy should be deceiving us like this! But that woman has deluded him."

"The woman beguiled me and I did eat," murmured Malcolm. Then Elizabeth looked at him rather sharply, as though she suspected a double meaning. But as he proceeded with his story, and she heard of Leah's noble act of self-sacrifice, her mood changed and her eyes filled with tears. Malcolm fancied that he heard her say softly under her breath, "She loved much, because much has been forgiven her."

But the climax of their wonder seemed reached when Malcolm told them that Leah was at the Manor House. Dinah seemed as though she could not believe her ears, and again Elizabeth looked at him curiously.

"Our dear Mrs. Godfrey!" she ejaculated. "I wonder what made you go to her. I thought," with a little laugh, "only a woman would have done that."

"Do you consider men so dense?" was his answer. "Mrs. Godfrey is the best friend I have in the world, and she has never disappointed me once. She is not only wise and almost masculine in her breadth of view, but she is also the most womanly of women."

"How well you have grasped her!" returned Elizabeth in an approving voice. "Yes, you are right, she will be a true friend to that poor Miss Jacobi. It was magnificent strategy. I do not believe any one else would have thought of it." But Malcolm only flushed at this eulogium.

"I promised you that I would do my best," he said in a constrained voice; but Elizabeth was too elated and excited by the good news to measure her words.

"Oh, but your best is so much better than other people's best," she said gaily. "Die, dear, why do you not make some pretty speeches to Mr. Herrick when he has achieved all this?" Then Dinah smiled and held out her hand.

"What should we have done without you!" was all she said, but Malcolm felt amply rewarded for his trouble.

They talked a little more about Leah Jacobi, and then Elizabeth said suddenly—

"I have an idea. I will go to the Manor House and talk to Mrs. Godfrey—it is our affair, and we must not shunt our responsibilities on other people's shoulders—and then I can judge of this poor Leah." And though Dianh was evidently startled by this bold suggestion, she did not attempt to gainsay it.

"Shall you go to-morrow?" she asked. "Perhaps I could go too." But Elizabeth promptly negatived this.

"You will do nothing of the kind," she returned decidedly; "I shall have you falling ill on my hands. Besides, you must be at the Wood House, in case Cedric comes;" and as Dinah perceived the force of this argument, she said no more about accompanying her sister.

Malcolm, however, was not so easily satisfied. "Are you sure that you had better do this?" he said rather gravely. "Would it not be wiser to leave Mrs. Godfrey to deal with Miss Jacobi?" But Elizabeth seemed quite indignant.

"Mr. Herrick, I did not expect this from you," she said severely. "I thought we were to do good to our enemies —and this poor soul is not our enemy after all. We have a debt to pay to her, have we not, Die? for she has set our boy free. We must do all we can to help her, and to free her from her terrible brother; for as long as she is with him there can be no peace for her."

"No, you are right," replied Malcolm slowly; "Saul Jacobi is her curse. He is a cold-hearted, selfish schemer. Well, I will not try to hinder your good work, for I see you are bent on doing it. You will go to-morrow, then?"

"Yes, I think so," but Elizabeth hesitated and looked

at her sister. "David is expecting his father to-morrow, and he will not want me until the next day——" but she broke off here as dinner was announced.

It could not be said that Malcolm enjoyed his meal. The presence of the servants prevented any freedom in the conversation, and as Dinah was still oppressed and weak from the effects of her headache, the brunt of the talk fell on Malcolm and Elizabeth, and neither of them seemed quite at their ease. The mention of his rival had affected Malcolm painfully, and Elizabeth was aware of this and was at once on her guard. She avoided all local subjects and plied him with questions about his mother and Anna and the Kestons; all of which Malcolm answered punctiliously. When a pause in the conversation seemed inevitable, he plunged into the breach with a description of Amias Keston's latest picture, and an anecdote or two about that infant prodigy Babs; he spoke of a book he had been reading, from which he gave them copious extracts; and then, dessert being placed on the table, he drew a sigh of relief. By that time he was sensible of fatigue.

He left them soon after this. When he bade Dinah good-bye, she took both his hands and looked wistfully· in his face. "I cannot say anything to-night," she whispered—"I am too giddy and confused; but I will write, and—and God bless you!"

To his surprise Elizabeth followed him into the hall. As she opened the door for him, the rush of raw, damp air came full in their faces.

"It is a regular November evening," she observed, with a little shiver. "It is the month I like least—the month of decay and——" then she checked herself abruptly. "Mr. Herrick, there is a question I wanted to ask, and that I did not wish Dinah to hear. You are going back to town this evening, are you not, because you expect that Cedric will come to Cheyne Walk?"

"I think he will be here," he returned reluctantly, for he had not wished to hint at this; in his own mind he was prepared for a stormy interview.

"I feel sure of it," she continued. "He is very unbalanced and passionate—he will say things that he does not mean, and that he will repent afterwards. You will bear with him—you will be patient, will you not?"

"Do you think you need ask me that?" Malcolm's voice was so full of reproach and meaning that a sudden flush crossed Elizabeth's face. "Have you forgotten already?" his expression seemed to say—"is he not your brother, and am I not your devoted and humble servant?" Then his manner changed.

"I will deal with him as gently as possible, you may be sure of that," he said kindly. But Elizabeth gave him her hand rather timidly and without looking at him.

This time there was no backward glance as Malcolm and his lantern disappeared into the dark woodlands; but Elizabeth stood so long in the porch that the dead leaves swirled round her feet and even blew across the hall.

"I wish I had not said that," she thought; "I might have trusted him. He will be firm, but he will be gentle too." And then she went back to Dinah, and they talked together of all that should be done on the morrow.

It was not long past eleven when Malcolm let himself into the house in Cheyne Walk with his latch-key, but Verity was evidently on the watch for him.

"Mr. Templeton is here," she said, and he detected a trace of anxiety in her manner. "He has been here quite two hours. Amias wanted him to come into the studio, but he preferred going to your room. I am afraid he is not well, or something is troubling him; he does nothing but walk about."

"I will go up to him," rejoined Malcolm. "I suppose there is a fire?" Verity nodded, and wished him goodnight.

The fire was burning cheerily; nevertheless, as Malcolm opened the door, the room felt as cold as a vault. The window opening on to the balcony had been flung up, and the damp air from the river pervaded the whole place. The sudden draught made the lamp smoke, and he moved it hastily. As he did so a dark figure came between him and the light, and seized him almost roughly by the arm.

"So it is you, Herrick, at last!" in a hoarse voice that was scarcely recognisable. "Now tell me, please, what have you done with Leah?"

The grip on Malcolm's arm was so painful that he winced. "Let me shut that window first, there's a good fellow," he returned coolly, "or we shall be blown into the street;" and as Cedric sullenly let him go, he fastened it and drew down the blind and turned up the lamp.

Cedric watched him savagely.

Verity might well have suspected that something was seriously amiss. Cedric's face was pale and his whole aspect disordered, and the strained, fierce look in his blue eyes almost dismayed Malcolm. There was something aggressive too in his manner that affected him unpleasantly.

"Well, are you going to speak?" in a defiant voice, "or do you wish to drive me crazy? What have you done with the girl who is to be my wife to-morrow?"

"Why do you imagine that I have done anything with her?" returned Malcolm steadily, for he wanted to find out what Cedric really knew. "I have just come from the Wood House. Your sisters are in great trouble about this."

"You have not taken her there," retorted Cedric, with a sneer, "and I am not in a mood to discuss my sisters. Herrick, I call this an infernal shame! What right have you to come between a man and his affianced wife? I will not bear it—you shall make me amends!"—stammering with passion. "Saul says you are at the bottom of this."

"Mr. Jacobi will have to prove it then," returned Malcolm quietly.

"Prove it! Do you think we have not sufficient proof?" exclaimed Cedric angrily. "I suppose you do not deny that you were at Gresham Gardens this morning."

"I was there certainly; Miss Jacobi sent for me. I had seen her in Kensington Gardens the previous day."

"I know all about that," interrupted Cedric rudely. "Saul told me you were bent on making mischief between me and Leah. You left the house with her this morning. One of the servants saw you go. You were carrying a Gladstone bag and a travelling wrap, evidently a lady's."

Malcolm bit his lip. They had been seen then.

"Before we go on with this cross-examination, will you allow me to explain matters," he observed. "It is no use your taking this tone with me, Cedric; I have done nothing of which I am ashamed. As far as I can, and up to a certain point, I will tell you the exact truth, and it may be well for you to hear me."

Malcolm's quiet tone was not without influence, and Cedric flung himself on a chair; but his attitude was still defiant.

"I own that I have done all in my power to induce Leah Jacobi to break off this disastrous engagement," continued Malcolm. "I did this not only for your sake, and because you were the tool of a designing and unscrupulous man, but also for your sisters' sake. When I left her yesterday it was impossible to know how far I had succeeded in my purpose." Cedric looked up when Malcolm said this.

"This morning Miss Jacobi sent me a note, and I went to her at once. She was in deep distress, and showed me her brother's telegram. To my astonishment, she told me that she fully intended to break off her engagement,

and entrusted this letter to my care;" and here he stopped
and handed it to Cedric, and withdrew to another part of
the room while he read it.

A long time afterwards Malcolm read that letter.

"My darling, I cannot marry you," Leah wrote. "I
am going to set you free. I pray God that I may never
see your dear face again, for this is the hardest piece of
work I have ever done in my life. Mr. Herrick has been
talking to me; he has made me see things in a different
light. I know now that I am no fit wife for you, my life
has been too soiled and degraded. In experience I am
twenty or thirty years older than you, and though I am
only nine-and-twenty, my heart is gray. Dear—dearest,
you are so young—perhaps that is why I love you—your
youth is so gracious and lovely in my eyes. But Mr.
Herrick is right. You must not be angry with him, Cedric. He has been so kind and gentle, and he is so true a
friend to you. I have sent for him—when he comes I
shall ask him to hide me in some safe place where you
and Saul cannot find me. I am so afraid of Saul—he is so
strong, he makes me do things against my conscience.

"Darling, let me say just this one thing more. It is
because of Saul that I am so determined not to marry
you. If you became my husband, he would be a drag
on you all your life. He has absolutely no conscience;
he would ruin you. No—no, you shall be free. I will
not hurt a hair of your head. Farewell.—Your loving
and unhappy   LEAH."

Malcolm had turned his back, and stood looking down
into the fire, until a choked sob reached his ears. Cedric's
head was sunk on his arms, and his whole frame was con-
vulsed with suppressed emotion; but when Malcolm put
his hand on his shoulder, he started up as though beside
himself.

"This is your doing," he said furiously. "I will never

forgive you, Herrick — never! Oh!" — as midnight chimed from a church near—" this is our wedding-day—, Leah's and mine, and you have hidden my bride away! But you shall give her up," with an oath, and for the moment Malcolm thought the lad would have struck him in his insane passion. Cedric was no mean athlete, and Malcolm was hardly a match for him, but he caught his uplifted hand and held it firmly.

"Don't be a fool, Cedric," he said quietly. "Do you suppose this violence will serve your purpose? Miss Jacobi has placed herself under my protection, and I shall certainly not betray her. Sit down and behave like a gentleman, and let us talk this out. Good heavens!" with a sudden change of voice, "do you suppose you are the only man in the world who cannot marry the woman he loves," and Malcolm's tone and manner seemed to check Cedric's passion. "Let us talk it out like men," he repeated, and Cedric sank back on his chair, still sullen but half subdued.

CHAPTER XXXIII

" HE WILL COME RIGHT"

If your eyes look for nothing but evil, you will always see evil triumphant; but if you have learned to let your glance rest on sincerity, simpleness, truth, you will ever discover deep down in all things the silent overpowering victory of that you love.—MAETERLINCK.

LONG afterwards Malcolm compared that night's work to a severe wrestling-match, and owned that it had taxed his mental and bodily strength to the utmost. The illustration was singularly apt. The whole force of his manhood and will were set to rescue this poor lad from the effects of his own infatuation and folly, but at first he made little progress.

Saul Jacobi's pernicious influence had done its work, and Malcolm, to his dismay and disgust, was forced to realise that his baleful and hated arguments had already poisoned Cedric's mind. More than once he was revolted by ideas which he knew had been inculcated by Saul Jacobi. "He has poisoned the wells," Malcolm said to himself indignantly—"Cedric's fresh young mind has been contaminated by his odious philosophy," and his heart grew sad as he remembered Dinah's faith in her boy.

More than once he was so sickened by Cedric's want of restraint and childish abandon of grief that he was tempted to give up the struggle. Only Elizabeth's pleading voice was in his ears—"You will bear with him—you will be patient with him, will you not?" and then again he would nerve himself to fresh effort.

All at once a thought came to him as an inspiration. Cedric had been giving way to a perfect paroxysm of

325

despair, and Malcolm had with some sternness remonstrated with him on his want of manliness and self-control. "You are making things worse," he said; "why don't you take your trouble like a man?" But the rebuke only exasperated Cedric.

"Oh, it is all very well for you to talk," he returned angrily, "but if you were in my place you would not bear it any better. You are so immaculate, Herrick, you can't make allowance for a poor miserable devil like me. I don't believe you have ever cared for a woman in your life. Good heavens!" as he caught sight of Malcolm's face, "do you mean that you have ever been in love?"

Then it was that the thought came to Malcolm—Cedric should know that he was a fellow-sufferer.

"I do mean it," he returned steadily, "and I also mean to say that your love is as water unto wine compared to mine; that is, if we can call such mad infatuation by so sacred a name." And there was a tone of contempt in Malcolm's voice that made Cedric wince.

"Don't be so hard on a fellow," he muttered.

"My dear boy, I would not be hard on you for worlds; if I speak of myself at such a moment, it is only that you may see that I am fully competent to sympathise with you."

"Won't you tell me more, Herrick?"

"No, dear lad, I think not, except that my case is even more hopeless than yours, for the only woman I have loved or can love will soon marry another man," and here Malcolm's face looked gray and worn. "I need not add," he continued hastily, "that all this is between us both."

"Of course—of course," was the eager answer. "I am awfully sorry—I am indeed. I wish I had not bullied you so."

Malcolm smiled a little sadly.

"Never mind that now. I only want to say this, we must take our punishment like men, and not whine like fractious children who want the moon—the moon is no nearer for all that." He sighed a little bitterly, for he was tired and depressed; and after that Cedric was more reasonable, and Malcolm regained some of his lost influence.

It was nearly morning before Malcolm could induce him to lie down on the couch; he had flatly refused to take possession of Malcolm's bed.

"I could not rest quietly in bed," he said piteously; "let me lie here while you write your letter;" for it had been arranged between them that Malcolm should send a note to Dinah by the early post; but long before the letter was written the worn-out lad was sleeping heavily. Malcolm covered him up with rugs before he slipped out to the post. Malcolm did not write a very long letter.

"I found Cedric here on my return home," he wrote. "He was very excited and unhappy, and I had great difficulty in bringing him to a reasonable frame of mind; but he is calmer now, and is at present asleep on my couch. I am going with him to Oxford to-morrow, and shall probably remain with him for a day or two. It will never do to leave him alone, or that fellow Jacobi will get hold of him again. I find he has already lent him money. I have been questioning Cedric, and I find that Saul Jacobi trumped up a false excuse for him to make to the Dean. Cedric was a little incoherent on the subject, but I understood him to say that he had begged for a three days' excuse on account of a sister's illness.

"As far as I can make out, Jacobi merely intended to have the marriage ceremony performed, and to allow Cedric to return to Oxford the next day. He had pacified him by promising to bring down his sister later, and to take lodgings for a week or two; but it is impossible to guess what the fellow really meant. As far as I can judge, there will be no further trouble with the authorities, but Cedric must not be left to himself.

"I know some excellent lodgings not a stone's throw from St. John's. Do you not think it would be a good thing if you and your sister were to take possession of them for a week or two? Cedric is not fit to be alone, and you will be a comfort to him. It seems to me that there is nothing else to be done. I cannot possibly remain beyond a night or two. If you wire I will engage the rooms, and they shall be in readiness for you." And when this letter was safely in the post, Malcolm sought the rest he needed so urgently, and was soon sleeping the heavy sleep of exhaustion.

Elizabeth was at the Manor House when Dinah received her letter, but she answered it and sent off her telegram without an hour's delay.

"I told him to take the rooms, Betty," she said, as she handed the letter to her sister the next day. "I have packed my things and shall go to-morrow. Of course, you will do as you like about coming too." Elizabeth considered the matter.

"If one could only have breathing-time," she murmured; "but to-morrow gives me so little time. Could you wait until the afternoon, Die?" she continued, "and then I could go across to Rotherwood and have a talk with David and his father. You see, dear, I am anxious to be with Cedric, and to settle you in comfortably, and I should also like to tell Mr. Herrick the result of my visit to the Manor House." Then Dinah rather reluctantly consented to put off her journey until the afternoon.

Elizabeth, preoccupied and anxious, hardly realised what the sacrifice of those few hours was to Dinah, who could literally hardly sleep or eat for her longing to comfort her darling.

Perhaps Elizabeth's thoughts were engrossed by the recollection of her conversation with Leah, for she spoke of little else that night; but just before they separated she asked to read Malcolm's letter again, and when she laid it down there was the old puzzled look in her eyes.

"Why does he always think of the right thing?" she said slowly. "What makes him so thoughtful and understanding? He leaves no margin for other people. This Oxford plan is just splendid. You will be such a comfort to the poor boy, Die. You will be there waiting and watching for him, and ready to fuss over him like a mother hen, and the sly old fox will not be able to get at him;" and she laughed, and bade her sister good-night. But when she was in her own room the thoughtful look returned. "He is always so wise and right," she said to herself. "He has only made one mistake—only one," and her face was very grave; for no one, not even her chosen lover, knew how the thought of Malcolm Herrick's patient sorrow oppressed Elizabeth's tender heart.

Dinah had good reason to regret their postponed journey, for they arrived at Oxford too late to see Cedric that night; but Malcolm was at the station to receive them, and accompanied them to their lodgings.

"I am glad you made up your mind to come," he said, as they drove from the station, "for I shall be obliged to go up to town to-morrow, and I feel happier to leave you in possession. I think Cedric likes the idea of having you. He is not looking well, but one must expect that; he has had rather a rough time of it. Oh, I forgot to say that he cannot possibly be with you until nearly twelve o'clock." Dinah tried not to give her sister a reproachful look when Malcolm said this. Malcolm only waited to hear how they liked the rooms he had taken before he went back to his hotel; but at their earnest request he promised to have breakfast with them the following morning, and also to take a later train, that they might have time for a good talk.

He kept his appointment punctually, and the conversation of course turned first on Cedric, but Malcolm was somewhat reticent on the subject of that stormy interview in Cheyne Walk.

"One must make allowances under such circumstances, and he was hardly himself that night," was all he said, but they fully understood him.

"Do you think he will get over it?" asked Dinah anxiously.

"Oh yes, he will get over it—he is so young;" but Malcolm avoided Elizabeth's eyes as he spoke; "youth has immense advantages. But you must give him time. If you will take my advice, dear Miss Templeton, you will not watch him too closely, or trouble if you find him a little altered, and not quite the old Cedric. He will come right by-and-by."

"Oh, if I could believe that," wistfully.

"You must make yourself believe it. Of course he will give you plenty of trouble at first. He will have his bad days, and try to make you as miserable as he is himself, but you must prepare yourself for that. Think what a boon it will be to him to turn in here and find some one ready to listen to his jeremiad." Then Dinah smiled faintly.

"I hope you intend to remain with your sister," he continued, turning rather abruptly to Elizabeth. She coloured and hesitated.

"I am afraid I can only remain a week, but I shall come down again later on. You need not fear that Dinah will be dull, Mr. Herrick; if she can only be sure of seeing her boy for an hour in the day, she will be perfectly happy. I always tell her that she is cut out for a hermit, she loves her own company so much. I am far more gregarious in my tastes—the society of my fellow-creatures is absolutely necessary to me."

Malcolm was quite aware of this, but he listened gravely. "I hope you mean to let me know your opinion of Leah Jacobi before I go," he observed presently. To his surprise she gave an embarrassed laugh.

"I have been dreading that question all breakfast time; I am so afraid I shall shock you. It is wicked of me, of course, but indeed I am only too ready to sympathise with poor old Cedric, for I have fallen in love with her myself."

"Do you know, I am not at all surprised to hear you say that," observed Malcolm.

"You were aware of my impulsive disposition," returned Elizabeth with another laugh. "But she is simply the most beautiful creature I ever saw in my life. All the time I was listening to her I thought of all those fair women the old patriarchs loved—Sarah and Rebekah and Rachel; but I think she is most like Rebekah."

"I daresay you are right there," replied Malcolm coolly —"I can imagine myself that Leah Jacobi would be equally clever at deception."

"For shame, Mr. Herrick!" in an indignant tone; "you know I did not mean that. I was thinking of the young Rebekah at the well at Damascus."

"It was too bad of me," he returned apologetically; "but of course I understood what you meant. There is a strange fascination about Miss Jacobi. It is not only her beauty, though that is undeniable."

"No, indeed," exclaimed Elizabeth eagerly; "but one can hardly say where the charm lies; but the moment I saw her deep-set, melancholy eyes, and heard her low, vibrating voice, I seemed to lose my heart to her. Poor dear Cedric, how could he help loving her?—how could any man resist her?" But Elizabeth checked herself as she became aware of Malcolm's keen, penetrating glance.

"You surely do not wish him to marry her?" he asked in a low voice. Then Elizabeth looked quite shocked.

"Mr. Herrick—our brother—Cedric; no, a thousand times no; neither would she marry him now. But oh, how my heart aches for her!"

" You need not tell me that."

" We were up half the night talking," she went on, " and she told me everything—everything," and here Elizabeth positively shuddered. " Oh, why are such things allowed? What a mystery life is! Mrs. Godfrey was with us at first, and then the Colonel carried her off; but I heard the clock strike three before I left Leah's room, and then I could not sleep a wink for thinking over some of the horrible scenes she had described."

" I wish she had not told you," murmured Malcolm. Elizabeth smiled a little sadly.

" It will not hurt me, and I shall be able to help her better. Mr. Herrick, Dinah agrees with me that we must never lose sight of her. I told Mrs. Godfrey so. Oh, that was a masterly stroke of policy, taking the poor thing to the Manor House. Mrs. Godfrey is so clever—she has an idea already. Did you ever see Mrs. Richardson, who lives in the red house on the road to Combe—Sandy Hollow, I think they call it?"

" Do you mean that very eccentric old lady whom Mrs. Godfrey always calls Mother Quixote, who is so rich, and always travels with a white Persian cat? Of course I have seen her at church. She is stout, rather addicted to gorgeous raiment, and wears a gold pince-nez."

" That is the very person!" exclaimed Elizabeth. " Oh yes, she is excessively rich, has not a relative in the world, gives half her income away, and, as dear Mrs. Godfrey expresses it, spends a good deal of her time in trying to wash her black sheep white, and weeping over her failures."

" And I am afraid does more harm than good in the long run," observed Malcolm; but Elizabeth would not allow this.

" She is the drollest old dear in the world," she went on, " and is quite a Mrs. Malaprop in some of her sayings, but she has the best and kindest heart in the world. Mrs. Godfrey means to enlist her sympathies on Leah's behalf, and we have no fear of the result."

"And you think this good lady will be able to help Miss Jacobi?"

"We are quite sure of it. Mrs. Richardson has a weak chest, and she always winters abroad, and she has been in the habit of engaging some young lady to accompany her as a travelling companion. Her maid is rather a crotchety old person, and very uneducated; besides, the cat gives her sufficient employment. I forgot to say he is blind, and rejoices in the name of Sir Charles Grandison. Mrs. Richardson is a descendant of the novelist, and always carries Clarissa Harlowe and Sir Charles Grandison about with her. She is full of amusing fads and fancies."

"And you mean Miss Jacobi to be her travelling companion?"

"Mrs. Godfrey means it—it is her idea. Anyhow, she promised to go round to Sandy Hollow the next day and give the old lady a full description of Leah, and if possible to arrange a meeting."

"I think it a very good idea," chimed in Dinah, her soft voice breaking the silence for the first time—she was always willing to leave the conversation in Elizabeth's hands. "Miss Jacobi seems very willing to do anything, poor thing, that will make her independent of her brother."

"Yes, indeed, she is terribly afraid of him," returned Elizabeth. "She has reason to dread his violence, I can see that. Once or twice he has treated her with absolute cruelty, but then she owned he had been drinking. You see," appealing to Malcolm, "it would be such a relief to us all to know she was abroad, and in such kind hands; and then, as Mrs. Godfrey says, she is so exactly fitted for the post. She is very accomplished, speaks French, German, and Italian fluently, and is a good reader. Oh, must you go?" as Malcolm looked at his watch with some significance.

"I am afraid I must not lose this train," he replied hastily, "but I shall hope to run down again in a week or two. You will let me know how things go on," addressing Dinah, "and if there be anything I can do for you?" and then he shook hands with Elizabeth rather hurriedly and went off to secure his luggage.

"I hope we did not keep him too long," observed Elizabeth anxiously, "for he is running as though he were late." But Dinah did not hear her; she had already taken up her position by the window, and was looking out for Cedric.

CHAPTER XXXIV

TRAVELLING THROUGH SAHARA

The hope I dreamed of was a dream—
Was but a dream; and now I wake
Exceeding comfortless, and worn and sad
For a dream's sake.
CHRISTINA ROSSETTI.

FOR the next few weeks Malcolm was much occupied with business, but he contrived to pay a flying visit to Oxford, and to spend a few hours with Dinah and Cedric. He had corresponded with Dinah regularly, and her letters told him all he most wished to know. At first they had been very sad. Cedric had broken down utterly on seeing his sisters, and both she and Elizabeth had been very much upset. The change in him was so great that they could hardly recognise their bright-faced boy, and Dinah owned that they had been shocked by the hard, reckless manner in which he had spoken. " I think Mr. Jacobi's influence has done great harm," she wrote; " Cedric says such extraordinary things sometimes, that I feel quite frightened to hear him. He never used to talk so—surely Oxford cannot have done this." Malcolm ground his teeth rather savagely when he read this. " He has poisoned the wells," he said to himself a second time. " There is no punishment too severe for one who tries to contaminate the innocence of youth !"

Dinah's letters became more cheerful after a time. Cedric liked having her near him, and she saw him for an hour or two every day. Elizabeth had not come down again. David Carlyon was not well. He had caught a fresh cold, and Elizabeth seemed worried about him, all the more that his sister was with him, and Theo did not

335

understand nursing. " Theo Carlyon is rather an unsatisfactory person," wrote Dinah.

By-and-by she gave him news of Leah Jacobi. Mrs. Godfrey's brilliant idea was certainly likely to be verified. Mrs. Richardson had been several times to the Manor House, she wrote, and had evidently taken a fancy to Leah. A few days later there was still more satisfactory news.

" It is all arranged," she wrote triumphantly. " Mrs. Richardson has engaged Miss Jacobi as a travelling companion, and will pay her a handsome salary. They are to leave England in about ten days' time. Mrs. Godfrey says that she and the Colonel will be quite sorry to lose their guest—Miss Jacobi is so gentle and affectionate that they have both grown fond of her; and Mrs. Godfrey predicts that Mrs. Richardson will never part with her."

Malcolm paid his second visit to Oxford soon after the receipt of this letter. Dinah was delighted to see him, and to hear that he intended to spend a quiet Sunday with them.

" I was just going to write to you," she said, when the first greetings had passed between them. " Cedric was so upset last night. He had a letter from that odious man Jacobi. Such a letter! written on a dirty scrap of paper in pencil. But I will show it to you; Cedric left it here;" and Dinah unlocked her writing-case.

Malcolm frowned as he read it.

" I am up Queer Street, my boy," wrote Jacobi; " 12 Gresham Gardens is in the hands of the bailiffs, and every stick of furniture is to be sold; and as England is rather too hot for me just now, I am going to make tracks for New York. If I could see that sister of mine, I would give her a piece of my mind. What a cursed fool the girl has been! But it is all that fellow Herrick's fault. He is a deep one, and he has a game of his own on hand; I am as sure of that as that my name is Saul Jacobi. Well, ta-ta, old fellow, I will let you know my diggings later on. Hang that fellow! if it had not been for him we should have pulled the job through, and you would have had the handsomest wife in Europe. Well, that game's played out, and I was never the one to cry over spilt milk. 'A short life and a merry one,' that's my creed.—Yours up to date,

"SAUL MELCHIOR JACOBI."

"So we are rid of the brute for the present," observed Malcolm. The expression seemed to alarm Dinah.

"For the present?" she repeated anxiously.

"My dear lady," he returned gravely, "do you suppose that we have seen the last of Saul Jacobi?"

"Indeed—indeed, I hope so," very earnestly.

"Then 'hope told a flattering tale,' and you must not believe her," replied Malcolm smiling. "The Jacobis of this life are not so easily shaken off. Like the horse-leech's daughters, they cry 'Give, give.' I should not be the least surprised if a series of begging letters with the New York postmark reached Cedric at due intervals."

"Oh, Mr. Herrick, what shall we do?"

"Do—why, put them in the fire unread. That will be my advice to Cedric. I know exactly the sort of letters that fellow will write. The first one will be jocular and friendly, and the business part will be in the postscript; the second will be pathetic and somewhat reproachful, and the demands more urgent; finally, if money is not forthcoming, he will bluster and threaten and make himself exceedingly unpleasant. Cedric must simply have no dealings with him; and above all things, he must take no notice of his letters."

"I hope you will tell Cedric this." And Malcolm promised that he would speak to him very plainly.

But Cedric was not the docile pupil of old. The lad's sweet disposition and milk of human kindness had soured

22

under the sudden shock of his trouble; the loss of his sweetheart and the consciousness of his own misconduct filled him with bitterness, and made him at times very irritable. Dinah's gentleness suited him better than Malcolm's bracing counsels, and her exceeding patience with him in his fits of despondency sometimes roused him to penitence.

By Malcolm's advice she had told him in guarded terms that Leah was well, and with friends who intended to take her abroad; but no entreaties on Cedric's part could induce her to reveal the names of Leah's protectors, or how she had received the information. Cedric complained bitterly to Malcolm that they were all treating him like a child.

" Not at all, my dear fellow," was Malcolm's answer; " it is by Miss Jacobi's wish that we keep silence. The lady who has engaged her as a companion is a stranger to all of us, but I believe she is a very kind-hearted woman, and that Miss Jacobi will be very comfortable with her."

" Comfortable—a companion—my beautiful Leah!" But the pain was too great, and Cedric burst into tears. After all, he was little more than a boy, and Malcolm remembered this and was patient.

On Sunday afternoon, as they were coming out of chapel, Dinah said suddenly, " I quite forgot to tell you that Mr. Rossiter has been at the Manor House again, and has seen Leah, and quite approves of the arrangement with Mrs. Richardson. He is going back to America, and has promised to keep an eye on Saul Jacobi. He was quite confidential with Leah."

" He is rather intimate with them," returned Malcolm; " indeed, I believe he is in love with the fair Rebekah himself"—for he had never forgotten Elizabeth's name for her. " Hugh Rossiter is a fine fellow, and would suit her a hundred times better than poor old Cedric. Oh well, he is too cunning a hunter to make a false shot, but I have a notion that he will try again some day;" and then Cedric came out and joined them, and they walked back to the lodgings.

Malcolm was going back to town that evening, and when Cedric had left them Dinah talked a little about her future plans.

"Cedric is so much better," she said, "that I think I can go home next week. He will follow me in another fortnight, and I do not like leaving Elizabeth so long alone."

"I think you told me that she was worried about Mr. Carlyon?" returned Malcolm with manifest effort.

"Yes, indeed, and she may well be," replied Dinah with a sigh. "Young men are so reckless and imprudent —at least David is. Just think of his madness, Mr. Herrick. He is not strong, and he takes cold more easily than other people. He got very wet taking a funeral for a clergyman at Dinglefield, and when he reached home, instead of changing his clothes, he went a mile farther to baptize a dying child. He was soaking by the time he got back, and a bad feverish cold set in. Elizabeth insisted that Dr. Randolph should see him; and she wrote to Theo herself, but I fancy from her letters that she rather repented of sending for her; but poultices were needed, and Mrs. Pratt, his landlady, is simply an impossible woman. However, things have worked so badly between them that Theo has gone back to Stokeley, and Elizabeth declares that even her brother is thankful to be rid of her. But he is better now.

"He is up and about again, but he doesn't lose his cough, and I can see Elizabeth is anxious. You look surprised, but I assure you my sister has some reason for her fears. David's mother was consumptive, and two of his sisters died young of the same complaint. Theo is the only robust one, and David knows well that he ought to take care. Mr. Carlyon is always worrying about him."

Malcolm tried to express his sympathy properly, but he felt he acquitted himself badly. Was this the reason, he wondered, why Elizabeth had looked so grave? but he thought it wiser not to dwell on the subject.

Malcolm was having a bad time just then. The excitement of the Jacobi episode had roused him for a while, but now natural reaction had set in, and the deadness and dulness of his daily routine oppressed him intolerably. Nothing interested him—nothing gave him pleasure. His literary work, the society of his friends, even his nightly " smokes " with the faithful Goliath, were like the dust and bitterness of the apples of Sodom. The present was like the desert of Sahara to him, and the future a perfect cavern of gloom.

He was tired of himself and every one else, and, though he did not know it, his nerves were unstrung, and he could not always control his irritability.

But he did his best, and fought his " foul fiend " gallantly. " He is a good divine that follows his own instructions," he would say grimly, when he compelled himself to make fresh efforts. Anything was better than brooding, he thought. And in the evenings he would resist the temptation to yield to his weariness and to take possession of his easy-chair.

For he knew too well that at such hours he was not master of his thoughts, and that in fancy the empty chair opposite to him would not long be unoccupied.

How often had he pictured Elizabeth there as the companion of his solitude—how often had her bright face, with its changing expression, come between him and his book! And in the gloaming her pleasant voice, with its quick breaks and hesitation, its characteristic abruptness, had sounded in his ears. Sometimes he would walk to and fro in a perfect agony of impatience and passionate rebellion against his fate. " I am possessed, but it is with an angel in woman's shape," he would say to himself; "and yet she is no angel either—she is far too human. And her faults—oh well," with a dreary laugh, " her faults are Elizabethan too." But once, when the bitterness of his pain was too great, he muttered to himself a strange thing.

" It is I who ought to be in his place," he said. " She is bewitched—David Carlyon's simplicity and goodness have bewitched her—but he is not her rightful mate." And then he struck himself fiercely on the breast and whispered, " He is here—he is here, Elizabeth!"

But in spite of his inward sadness he would not spare himself, and every week he went as usual to Queen's Gate to dine with his mother. But the long evenings tried him, and he found it difficult to hide his ennui and weariness from his mother's sharp eyes. One evening, just before Christmas, Anna made some remarks on his tired looks in her gentle, affectionate way, and he had checked her with unwonted irritability.

" I wish you would get out of that habit of commenting on people's looks," he said quite angrily. " It is very objectionable to me. I suppose every one is tired and out of sorts at times, but it does no good to notice it."

" I am sorry, Malcolm—I will try to remember next time," faltered Anna; but the tears were in her eyes, and a few minutes later she left the room.

Mrs. Herrick ventured on a remonstrance. " I am afraid you have hurt Anna," she said; " she is so sensitive, and you were quite rough with her."

" I am afraid I was," returned Malcolm penitently; " but if you only knew how it riles a man to be watched so closely."

" It was a very natural speech on Anna's part," replied his mother in her sensible, matter-of-fact way. " The truth is, Malcolm, you have not been like yourself for months—you are ill or worried, and ycu do not wish us to take any notice. Well, you shall have your way, but it is a little hard on us both."

"Mother, there is nothing that I can tell you. You know I have said that before. One must have worries in this life——" But Malcolm checked himself as Anna came back into the room. She was rather quiet and subdued all dinner-time, though she tried to appear as usual. And Malcolm's conscience pricked him unmercifully.

Later on he found himself alone with her. She was drawing at a little round table, and he went and stood by her.

"Annachen," he said caressingly, as he put his hand under her chin and made her look at him, "I was a brute to speak to you as I did. Of course you meant it kindly, dear, but it seemed to rub me up the wrong way. I think I am tired this evening; anyhow, my head aches." And Malcolm might have added with truthfulness that his heart ached too.

"Yes, and I worried you; it was very tactless and foolish on my part," and again the ready tears started to Anna's eyes. But Malcolm would not allow this—his dear little Anna was always kind and thoughtful, and he had no right to be so savage with her.

"My mother is always hinting at my changed looks, but indeed I try to be as usual. If I behave so badly, I must keep away." But this threat so alarmed Anna that he took back his words.

"He is very unhappy—I think he gets more so," Anna thought, as she stood by her window that night; "and of course it is Elizabeth who makes him so." And that night Anna again wept and prayed for Malcolm—her dearest brother, as she called him—for deep down in her girlish heart there was buried the pure virginal love that she had unconsciously given him—a love that no touch or breath would ever wake into life now.

Malcolm was very repentant for days over his unkind speech, and on Christmas Eve, when he paid his next visit, he brought Anna a peace-offering in the shape of a valuable proof engraving of a picture she had long coveted. Malcolm had had it beautifully framed. Anna was enchanted with the gift, but Mrs. Herrick privately called her son to account for his extravagance.

"There was no need to make Anna such an expensive present," she said seriously. "You must have paid twenty guineas for that engraving. You are too lavish in your generosity. She would be quite satisfied with some pretty trifle."

"I am quite sure of that," he returned; "but it is such a pleasure to give her things. Indeed, mother," as Mrs. Herrick still looked grave, "I can well afford it. I have more money than I know how to spend, and as I am not likely to marry, I see no good in hoarding."

Malcolm was right in saying that his income was too large for a bachelor, for in addition to the salary he drew from his literary post, his mother insisted on making him a handsome allowance, and every quarter day a large sum was placed to his account at his banker's, which Malcolm rarely touched.

"You are my only son, and there will be plenty for you when I die," she had said to him; "and Anna shall have her share too. Your father was a rich man, Malcolm, and there is no need for you to work unless you wish to do so;" but Malcolm soon convinced her that an idle life was not to his taste.

Just after the new year Malcolm received rather a reproachful letter from Mrs. Godfrey, accusing him of forgetting their existence.

"Of course you will say you are busy," she wrote, "but I do not mean to accept that excuse. You can spend a quiet Sunday with us as well as at Oxford, and I beg to remind you that I am an older friend than Dinah Templeton." Then Malcolm somewhat reluctantly made up his mind to accept the invitation for the following Saturday, although he was hardly in the mood for his old friend's lively talk.

To his surprise his genial hostess received him rather gravely, and it struck him at once that her cheerfulness was a little forced, and with the familiarity of their intimate friendship he at once taxed her with it. "Colonel Godfrey is well, and you are quite well," he said pointedly, "and yet something seems troubling you?"

"You are quite right," she returned with a sigh. "You know I am rather a sympathetic person, Mr. Herrick, and I have been very much upset this morning by a letter from Elizabeth Templeton. Mr. Carlyon has been up to town to consult Dr. Broderick. His father took him; and from what she says there is nothing to be done—the poor fellow is in a rapid decline," and as she said this Mrs. Godfrey's eyes were full of tears.

CHAPTER XXXV

VIA DOLOROSA

Bleed on beneath the rod,
  Weep on until thou see;
Turn fear and hope to love of God,
  Who loveth thee.

Turn all to love, poor soul;
Be love thy starting-point, thy goal,
  Be love thy watch and ward;
  And thy reward.
CHRISTINA ROSSETTI.

It was the Feast of the Epiphany, and morning service was just over in Rotherwood church, when Elizabeth Templeton came out of the porch and walked slowly towards the gate, as though she expected some one to overtake her.

At the sound of short, hurrying footsteps behind her she turned round and welcomed the new-comer with a faint smile, and they went on together. The Rev. Rupert Carlyon had been taking the service at his son's request, and now, as he walked beside Elizabeth and tried vainly to adapt his brisk, rapid step to hers, he looked more than ever like a gray-haired, shabby David Carlyon. The resemblance between father and son had always been striking, and even the mannerisms and tricks of speech were absurdly similar. "A dry, chippy little man," Cedric had once called him, and now, in his worn Inverness cape and slouched clerical hat, he seemed smaller and more shrunken than ever.

It was a lovely winter's day, and the hoar-frost on the hedges glittered in the sunshine; the air was crisp and

buoyant in spite of the cold; but Elizabeth, who so rev-
elled in the beauty of Nature, and thought every season
good and perfect, now only glanced round her with the
indifferent air of one whose thoughts were elsewhere.

"You are going to the vicarage?" she remarked at last;
"I must not take you out of your way."

"Oh, I will walk as far as the White Cottage with
you," returned Mr. Carlyon briskly. "You have promised to spend my last day with my boy and me, so I shall
be sure to turn up at tea. Charrington will give me some
luncheon, and then I have two or three visits to pay for
David; he is worrying himself dreadfully about that cobbler's child."

"Ah, poor little Kit," observed Elizabeth sadly; "how
sorry Mr. Herrick will be—Kit is his special protégée.
But Dr. Randolph says that she could never have lived
to grow up. Her stepmother is nursing her devotedly;
but it is so sad to see Caleb Martin: he is quite bound
up in the child, and it seems no use to try and comfort
him. 'Ay, it is the Lord's will,' he said to me yesterday,
'and maybe Kit will have a fine time when the angels
make much of her; but what will Ma'am and I do without her—that is what I want to know?'"

"To be sure—to be sure," returned Mr. Carlyon hurriedly, "that is what we all want to know. Well, Elizabeth, you will do your best to make my boy hear reason?
Theo and I have failed, and this is our last chance."

"I will do what I can," replied Elizabeth dejectedly;
"but David is a difficult patient, and I very much fear
that even I shall have little influence with him. It is so
strange," she continued sorrowfully, "that with all his
unselfishness he should think so little of our feelings in
this."

"Oh, you must make allowances for the morbidness of
disease," returned Mr. Carlyon, shaking his head. "Sick
people have their fancies. You must not lose heart, my

dear,—remember you are my chief comfort as well as David's." Then again she tried to smile. The next minute they came in sight of the White Cottage, and Mr. Carlyon left her to fulfil his self-imposed duties.

Elizabeth was right when she confessed that David Carlyon was a difficult patient, for his high spirit and energy had prevented him for a long time from owning he was ill.

Even in the early days of their engagement there had been symptoms that ought not to have been neglected; but he had fought his languor and fever manfully, and even Elizabeth knew nothing of an alarming attack of faintness that had followed an unusually hard day's work.

Afterwards he had taken cold, and his illness had been so sharp that Elizabeth in desperation had summoned his sister; but even then David had absolutely refused any further medical advice, and had also resisted all his friends' entreaties that he would be moved to the vicarage or the Wood House to be properly nursed. " His old diggings were good enough for the likes of him," he would say, " and though Mother Pratt had her failings, she was not a bad sort;" and when Elizabeth pressed him more closely he had seemed quite worried.

" Do give me my way in this," he said to her coaxingly. " If you knew how I love this dear old cottage! It was in this room I first saw you, dearest. You were standing by that window, in the sunshine, when the vicar brought me to see the place, and you turned round with such a beaming smile on your face. I think I loved you then. I could not be so happy anywhere else." And Elizabeth had reluctantly yielded her opinion.

But the humble cottage rooms had been beautified and transformed by hers and Dinah's thoughtful care for the invalid, and one comfort after another had found their way from the Wood House. The very couch that Dinah had used in her illness, with its soft silk cushions and eider-down foot-quilt, the gold and black screen from the inner drawing-room, and a favourite easy-chair that David had often praised, were all at the White Cottage. Nor was Mr. Charrington behindhand in his attentions. His housekeeper, Mrs. Finch, always prepared the invalid's dainty little dinners: the excellent beef-tea and soups, the jellies, rusks, and delicate puddings, were all Mrs. Finch's handiwork. Mrs. Pratt's cookery was not to be depended on, and though she pretended to grumble at other folks' interference, she was only too glad to be saved trouble.

It may be doubted whether David Carlyon really realized his own serious condition until the physician's opinion had been made known to him. "Advanced phthisis," he muttered thoughtfully. But when Dr. Broderick proceeded to recommend Mentone or some southern health resort for the winter, he had turned upon him almost abruptly.

"I suppose Davos Platz would not cure me?" he asked. Then, as the doctor hesitated with the natural dislike to give pain, David continued bluntly—

"It would be the truest kindness on your part, Dr. Broderick, to tell me the truth. If I take your advice and go to one of these places, may I expect to get well in time?"

"I am afraid not, Mr. Carlyon," returned the physician reluctantly. "It would be wrong of me to let you go away with this idea. You have consulted me too late—the disease is too far advanced. But it is my duty to tell you that life would certainly be prolonged in a warmer climate."

"There, David," and the Rev. Rupert Carlyon looked pleadingly at his son.

"Wait a moment, father," returned David firmly; "I have not quite finished my questions. Let us understand each other, doctor. If I go away, you tell me my life will be prolonged—do you mean for years?" Dr. Broderick shook his head.

"Oh, I see"—but David tried not to look at his father's pinched, white face—"you mean months probably?"

"Yes—yes," returned the doctor hurriedly; "with care, and under favourable circumstances, there might be no further breakdown for another year; but"—with a keen look at his patient—"I will not undertake to promise this."

"I quite understand," returned David quietly. "Dr. Broderick, I am sorry, but I cannot take your prescription. They sent my mother to Davos Platz—there seemed hope for her—and she died away from us all; and one of my sisters died at Mentone too. But I do not intend to follow their example;" and then he had risen from his chair and put an end to the interview.

Nothing would induce him to go abroad. Even when Elizabeth promised that she and Dinah would go too, his resolution to remain in England had been unshaken.

"Why should I let them sacrifice themselves for me?" he said to his father. "Am I not bringing trouble enough on Elizabeth? Why did I ever speak to her? I was mad to let her engage herself to me—I might have known how it would be!" And that day David's despondency was very great.

But at other times he made heroic efforts to hide his deep inward sadness from Elizabeth. He was so young, and the love of life was so strong within him, and the thought of disease and death so terrible. Sometimes in the dark hours of the winter's night, when his racking cough would not let him sleep, he wrestled with his despair as Christian wrestled with Apollyon.

"A soldier who refuses wounds and death," he would say to himself—"a minister of Christ who fears to tread in his Master's footsteps, what is he but a coward and deserter—and I am both!"

And then the torrent of his human passion would sweep over his soul—his love for Elizabeth, the knowledge that but for this hereditary malady he would have had the blessed certainty of calling her wife!

What a noble life they two would have lived! What plans of unselfishness they had formed! How the treasures of their happiness would have overflowed and fertilised other and more barren lives! And now not life but death claimed him!

Ah, no wonder if his human weakness blenched at the prospect, if his heart at times quailed and grew sick within him; for when one is young and happy it is not easy to die, and fuller life, not rest, is the thing desired.

But there were times when his fears seemed lulled and tranquillised, and when, with the strange hopefulness that was a feature of his disease, he would even delude himself with the idea that the doctors were wrong, and that he would surely get better.

These intervals of comparative brightness would come to him when the sun shone, or his nights had been less suffering, or when Elizabeth was with him. Her presence so rested and stimulated him that it was impossible for him always to realise the truth. " I can think of nothing but you," he would say to her—" I can think of nothing but you."

The sitting-room at the White Cottage looked snug and cosy that morning; the fire burned cheerily, and David Carlyon lay on his luxurious couch in the sunshine in a perfect nest of pillows, carefully screened from draughts, and with a small table beside him, with flowers and fruit and books—all carefully and tastefully arranged by Elizabeth's own hands, on her way to church, while the invalid was still in his bedroom.

It was a good day with David, and the old cheery smile was on his lips as Elizabeth entered; but as she knelt beside him to give him her usual greeting, the ravages of

the fatal disease were fearfully perceptible in the strong
light.

The hollowed temples and sharply-defined features, the
tightened skin, the hectic flush, the emaciation and short-
ness of breathing, and the constant cough, all told their
sad tale of rapid decline and decay. Too late—she knew
it well—for any human skill to arrest those symptoms;
no earthly care and love could preserve that cherished life
much longer!

" You are late, dearest," he said, holding her hand; " I
saw the church-goers pass a quarter of an hour ago. I
expect you and my father were gossiping as usual. But
all the same I know my good Fairy has been at work,"
with a glance at his flowers. " You must not spoil me
like this, my darling," and he raised her hand to his
lips.

" You know I love to do it," returned Elizabeth gently.
And then she brought a low chair to his side, and placed
herself where he could see her. He would lie for hours
contentedly watching her as she worked or read to him.
Sometimes the thin hand would touch a fold of her dress
caressingly, as though even that were sacred to him, and
not a change of the speaking face or an intonation of her
voice would be lost on him.

Perhaps no two men were more dissimilar than David
Carlyon and Malcolm Herrick, and yet they were alike in
this, that they each loved Elizabeth with a profound and
noble love.

" You are looking serious, dear," he said presently, as
Elizabeth made a pretence of sorting the silks of her
embroidery. That little piece of embroidery with its gay
silken flowers became one of Elizabeth's dearest relics.
It was David who helped her choose the shades, who insisted on a spray of his favourite lilies of the valley being
inserted. How he had praised her skill and made his
little jokes over her industry! But the screen would

never be used by him now, and the stitches were put in perfunctorily and with a heavy heart.

Elizabeth had made no answer to David's remark about her gravity. She was trying to collect her thoughts for the business she had in view; but the next minute a hand was laid upon her work.

"Tell me all about it," he said persuasively. "Of course I know you and my father have been brewing mischief. I think I can read your very thoughts," as Elizabeth looked up at him; "you need not try to hide things from me."

"I could not if I tried," she returned in a low voice. "David, I want you to do something for my sake. Your father and I—yes, and Dinah too—have been making such a nice little plan. We have heard of a delightful house at Ventnor; it belongs to a friend of Mrs. Godfrey, and it is so comfortable and so beautifully furnished, and with such a pleasant view. You are so fond of the sea, David, and your father loves it too; and we thought"— hesitating a moment, as she felt the grip of David's fingers round her wrist—"Dinah and I both thought it would be a capital arrangement to take Red Brae for three or four months. There would be plenty of room for you, and your father and Theo too," she continued as he remained silent; "and it would be so nice for us to be together, and our old nurse Mrs. Gibbon—you know Mrs. Gibbon, dear—would help us to take care of you."

David drew a deep breath. "Yes, I see," he returned slowly, "and all the expense and trouble would be for me. Don't I know your generosity, Elizabeth," in a choked voice. "But it is too much—I cannot do it. Don't you know, darling—don't we both know—that nothing really matters? Ventnor will do me no good. Let me bide where I am," and David's voice was pathetic in its pleading—"let me die in this dear old cottage."

"No, no," returned Elizabeth, bursting into tears.

"David, how can you be so cruel! Surely you wish to stay longer with me! Why need we be parted yet! Think of it, dear—that it is for my sake, and your father's and Theo's. If it is a sacrifice, it is a sacrifice for those you love. Oh, David, my David, it is such a little thing I ask —just for us to be a few months longer together. I know how you hated going abroad, and I would not have pressed it for worlds; but Ventnor—oh, David, you cannot have the heart to refuse me!" And Elizabeth broke down utterly and hid her face in her hands.

Perhaps it was as well that she did not see David's expression that moment; as he lay back upon his pillows his face was deathly. Why did they ask this of him? He was just growing more resigned and peaceful. Those agonised prayers of his for aid and succour had been answered, and the deep blessedness of an accepted cross seemed to fill his soul with a strange calm. He must die, and he knew it; but his Heavenly Father had been merciful to him, and death had lost its terrors; and now his longing was to die in the village he had chosen as his home, and under the shadow of the church where he had ministered as God's priest.

He knew where they would lay him: he and Elizabeth had chosen his last resting-place, and she had listened dry-eyed to his simple directions and wishes. He had talked out his heart to her, and her unselfish sympathy had been his greatest comfort. But now she was asking this sacrifice of him, and how was he to refuse her? And yet, if Elizabeth had guessed how the thought of that exile filled him with dismay and desolation, she would surely have denied her own craving for a few more weeks of life. But David knew better than to tell her.

Presently the hot hand was laid on her head.

"Elizabeth, let me see your dear face. You and my father shall have your way, darling; I will go to Ventnor." David's breathing was so laboured that he was obliged to stop here; but Elizabeth, with a cry of joy, threw her arms round him.

"Oh, David dear, thank you—thank you! You have made me so happy!" and the smile he loved so well beamed through her tears. But David's answering smile was rather forced.

"There is little cause for thankfulness," he replied wearily—"a poor helpless invalid who will only give you trouble! But there is one thing you must promise, dearest." And, as she looked at him expectantly, he whispered, "You must promise to bring me back here." Then Elizabeth bowed her head in silence, for she knew too well what he meant.

CHAPTER XXXVI

"I HAVE BEEN A COWARD"

Father! we need Thy winter as Thy spring;
We need Thy earthquakes as Thy summer showers;
But through them all Thy strong arms carry us,
Thy strong heart bearing large share in our grief.
Because Thou lovest goodness more than joy
In them Thou lovest, Thou dost let them grieve.
GEORGE MACDONALD.

AND so it was settled—Elizabeth had her way; and after a little they talked quietly of their future plans. The flitting was to be accomplished as soon as possible. The house would be ready for them in another week. Dinah would go down first to make arrangements, and Cedric would accompany her, and stay at Ventnor until it was time for him to return to Oxford. The change of scene would be good for him, and in many ways he would be useful to Dinah. Elizabeth also told David that his father had promised to travel down with them; that he intended to find a *locum tenens* for Stokeley, and that he would probably remain with them for a month or six weeks; and this last item of information seemed to afford David much satisfaction. But the next moment he observed, in rather a worried tone, that it would be a great expense, and that he was afraid Theo would object.

"Theo will have to mind her own business," returned Elizabeth severely. "Your father means to tell her that you are his first duty, and of course he is right." But Elizabeth carefully forbore to tell David that she had already undertaken to pay the expenses of the *locum tenens* for three months, and by dint of sheer obstinacy and feminine persuasions she had at last induced Mr. Carlyon to accept her bounty.

355

" My poverty and not my will consents," he observed sadly. But Elizabeth would not listen to this.

" Dear Mr. Carlyon," she had said earnestly, " if you only knew the pleasure this will give me. Can you not understand that I only cared for my money because it would be his, and now what good will it be to me? Let me use it for him as long as I can. Let me do all in my power for him and you too—as though—as though I were already your daughter." And then, as she wiped away a few quiet tears, Mr. Carlyon had yielded.

David strove with his wonted unselfishness to interest himself in Elizabeth's plans for his comfort. He heard how the inner drawing-room at Red Brae was to be converted into a bedroom, that he might be able, without fatigue, to take possession of the drawing-room couch by the pleasant window, with its view of the sea; and how a smaller room on the same floor was to be prepared for his father. But by and bye, in spite of his efforts, his attention flagged, and he looked so exhausted that Elizabeth refused to say another word.

" I shall give you your luncheon, and then read you to sleep," she said, in what David called " her Mother Gamp tone;" but he was too worn out to resist, and though forgetfulness was not to be obtained, it was certainly a comfort to lie with closed eyes and listen to Elizabeth's dear voice, till the twilight compelled her to close the book, and then she sat by him in silence until he asked her to light the lamp.

Tea was ready before Mr. Carlyon returned. As he opened the door he gave a quick, anxious glance at Elizabeth.

" Come in, dad, it is all right," observed David in a weak voice, but he spoke with his old cheeriness. " Wilful man, and wilful woman too, must have their way, and I have given in like a good boy."

" That's a dear lad," returned his father, rubbing his

cold hands gleefully together. " I knew you would make him hear reason, Elizabeth. She is worth the rest of us put together, is she not, Davie?"

" Mr. Carlyon," interrupted Elizabeth, " David is tired and must not talk any more, and some one else is tired too." And then she drew up an easy-chair by the fire and gave Mr. Carlyon his tea, and talked to him softly about Mr. Charrington and Kit, until it was time for her to go; but even then she refused to bid him good-bye. " I shall be at the station," she whispered, as he kissed her forehead; " we can say things to each other then," and he understood her and nodded.

But later on, as Mr. Carlyon sat beside his son's bedside, with the worn little book of devotions out of which he had been reading to him still open in his hands, he was struck with the strained, troubled look in David's eyes.

" What is it, my dear?" he said wistfully, for the curate-in-charge of Stokeley had homely little ways and tricks of speech that endeared him still more to those who loved him, and Elizabeth would often praise the simplicity and unobtrusive goodness that reminded her of David.

" There is something on your mind," he continued tenderly; " make a clean breast of it, my boy. You and I understand each other—don't we, Davie?" and Mr. Carlyon gently patted his son's hand, as though he were still a little child. " Out with it, lad—you are not quite happy about Ventnor?"

" Father, how could you guess that?" returned David in a deprecating voice. " If you knew how I hate myself for being so cowardly and ungrateful. Promise me— promise me, dad, that you will never let Elizabeth know how badly I feel about it; it would make her so unhappy."

" So it would, poor girl—so it would," rejoined Mr. Carlyon, for in his eyes Elizabeth was still a girl, and the very dearest of daughters to him.

"She and Dinah have planned it all for me," continued David. "I know what a sacrifice it is to Dinah, for she does so dislike leaving home; but she is doing it for Elizabeth's sake."

"You are doing it for Elizabeth's sake too, are you not, David?" asked his father quietly. Then the harassed face brightened at once.

"Let me tell you all about it, dad," he returned eagerly —"it will be such a comfort; you have often been my father-confessor before. If you knew how my heart sank when Elizabeth begged me to go to Ventnor, and yet how was I to refuse her when she said, with tears in her eyes, that my consenting to the plan would probably give her a few more weeks of happiness. You know how she meant it?"

"Oh yes, I know, David," in the same quiet tone.

"Of course, I could not refuse. I dared not be guilty of such selfishness, for—after all, what does a little more pain matter?" and here David drew a heavy sigh of intense weariness. "But I was so tired, and then I knew that the battle would have to be fought all over again."

"I am not sure that I understand you, dear lad."

"No, because I am not making things clear; but I will try to do so, and then you must help me. I have been a coward, father—that's the truth—and have rebelled against my hard fate—God's will was not my will, and I wanted to live and marry Elizabeth."

"Ay, David boy, I know."

"Yes, you know," with a sad, yearning look at the gray head bent now upon the trembling hands. "You know that was how my mother felt when she went so far away from us to die—she only consented to go because she wanted to live."

"And it broke her heart to leave us," returned his father huskily. "Dear heart, how she prayed that we might be spared that parting; but the Divine Will ordered otherwise."

"I have prayed too," murmured David, "and then, thank God! the strength and help I needed so sorely came. I have felt so peaceful lately, and now the struggle will begin again."

"Oh no, surely not, David."

"Yes, father, it must. I shall get better for a time, and I shall have the sunshine, and Elizabeth's dear love, and life will grow too precious to me again, and I shall dishonour my Master, and put Him to shame, by wanting to lay down my cross."

"No, David, I am not afraid of that," returned his father gravely. "My own boy, this is only one of the dark hours, when the evil one tempts you in your weakness; need I remind you of what you have so often preached to others, that as thy day thy strength will be, and that help never comes beforehand?"

"True, but I seem to forget everything." Then a warm, comforting hand was laid tenderly upon David's forehead.

"I shall remind you. We shall not be parted yet, my son, and God will help me to say the right words to you. Ah, David," in a reverent tone, "many lives have their Gethsemanes, but only one ever drank the bitter cup of sorrow to the dregs without a murmur, and only one had an angel to comfort Him. He will not be hard on us because our human will shrinks from some hard cross of pain, for 'He knoweth our frame,' and in our weakness and extremity He will be our staff and our stay." And in trembling tones he blessed his boy, and sat beside him in voiceless prayer and the deep, inward supplication of exceeding love, nor did he leave him until David had sunk into an exhausted sleep.

David was very feverish and unwell the next day, and Mr. Carlyon could not leave him; but after a few hours he grew better again, and as the days went on he seemed to recover his old cheerfulness.

One afternoon, as Elizabeth was sitting with him as usual—for she always spent her afternoons at the White Cottage—he surprised her by asking if Malcolm Herrick never came to the Wood House now.

"How strange that you should ask that question," returned Elizabeth, colouring slightly at the mention of Malcolm's name, "for he is coming down this very evening, and Cedric is driving to Earlsfield to meet him. Dinah asked him to come," she went on; "she wanted to talk to him about Cedric."

"Herrick is Dinah's right-hand man of business—she quite swears by him," replied David, smoothing tenderly a ruffled lock of brown hair that the wind had disordered. "I suppose he will remain the night?"

"Oh yes, of course. Dinah has got a room ready for him; she told him that she should not allow him to go to the 'King's Arms.'"

"It was right for her to put her foot down," returned David approvingly. "Why on earth need he scruple to accept your hospitality! Somehow I always liked Herrick, though I am not so sure that he returned the compliment; perhaps under the circumstances one could hardly expect it."

Elizabeth's face grew hot—the subject was a painful one to her. "Never mind about Mr. Herrick, dear," she said hurriedly; "Dinah and he are great friends."

"You need not tell me that," in rather a meaning tone; "Dinah has excellent taste. Dearest," his voice changing to seriousness, "I want you to give Herrick a message from me. Tell him I should like to shake hands with him when he goes to the vicarage."

"Do you really want me to say this to him?" and there was little doubt from Elizabeth's face that she was reluctant to give the message. But David meant to have his way.

"Yes, tell him," he repeated. "He and Cedric are sure to walk over in the morning—the vicar and Herrick are such cronies; and why should he pass my door?" And this seemed so plausible that Elizabeth said no more; but as she walked home she wondered more than once over this strange fancy on David's part. There had been so little intercourse between the two young men—a secret sense of antagonism on Malcolm Herrick's part had been an obstacle to David's proffered friendliness. It was true that Mr. Herrick must pass the White Cottage on his way to the vicarage, and even without the message his good feeling would probably have induced him to stop and inquire after the invalid, but she felt David's request would surprise him. Nevertheless, she must do his will and give the message.

Elizabeth was later than usual that evening, and she found that Malcolm had just arrived, and was talking to Dinah in the drawing-room. He was standing before the fire warming himself after his cold drive, and as Elizabeth entered he broke off in the middle of a sentence and silently shook hands with her. Elizabeth felt at once conscious that his manner was even more constrained and guarded than usual, and this made her nervous, and for the moment she could find nothing to say. It was a relief to them both when Dinah observed in her quiet, matter-of-fact way—

"Mr. Herrick is so kind and obliging, Betty; he has promised not to leave us until quite late to-morrow afternoon—that will give us plenty of time for a nice talk. You see, Cedric will be with us this evening, and we may find it difficult to get rid of him, and there is so much that I want to say."

"I think I can take him off your hands," replied Elizabeth; and then she turned to Malcolm, though he no-

ticed that she avoided looking at him, and there was a
curious abruptness in her manner that almost amounted
to awkwardness.

"Mr. Carlyon has sent you a message, Mr. Herrick.
He thinks you will be sure to call at the vicarage, and
he would like you to look in at the White Cottage as you
pass. He says that he would be pleased to shake hands
with you."

There was no doubt that Malcolm was surprised. He
unconsciously stiffened.

"He is very kind," he said rather formally; "but of
course I meant to call, or at least leave my card—I had
just told your sister so."

"Perhaps you had better call at the vicarage first," returned Elizabeth hurriedly. "Mr. Carlyon is rarely out
of his room before mid-day, and all hours are alike
to Mr. Charrington." And when Malcolm had gravely
agreed to do this, Elizabeth went upstairs to prepare
for dinner, and did not appear again until the gong
sounded.

She did not forget her promise, however, of taking
Cedric off Dinah's hands, and as soon as they had finished
their coffee she challenged him to a game of chess in the
inner drawing-room, where on cold nights a second fire
generally burned.

The rooms were so large that unless Dinah and Malcolm raised their voices it was impossible to hear their
conversation, and as Cedric had his back to them he had
no idea that they were talking more confidentially than
usual; but from Malcolm's position Elizabeth's face stood
out in full relief, and in spite of all his efforts his attention often wandered.

Even in those few short weeks since they had last met
he could see a change in her. She had grown thinner and
paler, and there was a deepened sadness in her eyes; and
yet in his opinion she had never looked more lovely,

though it was more the inward than outward loveliness that he meant.

He noticed how mechanically she played, and how the game failed to interest her. When Cedric checkmated her twice, she only rose with an air of relief, as though she had finished a wearisome task, and came towards them.

"I am cold," she said simply, as Dinah made room for her; "we nearly let the fire out between us." But as she sat in her snug corner warming her hands, she did not attempt to join in the conversation. Indeed, her manner was so absent that Malcolm felt convinced that she heard little of what they said, and he was not surprised that Dinah noticed it at last.

"You are tired, Betty dear," she said kindly; "I am quite sure that Mr. Herrick will excuse you;" and Elizabeth availed herself at once of this permission to withdraw.

"She is not at her ease," Malcolm thought bitterly. "She seems afraid of me somehow; she will not meet my eyes, and she has scarcely spoken a dozen words to me." And he sighed, for it seemed the saddest thing to him that she should suffer, and that he should be powerless to help her; and in his fanciful way he said to himself, "We are like two travellers walking along stony paths with a high wall between us, so that no helping hand can be stretched out, and no voices of comfort can be heard." And then he added, "I dare not even tell her that I am sorry for her, and for him too."

Malcolm was alone when he paid his visit to the White Cottage. There was no doubt that the change in David Carlyon shocked him greatly, though he strove to hide this from the invalid.

David welcomed him with his old cordiality; but Malcolm, who was exceedingly nervous, could only stammer out a few commonplaces.

The bright, eager young face that Elizabeth so loved

was shrunken and wasted, the lips seemed drawn from the teeth, and yet at times the old cheery smile played round them; but the voice was weak and toneless, and every now and then the hard, dry cough seemed to rack him cruelly.

"If you knew how sorry I am to see you like this," observed Malcolm kindly.

"Well, I am rather a poor specimen just now," returned David with a feeble laugh; "but what can't be cured must be endured—eh, Herrick? I told Elizabeth" (here a shade came over Malcolm's face) "that I should like to shake hands with you. When a fellow is going a long journey"—and here David's hollow eyes grew a little sad and wistful—"it seems natural to bid one's friends good-bye. We did not know each other much, Herrick, but I always wanted to see more of you."

"You are very good to say so"—but if his life had depended on it Malcolm could not have brought himself to say more at that moment. He wished himself a hundred miles away.

A quaint, sweet smile flitted across David's face; he could read Malcolm's thoughts.

"You have been such a good fellow, Herrick, and have done so much for them all. That was a bad business with Cedric, but at his age he will get over it—you and I know that."

"We do indeed," returned Malcolm gravely.

"Dinah comes and talks to me sometimes," went on David. "She says that if you had been their own brother you could not have done more; she is so grateful to you, Herrick." Perhaps he would have said more, but Malcolm checked him.

"Never mind that, Carlyon; it was a great pleasure to me to do it. Now let us talk of something more interesting." And then for a short time they talked of Oxford and the boat-race; and then of Ventnor, which Malcolm knew well—he had even spent an evening at Red Brae when the Godfreys were staying there. "The house is charming," he said quite enthusiastically; "I know the rooms you will have, Carlyon, and they are delightful."

David did not respond, and he was evidently getting tired, so Malcolm rose to take his leave.

"I wish—I wish I could do something for you too," he said with such sincerity that David was quite touched.

"I have had my good things," he returned in a low voice, "and now I must dree my weird. Don't worry, Herrick—things generally come right in the long run, but we must not try to act Providence too much. Goodbye—God bless you." The thin hand wrung Malcolm's with surprising force; but Malcolm's eyes were a little misty as he went out of the room, for he knew—he knew too well—that in this life he should never see David Carlyon's face again!

CHAPTER XXXVII

THE PARTING OF THE WAYS

Shall I forget on this side of the grave?
I promise nothing: you must wait and see,
    Patient and brave.
(O my soul, watch with him and he with me!)

Shall I forget in peace of Paradise?
I promise nothing: follow, friend, and see,
    Faithful and wise.
(O my soul, lead the way he walks with me!)
CHRISTINA ROSSETTI.

A FEW days after the invalid had safely reached Ventnor, Dinah wrote one of her pleasant, chatty letters to
Malcolm. She told him that David had borne the long
journey fairly well, and that he and Mr. Carlyon were
charmed with Red Brae. "I wish Cedric could have
stayed longer," she finished. "He has been such a dear
good boy; but I am afraid he is still very unhappy. Elizabeth heard from Mrs. Godfrey yesterday. Leah has
been ill with influenza, but Mrs. Richardson has nursed
her like a mother. Leah seems devoted to her already.
The poor girl told Mrs. Godfrey that she had never had
such a kind friend in her life."

As the weeks went on, Dinah wrote still more cheerily.
"The improvement in David is quite surprising," she said
in one of her letters. "Even Dr. Hewlitt seems astonished. He is able to be out in his bath-chair every day,
and on sunny afternoons he spends hours on the balcony.
Mr. Carlyon is always with him. It is beautiful to see
their devotion to each other. They seem to think alike on
every subject. He and Elizabeth read aloud by turns,
and I like to take my work there and listen to them.

366

" A happy family party," thought Malcolm a little bitterly, as he put down the letter. Even now he could have found it in his heart to envy his rival; but the next moment he dismissed the unworthy thought.

But it was only a temporary rally. Dr. Hewlitt told Dinah privately one day that there was no real improvement in the patient's condition, and that at any time there might be a sudden change for the worse; when they least expected it, hæmorrhage or collapse might set in. And the doctor's fears were verified.

One day, late in March, David seemed unusually well. A gale had blown all night, but towards morning the wind had lulled and a heavy rain had set in, and David had expressed some disappointment at having to remain indoors; but Mr. Carlyon, who considered himself weather-wise, assured him that the weather would improve later.

The gale had disturbed Elizabeth, and she had found it impossible to sleep for hours, and when she rose the next morning she felt unusually weary and depressed. A strange foreboding—a sense of separation and loss— seemed to oppress her, and no efforts on her part could enable her to maintain her wonted cheerfulness. Her dejection was so evident that David noticed it at last, and when Mr. Carlyon had put on his old mackintosh and gone out for a blow on the parade, he gently rallied her on her depression.

" What is it, dearest?" he asked rather anxiously. " You are not your bright self this morning. You are so good and unselfish, darling, that you never let me see when you are unhappy, but to-day you cannot hide it from me." Then he took her hands and held them so that he could see her face.

" I do not know what has come over me," returned Elizabeth in a mournful voice, " but all night long and this morning my heart has felt as heavy as lead." Great tears welled in her eyes, and she suddenly laid her head down on his shoulder. "Oh, David—David, if I could only go too; life will be so long and difficult without you." He stroked her hair for a few minutes without speaking. She was thinking of the parting that must surely come, and he must find some word to comfort her. "If I could only feel that you were near me," she whispered, "even though I could not see you or hear your voice—that you were still loving me and watching over my poor life!"

"Dearest," he returned tenderly, "I have often had these thoughts. More than once my father and I have spoken of it. It is his idea that nothing can divide us from those we love. Continuity of life—continuity of love, that is his creed."

"Is it yours too, David?"

"Dear Elizabeth," returned the young man simply, "the future is so veiled in mystery and silence that one hardly knows what one believes, except that all will be well with us. It seems to me that even in paradise we must still love our dear ones and pray for them, so tossed and buffeted by the waves of this troublesome world; but more than that I dare not say. I think I must always love you—there as well as here." Then she smiled at him through her tears.

"Dear love," he went on a moment later, "there is something I have often wanted to say, and yet the words were difficult to utter. Elizabeth, life is long as you say, and your great loving heart must not remain unsatisfied. Do not mourn for me too long—do not refuse comfort that may be offered to you, if you can be happy, dear." But here Elizabeth's hand was laid over his lips.

"No—no, you shall not say it—I will not hear it;" and Elizabeth's eyes were wide with trouble. "David—David——" and then she could say no more for her wild weeping.

"Hush—hush, my darling—I cannot bear this," and David's lips grew so white that Elizabeth in alarm controlled herself. But as she gave him a restorative, he held out his feeble hand to her. "Forgive me if I said too much," he pleaded; "I thought perhaps it might be a comfort afterwards. Dear Elizabeth, be true to yourself as you have been true to me, and may God bless and reward you for all your goodness to me and mine!" David spoke with strange solemnity, for, though neither of them guessed it then, this was their last farewell before the parting of the ways.

The evening passed tranquilly. Elizabeth seemed less dejected, but her head ached, and she sat silently beside David, while Mr. Carlyon went on with the book they were reading. Once, when there was a pause, she looked up and saw David's rapt gaze fixed on the sunset, while a look of almost unearthly beauty seemed to transform his emaciated features. She would have spoken to him; but he made a gesture as though for silence, and again that awful sense of separation seemed to pass between them. Mr. Carlyon put down his book, and looked too at the wondrous pageant of the sea and sky. "The bridegroom has run his race," murmured David in a strange voice. "What regal robes of gold and crimson! Father, this is the best sunset we have seen yet."

"Ay, that it is, David," returned Mr. Carlyon; "but you are looking weary, my boy, and I must be getting you to bed. Will you ring for Nurse Gibbon, Elizabeth?" But as she did so she noticed how feebly David walked, and how heavily he leant on his father's arm.

Half an hour later, as Elizabeth was standing on the balcony enjoying the cool spring air, she heard Mr. Carlyon call her loudly. Then a bell rang, and she and Dinah rushed into David's room. One look at the changed, livid face told them the truth. Dinah sent off for the doctor, and she and Elizabeth tried all possible remedies, but in

24

vain. Sudden collapse had set in. David could not speak; but for one moment his dying eyes rested on Elizabeth's face, and his last act of consciousness was to try to put her hand in his father's.

"I understand, David," Elizabeth stooped and whispered into his dull ear. "Yes, we will take care of each other, and comfort each other;" and then a faint, flickering smile seemed to cross his face, but the next moment unconsciousness set in. For hours Elizabeth knelt beside him with her arm supporting the pillow under his head, while on the other side the stricken father offered up supplications for his dying son. When his voice quavered and broke with human weakness, and Dinah begged him to spare himself, he shook his gray head. "Maybe he hears me—I will go as far as I can with him down the valley of the shadow of death." And then he folded his trembling hands together. "Oh, David—David, would God I had died for thee, my son—my son!"

"It was very sudden," wrote Dinah to Malcolm the next morning. "Dear David had seemed so much better that day; but Dr. Hewlitt had warned us of probable collapse and heart-failure.

"He had only left us half an hour, and Mr. Carlyon was reading the Evening Psalms to him, when he saw a change in him and called to us.

"I am sure David knew us when we went in, but he could not speak, and then unconsciousness came on. The end was so quiet that we hardly knew when he left us. We have telegraphed to Theo; there is much to be done. Dear Elizabeth is very good and calm. She and Mr. Carlyon are never apart; he can do nothing without her.

"He looks quite aged and broken, and no wonder: he has known so much trouble, and David was his only son."

Dinah secretly marvelled at Elizabeth's wonderful self-control and calmness. During those trying days no one saw her shed tears: it seemed as though her grief was too deep and sacred for outward manifestation. But when Dinah gently hinted at her surprise, Elizabeth looked at her almost reproachfully.

"I thought you would have understood, Die," she returned in a low voice. "David, my David, is a saint in paradise, and one must be still and reverent in one's grief. When one has to mourn all one's life, there need be no excitement." And then she murmured, "I shall go to him, but he shall not return to me;" and then, as Dinah took her sister's hand and kissed it almost passionately in her love and sympathy, one of the old beautiful smiles lighted up Elizabeth's face.

"I was as one who dreamed," she said later on; and indeed it was a strange dual life that she lived. There were the quiet hours when she knelt beside the coffin—when her thoughts seemed winged, and carried her to the still land where her beloved walked in green pastures and beside still waters; when in fancy she seemed to hear far-off echoes of melodious voices; when for David's sake she would feel comforted and at rest.

"He did not want to die," she would say to herself— "life was sweet to him—but God gave him grace to offer up his will, and then peace came. Darling—darling," laying her cheek against the coffin, "you will never suffer again—no more pain or weariness—no more conflict and temptation—only fuller life and more faithful service— for His servants shall serve Him, and they shall see His face." Elizabeth marked those words with a red cross on the margin of her Bible on the day David died.

But there was another reason for Elizabeth's self-control and unselfishness. She was anxious on Mr. Carlyon's account. Dinah was right when she told Malcolm that he was much aged and broken. "I have lost my Benjamin, the son of my right hand," he had said to her— "God's hand is heavy upon me;" and though he strove to bear his sorrow with resignation, his feebleness alarmed

372 HERB OF GRACE

them all. Theo, as usual, was undisciplined in her grief. "He will die too," she lamented. "Elizabeth, David has gone, and now poor father will follow him. I have never seen him look so ill. David and he were everything to each other."

"Hush, Theo," returned Elizabeth quietly, "we must give him time. It has been a great shock. We must not let him know that we are anxious." And, forgetful of her own trouble, Elizabeth ministered to him with filial devotion. No one else could induce him to take food. She would bring the cup of soup, or the glass of wine, and sit beside him as he took it; or lure him gently to talk to her of David—of his childhood or boyhood. "No one does him so much good as Miss Templeton," Dr. Hewlitt observed one day to Dinah. "I confess I was a bit anxious about him for two days—he has a weak heart, and I did not quite like his look; but your sister has brought him round."

Elizabeth smiled happily when Dinah told her this.

"I am glad Dr. Hewlitt said that, Die. I do love to take care of him; it is the only thing I can do for David now."

"Father," she said to him one day—for when they were alone she always called him by that name—"I think you have still some work to do before your rest time comes. You are getting better, are you not?"

Then he looked at her with sad wistfulness.

"I think I am not worthy to go yet," he returned humbly. "I must do my Master's work as long as He gives me strength to do it. Oh, Elizabeth, they are all there—all but Theo and I—David's mother, and Alice, and Magdalene, and our little Felicia, and now David has joined them in that heavenly mansion."

"But you will go too, dear, when the Master says, 'Go up higher,'" whispered Elizabeth.

Then the slow tears of age gathered in Mr. Carlyon's

eyes. " Yes—yes, I know it; but the flesh is weak, Eliza-beth. Pray for me that I may have patience;" and then he rested his gray head against her as she knelt beside him, as though the burden of that sorrow were too heavy for him to bear.

Malcolm was in the churchyard that sunshiny April day when they buried David in the tranquil spot that he had chosen for his last resting-place. Not only the people of Rotherwood, but friends from Staplegrove and Earlsfield, and from the villages for miles round, were gathered there—for the young clergyman had been much beloved. Very near the newly-made grave was a tiny grassy mound where little Kit lay; and at Malcolm's side stood a small, shabbily-dressed man, with pale watery blue eyes and an air of extreme dejection, nervously fumbling with the crape band on his hat. Malcolm had just laid a little spray of violets and lilies of the valley on the mound, as they waited for the funeral procession.

" She was fond of flowers, Caleb."

" Ay, that she was, sir," brightening up. " Kit loved everything that was bright and pretty, bless her dear heart! I hope they'll give her lots of flowers where she's gone, and that they will let her pick them for herself. You mind her last words to me, Mr. Herrick—' Good-bye, dad, I am a-going to be an angel, and I mean to be a real splendid one,' and all the time her poor throat would hardly let her speak."

" Poor little soul," murmured Malcolm compassion-ately; for Kit had suffered greatly in her heroic childish fashion. " Hush, here they come, Caleb."

Malcolm grew quite white when he saw Elizabeth looking like a widow in her deep mourning and crape veil, leaning on Mr. Carlyon's arm. She had chosen the two hymns that David's favourite choir-boys were to sing— " For all the saints who from their labours rest," and " How bright those glorious spirits shine." They were

singing the last when the breeze caught Elizabeth's veil
and blew it aside, and he had a glimpse of her face. The
beauty of her expression—its patient sadness, its calm
faith—moved him strangely. "He is not here," it seemed
to say—" he has gone to a world where there are no more
sorrow and sighing, and God shall wipe away all tears."
And then the boys' voices rang sweetly through the
churchyard:

> " 'Midst pastures green He'll lead His flock,
>   Where living streams appear;
> And God the Lord from every eye
>   Shall wipe off every tear."

Malcolm lingered behind until the crowd had dispersed,
and then he and Caleb looked down at the flower-decked
coffin. Loving hands had lined the walls of the grave
with grasses and spring flowers, Lent lilies and blue hya-
cinths, until it looked like a green bower decked with
blossoms. Countless wreaths and crosses and rustic
bunches of flowers lay on the grass waiting until the
grave was filled. Malcolm looked at them all before he
went back to town; but all that evening the remembrance
of Elizabeth's rapt, uplifted look remained with him.

"She did not know I was there," he said to himself.
But he was wrong. The very next evening he had a
note from Dinah.

"Elizabeth wants me to thank you," she wrote, " for
your lovely cross. She thought it so kind of you to be
there with us. We both saw you. Was it not all peaceful
and beautiful? Next Thursday Elizabeth is going to
Stokeley with Mr. Carlyon. He is better, but still very
weak and ailing, and she dare not leave him to Theo.
When I am alone, will you come down for a night? it
would be such a comfort to talk to so kind a friend." And
then when Malcolm read this he made up his mind that
he would go to the Wood House as soon as Elizabeth had
left for Stokeley.

CHAPTER XXXVIII

TANGLED THREADS

God has furnished us with constant occasions of bearing one another's burdens. For there is no man living without his failings, no man that is so happy as never to give offence, no man without his load of trouble.

A loving heart is the great requirement.—*Teaching of Buddha.*

CEDRIC had spent the Easter vacation with Malcolm at Cheyne Walk. Malcolm had previously sounded Dinah before he gave the invitation, and found that she fully appreciated the thoughtfulness that prompted it. "It is so like your usual kindness, dear friend," she wrote. "You felt, as we do, that the Wood House would be too quiet and dull just now for Cedric. It is so much better for him to be with you. Indeed, I shall not mind being alone; and when Cedric goes back to Oxford you will run down to see me as you promised."

Malcolm was relieved to find a great improvement in Cedric. Though his love-affair had ended so disastrously, he had achieved his pet ambition, and had been in the winning boat in the Oxford and Cambridge boat-race. The excitement and months of training had done him good morally and physically, and though he was still depressed and melancholy, and had by no means forgotten Leah, he showed greater manliness and self-control, and Malcolm's influence was again in the ascendant.

Malcolm took him to Queen's Gate and introduced him to his mother and Anna. He had previously acquainted his mother with the story of his unfortunate infatuation for Leah Jacobi. To his surprise she was deeply interested, and begged to be allowed to tell Anna.

" Anna cares so much more for unhappy people," she said. " You will see how kind she will be to the poor fellow."

In her way Mrs. Herrick was kind too. Malcolm, who knew young men were seldom welcome at 27 Queen's Gate, was secretly amazed at the graciousness with which Cedric was received.

Mrs. Herrick's stoicism was not proof against the lad's handsome face and deep melancholy. Her manner softened and grew quite motherly; and as for Anna, Malcolm took her to task at last, when he found that Cedric was in the habit of going over to Queen's Gate at all hours in the day.

Anna thought Malcolm was serious, and flushed up in quite a distressed manner at his bantering tone.

" Mother asked him," she said, defending herself quite anxiously. " It is so dull for him at Cheyne Walk while you are in town, and so mother said he could come here to luncheon whenever he liked."

" That was kind of her," returned Malcolm; " but as for dulness, there is not a more jovial old fellow than Goliath of Gath. He and Verity would look after him right enough during my absence. Cedric used to be quite chummy with them when he was with me before."

" Yes, I know, dear, but Mr. Templeton says things are so different this time. He likes the Kestons tremendously, but somehow he says he does not feel up to the studio life. I know what he means, Malcolm," rather shyly—" when one is unhappy one must choose one's own companions."

" And so Cedric prefers being here, and talking to you about his troubles." Perhaps Malcolm's tone was slightly mischievous, for Anna blushed violently.

" Oh, Malcolm, surely you understand," she returned nervously. " Don't you see, Mr. Templeton knows we are sorry for him, and he is grateful for our sympathy, and he likes to come and talk to us. He made me feel quite bad yesterday. I could hardly sleep for thinking of all he went through, and thinking of the death of that poor Mr. Carlyon. He does seem so sorry for his sister, though he declares that he never thought him good enough for her. That is how people talk," went on Anna, frowning thoughtfully over her words; " they will judge by outward appearance, as though anything matters when two people love each other. Mr. Templeton has been talking so much about his sister Elizabeth that he quite makes me long to see her, but all the same he seems to care most for his elder sister."

" I believe he does," returned Malcolm; " but then she has taken the place of a mother to him. Anna, dear, I was only in jest. I am really very grateful to you and my mother for making Cedric so happy and at home. I do quite understand, and I believe the society of two such good women will do much for him. Like the rest of us, he has found out that you are a friend born for adversity —a veritable daughter of consolation," and Malcolm's words made Anna very happy.

When Cedric returned to Oxford for his last term, Malcolm paid his promised visit to the Wood House; but he only stayed two nights. The place was too full of painful associations. Elizabeth's presence haunted every room, the emptiness and desolation of the house oppressed him like a nightmare, and though Dinah's gentleness and tact made things more bearable during the day, at night he found himself unable to sleep; and Dinah, who read his weary look aright, forbore to press him to remain. " It is not good for him to be here," she said to herself; " he is so kind and unselfish that he will not spare himself, but I will not ask him to come again," and Dinah kept her word.

But they had much to discuss during those two days. There was now no longer any talk of the Civil Service

Examination for Cedric. At the end of June he was
to go abroad for six or eight months. A friend of Malcolm's, a young barrister, who had also been crossed in
love—a sensible, straightforward fellow—was to accompany him. "He is sure to like Dunlop," Malcolm observed, as he and Dinah paced the terrace together in the
sweet spring sunshine. "Charlie is a good-hearted fellow, and one of the best companions I know, though he
is a bit down in the mouth just now, poor old chap."

I think you said the lady jilted him?" asked Dinah
sympathetically.

"Yes, and he is well rid of her, if we could only get
him to believe that. She was a handsome girl—I saw
her once—but she came across an American millionaire,
and sent Charlie about his business. Oh, he will get over
it fast enough," as Dinah looked quite sorrowful; "when
a woman does that sort of thing, she just kills a man's
love. Of course he must suffer a bit—his pride is hurt
as well as his heart—but in two or three years he will
fall in love again, and will live happy ever after."

"Oh, how I hope Cedric will care for some nice girl
by-and-bye," exclaimed Dinah earnestly; but Malcolm
only smiled.

"You need have no doubt of that, my dear lady," he
returned; "but you must give him time to be off with the
old love. That is why I am so anxious that he and Miss
Jacobi should not meet. You tell me that she and Mrs.
Richardson return to Sandy Hollow early in June?"

"Yes; Mrs. Godfrey told us that."

"Then the sooner he is out of England the better. In
London one is never sure of not coming across people."
And then he rapidly sketched out the details of the proposed trip, which was to include Germany, Switzerland,
the Austrian Tyrol, the Italian Lakes, and probably
Greece and Constantinople. Cedric had a great desire to
visit the Crimea and the shores of the Bosphorus, and to

see something of Eastern life. In all probability Christmas and the New Year would be spent in Cairo. "We had better leave Dunlop to work out details," continued Malcolm, "as money or time seem no object. You may as well give them a long tether. Change of scene will do Cedric a world of good, and when he is tired of wandering he will settle down more happily. Very likely by that time he will have some idea of what he wants to do;" and Malcolm's sound common-sense carried the day.

Dinah spoke very little of her sister. She was well, she said in answer to Malcolm's inquiries—Elizabeth was so strong that her health rarely suffered; but she was grieving sorely for David. "Mr. Carlyon is better," she continued. "Elizabeth is the greatest comfort to him. She goes with him when he visits the sick, and sits beside him when he writes his sermons. Indeed, Theo says they are never apart. Theo is very much softened and subdued by her brother's death," went on Dinah. "I think Elizabeth's influence and example will do good there. I believe that, with all her faults, Theo Carlyon is really a good-hearted woman."

Malcolm paid a flying visit to Oxford soon after he got back to town—somehow movement seemed necessary to him in those weary, restless days—and he took Mr. Dunlop with him, and had the satisfaction of seeing that Cedric appeared to like him at once.

"He does not seem to stand on tiptoe and look over a fellow's head, don't you know," observed Cedric. "He meets one on equal terms, though he is ten years older. He is a chip of your block, Herrick, and I expect he is a good fellow too"—and all this speech did Malcolm retail to Dinah in his next letter.

Cedric spent three or four days at Cheyne Walk before he started for the Continent, and again most of his time was devoted to his friends at 27 Queen's Gate.

Malcolm was secretly glad that he was in such safe

hands, for, as the time of Cedric's departure drew near, he could not divest himself of an uneasy fear that all their precautions might be unavailing, and that, when they least expected it, he and Leah Jacobi would come face to face. He knew that she and her new friend Mrs. Richardson were now settled at Sandy Hollow for the summer, and that Mrs. Richardson came frequently to town for sight-seeing or shopping expeditions.

Malcolm little knew what good reason he had for his fears.

On Cedric's last day in Cheyne Walk, Mrs. Herrick proposed that he should drive with her and Anna to Pall Mall to see some pictures that were being exhibited. She would leave them at the gallery for an hour, and call for them when she had done her shopping. Malcolm had promised to be there at the same time, and they would all go back together to Queen's Gate for the remainder of the day. It so happened that Mrs. Richardson had planned one of her favourite shopping expeditions for the same day, and in the course of the afternoon the hansom she had chartered drew up at a shop exactly opposite the gallery, where at that very moment Anna, Cedric, and Malcolm were coming down the staircase to join Mrs. Herrick, who was waiting for them in her carriage.

Leah, who had not recovered her normal strength since her attack of influenza, was excessively tried by all the noise and bustle of the West End, and begged to remain in the hansom while Mrs. Richardson finished her purchases. When Mrs. Richardson came out of the shop a quarter of an hour later, the handsome carriage with its pair of bay horses had driven off, and Leah was leaning back in the hansom looking white as death, with a pained, startled expression in her beautiful eyes.

Mrs. Richardson told the man to drive to the station. Then she took the girl's hand kindly. " What is it, my dear?" she said in a motherly voice. "Are you ill, or has something frightened you?" but it was long before Leah could gasp out her explanation.

"She had seen him, and he looked quite bright and happy, and he was talking to a fair haired-girl with a sweet face, and Mr. Herrick was with them;" but poor Leah could say no more, for the jealous pain seemed to choke her. That was the way he had smiled at her, and now she was forgotten, and this other girl had taken her place!

Mrs. Richardson, with all her eccentricities, had a warm, true heart, and she was very patient and tender with the poor girl.

But late that night, as she sat in her dressing-room, there was a timid knock at her door, and Leah entered in her white wrapper, with all her glorious dark hair streaming over her shoulders; but her eyes were swollen with weeping.

"I felt I must come and speak to you or I could not sleep!" she exclaimed in her deep voice; and kneeling down by her friend—"Oh, I have been so wicked! but I will try to be good now."

"Tell me all about it, dearie," returned Mrs. Richardson in her kind, comforting voice; and she drew the dark head to her shoulder, and a sort of wonder filled her eyes as she saw the glossy lengths of hair that swept the floor.

To an onlooker Mrs. Richardson might have seemed a somewhat grotesque figure in her quilted magenta silk dressing-gown, with her gray fringe pinned up by her maid in little twists and rolls, but her honest eyes beamed with kindness and sympathy.

"Oh, I have been so wicked!" repeated Leah. "All these months I have been praying that he might not suffer as I have been suffering, and that in time he might forget me and be happy; and yet, because my prayer has been answered, and that girl is helping him to forget, I felt as though I hated her;" and then she hid her face in the folds of the gaudy dressing-gown and shed tears of bitter shame and self-loathing.

" My dear, if you cry so you will make yourself ill," observed Mrs. Richardson soothingly. " You have been sorely tried, you poor child, but you are not wicked; on the contrary, I think few girls have behaved so well. Do not call yourself names, dearie; Mrs. Godfrey and I both think you good, and we mean to do our best to make you happy."

" Yes, and I am so grateful to you both, you dear, dear friends," and Leah raised her tear-stained face and kissed her with all the warmth of her loving nature. What was it to her that Mrs. Richardson was an odd-looking, eccentric old lady, whose curled gray fringe and gay attire scarcely harmonised with her homely, weather-beaten features; to Leah her face was transfigured by the loveliness of a kind and tender nature. " I think I saw her as the angels did," she said long years afterwards to one who had served for her as Jacob did for his beloved Rachel; " for I loved every line of her dear homely face. Oh, how she mothered me, who had never known mother love, and how good and patient she was with me in my bad times! If God had not taken her, I could never have left her—never!" For when Mrs. Richardson died some years later, her hand was locked in that of her adopted daughter.

Leah drooped for some time after this encounter. Then, as the summer went on, she recovered her spirits gradually; new duties and interests demanded her attention, and in the wholesome and active life led by the mistress of Sandy Hollow she found plenty to distract her sad thoughts.

Mrs. Richardson was a great gardener, and on warm days she spent most of her time in the open air; they breakfasted under a spreading chestnut, and often dined in foreign fashion on the terrace facing the sunset.

When Malcolm went down to the Manor House in August before he started for Norway, he walked across to Sandy Hollow with Mrs. Godfrey. They found Mrs. Richardson sitting in a shady retreat, with all her various pets round her. Leah was gathering flowers in the lower garden, she said. She received Malcolm very kindly, for he was one of her favourites, and talked to him a great deal about the girl—of her sweet temper, her docility, and her patience.

" She has heard nothing of that wretched brother of hers," she continued. Then Malcolm shrugged his shoulders; he could give her information on that subject, he said drily—at least a score of begging letters had reached him and Cedric from New York, and had been consigned to the flames. Saul Jacobi was evidently playing his old tricks and living on his wits; he was utterly irredeemable. Hugh Rossiter always prophesied that he would never die in his bed; and this prediction was unfortunately verified some three years later, when, in a drunken brawl, a tipsy sailor lurched up against him one dark night and pushed him over the quay. No one heard his cry for help for the oaths and curses that were filling the air; neither was his body found until the next day. Strange to say, it was Hugh Rossiter who identified it; and it was he who later on brought Leah a pathetic little proof that Saul had not wholly forgotten his sister.

In the pocket of his shabby old coat—how shabby and how ragged it was Hugh never ventured to tell her—there was a cheap little photo of Leah, taken when she was eighteen, and in the first bloom of her young beauty; and on the soiled envelope was written, " My little sister Leah," and the date of her birth. For no nature is wholly evil and irreclaimable, and perhaps, in spite of his tyranny and cruel tempers, there was a spark of affection in the man's heart for the young sister dependent on him. Leah always believed this, and she wept the saddest, tenderest tears over the little photo. " My poor Saul," she said, " his nature was strangely warped, and he did not know how to speak the truth, and he could be hard and cruel— as I know to my cost—but there were times when he was very good to me;" and so even Saul Jacobi had one human being to mourn for him.

CHAPTER XXXIX

THE NEW CURATE-IN-CHARGE

While I? I sat alone and watched;
  My lot in life, to live alone
In my own world of interests,
  Much felt but little shown.

   .   .   .   .   .

Yet sometimes, when I feel my strength
  Most weak, and life most burdensome,
I lift mine eyes up to the hills,
  From whence my help shall come.
                   CHRISTINA ROSSETTI.

MALCOLM sat for some time talking to the two ladies; then he made an excuse and set off in search of Leah. He was well acquainted with the grounds of Sandy Hollow, and could have found his way blindfolded to the lower garden.

It was a quaint old plaisance shut in with high walls, which were covered with fruit trees, where downy peaches, and nectarines, and golden apricots, and big yellow plums nestled their sun-kissed cheeks against the warm red bricks. In the oddly-shaped beds all manner of sweet growing things seemed to jostle each other—not forming stately rows, or ordered phalanx, or even gay-patterned borders after the fashion of modern flower-beds, but growing together in the loveliest confusion—peonies and nasturtiums, sweet-peas and salvias; and everywhere crowds of roses—over arches, climbing up walls, hanging in festoons over the gateway, long rows of Standards guarding the path like an army of beauteous Amazons; while all day long the heavy brown bees hummed round them, and filled their honey-bags with rifled sweets.

There was a small green bench placed invitingly in a shady corner, where Leah had seated herself to rest after her labours. Malcolm thought that her figure gave the finishing touch to the picture. She wore a white dress and a large shady hat, and a basket of Marshal Niel roses was in her lap; but when she caught sight of the visitor she rose so hastily that the basket was upset and the roses strewed the ground at her feet. Malcolm felt concerned when he saw how pale she had grown, and how she was trembling from head to foot, but he thought it better to take no notice and to give her time to recover herself.

" Have I startled you?" he said lightly. " Let me pick up your roses for you. May I have this bud for myself?" showing her his spoil. Then, when the basket was full again, he sat down beside her; but it was Leah who broke the silence. She had not regained her colour, and her voice still trembled a little.

" I did not know you were in the neighbourhood," she faltered, " and it startled me so to see you at the gate. I have not been strong since the influenza, and even a little thing like that brings on palpitation; but you must not think that I am not glad to see you."

" Thank you," returned Malcolm in a pleasant, friendly voice. " I only arrived at the Manor House last evening, so you see I have lost no time in coming over to Sandy Hollow. I wanted to see for myself how you were. You are rather too thin and unsubstantial-looking, Miss Jacobi;" but all the time he was saying to himself that he had never seen her look more lovely.

" What does it matter how one looks?" she returned indifferently. " You are thinner too, Mr. Herrick; but then you work so hard. Do you know"—and here her voice changed—" that I saw you a few weeks ago. You did not see me, and I could not speak; you were with some friends." Leah's manner was so significant and pregnant with meaning that Malcolm gazed at her inquiringly.

"I do not remember; I have so many friends," he observed in a puzzled tone.

"You had been to see those French pictures in the new gallery," she returned, "and a lady was waiting for you in her carriage." Then a sudden light broke in upon Malcolm.

"It must have been my mother!" he exclaimed, and then he stopped a little awkwardly, for of course he remembered now; but she finished his sentence quite calmly.

"Yes, he was there—Mr. Templeton, I mean; he was talking to a girl with fair hair, and with such a nice face —not pretty, but sweet and good; and they were laughing together. I could hear him laugh quite distinctly—my hansom was so close."

"Good heavens! what an escape," Malcolm said to himself inwardly; "it was a near thing." Then aloud, "That was Anna Sheldon, my adopted sister; she is the dearest girl in the world; but you are right, she is not really pretty."

"They seemed very happy," returned Leah, but her voice was full of wistful pain.

Malcolm, who was a fellow-sufferer, understood in a moment what she was feeling, and his kind heart prompted the remedy.

"Cedric has been a great deal with them lately," he said quietly; "my mother and Anna know all about his trouble; and they are very kind to him. It is good for him to be with friends who can make allowances for him, and help him."

"But he seemed happy," persisted the poor girl; "and —and—Miss Sheldon will soon make him forget things." But Malcolm shook his head.

"I am afraid not," he returned rather sadly; "Cedric

is by no means happy, though we all do our best to make him so. He has had a great shock, Miss Jacobi, and in spite of his youth he has suffered much. I wish I could tell you truthfully that he has forgotten you, but it would be a useless falsehood. We can only hope that time and change will be beneficial;" and then, in the kindest manner, he sketched the outline of Cedric's projected travels. and gave her a full description of his travelling companion.

Malcolm's confidence was not thrown away; before many minutes were over Leah's wan face brightened a little, and her eyes lost their strained look.

"Thank you—thank you so much, Mr. Herrick," she said gratefully, when he had finished; "no one has told me anything about him, and it does me good to know. And now will you do me a favour"—turning to him—"when you write next to Mr. Templeton, will you give him a message from me?"

"May I know the message first?" replied Malcolm cautiously. Then she smiled a little sadly.

"Ah, you do not trust me. Well, I cannot wonder at that. But my message will not hurt him; indeed, I think it may do him good. I want you to tell him that I have been ill, but I am getting well and strong now, and that I am with a dear friend who mothers and takes care of me, and whom I love better every day; and that I am content and at peace. Tell him that I never forget to pray for him, and that my one prayer and wish is for his happiness; that I entreat him with all my heart not to let his disappointment shadow his life; that if he can forget me, it would be wiser and better to do so; but if he remembers, let him think of me as though I were dead, and already praying for him in paradise. Will you tell him this?"

Malcolm was silent for a moment, then he bowed his

head, and Leah saw him pencil the message rapidly in his note-book.

"He shall have it—not a word shall be missed," he said briefly. Then he saw the tears of gratitude in her eyes.

"It will make him happier to know I am content," she whispered; "Cedric has such a kind heart."

"You are right—I think that message will do him good," agreed Malcolm. And then Leah lifted her basket and they walked back to the others.

It was during this visit to the Manor House that, in an unguarded moment, Malcolm's jealously-kept secret was betrayed to Mrs. Godfrey's sharp eyes, though Malcolm never guessed the fact then or afterwards.

They had been having tea in the alcove as usual, and the Colonel had just gone to the stables to give an order for the next day. Malcolm had made some humorous speech or other about his wonderful agility for a man of his age, when Mrs. Godfrey remarked innocently—

"How strange that you should say that, Mr. Herrick! It is just word for word what Elizabeth said when she was last here. I never saw two people think so alike;" and here Mrs. Godfrey laughed quite merrily, for once before she had accused Malcolm of making Elizabethan speeches. But her laugh died away when she saw Malcolm's face. It was too sudden, and he was not prepared; but the next moment he was hanging over the parapet trying to catch a peacock butterfly, and was actually joining in the laugh.

"That reminds me of a funny story," he said, speaking rather rapidly, "of two fellows who coined each other's ideas and got rather mixed sometimes;" and he told her the story from beginning to end with his old vivacity, and when he had finished it he went off in search of the Colonel.

But Mrs. Godfrey looked thoughtfully at the distant

prospect until Malcolm's footsteps were no longer audible.

" I feel like a burglar," she said to herself—" as though I had picked a lock and stolen something. I, to call myself a clever woman and never to guess it! But he has been too deep for me. He is very strong; one might as well try to open an oyster with one's nails as to find out anything Malcolm Herrick wishes to hide."

Mrs. Godfrey's face grew more troubled. " His mouth was like iron," she whispered, " but his face was so white in the sunshine. Poor fellow—poor fellow," in quite a caressing tone. " But you will be safe with me—even Alick shall not know. I wonder if he guesses anything; he only said yesterday that Mr. Herrick was different somehow. Ah, Elizabeth," she went on, pacing the terrace restlessly, " even wise women like you and me make mistakes sometimes. Yes, yes, you have made a great mistake, my dear;" and then she went into the house to get ready for her walk.

Malcolm went to Norway, and wondered why he did not enjoy himself more. He had congenial companions, good sport, and the weather was distinctly favourable, but he could not get rid of his trouble. Wherever he went, in sunlight or moonlight, the shadowy presence of the woman he loved so passionately walked beside him. On the shores of the lonely fiord or in the pine forests, Elizabeth's bright, speaking face seemed to move before him like a will o' the wisp; even in the rustle of the summer breeze in the leaves he could hear her voice, with its odd breaks and sibilant pauses, so curiously sweet to his ear. " I am possessed," he would say to himself—" I am possessed!" and indeed with all his strength of will he was powerless to resist that influence.

Dinah still wrote to him from time to time. The Wood House was empty, she told him; they had taken a house at Ullswater for three months. Mr. Carlyon and Theo were to be their guests. "Mr. Carlyon is very far from well," she wrote, "and his doctor has ordered complete rest for some months; and we think Elizabeth needs rest and change too, so altogether it is an excellent plan."

The Ullswater scheme seemed to work well. Dinah told Malcolm that Mr. Carlyon and Elizabeth were out together most of the day—fishing, boating, or roaming over the country in search of ferns and wild-flowers. "The life just suits Elizabeth," she went on; "she likes the quiet and freedom. And then she and Mr. Carlyon do each other so much good. He was so weak after the funeral that it is my private opinion that but for Elizabeth's care and devotion he would soon have followed David. I know he thinks so himself. 'Father has two daughters now,' Theo often says, 'but Elizabeth suits him best.' She says it quite amiably. Theo and I keep each other company. Her favourite amusement seems visiting the cottages and talking to the women and children; they get quite fond of 'the red-headed lady,' as they call her. But in the evening we are all together, and then Mr. Carlyon or Elizabeth reads aloud."

Malcolm was hard at work in his chambers long before the sisters returned to the Wood House. His book had proved a great success, and the leading papers had reviewed it most favourably. He had now commenced fresh work, and spent all his leisure hours at his desk. When Amias Keston complained that the studio evenings were things of the past, Malcolm looked at him a little sadly. "I can't help it, old fellow," he said gravely; "my social qualities are a bit rusty, but I will behave better by and bye;" and then he nodded to Verity, and went back to his papers and wrote on grimly, as though some unseen taskmaster were behind him, ready to scourge him on if he loitered.

"My work saved me—I had nothing else to live for," he said long afterwards; "nothing else fully occupied

my thoughts and made me forget my trouble. When I
was turning out copy I was almost happy. I was not
Malcolm Herrick: I was the heir of all the ages entering
into my kingdom."

" Yes, I know what you mean," replied the friend to
whom he had said this: " the children were strewing
flowers, and there were timbrels and harps, and they had
crowned you with laurel leaves, as though you were a
conquering hero."

" Something of that sort," he returned laughing. " But
you must not make fun of my sweet mistress from Par-
nassus; it kept me sane and cool to woo my reluctant
Muse. At times she frowned, and then I set my teeth
hard and worked like a navvy; but when she smiled my
pen seemed to fly in the sunlight, and I was warm and
happy."

Malcolm sent a copy of his book to Dinah, and she was
not long in acknowledging it. " We have both read it,
and think it beautiful," she wrote. " I tried to read it
aloud to Elizabeth, but I got so choky over it, and stopped
so often, that she grew impatient at last and carried off
the book to finish it in her own room. She wants me to
tell you how much she likes it. She has sent a copy to
Mr. Carlyon. Now I am going to tell you a piece of
news that will rather surprise you, but Elizabeth did not
wish me to drop a hint until things were definitely settled.

" Mr. Carlyon has resigned his living. The doctor has
told him plainly that another winter at Stokeley will be
too great a risk: the place is very bleak and cold, and
the work far too hard. The Bishop is going to put in a
younger man.

" Mr. Carlyon is actually coming to Rotherwood, and
is to take David's place"—Malcolm started and frowned
when he came to this." You will be surprised, of course
—every one is—but it is really a most excellent arrangement.

" You see, Mr. Charrington's health is not good, and as he will have to winter abroad, he really requires a curate-in-charge who will be responsible for the parish. The salary will be very little less than the income of Stokeley; there is no house, but we have got over this difficulty. Do you remember that low gray house, with the rowan tree over the gate, just by Elizabeth's Home of Rest, where little Kit died? It is scarcely more than a cottage, but it is very cosy and comfortable, and quite large enough for Theo and her father. There are two sitting-rooms—the larger one is to be Mr. Carlyon's study, they will not need a drawing-room—and four bed-rooms, and the garden is really charming. Rowan Cottage belongs to us, so we can ask a nominal rent. I cannot tell you how happy all this makes Elizabeth. Mr. Carlyon has been her one thought since David died. She feels it such a privilege to watch over him and attend to his little comforts. She is at work now at the cottage, getting everything ready for them, for they are expected in about a fortnight's time. But what a volume I am writing, my dear friend, and as usual about our own affairs. By the bye, I have never given you Elizabeth's message. She says that now you have become a celebrated author, she hopes you will not forget your old friends at the Wood House. Of course, this was only one of her joking speeches; she makes her little jokes now and then. What she really means is that you have not been to see us for a long time, and that when you come you will be welcome."

Malcolm read this letter at least a dozen times, and each time he came to the message he smiled as though he were well pleased; nevertheless he made no attempt to go to Staplegrove.

With the exception of that half-hour in the church-yard, he had not seen Elizabeth since her trouble—an instinctive feeling of delicacy had warned him to keep his

distance.   Nearly eight months had passed, but he was
still unwilling to force himself upon her, and the present
moment seemed to him peculiarly unpropitious.   Elizabeth's thoughts would be occupied with the preparations
at the cottage.   He knew her so well: she never did
things by halves, and she would be at Rotherwood all
day long.   No, he would not go yet, he said to himself;
it would be time enough when Cedric came back, and then
he would go down to the Wood House as a matter of
course.   It cost Malcolm some effort to keep this resolution when Cedric deferred his return week after week.
When the New Year opened he was at Cairo, and having
" a rattling good time," as he expressed it.   It was not
until the end of March that he and Mr. Dunlop turned
their faces homeward; but Malcolm made his work an
excuse and held grimly to his post.

CHAPTER XL

" HE IS MY RIVAL STILL"

Fire that's closest kept burns most of all.

. . . .

Ay, so true love should do: it cannot speak;
For truth hath better deeds than words to grace it.
SHAKESPEARE.

Love is patient and content with anything, so it be together
with its beloved.—JEREMY TAYLOR.

IT was on a bright sunshiny April afternoon that Malcolm at last paid his long-deferred visit to Staplegrove.
Cedric had been at home for nearly a week then, but he
and Malcolm had already met. Cedric had spent a night
at Cheyne Walk before going down to the Wood House,
and had extracted from his friend a reluctant promise
that he would come down as early in the week as possible.
Malcolm's assurance that he could only spare two nights
was treated by the young matron with incredulity.

" Look here, Herrick," he returned in a lordly manner,
" it is no good putting on side with me. You may be a
brilliant essayist, as that fellow called you, and a tiptop
literary swell, but you are not going to chuck up old
friends in this fashion. You are going to pay us a decent
visit, or your humble servant will kick up no end of a
shindy." But to all this Malcolm turned a deaf ear. He
repeated gravely that his engagements would only allow
him to sleep two nights at the Wood House; and as Malcolm had made the engagements himself for the express
purpose of shortening his visit, he probably knew best.

Cedric grumbled a good deal, and used some strong
language, but he quieted down after a time, and they went
on with their conversation; for Cedric had a plan in his
head, and he wanted his friend's advice and co-operation.

As Malcolm listened, he wondered what Dinah would think of her boy. Cedric looked at least two or three years older; he was broader, stronger, and Malcolm even fancied he had gained an inch in height; he was certainly a magnificent specimen of an athletic young Englishman.

He had always been handsome, but in Malcolm's opinion he had never appeared to greater advantage than now. His skin was slightly tanned by sun and wind, and his hair had darkened a little; he had lost the expression of weak irresolution which had marred his face, and he had evidently grown in manliness and self-restraint. His manner was still boyish at times, and Malcolm was glad to hear the old ringing laugh. Cedric's wound had been deep, but it was not incurable—time and change of scene had been potent factors in the cure. Malcolm listened with a great deal of interest to the scheme that Cedric intended to lay before his sisters.

It appeared that in the Bavarian highlands he had stumbled across an old school-fellow, Harry Strickland.

"We were chums at Haileybury," went on Cedric. "Harry was always a good sort; but his people sent him to Cambridge, so I lost sight of him. I knew his father was dead and that an uncle had offered him a home—his mother had died when he was quite a little chap, and he had no brothers or sisters—but when we met in the inn that wet night—when Dunlop and I were nearly drowned getting down from the Alp—he told me that a fit of gout had carried off his uncle quite unexpectedly."

"Poor chap, he seems a bit lonely," observed Malcolm sympathetically.

"Yes, he was mooning about, and rather bothered what to do next. So he was delighted at the idea of joining some of our excursions. But I will keep all that for the Wood House, for we had no end of adventures—the dare-devil Englishmen as they called us. But never mind that, I must hurry on.

"Harry is his uncle's heir—not that that amounts to much—but he has come into possession of a fine old farm that has been in the family for a hundred years at least, with plenty of good land, but, alas! little capital. The facts of the case are these, Herrick. Roger Strickland was not a rich man, and for want of a little ready money the farm has deteriorated in value. There is plenty to be got out of the land if only more could be spent on it; they want a new barn and some outhouses, and some of the fencing is disgraceful. As for the Priory itself—it is the Priory farm, you know—it is an old ramshackle place and in sore need of repair; some of the floors are rotten, and there are holes and crannies, and the mice and rats hold high revel in the disused rooms."

"My dear fellow, your description is not alluring," remarked Malcolm, wondering what all this meant.

"Oh, I am telling you the worst; it really is a lovely old place. Only Harry declares he would not live there alone for anything; it is supposed to be haunted by a certain evil-minded Strickland, in a green velvet suit and a powdered periwig, who drags one leg——but I will tell you the story another time; it will make your hair stand on end. Now Harry's difficulty is this: he has so little capital that he is half afraid of taking up the farm himself, and yet it is the only life he cares about; and he wants to find some one, with money to spare, who would join him in working the concern"—and here Cedric stopped and looked significantly at Malcolm.

"Ah, I understand now," returned his friend; "it is to be a sort of partnership. And so you think you would like to take to farming—eh, Cedric?"

"Like it," returned Cedric, colouring with excitement, "it is the very life I should choose. It would be just splendid for Harry and me to work together! Oh, I know what you are going to say"—as Malcolm opened his lips—"but wait a moment and let me finish first. Of course I know nothing of farming, and Harry knows precious little either; but he has a good bailiff whom he can trust, and whose wife manages the dairy. What I am going to propose is this, that Harry and I should go to the Agricultural College at Cirencester for a few months and get an idea of the business; and then, if Dinah would start me with a good round sum we could begin to get the place in order. I have set my heart on it, Herrick," and here Cedric's voice was very persuasive, " and I want you to come down and talk it out with her, like the good fellow you are."

" I will come, of course," returned Malcolm slowly, " and on the whole I am inclined to approve of your plan; but I do not think we can decide anything in this off-hand way. I think the best thing would be for us to reconnoitre the place, and perhaps Mr. Strickland could accompany us. The bailiff could give us full particulars, and we might consult Mr. Strickland's lawyer if we are in any difficulty."

And Cedric made no objection to this arrangement. They would go into the thing properly, of course, and there was no need to hurry matters; he only stipulated that Malcolm should come down and talk to Dinah without delay. This Malcolm had already promised; and when Cedric went to bed he felt assured that Malcolm's interest and sympathy were fully enlisted on his behalf.

" It is a foregone conclusion as far as Dinah is concerned," he thought, as he laid his head on his pillow. " Herrick can make her believe anything he likes, she has such faith in him; he has only to say that it is a capital plan, and that I shall make a first-rate farmer, and she will be ready to take out her cheque-book at once."

Cedric went round to 27 Queen's Gate to pay his respects to the ladies before he started for Staplegrove. Malcolm, who dined there that night, was amused by his mother's openly-avowed admiration of their young friend.

"Cedric Templeton is one of the most attractive-look-ing men I have ever seen," she said in her most serious voice; "he is very much improved in every way, and is altogether charming."

"I hope you agree with my mother, Anna?" observed Malcolm, laughing. "I think Cedric's ears must be burn-ing at the present moment." But Anna only returned rather shyly that she thought Mr. Templeton looked ex-tremely well.

Malcolm had fixed his day, but he refused to state any hour for his arrival. There was no need to send the dog-cart for him; he would prefer taking a fly from the station. Of course, he put forth business as his plea; but in reality he did not wish Cedric to meet him, the lad's incessant chatter all the way to Staplegrove would have worried him excessively. It was just a year since he had seen Elizabeth, and in his heart he was secretly dreading that first meeting. Perhaps he had left it too long, he ought to have gone sooner; they would be like strangers, and the first interview would be very embarrassing to them both. Yes, he had been a fool to spare himself the pain of seeing her grief. He had kept away, banishing himself for all these months, and yet what good had it done him? it had only increased his nervousness and dis-comfort tenfold. He was haunted by the fear that he should find her changed, that she would be cold and distant with him. He worked himself up into such a fever at last, that half-way up the Staplegrove Hill he stopped the fly and told the driver that he wished to walk, and directed him to take his bag to the Wood House.

The walk certainly refreshed him, and by the time he reached the Crow's Nest he felt more ready for the ordeal. When he came to the gate that led to the Wood House, he hesitated, and then crossed the road and stood for a few moments looking down the little woodland path he remembered so well. No other place was so associated with Elizabeth. How often he had met her at this little gate, or waited for her when he knew she was coming back from Rotherwood! That day, for example, when she wore her white sun-bonnet, and came along swinging her arms like an imperial milkmaid, a "very queen of curds and cream." At that moment a little sharp clang of a distant gate made his heart beat suddenly. There were footsteps—yes, without doubt, there were footsteps —it was no fancy. Then at the bend of the road he could see distinctly a tall black figure, walking rather slowly and wearily along, and though he could not see her face he knew it was Elizabeth.

The next minute he unlatched the gate a little noisily; he would not steal a march on her—she believed herself alone; then she looked up and quickened her pace, and when he came up to her, there was actually a smile on her face.

"You are fond of surprises," she said, looking at him as she gave him her hand. "Am I late, have you come to meet me; and what have you done with your luggage?"

"I have sent it on," he returned quietly; "it is such a lovely afternoon that I preferred to walk. No, I did not come to meet you; for all I knew, you might have been at the Wood House. I only had a fancy that I should like to see the woodlands again, and then I saw you coming."

"It is not my usual afternoon for Rotherwood," she returned quickly, but a faint colour had come in her face at his words; "but I am there most days. You know, of course—Dinah will have told you—of the new interest I have there. I think Die tells you most things," she continued, with the same glimmer of a smile on her lips.

"Yes, she is very good," he returned gravely. They were walking side by side now. Malcolm had hardly trusted himself to look at her, and yet nothing had been lost on him. How changed she was! that was his first thought. She looked years older; mourning did not suit her; the black hat with its heavy trimming seemed to extinguish her somehow. She was paler and thinner, he was sure of that, and had lost some of her splendid vitality; and yet in spite of all this it was to him the dearest face in the world.

As she made that poor little attempt at a smile, his whole heart went out to her in profound love and pity, and he forgot his own pain in remembering her trouble.

"Your sister told me about Mr. Carlyon," he said, as they crossed the road; "I was very glad to hear from her how well it answered."

"He is very happy at Rotherwood," returned Elizabeth. "The people seem to take to him, and he and the vicar are like brothers, and the work exactly suits him. Theo is happy too, and that is a great blessing. And we have made the cottage so pretty that I should like you to see it." Elizabeth's manner had become more natural; she spoke now as though she were sure of Malcolm's interest. He did not disappoint her.

"I shall certainly call there when I go to the vicarage," he returned, and then he stopped as though to take breath. "I was very glad when I read your sister's letter, and knew that this new work was to come to you; it must make you so much happier."

Malcolm's words were almost magical in their effect, for Elizabeth turned to him with her old eagerness.

"Oh, you always understand," she said gratefully; "that is why it is so easy to talk to you. Yes, indeed, it has made me so much happier. Life is worth living when one knows there is some one in the world who is dependent on one for earthly comfort. Of course Mr. Carlyon has Theo, but she does not know him as I do. I am at the cottage nearly every day."

Malcolm listened and smiled, but he could not have spoken at that moment. How little she guessed how her

26

words stabbed him! She could tell him to his face that life was worth living " because there was some one dependent on her for earthly comfort," and yet she could leave him hungering and thirsting in that sad pilgrimage of his. All her thoughts and sweet ministries were for David's father. " It is for him," he thought bitterly; " he is my rival still—dead as well as living. She is very faithful: she will not forget him, and her heart is still closed to me."

Elizabeth did not seem to notice his silence; she talked on about Mr. Charrington, and the new schools; and then Cedric came flying down the path to meet them, and the next moment Malcolm saw Dinah smiling in the porch.

After dinner that evening they gathered round the fire, for the nights were still chilly, and Elizabeth joined the circle to hear Cedric's scheme discussed.

From his dark corner Malcolm watched her. In spite of her unrelieved black and absence of ornaments, she was looking more like the old Elizabeth. She grew interested and then quite absorbed in Cedric's project, and soon began discussing it with her wonted vivacity. When Malcolm made some damping remark, she argued the point with him in a most peremptory fashion, and was quite Elizabethan in her rebuke.

" That is the worst of talking to a lawyer," she said severely: " his legal mind takes such cut-and-dried views. Granted that it is a speculation, it seems a promising one; and nothing venture, nothing have. I don't know how you feel, Die, but I am quite willing to do my share." Then Dinah, who was in quite a flutter of excitement and pleasure, looked at her adviser in a timid, deprecating fashion.

" If Mr. Herrick thinks we are not imprudent, I should like to do as Cedric wishes," she replied; " though there is no need to touch your money, Betty." But Elizabeth took no notice of this remark.

"I have a proposal to make," she went on in such an animated voice that Malcolm quite started. "Why should we not all go down and see the place? And Mr. Strickland could come too. Donnarton is only three hours from town; it would be a sort of picnic excursion, and I know Dinah would like it."

"Bravo, Betty, what a brick you are!" exclaimed Cedric boisterously; and Malcolm observed in a low voice that it was an excellent idea.

But when they talked it over quietly they found an amendment was necessary. It would be impossible to go and return the same day; there was the farm to inspect, and most likely they would have to consult the lawyer. The matter ended by Cedric volunteering to go back with Malcolm when he returned to town, and talk the matter over with Harry Strickland; and if any decent lodgings could be found in the little town of Donnarton, they would stop at least one night.

As early a day as possible was to be fixed, and all the arrangements were to be made by the gentlemen. Dinah was evidently charmed with the prospect of seeing the Priory; but Elizabeth's ardour quickly cooled when she found it would be necessary to remain the night. "I suppose you could not go without me, Die?" she observed when alone with her sister. Then Dinah's face fell.

"Oh, Betty dear, that would spoil everything," she said in a distressed tone. "Surely you want to see dear Cedric's future home."

"Of course I want to see it," returned Elizabeth rather shortly; "only I should have preferred going down quietly a little later on"—which was somewhat contradictory, as she had herself proposed the plan. But perhaps the delighted look on Malcolm's face when he heard her proposition had somewhat alarmed her; for the next day she was a little cool and distant in her manner to him, and left his entertainment to Dinah and Cedric.

CHAPTER XLI

"YOU CAN BE DINAH'S FRIEND"

Sometimes I said: This thing shall be no more;
My expectation wearies and shall cease;
I will resign it now and be at peace:
　　Yet never gave it o'er.
　　　　　　　　　CHRISTINA ROSSETTI.

VARIOUS complications prevented the Templeton—Strickland picnic, as Cedric termed it, from being speedily carried out, and it was not until the middle of May that a day was definitely fixed, and Cedric brought his sisters up to Waterloo, where Malcolm and Mr. Strickland met them. The whole party were to be housed at the Priory, where they were to sleep two nights. There were plenty of good bedrooms, Harry Strickland told them, and in a rough, homely fashion he could undertake that they should be comfortable. He had already been down to the Priory to look after things, and to tell Mrs. Renshaw that she must find some temporary help. He would have brought down a hamper of delicacies from Fortnum and Mason, but Cedric remonstrated with him and said his sisters would much prefer simple country fare. And then Harry gave orders to his bailiff that the plumpest chickens and the fattest ducks were to be sacrificed, and new laid-eggs and cream served *ad libitum*.

Malcolm always looked back on those two days as the saddest and yet the most beautiful he had ever known. For what sadness can be equal to that of being with the person one loves best in the world, and yet being conscious of a great dividing gulf, that never narrows; and yet in spite of this, what happiness to know that one roof

404

would cover them for two days! Malcolm was in that condition when he was thankful for even fragments and crumbs—a kind smile, an approving word from Elizabeth made his heart beat more quickly. As for Dinah, she was in the seventh heaven. The country was lovely, the Priory a beautiful, picturesque old place, with leaded casements and a deep porch, and a wonderful neglected garden, a veritable wilderness of sweets. She liked everything, admired everything; she thought Harry Strickland a thoroughly nice fellow; and she and Elizabeth wandered all over the house, suggesting improvements in their practicable, sensible way; and full of admiration for the fine oak staircase and some really beautiful cabinets, and benches, on the landing-place and in the best parlours. Roger Strickland had always called them parlours—the oak parlour and the cedar parlour—the latter a charming room with a fine ceiling, cedar-lined panels, and a cosy nook by the fireplace covered with quaint tapestry. Elizabeth fell in love with this room directly. She insisted that a certain cabinet she had seen upstairs should be brought down to the cedar parlour, and that an empty recess should be fitted up for books; and the young men listened to her quite meekly. Her reforms and alterations became so sweeping and extensive at last, that Malcolm, who at first had been only amused, grew seriously alarmed. "We must see what Mr. Atkins thinks," he kept observing; "we must decide on nothing without him." Mr. Atkins was the lawyer who had managed all the Strickland business, and they were to drive into Donnarton that very afternoon to consult him. Nevertheless, when Malcolm made his little protest, Elizabeth only shrugged her shoulders and muttered something about "cautious legal minds" under her breath.

"Good for you, Betty, that we have a lawyer handy," observed Cedric in high good-humour, "or you would be ruining yourself and Dinah too. No—no, Herrick is

right : we will mend the holes and lay down fresh floor-
ing where it is absolutely necessary, and do any cleaning
and painting that are required, but the rest can keep for a
while; the parlours and two decent bedrooms are all we
shall require." And then they went off to see the dairy.

They drove into Donnarton after an early dinner; but
on arriving at the lawyer's Elizabeth suddenly remarked
that they were far too large a party, and that she meant
to do a little sight-seeing on her own account. So, as
they knew of old that it was useless to argue with her,
they went inside, and from over the wire blind in the
dingy front room Malcolm watched her crossing the butter market in the direction of the ancient churchyard that
skirted one side of it.

It troubled him to hear a bell toll as she passed through
the little gate, and a moment later a funeral procession,
following a small coffin, evidently of a child, climbed
slowly up the steps.

After that he resigned himself to a long, tedious hour.
The room was hot and airless, the lawyer very prosy and
unnecessarily fluent; but he seemed a straightforward,
honest man, and gave them good counsel. Malcolm was
soon put into possession of all the Strickland bequest, and
after this it was all plain sailing.

The land was good, and though the farm had deteriorated, a little judicious management and a moderate out-
lay would soon put things on a different footing. This
was Mr. Atkins's opinion; he had himself suggested that
a partner with some capital should be found.

Some final arrangements were made after this; then
Cedric suggested that they should have tea at the inn,
and Malcolm volunteered to go in search of Elizabeth.

He felt sure that he should find her still in the churchyard, and he was right. She was standing near one of
those dreary monuments which affectionate relatives
loved to raise to their departed friends in the early Vic-

torian era. There was old Time with his beard and scythe, a broken column, veiled mourners and a dejected-looking cherub, and the stiff funereal urn; but Elizabeth was looking at a cluster of grassy mounds under a yew tree, with simple headstones, and here and there a cross. She looked up at Malcolm with a quiet smile.

"Have they sent you to find me?" she asked. "It is so nice and peaceful here; I like to think of all those tired workers resting after their labours—their work done."

"I think you make a mistake there," returned Malcolm, falling at once into her vein of thought. "Resting, true, but their work is certainly not finished: it is only broken off, because probably they have reached a part that can only be carried on under certain conditions."

Elizabeth turned round in her quick way. "Say that again!" she exclaimed eagerly, and Malcolm repeated his speech.

"I like that," she murmured: "if one could only grasp that thought."

"There is no difficulty, surely," he replied. "People often talk of continuity of life, and continuity of love, and why not continuity of work? Think of all the thousands of workers who have gone hence, many of them in the prime of their youth or manhood—votaries of science, of art, pioneers and missionaries, soldiers of the Cross, and soldiers of the Queen— a vast army that no man can number!" Here Malcolm paused.

"Yes, yes—oh, please go on!" Elizabeth was drinking in his words as though they were new wine.

"You know what the Wisdom of Solomon says: 'In the sight of the unwise they seemed to die, and their departure is taken for misery;' but," looking at her with a smile, "you and I know better than that."

"And you think, as Mr. Carlyon does, that there will be active life and work there?" and Elizabeth's large sad eyes were full of yearning as she asked the question.

"How could I face the future if I did not believe it?" returned Malcolm earnestly. "Why are these talents, these gifts of genius, this thirst for knowledge given to us, if they are not to be developed and turned to account hereafter? Think of the conditions under which such work will be done"—and here Malcolm's voice was full of enthusiasm—"the wisdom of the ages around us, the great ones of the earth—in whose footprints we have striven to walk—beside us in the fulness of their majesty —no hindrances, no physical weakness, no painful conflict between the human will and the clouded intellect: the heir of all the ages will have entered his goodly heritage. Oh, forgive me," checking himself abruptly, for the tears were streaming down Elizabeth's cheeks.

"No—no, it has been such a comfort! I shall not forget; you have done me so much good;" and then she wiped away her tears, and tried to smile, and by the time they reached the inn she had regained her composure. During their drive home Malcolm occupied the seat next her in the waggonette, and Dinah, who was opposite to them, noticed that Elizabeth talked more to him than she had done since that unlucky afternoon at the Pool, and that Malcolm looked unusually happy.

But his content was of short duration. The next morning, as they were waiting for the waggonette to take them to the station, Elizabeth wandered into the deserted garden, and Malcolm, who followed her, found her standing under a Guelder rose-tree, picking some of the snowy blossoms.

She greeted him with a smile. "This reminds me of Cedric's nursery days," she observed. "He used to love to pelt me with these soft white balls when he was a mite of a thing in a white frock and blue ribbons. Powder-puffins," he used to call them. "What a pretty little fellow he was, to be sure! Well, Mr. Herrick," as Malcolm made no reply, "so our little jaunt is at an end. It has really been very pleasant, don't you think so?"

"I have enjoyed it," returned Malcolm. He spoke with marked emphasis.

"Oh, so have we all," she replied lightly. "It is so delightful to see those two boys so ridiculously happy;" for both Cedric and Harry Strickland had behaved during breakfast time like a couple of crazy schoolboys.

"You have helped to make them so," observed Malcolm meaningly.

"Oh no," in a careless tone; "Dinah is taking the lion's share. If I had had my way, I would have restored . this beautiful old place—but two lawyers are enough to crush any woman."

"I am only thankful that we were able to check such sinful extravagance," he returned calmly; "I believe generosity can degenerate into positive vice." But Elizabeth refused to listen to this.

"If it had been Cedric's house, I would have done it up from garret to basement," she said wilfully. "Anyhow, I mean to take the garden in hand. When you come down to the Wood House next, you shall hear all my plans, and of course we shall have one of our old fights over them."

Now what was there in this speech to cause such a curious revulsion in Malcolm's mind? Elizabeth was speaking with the utmost good-humour, and at any other moment he would have thought her imperiousness charming—so what possessed him to draw himself up and say rather stiffly that he feared that it would be some time before they saw him at Staplegrove. "You know, I am going abroad this summer with my mother and Anna Sheldon," he continued gravely; "we are going to the Engadine and the Italian Lakes."

"But that is not until August," returned Elizabeth, rather taken aback by Malcolm's sudden gravity. She had been so pleased with him the previous afternoon; her liking for him had deepened, and she had felt a genuine desire for his friendship. In her secret heart she knew how well he had behaved, and was grateful to him for his delicacy and tact; but at this moment she felt as though she had received a douche of cold water. "That is not until August, and it is only May now," she repeated rather seriously.

"Yes, I know"—but here Malcolm lost his self-command. Perhaps the May sunshine dazzled him, or the soft friendliness in Elizabeth's eyes and that unvarying kindliness tried his endurance, but for once the underlying bitterness found vent.

"I cannot come before I go abroad—you, of all people, ought not to expect it! You must know how I feel—that it is not good for me! When I am with you, I can scarcely endure my pain!" He spoke harshly, almost flinging the words at her; but she answered him quite humbly.

"Forgive me, I did not want to hurt you," in a trembling voice—"I did not understand."

"No, you have never understood," but there was no conciliation in his tone; "you make things harder for me. Elizabeth, I ought not to have said this, but the happiness of these two days has been too much for me. I will keep away until I have regained mastery over myself, and then I will come. If you want me—if there be anything that I can do for you or your sister, you must send for me."

"I could not do that," she returned, averting her face, and showers of white petals powdered the ground at her feet, as her nervous fingers unconsciously stript the stalks —"you have made that impossible." And then she continued impulsively, "Mr. Herrick, you must believe how sorry I am. You have been such a friend—such a true, kind friend, and I have been so grateful to you!"

"I can never be your friend, Elizabeth"—there was a sad finality about Malcolm's tone that made Elizabeth shrink from him almost timidly.

"Can you not?" she returned with a little sob. "But you can be Dinah's friend. Do not let her suffer because of this; if we are both unhappy, there is no need that she should be, and you are one of her greatest comforts."

"You are right," replied Malcolm more gently, "and I shall always be at Miss Templeton's service. I know you tell her everything, will you let her know this?—when she wants me, when either of you want me, I will come if needs be from the ends of the earth. You will believe this?"

"I always believe Dinah's friend," she returned, in a voice he hardly recognised—it was so soft and full of feeling; "but how I shall miss mine!" and here Elizabeth's eyes were very sad. She looked at the bare flower-stalks in her hands rather remorsefully before she threw them away and returned to the house.

On their way to the station Malcolm occupied a seat next to the driver. Now and then Elizabeth glanced up at the broad shoulders a little wistfully. How silent he was, she did not once hear his voice! While they waited for the train, he and Harry Strickland paced up and down the platform. The train was rather full, one or two strangers were in their compartment, and whether accidentally or by purpose, Malcolm was shut off from the rest of his party.

At Waterloo a silent hand-shake was all that passed between him and Elizabeth, and even to Dinah he said little; but as he drove off in the hansom, he told himself that he had done right, and that he did not regret a single word he had spoken.

It was far better for her to know the truth: he understood her so well—she was not dense, but she was wilfully blinding her eyes; very likely she was misled by his calm, matter-of-fact manner.

"She thinks I have got over it—that I have come to my senses, and accepted the inevitable—that we can be friends in the comfortable, approved fashion"—here Malcolm's eyes flashed with sudden fire—" but she has found out her mistake. No, there shall be no more deception. When I see her again I shall wear my true colours—though Heaven forbid that I should persecute her with attentions that only embarrass and distress her. No, you are safe with me, dear," he murmured inwardly; "but even for your sweet sake I will not act a lie. I am Dinah's friend, but your lover, Elizabeth—and must be as long as I have life and breath"—and somehow this solemn avowal of his heart's secret did Malcolm good. But Dinah noticed that Elizabeth was more than usually depressed for some time after their return to the Wood House.

CHAPTER XLII

THE WHIRLIGIG OF TIME

Give what you have; to some it may be better than you dare
to think.—LONGFELLOW.

The Possible stands by us ever fresh,
Fairer than aught which any life hath owned,
And makes divine amends.

JEAN INGELOW.

Two years had passed away since Malcolm had uttered
his passionate protest in the Priory garden that May
morning, when the white petals of the Guelder roses in
Elizabeth's hand lay like snow on the gravel path, and all
this time he had sternly adhered to his resolution.

In those two years he had only paid four visits to the
Wood House, and on two of these occasions Elizabeth
had been absent. Each time he had come on Dinah's invitation, to give her the help and counsel she needed, and
more than once he had met her at 27 Queen's Gate.

For Cedric had had his way, and had effected an introduction between his sisters and Mrs. Herrick; and as they
had mutually taken to each other, a pleasant intimacy had
been the result, and Anna had paid two or three visits to
the Wood House. From the first moment of their meeting Anna had fallen in love with Dinah. "You must not
think that I do not care for Miss Elizabeth Templeton,"
she had observed rather shyly to Malcolm, after her first
visit to Staplegrove—"for I admire and like her more
than I can say, and I am never tired of talking to her—
but I do love my dear Miss Dinah!" And indeed Dinah
accepted the girl's innocent worship with great kindness.
"She is a dear child, and Elizabeth and I are very fond

of her," she wrote once to Malcolm; "the thought that some one else is fond of her too makes me very happy." For at this time it was evident to all Cedric's friends that a mutual attachment was growing up between him and Anna.

The years had not been unfruitful to Malcolm, and his name as a powerful and successful author was firmly established. He no longer held his appointment, and had given up his dingy chambers in Lincoln's Inn. His own work fully occupied him, and thanks to his literary receipts and his mother's generosity, he realised a good income.

To his own regret and to his friends also, he was no longer a member of the Keston ménage. He had outgrown his homely quarters, and now occupied one of the new flats in Cheyne Walk, and lived in quite a palatial fashion, though many a pipe was still smoked in Amias's studio. Malcolm had emerged from his shell, and mixed freely in society. His was a name to conjure with, and all the people best worth knowing gathered round him and delighted to do him homage. Elizabeth used to read his name sometimes in the columns of the *Times* and the *Morning Post*. "He seems to go everywhere, and to know every one," she observed once to Dinah; "I am afraid he will be terribly spoiled." But she only said it to tease Dinah. She knew that Malcolm Herrick had no overweening estimate of himself—that, in spite of his success and his many friends, and all the smiles and adulation lavished on him, at heart he was a lonely man. Perhaps in her way Elizabeth was lonely too. In spite of her devotion to David's father, there were times when the narrowness of her life oppressed her—when her broad sympathies and strong vitality seemed to cry out for a larger life, for a wider outlook—when she trod the woodland paths with a sense of weariness—the same path day after day.

" How tired one gets of it all!" she said to herself one May afternoon, as she came in sight of the porch where Mr. Carlyon was reading tranquilly and enjoying the sweet spring air. The curate-in-charge looked slightly older and had taken to spectacles, but otherwise there was little change in him. On the whole, his existence was a very peaceful one. He loved Rotherwood and the simple, kindly folk amongst whom he lived. His books and Elizabeth's society were his chief pleasures. If the day passed without seeing her, Theo noticed that he grew restless and preoccupied, and finally went across to the Wood House on some excuse or other, to assure himself that nothing was amiss.

" Father thinks that there is no one like Elizabeth," Theo would observe: " nothing that she says or does is wrong. If he had his way they would never be apart;" and Theo was right.

In spite of his short sight, Mr. Carlyon soon detected the signs of mental weariness on Elizabeth's pale face; for as she seated herself on the wooden bench beside him, he patted her hand in his tender, homely way.

" What is it, my dear?" he asked gently. " You look tired, Elizabeth."

" Do I?" she returned absently; " I feel as though I could walk ten miles with pleasure. That is the worst, I am so strong that nothing tires me. Sometimes I fancy it would be a pleasant experience to be honestly fatigued in some good cause. How one would sleep after it!"

" I thought you always slept well, dear?"

" Oh, so I do: often I fall asleep as soon as my head is on the pillow. But I wake early—the first twitter of the birds rouses me—and then life looks so long." Elizabeth spoke in a dejected tone.

" Come and walk," was Mr. Carlyon's only answer to this; " I have been writing my sermon all the morning, and I feel a bit stiff and headachy. Let us go down the valley;" and as Elizabeth made no objection to this, he got his hat and stick, and they sallied forth together. Outside the gate they came upon the vicar, and the three walked on together, as Mr. Charrington intended calling at the Crow's Nest. Elizabeth had been very silent all the way, and had left the conversation to the two gentlemen. When Mr. Charrington had quitted them, they turned into the long woodland path that skirted the valley. It was a beautiful spot, and a favourite resort of Elizabeth's. She loved to breathe the spicy incense of the pines, and to watch the shadows move across the valley. As they seated themselves under a little clump of firs, they could look down into the dark woods far below. All round them were heather, bracken, whortleberries, and brambles, and later on the hillside would be a glory of purple.

"Well, Elizabeth, what is it?" asked Mr. Carlyon, as she still sat beside him in a brown study, and her brow puckered and lined with thought. "I am sure I have been patient enough." Then she started and laughed a little nervously.

"How stupid I am this afternoon! And I have so much to tell you. I am so ashamed of myself, for I ought to be in such good spirits. The young people have come to an understanding at last. Cedric and Anna have written to Dinah; I left her crying for joy over their letters.

"I do not wonder at that—Miss Sheldon is a sweet girl."

"Cedric thinks she is perfect. I wish you could have seen his letter: he is rapturously happy. And Anna writes so sweetly: she says it seems like a dream; that she can hardly believe in her happiness; that she does not deserve it, and that Cedric is everything that she could desire."

"Ah, they are young—life does not seem long to them, does it, Elizabeth?" She smiled and shook her head.

"Cedric is going to bring her down on Wednesday,

and he wants Mr. Herrick to come too. Dinah means to ask him, I believe. I tell her that he is far too busy and important a personage to trouble with our small family concerns; but Dinah was quite indignant when I said that."

"She has greater faith in his friendship, you see." But to this Elizabeth made no answer. She went on talking with assumed eagerness of the young couple.

"Cedric intends to be married soon," she said. "Mr. Strickland is going to let them have the Priory, and has taken a cottage for his own use. How charmed Anna will be when she sees it—the garden is a dream of beauty, and the house is delightful!" For each summer she and Dinah had spent weeks at the Priory, and had succeeded in transforming the place. Anna would have a lovely home, and the simple country life would be far more to her taste than ever town had been. Even Mrs. Herrick. who would feel her loss keenly, owned this.

"And Mr. Herrick is to be asked on this grand occasion? I am glad of that, Elizabeth;" and here Mr. Carlyon pushed up his spectacles and peered at her in his mild. short-sighted way. "Do you know, my child, there is something I have been wanting to say to you for a long time, and I may as well say it now."

Elizabeth looked at him rather apprehensively: there was something significant in his manner.

"Something? What do you mean?" she faltered.

"You have been a dear good daughter to me," he went on, clearing his throat from a slight huskiness, "and if you were my own flesh and blood you could not be more to me. We have so much in common, have we not, my dear—and then we both loved David."

"Yes—yes," she murmured, and the ready tears sprang to her eyes.

"We mourned for our dear boy together," he went on slowly, "and groped our way hand in hand through the

27

darkness. How unhappy we were three years ago! Even now it is painful to look back on those days, but, thank God! time and His grace have helped us, and we no longer suffer."

"I am not so sure of that," returned Elizabeth in a low voice; but he seemed not to hear her.

"You have been very faithful, Elizabeth. If you had been David's widow you could not have mourned for him more deeply; but, as David's father, I would bid you mourn no more."

She stared at him with parted lips, but the words would not come.

"Why should you spoil your life, Elizabeth? You are only thirty-five, and please God there are many, many years before you. Why is your heart to be empty and your arms unfilled because our precious boy is in paradise? Do you know, my dear, we often spoke of this—he and I. Thank God, there were no secrets between us. and he told me more than once that the thought of your future was always on his mind."

Elizabeth bowed her head on her hands. She was weeping now, though the tears came very quietly. "If he had only talked to me!" she murmured.

"He tried to do so more than once," returned Mr. Carlyon, "but each time you stopped him. Would you like me to tell you what he said as well as I can remember his words?" She nodded, but her face was still hidden.

"It was at Ventnor, and very near the end, and he was talking about you—living or dying you were his one thought. 'I know how she will grieve,' he said to me, 'but, father, you must not let her grieve too long. I think it would trouble me even in paradise—if such a thing could be—if I thought I had spoilt her life. Elizabeth is made for happiness—she must not waste her sweetness.' And then—shall I go on?" but all the same he did not wait for consent—"it was then that David told me something that I had guessed before—that some one else loved you, and loved you dearly. I am right, am I not, Elizabeth?" No answer, but he could see how her hands clutched each other, as though in sudden agitation.

"'I was beforehand, and he had no chance,' David went on, 'but he is my superior in everything'—he was always so humble in his own estimation, dear fellow. 'Father, Malcolm Herrick worships the ground she walks on. One day he must have his reward.'"

"Oh, hush—hush, for pity's sake," and Elizabeth stretched out her hand to stop him, but he detained it gently.

"Elizabeth, three years are long enough for mourning, and Mr. Herrick has been very patient. Why should another life be spoiled? Why should you doom him as well as yourself to loneliness? I have not forgotten his look that evening when you were singing to us—it was the look of a man who is starving for a little happiness, for the comfort and sweet sustenance that only a wife can give him. There, I will say no more—I have discharged my conscience, and repeated my boy's words. I trust they have not been spoken in vain." His hand rested lightly on her head for a moment as though in blessing, but no word escaped his lips. Then he rose, and after a moment Elizabeth joined him, and they walked back silently together.

"You are not vexed with me, my dear?" he asked anxiously, when they parted at the gate of Rowan Cottage. Then Elizabeth raised her sad eyes to his.

"Why should I be vexed? You are always so kind—so kind; but you have said things that have troubled me;" and she left him, and walked on rapidly until she found herself in the familiar woodland path, and then she unconsciously slackened her pace.

She felt strangely shaken and agitated. The words her old friend had spoken had thrilled her as though by an electric shock. It was a message from the dead. Half-involuntarily she sank down on the bank in the very spot where Malcolm had picked the honeysuckle. She knew what it was to be tired now—for the moment she felt weak and powerless as a little child.

Over and over again she repeated dumbly Mr. Carlyon's words. How could she doubt that David had spoken them when he had tried with loving unselfishness to say them to her! Would she ever forget the tender solemnity of his manner?—

"Elizabeth, life is long as you say, and your great loving heart must not remain unsatisfied. Do not mourn for me too long—do not refuse comfort that may be offered to you, if you can be happy, dear;" but she had stopped him, and he could say no more. Truly, as his father had said, "living or dying she had been his one thought." "Oh, how good you were to me, David!" she whispered.

She rose and paced restlessly to and fro, while a bright-eyed robin watched her from a hazel twig; for other words besides David's were haunting her, and had been haunting her for two years, thought she had vainly tried to forget them. Sometimes she would wake from sleep with her heart beating, and those sad, reproachful words sounding in her ears—

"I can never be your friend, Elizabeth." And again, "If either of you want me, I will come if needs be from the ends of the earth." Would she ever forget the look on his face as he said this!

She had told him then that she should miss him. In these two years she had only seen him twice, and each time some strange embarrassment on her part had seemed to estrange them still more. He was Dinah's friend, not hers—from her he would have all or nothing. And yet, as time went on, and that vast loneliness of life pressed on her more and more, and her woman spirit seemed to wander through waste places seeking rest and finding none, that silent, patient love, that seemed to enfold her from a distance, began to appeal to her more strongly. " Why should another life be spoiled?" Mr. Carlyon had said. " Ah, why indeed?" she murmured.

Then her mood changed; her face grew hot, and there was a pained look in her eyes. " I have tried him too much," she thought; " there are limits even to his patience. Last time I noticed a change: he is growing weary—perhaps he has seen some one else;" and here she choked down something like a sob and hurried on.

Dinah wondered what was amiss with her that evening; she seemed so listless and silent, and took so little interest in the absorbing topic of Cedric's engagement.

The young couple were to arrive the following afternoon, and Dinah had arranged to drive to Earlsfield to meet them. As they sat down to luncheon, she said to Elizabeth, " I am so glad that Mr. Herrick has promised to come to-morrow; I have just had a telegram from him;" and she handed it to her sister. Elizabeth was rather a long time reading it. " Shall be with you by dinner-time. Shall take fly. Stay two nights."

" Is it not good of him to come, when he is so dreadfully busy?" continued Dinah in her placid, satisfied voice. " Cedric will be delighted to have him! Do you think we ought to ask Theo and Mr. Carlyon to dinner, or would Mr. Herrick prefer just a family party?"

" Oh, I think a family party will suit him best," returned Elizabeth gravely; " Theo rather bores him with her parish talk;" and Dinah said no more.

CHAPTER XLIII

A MAY AFTERNOON

What is this love that now on angel wing
Sweeps us amid the stars in passionate calm.
                                    MacDonald.

ELIZABETH stood on the terrace in the sweet stillness of a May afternoon. She had been gathering flowers for the dinner-table and drawing-room—masses of white and mauve lilac, long golden trails of laburnum, dainty pink and white May blossoms—but though the Guelder roses almost dropped into her hand, she passed them by untouched and with averted eyes. All her life they had been her special favourites, but now they recalled too vividly a painful episode—the day when Malcolm Herrick so sternly and so sorrowfully refused her his friendship.

Malcolm had been nearly twenty-four hours at the Wood House, and she had hardly exchanged a dozen words with him, and already he had signified his intention of returning to town the next morning, in spite of Cedric's vehement protestations. He had arrived so late the previous evening that he had had only time for a hasty greeting before he went to his room to prepare for dinner. During the evening the young couple had naturally engrossed his attention. A harder-hearted man than Malcolm would have been touched by Anna's innocent happiness and her shy pride in her handsome young lover. "Does she not look lovely!" Elizabeth had said to him in a low voice as they were all gathered on the terrace after dinner. And indeed the girl looked very fair and sweet in her white silk dress, with a row of pearls clasped round her soft throat. "You are right; and yet I never thought

422

Anna really pretty," he returned in a cool, critical tone. "Happiness is generally a beautifier, and my little girl certainly looks her best to-night." And then he went after them; and Elizabeth saw that Anna was hanging on his arm as they went down the steps and that Cedric's hand was on his shoulder.

"How happy they are!" she thought a little enviously; "they are both devoted to him, and he certainly returns their affection. He is good and kind to every one but me," she continued resentfully: "if Dinah had said that, he would not have answered her so curtly and then turned on his heel and left her." Here Elizabeth wilfully ignored the fact that Cedric had signalled to him somewhat impatiently.

"I believe that he has made a vow not to speak to me if he can help it."

Elizabeth was in a restless, irritable frame of mind that prevented her from taking a reasonable view of things. If she had been less alive to her own embarrassment and discomfort, she would have discovered for herself that Malcolm was ill at ease too.

If he had not talked much to her, he had watched her closely, and it had troubled and pained him to see how thin and worn she looked; in the strong light he had even noticed a faint tinge of gray in her bright brown hair.

"She is pitiless to herself as well as to me," he said to himself bitterly; "if she goes on like this, she will be an old woman before her time. Her life is too limited: it suits Dinah, but it does not suit Elizabeth. Why should she spend her time teaching village children and fagging after that old man"—for Malcolm was growing hopeless and embittered.

The evening had not been productive of much comfort to either of them; a sense of widening estrangement, of ever-deepening misunderstanding kept them apart.

When Elizabeth went to the piano—for she had been induced to resume her singing—Malcolm did not follow
her; neither did she sing one of his favourite songs.
Even when Dinah innocently recalled one that she remembered he loved, and begged her sister to sing it, Elizabeth obstinately refused. "Oh, that old thing!" she said
contemptuously; "I am so tired of it." But Malcolm
was quite aware of her reason for refusing: she would
make no effort to please him, for fear he should be encouraged to repeat his offence.

The next morning things were no better. Cedric had
asked Malcolm to walk with them to the valley. It was
a glorious morning—bright and fresh and sweet—"just
the day for a prowl," as Cedric said. "You will come too,
Betty?" he continued; but to every one's surprise Elizabeth demurred to this.

"She was very sorry," she stammered, "but she had
promised to go to Rotherwood."

"Why, we are all going there after luncheon!" exclaimed Cedric. "Herrick wants to call at the vicarage,
so we can leave him there, and you can go on to Rowan
Cottage."

But again Elizabeth hesitated. "It was a great pity,"
she returned hurriedly, "but Mr. Carlyon and Theo were
going to Earlsfield in the afternoon, and she wanted to
see Theo particularly about the new school-books that
they were to order at Thornton's. Theo makes such mistakes," she went on: "the last batch was all wrong and
had to be sent back;" and though Cedric argued with
her, and Anna put in a persuasive word or two, Elizabeth
was firm. The afternoon would not do. She was very
sorry to be so unsociable; but it could not be helped—
she must go alone.

All this time Malcolm had said no word. Perhaps if
he had, Elizabeth might have been induced to reconsider
her decision. The fact was, she was getting sore as well

as unhappy. "If he had wanted me, he would have asked me to accompany them," she said to herself, never dreaming that her brusque, decided manner made any such invitation on his part a sheer impossibility.

So Elizabeth had her way, and spent a long pottering morning in the schools and in going over accounts with Theo. More than once she put back her hair from her hot forehead with a gesture of weariness. How lovely the valley would look! she thought. How dark the shadows of the firs would lie! while golden shafts of sunlight would penetrate between the slender stems! She knew where they would be sitting—on a shady knoll overlooking the Dale farm and the range of hillside beyond. They would be talking to him about the Priory, and their future life, and all their hopes and fears; and he would be listening to them with that kind smile she knew so well on his lips.

"What is the matter with you, Elizabeth?" cried Theo rather pettishly; "do you know, you have added up all those figures wrongly?"

"Have I, dear? I am so sorry;" and Elizabeth, with a tired little sigh, worked her way up the column again. When she had entered the sum-total, she took up her hat.

"Surely you will wait for father," observed Theo, rather surprised at this unusual haste; "you know he promised us that he would be back soon after twelve."

"Yes, I know; but we have a guest staying with us, and I ought not to absent myself too long. I have seen Mr. Carlyon already and he will understand. Please give him my love."

Elizabeth could not have told why she was in such a hurry to be home, or why the morning seemed so endless to her. Theo's tactless remarks irritated her more than usual; she could hardly control her impatience as she answered her.

"Theo is very wearisome at times," she thought, as she walked rapidly through the woodlands.

But after all there had been no need for haste. She found Dinah alone; the walking party had not returned.

"Oh, how tired you look, Betty dear!"—this had been Dinah's constant remark of late. "You have been shut up with those noisy children and Theo all the morning, instead of sitting on the hillside enjoying the breeze from the moor. I am afraid'—here Dinah hesitated—"that Mr. Herrick was a little hurt about it. Don't you think one ought to do something to entertain one's guests?"

This was quite a severe reproof from her gentle sister; but Elizabeth only laughed a little mirthless laugh.

"He is your guest, not mine, Dinah—you ought to have gone to the valley yourself"—which was carrying the attack into the enemy's country. "No one wanted my society—a disagreeable, cross old maid—eh, Dinah?" Elizabeth's poor little joke nearly ended disastrously, for her lip quivered and she was very near a sob; but in another minute she recovered herself, and Dinah wisely said no more.

But the moment Elizabeth saw Malcolm's face at luncheon she knew her sister was right: he was unusually silent, rather constrained in manner, and hardly addressed her.

Then an evil spirit of contradiction entered into Elizabeth, and she became suddenly extremely talkative. To listen to her, Rotherwood might have been a rustic paradise, full of "village Hampdens and mute, inglorious Miltons," and that in its idyllic streets peace and simplicity reigned. Even the heavy, loutish Tommies and Jacks, who had exasperated her by their dense stupidity that morning, were only subjects for a humorous anecdote or two, with little effective and sprightly touches which made Cedric throw back his head with a boyish laugh. But Malcolm never raised his eyes from his plate.

To him Elizabeth's graphic descriptions were far from amusing. He was thankful when the meal was over and they were ready to set out for Rotherwood.

Dinah had some calls to pay, so Elizabeth had the house to herself for an hour or two; but she would not be idle for a moment. The sun was hot on the terrace and flower-beds, but the vases were to be replenished. Dinah had returned and brought her a cup of tea before she had finished. " I should not be surprised if they all had tea at the vicarage," she observed, and Elizabeth assented.

But a little later, as she stood on the terrace with a few sprays of lilac in her hand, which she meant to carry off to her own room, she heard Cedric's laugh distinctly from the drive. Her cheeks burned suddenly and a curious revulsion came over her. She had not expected them back so soon: she was not ready to meet them. She glanced at the drawing-room windows behind her. It would not do to go in that way; they would come face to face in the hall. She would go down to the Pool; no one would look for her there. He—Mr. Herrick—had never once been there since that day. She knew how he avoided the place. Yes, she would be safe there, and could get cool and collect her thoughts, and to-night she would behave better and sing some of the old songs. Elizabeth was half over the rustic bridge as she made this resolution; then she walked quickly through the little gap which led to the shady pool, with its moss-grown boulders; but the next minute she recoiled in absolute terror. Some one was standing there, gazing down into the still water, with bent head and folded arms. It was Malcolm!

She would have crept away; but at the sound of her footsteps he turned round, and her retreat was cut off.

" You quite startled me, Mr. Herrick," she said rather nervously; " I thought you never came here." It was the last thing she ought to have said, but she was confused by the sudden surprise. A faint smile crossed Malcolm's pale face.

"You are right," he said in a curious undertone, "I have never seen it since that day, three and a half years ago. But it has haunted me: more than once I have dreamt of it—such foolish dreams! You were Ophelia, and the water-weeds were strangling you and dragging you down, and I was trying to help you."

"Well," with a forced laugh, "did you succeed in saving me?"

"I think not; I have a fancy that you told me that you preferred strangling to my help. Oh, it was only a dream," as Elizabeth looked rather horrified at this; "my dreams of the Pool were never happy ones."

Elizabeth made no reply to this—perhaps words were a little difficult at the moment. But as Malcolm said no more, she observed presently—"I suppose you thought you could exorcise the nightmares by seeing the place again?" Then he turned round and looked her full in the face, and the lines round his mouth were fixed and stern.

"No," he said with unnatural calmness, "any such exorcism would be useless in my case; I have only come to take a last look at it."

Elizabeth's strength seemed to forsake her, and she sank down on the boulder. "What—what do you mean?" she asked faintly.

"What do I mean?" with a bitter laugh, but his eyes flashed ominously. "I mean that I am a coward. Cowards run away, do they not? Elizabeth, I am beaten —I confess it—I am going to give it up. I shall come here no more."

"No more—not come to the Wood House?" Elizabeth could scarcely gasp out the words.

"No," he replied quietly, "not even to see your sister. I mean to tell her so before I leave; she will understand me. Why should I come here to be treated as you have treated me to-day? Each time I come you show me more plainly that my love and devotion are nothing to you. Well, dear as you are to me—God only knows how dear —I can lead my life without you. Yes, I will free myself from my bonds—I will be no woman's slave."

If she could only speak! The tears were running down her face now; he must have seen them if he had looked; but as she put up her hands to hide them, a little choking sob escaped her and reached his ear.

He bent over her and spoke in a gentler tone. " Why are you weeping, Elizabeth? Are those tears for yourself or me?"

" For myself," she whispered; " because you are leaving me, and I want you—I want you so."

Strong man as he was, Malcolm trembled from head to foot with the sudden shock and revulsion. What could she mean? The next minute he was kneeling on the ground beside her, and had drawn away her hands, so that she was as defenceless as a child.

" I must see your face, Elizabeth," very firmly. " You are a truthful woman, you never deceived any one; let me read the truth in your eyes. You want me you say— does that mean you are beginning to care for me?"

" I think so;" but Elizabeth's eyes refused to meet his.

" Does it mean that you love me well enough to be my wife?" he asked again, and his voice thrilled her through and through. Then a lovely colour came to Elizabeth's face.

" I think I do, Malcolm," she whispered timidly. " I believe I have been caring a long time, but I would not let myself believe it. Oh," dropping her hot cheek against his shoulder, " it nearly broke my heart when you said you would never come again."

" I meant it, dearest; it seemed to me that my last hope was gone. Oh, my beloved—my own at last!" and then Malcolm's long, passionate kiss set the seal to their betrothal, and for a little while there was the silence of a great peace.

An hour had passed—no one had come in search of them, and the evening shadows were beginning to steal over the Pool—but still they sat hand in hand, talking earnestly and lovingly after the manner of lovers, until the gong warned them that it was time to return to the house. But even then they lingered.

" Is the spirit of the Pool properly exorcised now, Malcolm?" asked Elizabeth, with her old playfulness. Then he clasped her close.

" I have her safe in my own keeping. Dearest," in a low, vibrating tone full of tenderness, " if I ever grow supine or forgetful in my great happiness, and the memory of these long years of misery and unrest fade away, you must bring me here and I shall remember."

" You shall remember nothing but that I love you," she whispered. " Malcolm, you will not leave me to-morrow? I cannot part with you so soon." And he promised that he would certainly remain over Sunday.

Elizabeth had not entirely laid aside her mourning, but the black silk dress she selected that evening fitted her exquisitely, and the dull, heavy folds suited her tall, queenly figure. She looked at herself for a moment, then with a hesitating hand she fastened a spray of white lilac in her dress. The next moment there was a familiar tap at her door, and Dinah, flushed and agitated, came into the room.

Elizabeth watched her smilingly; then she opened her arms without a word, and for a few moments the sisters held each other very closely.

" Oh, Betty, my darling—my darling, if you knew how happy this has made me!"

" How did you know, Die—have you seen him?"

" Yes, just now; he was crossing the hall, and I saw his face. We were alone, there was no one near, and he caught hold of my hands—oh, such a grip. 'Dinah,' he said—'you will let me call you Dinah now? for I am going to be your brother.' But we had no time for another word, for Cedric and Anna came out of the drawing-room."

"We shall not tell them this evening," returned Elizabeth. "Malcolm has promised to keep it quiet. I told him that only you—my other self—must know to-night. You will be careful, will you not, Die?"

"Yes, dear, but you must let me hear more. How did it happen, Betty? I thought you and Malcolm Herrick never meant to speak to each other again. It has been such a tiresome, uncomfortable day. When I brought you that cup of tea on the terrace I did so long to say a word to you; but I saw by your face that I should only make things worse."

"I am glad you refrained. Do you know, Die, I thought I heard them in the drive—I had no idea that Malcolm had returned an hour before—and I got into such a panic that I went down to the Pool to recover myself, and—and he was there."

"At the Pool?"

"Yes, and he heard me, and I was obliged to stay; and then he told me that the place haunted him, and gave him bad dreams—oh, such ghastly dreams; and then all at once he said he was taking his last look at it—that he never meant to come here again."

"Poor fellow, did he really say that?"

"It was poor Betty, I think, then. Oh, Die, if you knew how limp and helpless I felt when he said that; I trembled so that I was obliged to sit down, and—and I could not help crying. I know I acted like a fool, but the next moment I could feel him bending over me, and his voice was quite changed and gentle when he asked me why I was crying."

"Of course you told him?"

" Yes, I could not keep it back; and then somehow it all came right, and we were both so happy. Oh, Die, how wonderful it seems that two such men should love me—my own dear David, and now Malcolm! I am not young or beautiful, or even clever."

" I think I understand it," returned Dinah, affectionately. And then Elizabeth put the last touches to her toilet, and a moment later they went downstairs, and found Malcolm still pacing the hall. He put out his hand silently to Elizabeth as they followed Dinah into the dining-room. That warm, quiet grasp was full of comforting assurance: as long as life lasted Elizabeth would have her lover and her friend; she had found her rightful mate, and the old restless days were over.

CHAPTER XLIV

"MY DEAREST REST"

She loves thee even as far-forth than
As any woman may a man;
And is thine own, and so she says;
And cares for thee ten thousand ways.

SURREY.

SOMETHING in Elizabeth's aspect seemed to attract Cedric's attention; perhaps it was the veiled brightness of her expression, or the white flowers at her breast, but more than once he eyed her in a puzzled fashion.

"What have you done to yourself, Betty?" he burst out at last; "you look scrumptious—ten years younger, and as though you had turned up trumps;" and though Elizabeth pretended to frown at these personal remarks, it was impossible not to laugh. Cedric had no idea how nearly he had gauged the truth: he little knew the good news that awaited him the next day. The knowledge that his dearest and most honoured friend was to be his brother-in-law would fill his cup of bliss to the brim.

Anna was somewhat weary with her unusual exertions that day, and after dinner Dinah established her in a cosy corner of the drawing-room, promising that Cedric should come and talk to her there.

"I will stay with you till he comes, and then I have a letter to write," she observed, for Dinah's tact was never at fault.

Elizabeth kissed her hand to them smilingly; then she wrapped herself up in a soft fleecy shawl and went out into the moonlight, and presently Malcolm joined her.

"I had some difficulty in shaking off Cedric," he re-

marked, as he took her hand and placed it on his arm;
" he was in a talkative mood, but I told him his ladye-love
would be waiting for him. He little knew my ladye-love
was waiting for me too."

" No; how pleased he will be when we tell him." How
sweetly that " we" sounded in Malcolm's ears! " Malcolm, there is something I want to ask you. Will you
go with me to Rotherwood to-morrow? I must see Mr.
Carlyon. He will be so happy about this"—with a light
emphasising pressure on his arm—" and he is like my
own father. And then I want you to come with me to
David's grave."

" Did you fear I should refuse?" for Elizabeth's voice
had been somewhat hesitating. " Do you think I should
refuse any wish that it is in my power to gratify?"

" No," she said gently; " I know how good you will
be to me—that if it were possible you would strew my
daily path with thornless roses. But it is not possible,
Malcolm."

" Then we will take our share of the briars and thorns
together."

" Indeed we will. Malcolm, there is something I want
to tell you before we stand by that grave to-morrow—
something I should like you to know;" and then, in a
voice broken by emotion, Elizabeth repeated the substance
of her conversation with Mr. Carlyon.

" It has made me so much happier," she faltered, when
she had finished. Then Malcolm drew her closer to him.

" I am glad you told me this," he said in a moved tone.
" Dear Elizabeth, I have a confession to make. In those
old unhappy days I used to wonder how you could care so
much for him. He was good and true and earnest, and
he loved you dearly; but all the same I could not understand."

" Dinah and Mrs. Godfrey could not understand
either," she replied gently; " but you none of you knew

my David: it made me a better woman only to be near him. His father has just the same simple, guileless nature—my two Nathanaels I used to call them."

"Dear, I understand better now," returned Malcolm kindly; "but I ask myself, could I have done the same in his place? I fear—I greatly fear, my love is not so selfless. If I had to die and leave you——" but Elizabeth would not listen to this.

"If you had been in his place you would have been equally generous; I know your good heart far too well to doubt that, Malcolm." Elizabeth was a tall woman, and as she bent involuntarily towards him, her cheek rested for a moment against his; that simple womanly caress seemed to set the seal to her sacred confidence. But when she would have moved away he held her fast.

"Elizabeth—Elizabeth," it was all he could say; but it was enough—no words were needed. Silently they said their Te Deum together, and the fair white moonlight lay on their bowed heads like a benison.

Two or three days later Malcolm found his way to 27 Queen's Gate, and entered his mother's study unannounced. Mrs. Herrick was writing as usual. Her keen gray eyes lighted up with pleasure when she saw him.

"My dear boy, at this hour—what a delightful surprise! I was just writing to Anna. Cedric will not hear of bringing her back until Thursday."

Malcolm smiled at his mother's tone. Strong-willed woman as she was, he knew that Cedric would rule her utterly; the lad's wheedling ways and blarneying tongue had already won her heart. Cedric never could be made to understand why people were afraid of Mrs. Herrick.

"Have you come to spend the afternoon with me, Malcolm?"

"Yes, if you will have me. I have some news for you, mother." Malcolm was little nervous, and spoke with some abruptness. Mrs. Herrick laid down her pen and looked at him intently.

"You need not tell me," she returned quietly. " I know your news—I can read it in your face—Elizabeth Templeton has promised to marry you."

"Mother, are you a witch?" in an astonished tone. "It is not possible that any one has betrayed me; Anna and Cedric promised not to say a word."

"No one has betrayed your confidence, Malcolm; and a mother does not need witchcraft to enable her to read her children's hearts.

"My dear boy," she continued—her strong features working a little with emotion,—"do you really imagine that I have been blind all these years—that, although you chose to withhold your confidence from me, I was not aware of your trouble. You are a reserved, self-contained man like your father, Malcolm—he always kept things to himself too—but all the same you could not hide from your mother that your poor heart was almost broken because the woman you wanted refused to marry you."

Malcolm took his mother's hand and kissed it. "You have been very good to me," he murmured; "but I could not speak, the pain was too great. Thank God, Elizabeth is mine now."

"I say, thank God, too"—and the keen eyes filled with tears. "Will you bring her to me, Malcolm?"

"Will I not, mother! But you must send her a message."

"Tell her, that from this hour she shall be the dearest of daughters to me, and that, for your sake, I shall love her dearly. And tell her—no, I will keep that for my own lips when we meet—that my son, God bless him! is worthy of any woman's love." And then, as Malcolm bent over her, she folded him in her motherly embrace. At that moment Malcolm and his mother fully understood each other.

Malcolm was anxious to be married as soon as possible; and as his mother and Dinah were on his side, and there was really no reason for delay, Elizabeth soon yielded to his persuasions, and a day was fixed early in August. Cedric and Anna were to wait until the elder couple returned from Scotland, and then Malcolm would give his adopted sister away; and after a fair amount of grumbling, Cedric acquiesced in this arrangement.

In the middle of June, Dinah and Elizabeth paid a long visit to 27 Queen's Gate, and Elizabeth did her shopping and saw the house in South Kensington that Malcolm had described to her in such glowing terms. A friend of his had recently bought it and furnished it in admirable taste; and now his wife's ill-health obliged him to part with it, and Malcolm was in treaty for it. The sisters were charmed with the house when they saw it, and Elizabeth strongly advised Malcolm to take most of the furniture. "It suits the house so exactly, and it will save you so much trouble," she observed sensibly; "I know Dinah agrees with me." And Dinah smiled and nodded.

"Die has made such a charming suggestion," continued Elizabeth, as she stepped out through the French window at one end of the long drawing-room on to a balcony, pleasantly shaded by an awning and prettily fitted up with flower-boxes and Indian matting and delightful lounging-chairs. "She says we must call this our town house, but that the Wood House must be our country house. She wants us to be there all the summer and autumn;" and here Elizabeth looked at Malcolm rather wistfully.

"And you think that arrangement would suit you?" he asked with a smile; but he knew her answer before hand.

"Oh, I should love to be with Die;" she replied earnestly. "Dear, do you mean that you will consent? Think what it would mean to me. I shall not be separated from Mr. Carlyon and my poor people; and I do so love the country; and we should have our winter and spring in town."

"I think it will work excellently," returned Malcolm in a tone of such conviction that Elizabeth's doubts vanished. "I can do my work as well at Staplegrove as here, and I love the country too. As long as we are together and you are happy, I shall be satisfied."

"Dearest, how good you are," she whispered, with one of her rare, shy caresses. "Die has planned everything so beautifully. You know the large end room we call our morning-room, that is to be your study. You are to have all your own books and things. Die is going to fit it up; she says it is to be her wedding present to you. The smaller room near it is to be the morning-room."

"But you will not leave me alone in my study!" observed Malcolm in an alarmed voice. "Your writing-table must be there too, Elizabeth. Do you think I could bear you out of my sight?"

Elizabeth laughed and blushed, and called him a foolish, jealous boy; but in her heart she loved to think that she was the delight of his eyes, and that every day she grew dearer to him.

It was the evening before the wedding, and a quiet little house-party had assembled at the Wood House— Mrs. Herrick and Anna, Colonel and Mrs. Godfrey; and Malcolm, who had taken up his quarters at the "King's Arms," had joined them at dinner. The wedding was to be at an early hour the next morning, and no other guests were to be invited. Colonel Godfrey would give the bride away, and the vicar and Mr. Carlyon would perform the ceremony between them. Anna would be the solitary bridesmaid.

The sunset clouds were fading behind the little fir wood

when Elizabeth and Malcolm came out on the terrace. Elizabeth had been a little grave and thoughtful during dinner, and Malcolm, who could read her perfectly, knew that she was somewhat oppressed by all the talk. The still peacefulness of the evening, only broken by the sleepy twittering of the birds, seemed to calm and refresh her.

"Malcolm," she said presently, "did you hear what Mrs. Godfrey was telling me at dinner—that Mr. Rossiter is coming to the Manor House?"

"Yes, I heard her," was the reply. "The Colonel was talking to me this afternoon; he says it is a foregone conclusion that Leah Jacobi will not refuse him a third time. His kindness and devotion after her brother's death have already won her gratitude. Hugh Rossiter is one of the best fellows I know," he observed, "and Leah will be a happy woman the day she marries him. And marry him she will, you may take my word for it."

"Poor Leah, I am so glad he cares for her. Of course you know Mrs. Richardson is dying, Malcolm, and that she is likely to be left alone in the world?"

"Yes, and then Hugh Rossiter will have his innings." And Malcolm was right, for before long the news of Leah's marriage reached them.

"I am so glad Mrs. Godfrey told me that," went on Elizabeth. "I want every one to be as happy as we are to-night. But for saying good-bye to Die and Mr. Carlyon I should not have a care. I can think of David without sadness, and life looks so beautiful. "Dear," with the vivid, bright smile he loved so well, "I am so glad you are an author and a famous man—I shall be so proud of you; and though I cannot share your work as some women could, I can help you in other ways. I must be your right hand, Malcolm."

"Shall I tell you what you will be to me," he returned, in a voice of deep, vibrating tenderness that thrilled her through and through. " I once read an old Scandinavian ballad where a warrior calls his love ' My dearest Rest.' ' Three grateful words,' the annotator goes on to say, ' and the most perfect crown of praise that ever woman won.' Shall I call you that, Elizabeth?—' my dearest Rest.' "

" It is far too beautiful for me," she whispered; " I do not deserve it." But even as Elizabeth said this, her woman's heart registered its first wifely vow.

Yes, she would be that to him—his haven and comfort when he was weary with the storm and stress of life— God helping her, now and for ever " his dearest Rest."

THE END

Lightning Source UK Ltd.
Milton Keynes UK
UKOW021804130313

207603UK00007B/389/P